Story & Art by
Chika Shiomi

4

[Cast of Characters]

Yukari Kobayakawa

A 17-year-old high school student and author of historical novels. Most of his stories are set in the Edo period. One day, he meets a girl named Mahoro at school. It's their first time meeting, but he feels as if he knows her and suddenly becomes dizzy. Later, his spirit enters the body of Yumurasaki, who he was in a past life.

Katsuhiko Satomi

The new housekeeper at Yukari's house. He and Mahoro have been at each other's throats ever since they met. He was Kazuma in his past life. As his connection to the past deepens, he suddenly finds himself able to handle a *katana* sword.

Mahoro Tachibana

Yukari's classmate and a big fan of his novels. She worries about Yukari's tendency to skip school due to illness, so she begins visiting him at his home. She was Takamura in her past life, and she's beginning to act more like him now.

The Present

The Past

Yumurasaki

The *oiran* of an establishment called Tatsutaya in the Yoshiwara pleasure district of Edo (present-day Tokyo, Japan). Due to his memories of her as his previous incarnation, Yukari knows that someone murdered her...

Shizuka Takamura

A frequent customer of Yumurasaki's and a powerful witch doctor. He truly cares for Yumurasaki and has proposed to buy her freedom.

Kazuma

A bodyguard at Tatsutaya where Yumurasaki works. He is Yumurasaki's long-lost brother.

The Story

At the young age of 17, high school student Yukari Kobayakawa is a genius author of historical novels set in the Edo period. One day, he meets a girl named Mahoro Tachibana at school. Despite meeting her for the first time, he feels like he knows her... Afterward, he suffers dizzy spells and enters the body of Yumurasaki, an oiran in an Edo period pleasure district. Yukari instinctively realizes she is himself in a past life, and he begins going back and forth between the past and present despite a warning from the witch doctor Takamura not to. He learns that Mahoro and Satomi were, respectively, Takamura and Kazuma in the past, and then scenes from the past begin overlapping with the present. What's worse, Yukari begins to show signs of suffering from Yumurasaki's illness!

Yukarism

[Volume 4 Contents]

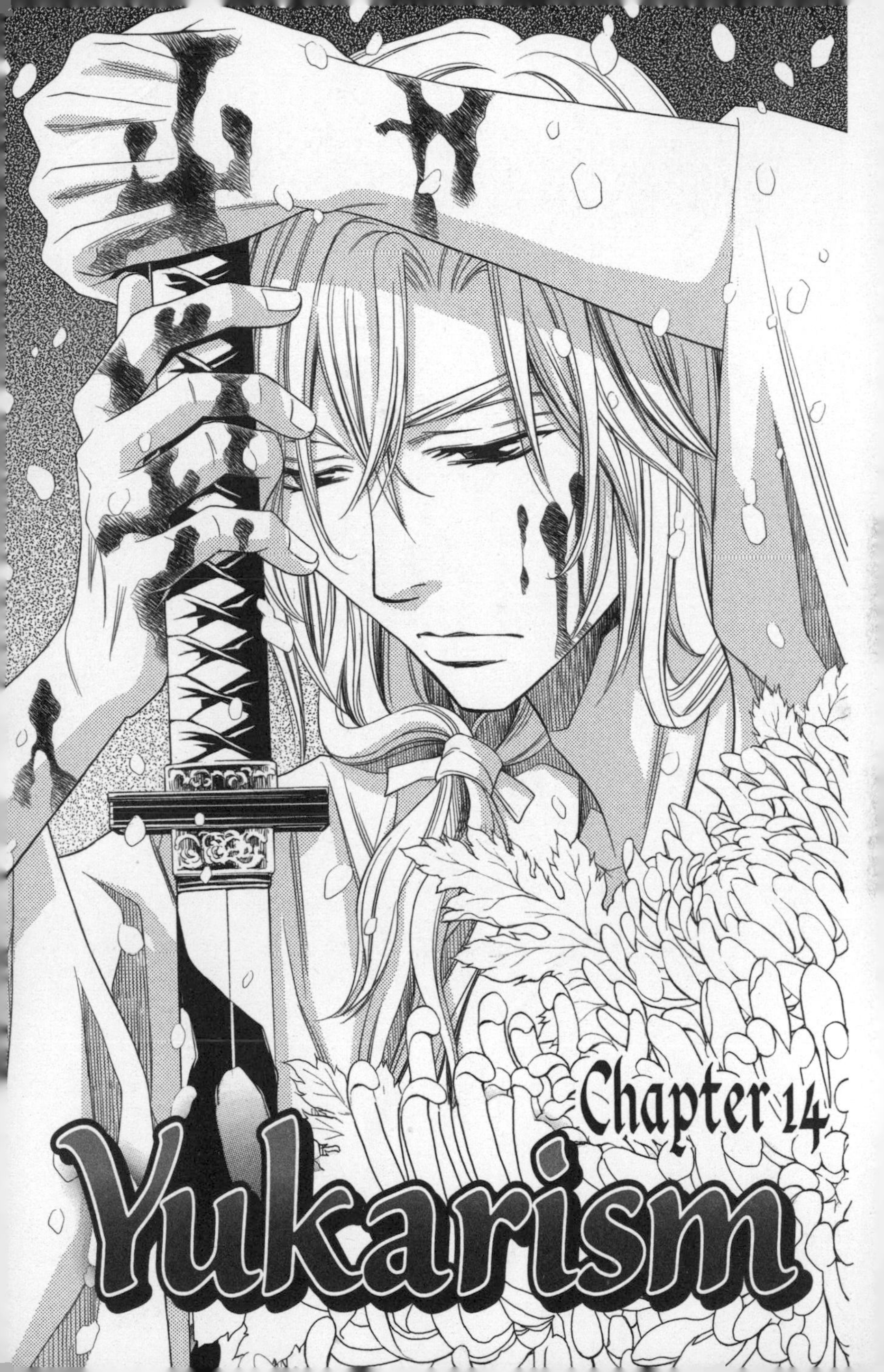
Chapter 14
Yukarism

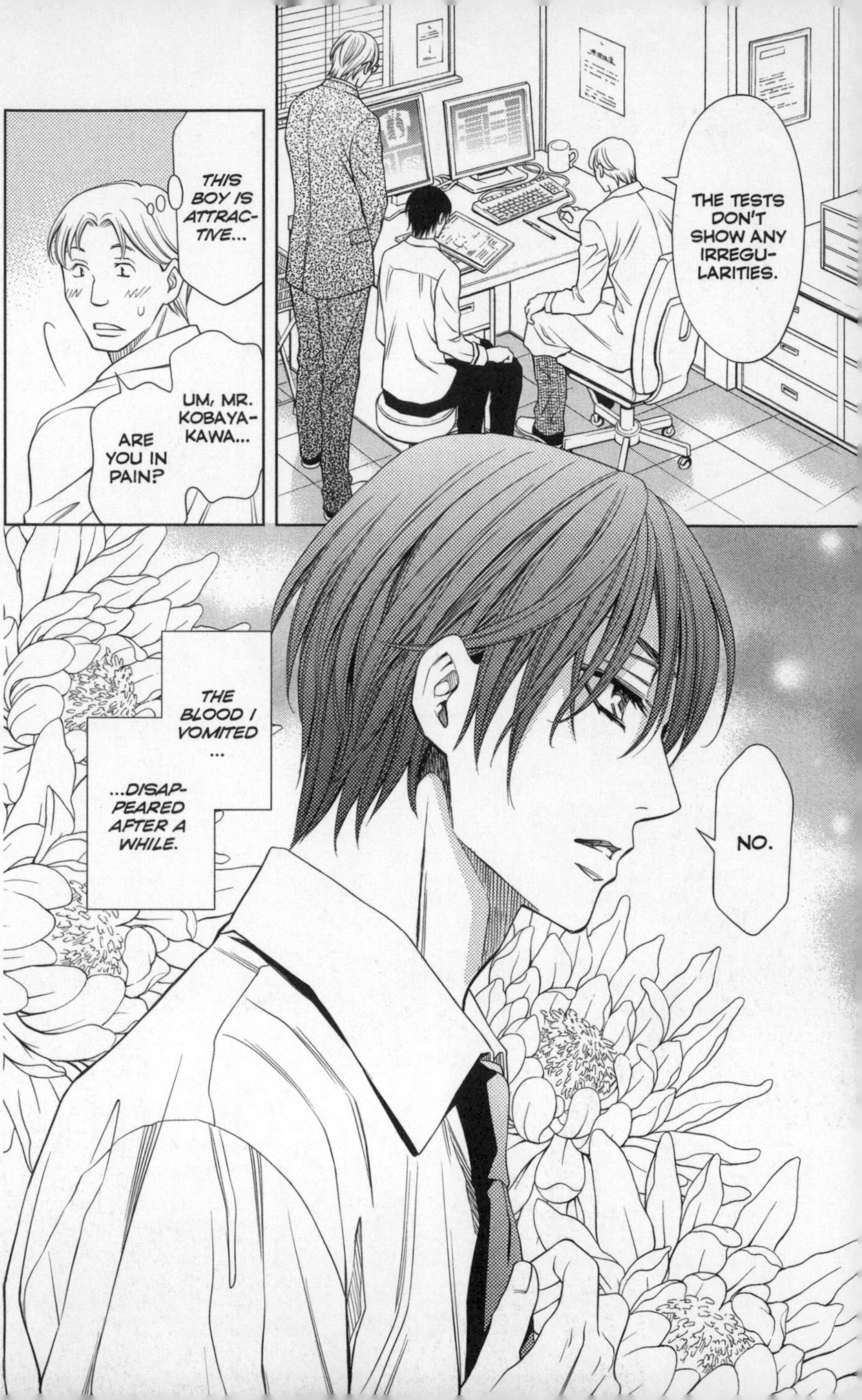
THE TESTS DON'T SHOW ANY IRREGULARITIES.
THIS BOY IS ATTRACTIVE...
UM, MR. KOBAYAKAWA...
ARE YOU IN PAIN?
NO.
THE BLOOD I VOMITED...
...DISAPPEARED AFTER A WHILE.

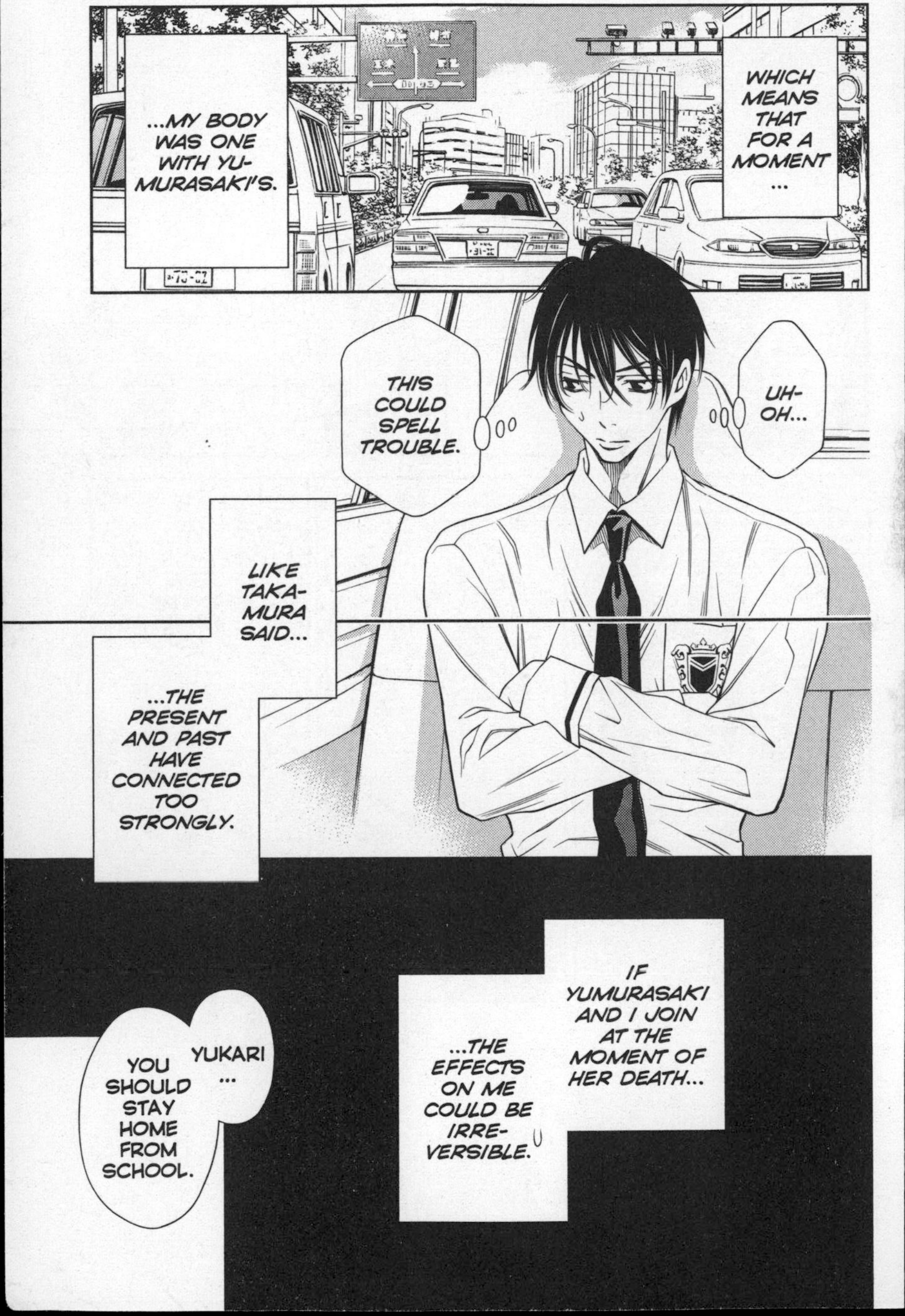
WHICH MEANS THAT FOR A MOMENT ...
...MY BODY WAS ONE WITH YU-MURASAKI'S.
UH-OH...
THIS COULD SPELL TROUBLE.
LIKE TAKA-MURA SAID...
...THE PRESENT AND PAST HAVE CONNECTED TOO STRONGLY.
IF YUMURASAKI AND I JOIN AT THE MOMENT OF HER DEATH...
...THE EFFECTS ON ME COULD BE IRRE-VERSIBLE.
YUKARI ...
YOU SHOULD STAY HOME FROM SCHOOL.

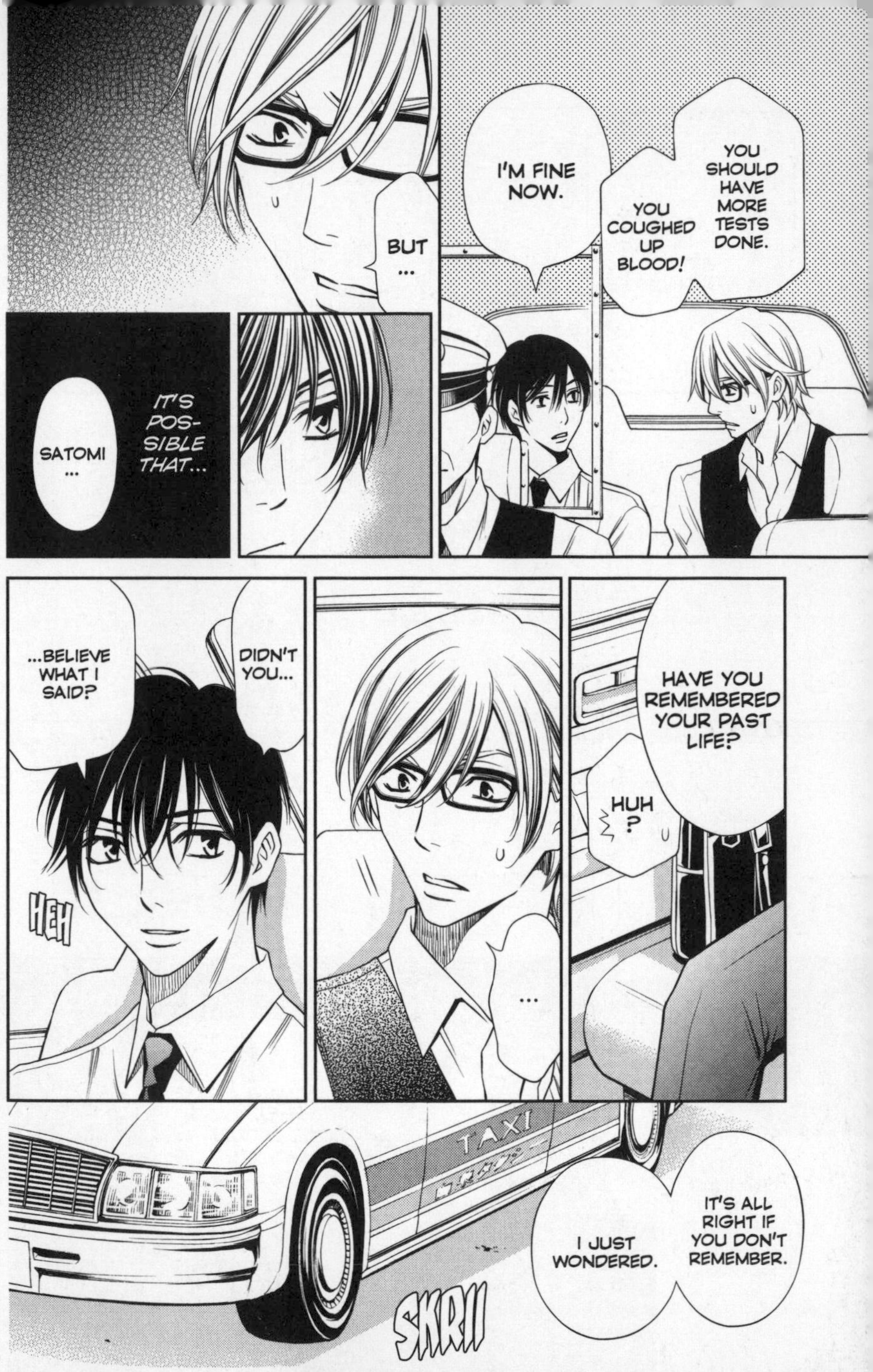
YOU SHOULD HAVE MORE TESTS DONE.
YOU COUGHED UP BLOOD!
I'M FINE NOW.
BUT ...
IT'S POS-SIBLE THAT...
SATOMI ...
HAVE YOU REMEMBERED YOUR PAST LIFE?
HUH ?
...
DIDN'T YOU...
...BELIEVE WHAT I SAID?
HEH
TAXI
IT'S ALL RIGHT IF YOU DON'T REMEMBER.
I JUST WONDERED.
SKRII

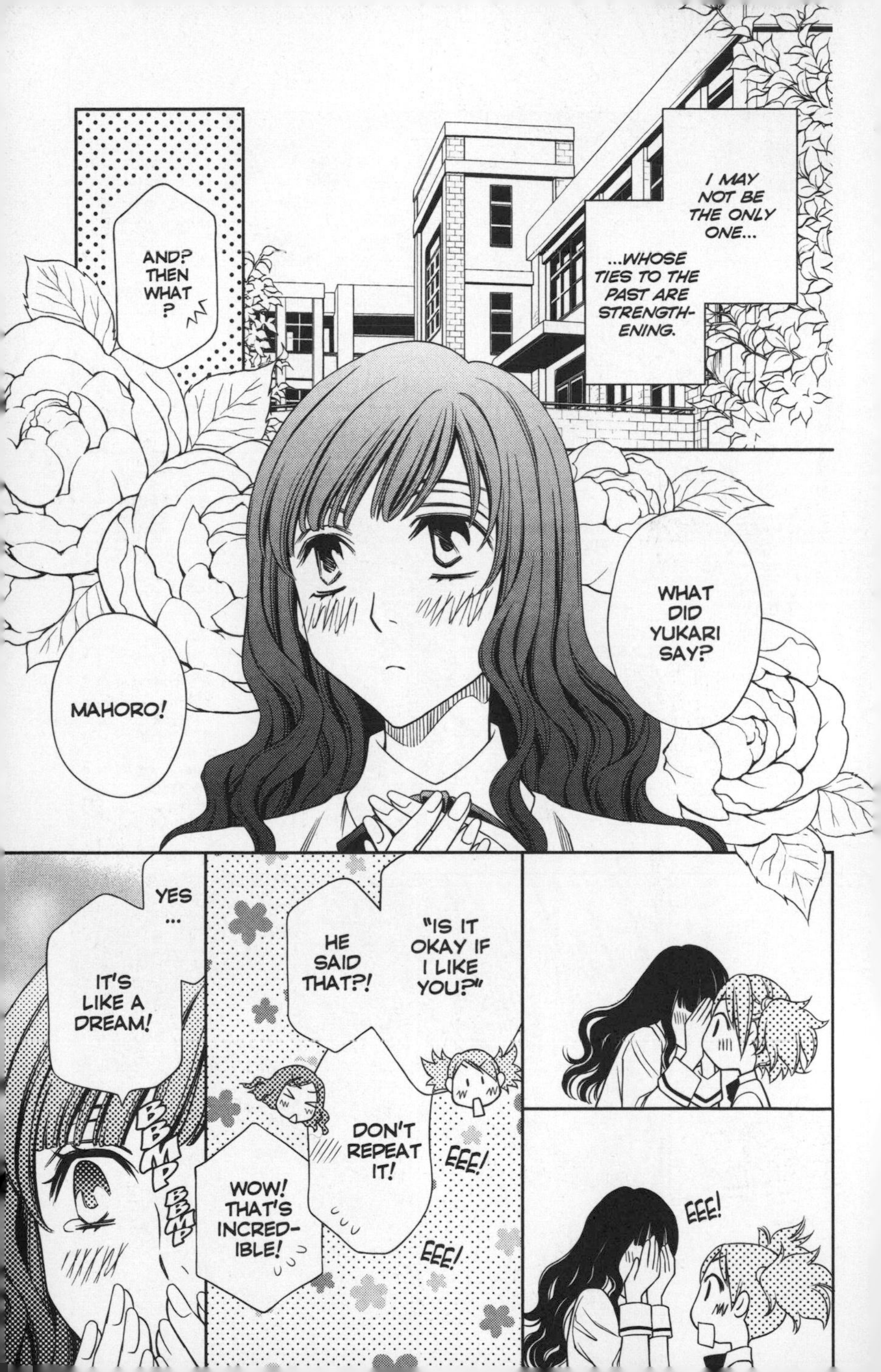
I MAY NOT BE THE ONLY ONE...
...WHOSE TIES TO THE PAST ARE STRENGTHENING.
WHAT DID YUKARI SAY?
AND? THEN WHAT?
MAHORO!
EEE!
"IS IT OKAY IF I LIKE YOU?"
HE SAID THAT?!
DON'T REPEAT IT!
EEE!
EEE!
WOW! THAT'S INCREDIBLE!
YES ...
IT'S LIKE A DREAM!
BBMP BBMP

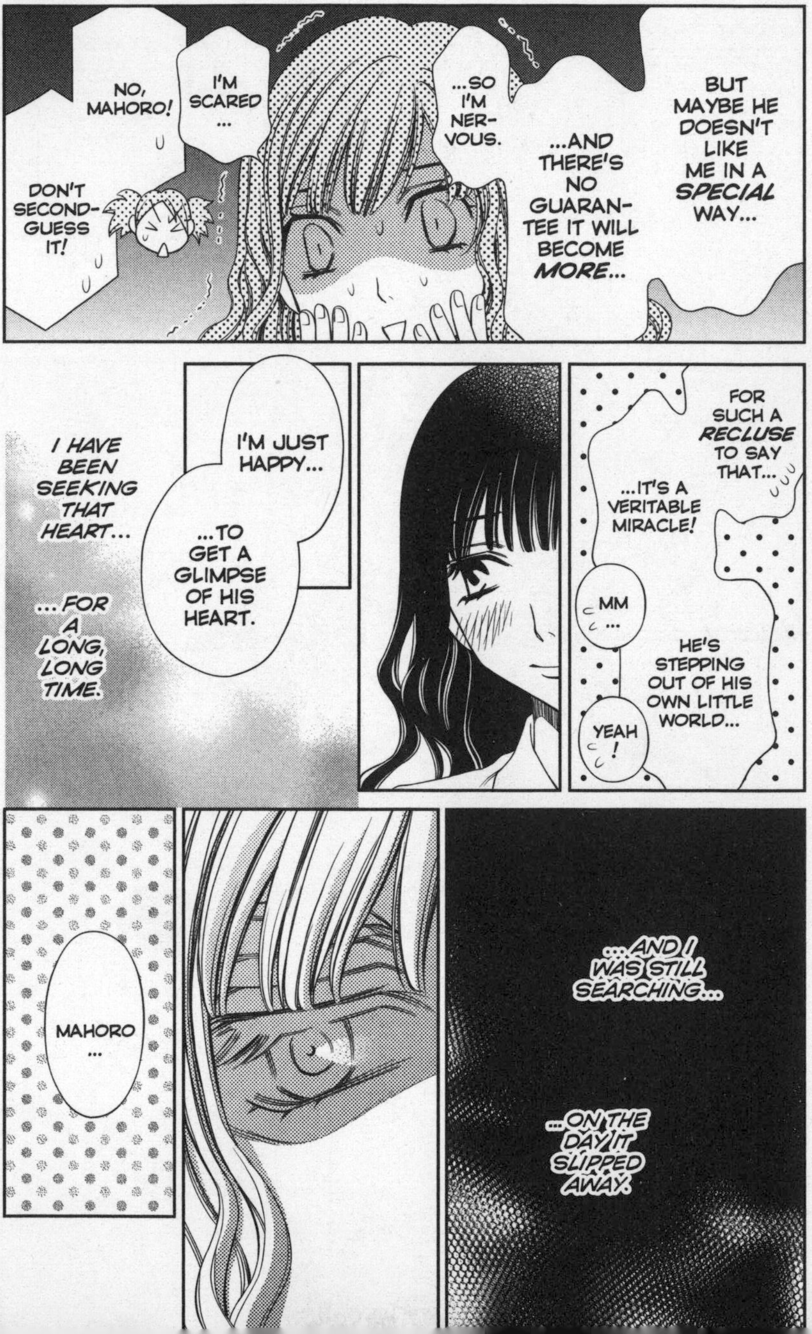
BUT MAYBE HE DOESN'T LIKE ME IN A *SPECIAL* WAY...
...AND THERE'S NO GUARANTEE IT WILL BECOME *MORE*...
...SO I'M NERVOUS.
I'M SCARED...
NO, MAHORO!
DON'T SECOND-GUESS IT!
FOR SUCH A *RECLUSE* TO SAY THAT...
...IT'S A VERITABLE MIRACLE!
HE'S STEPPING OUT OF HIS OWN LITTLE WORLD...
MM...
YEAH!
I'M JUST HAPPY...
...TO GET A GLIMPSE OF HIS HEART.
I HAVE BEEN SEEKING THAT HEART...
...FOR A LONG, LONG TIME.
...AND I WAS STILL SEARCHING...
...ON THE DAY IT SLIPPED AWAY.
MAHORO...

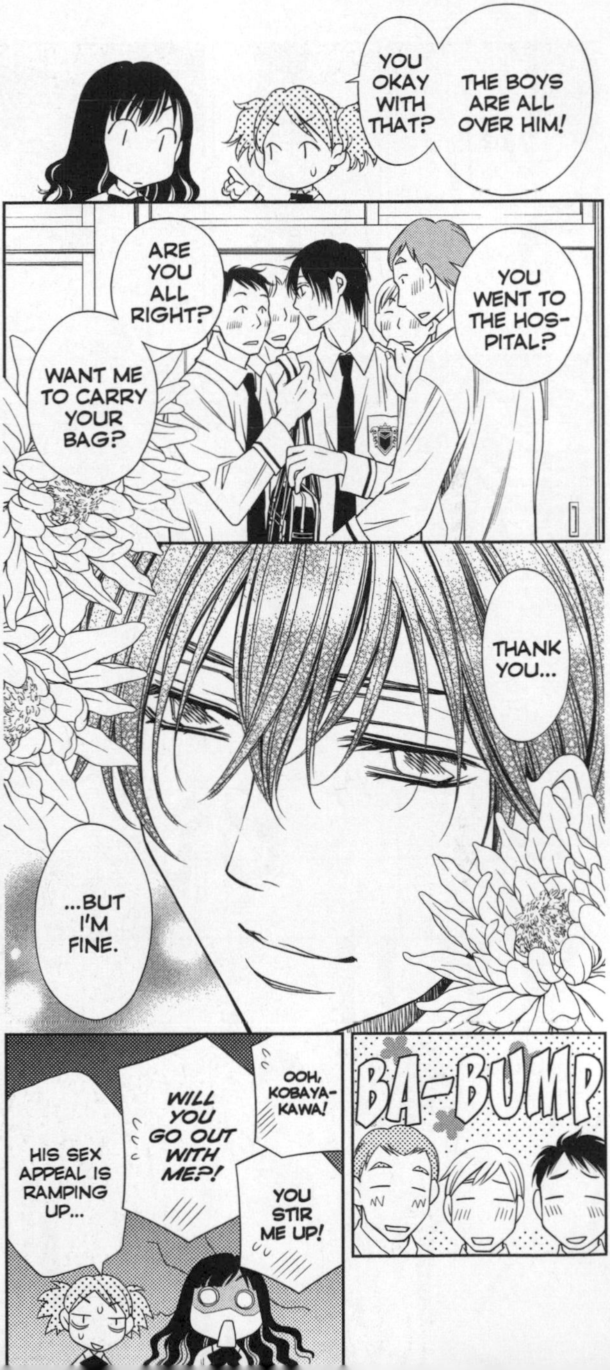
THE BOYS ARE ALL OVER HIM!
YOU OKAY WITH THAT?
YOU WENT TO THE HOSPITAL?
ARE YOU ALL RIGHT?
WANT ME TO CARRY YOUR BAG?
THANK YOU...
...BUT I'M FINE.
BA-BUMP
OOH, KOBAYAKAWA!
WILL YOU GO OUT WITH ME?!
YOU STIR ME UP!
HIS SEX APPEAL IS RAMPING UP...

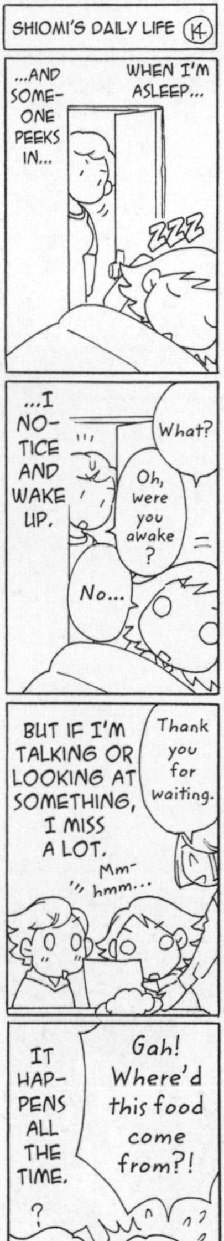
SHIOMI'S DAILY LIFE (14)
WHEN I'M ASLEEP...
...AND SOMEONE PEEKS IN...
ZZZ
What?
Oh, were you awake?
...I NOTICE AND WAKE UP.
No...
Thank you for waiting.
BUT IF I'M TALKING OR LOOKING AT SOMETHING, I MISS A LOT.
Mm-hmm...
Gah! Where'd this food come from?!
IT HAPPENS ALL THE TIME.
?

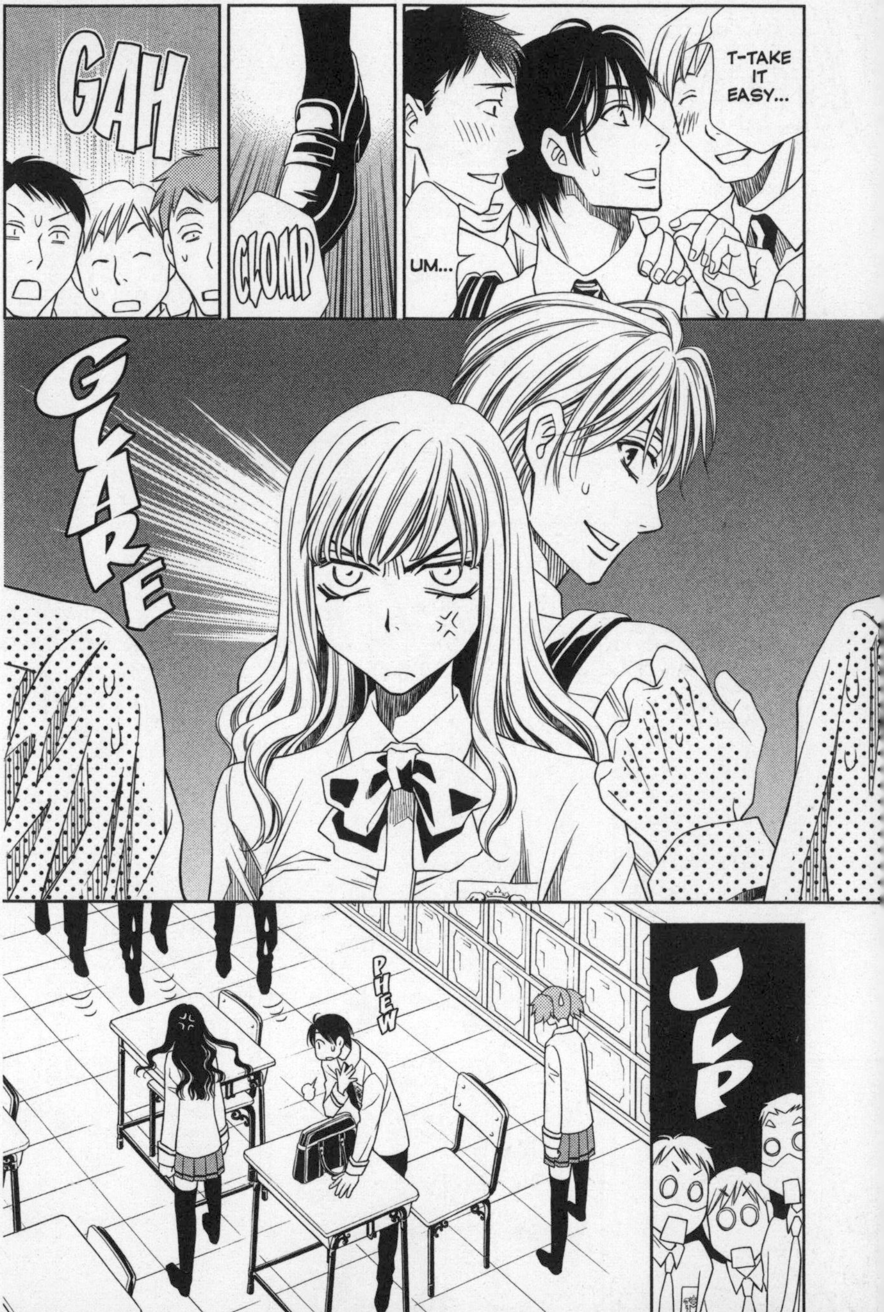
T-TAKE IT EASY...
UM...
CLOMP
GAH
GLARE
ULP
PHEW

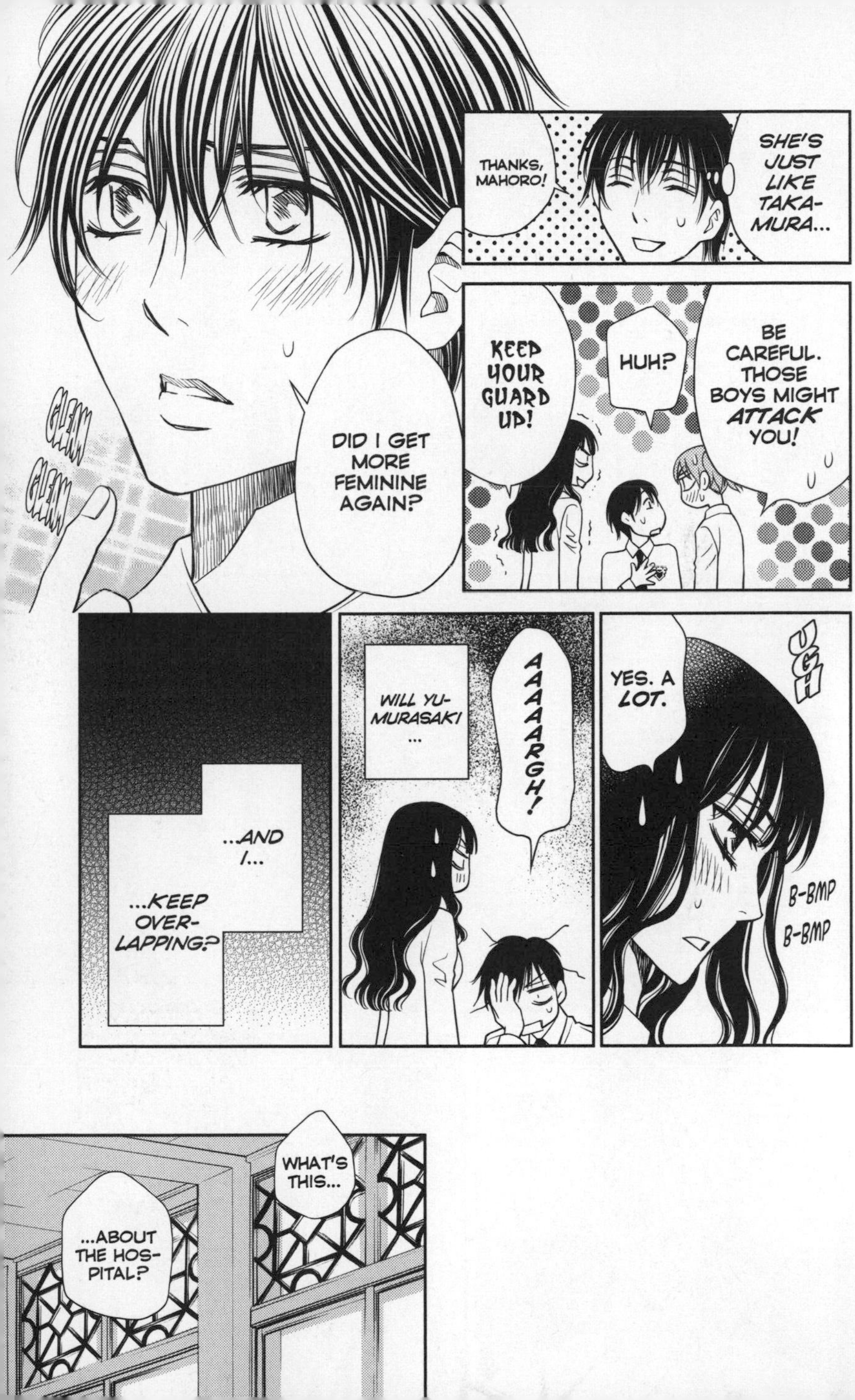
SHE'S JUST LIKE TAKA-MURA...
THANKS, MAHORO!
BE CAREFUL. THOSE BOYS MIGHT ATTACK YOU!
HUH?
KEEP YOUR GUARD UP!
DID I GET MORE FEMININE AGAIN?
GLEAM
GLEAM
UGH
YES. A LOT.
B-BMP
B-BMP
AAAAAARGH!
WILL YU-MURASAKI ...
...AND I...
...KEEP OVER-LAPPING?
WHAT'S THIS...
...ABOUT THE HOS-PITAL?

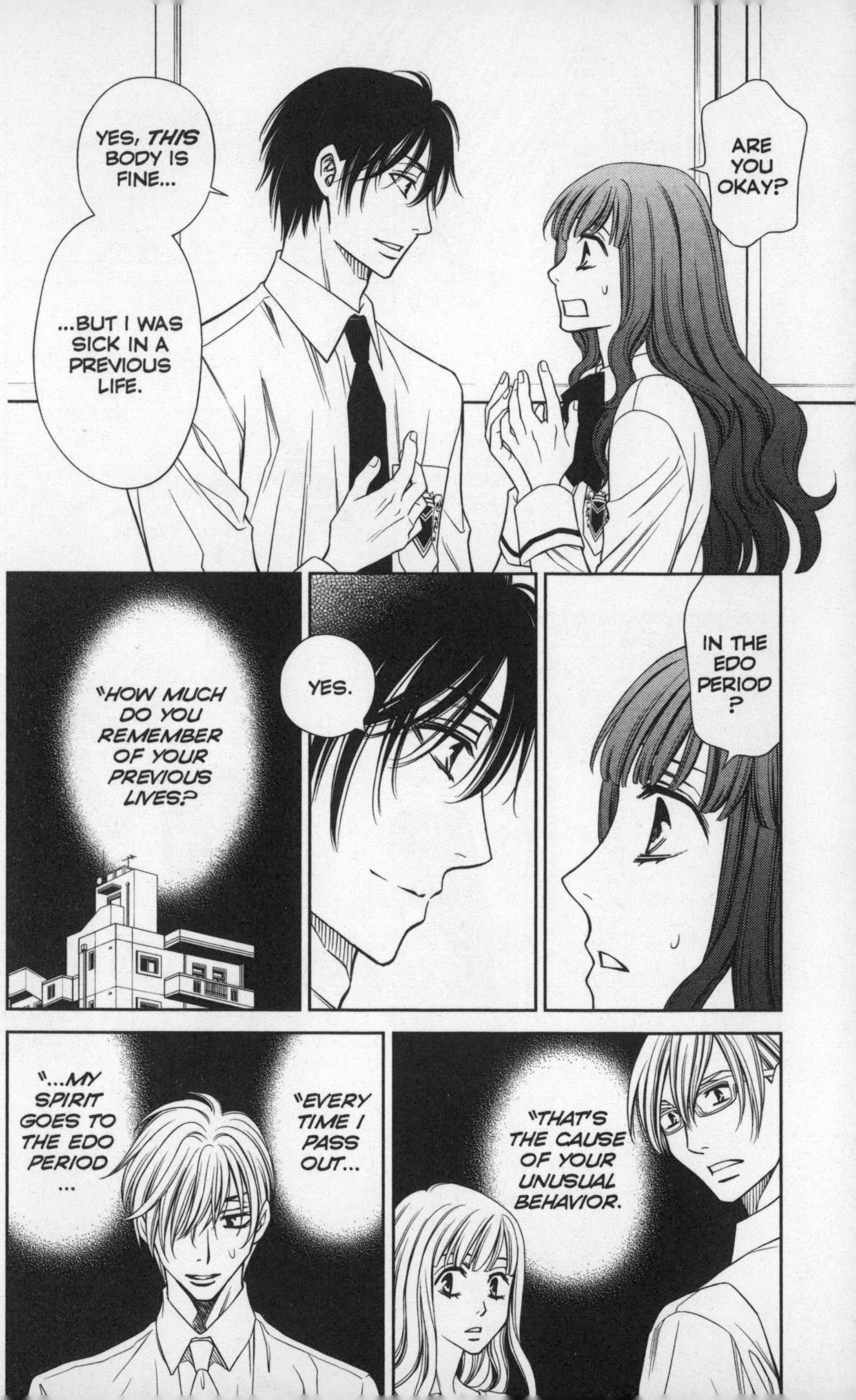
ARE YOU OKAY?
YES, *THIS* BODY IS FINE...
...BUT I WAS SICK IN A PREVIOUS LIFE.
IN THE EDO PERIOD?
YES.
"HOW MUCH DO YOU REMEMBER OF YOUR PREVIOUS LIVES?
"THAT'S THE CAUSE OF YOUR UNUSUAL BEHAVIOR.
"EVERY TIME I PASS OUT...
"...MY SPIRIT GOES TO THE EDO PERIOD...

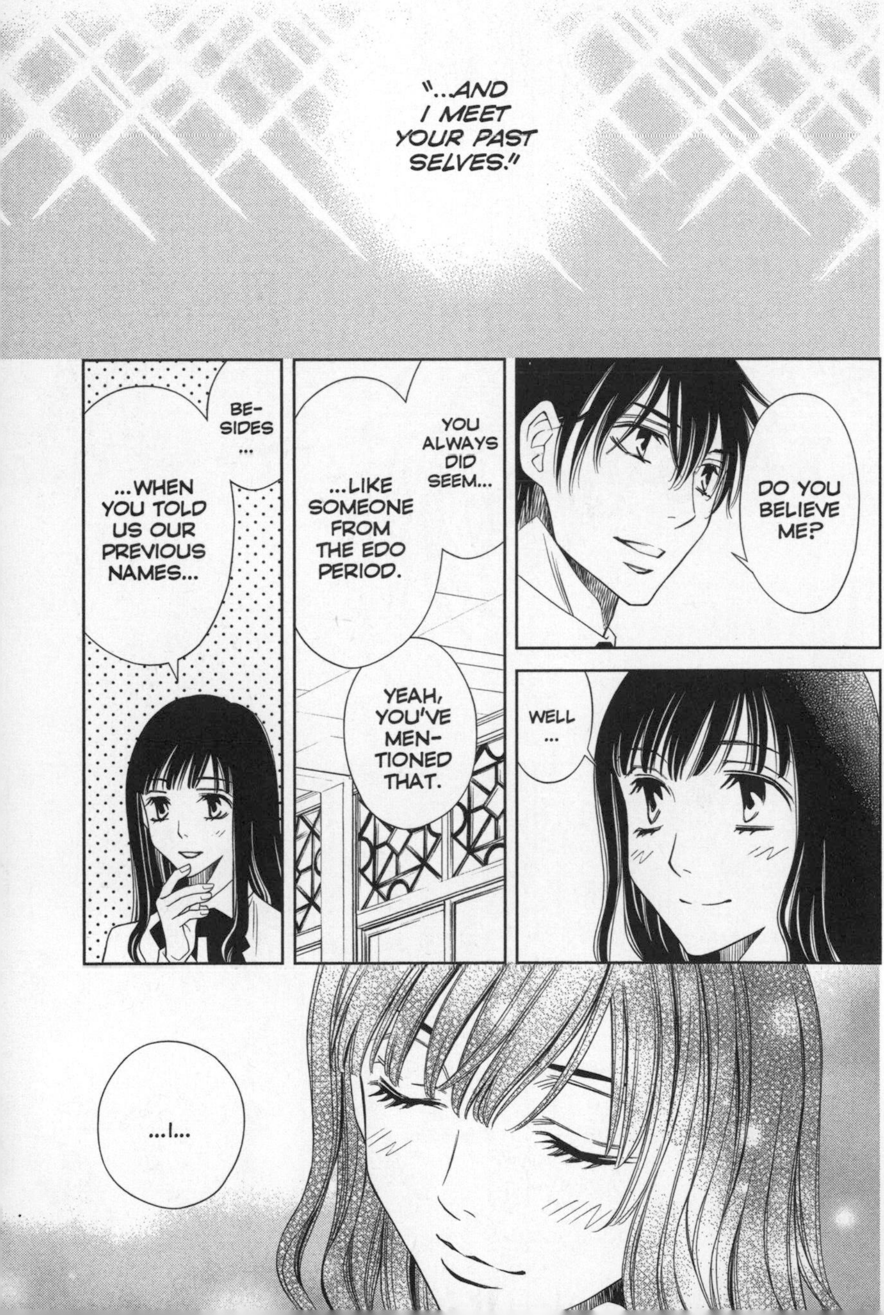
"...AND I MEET YOUR PAST SELVES."
DO YOU BELIEVE ME?
WELL ...
YOU ALWAYS DID SEEM...
...LIKE SOMEONE FROM THE EDO PERIOD.
YEAH, YOU'VE MEN-TIONED THAT.
BE-SIDES ...
...WHEN YOU TOLD US OUR PREVIOUS NAMES...
...I...

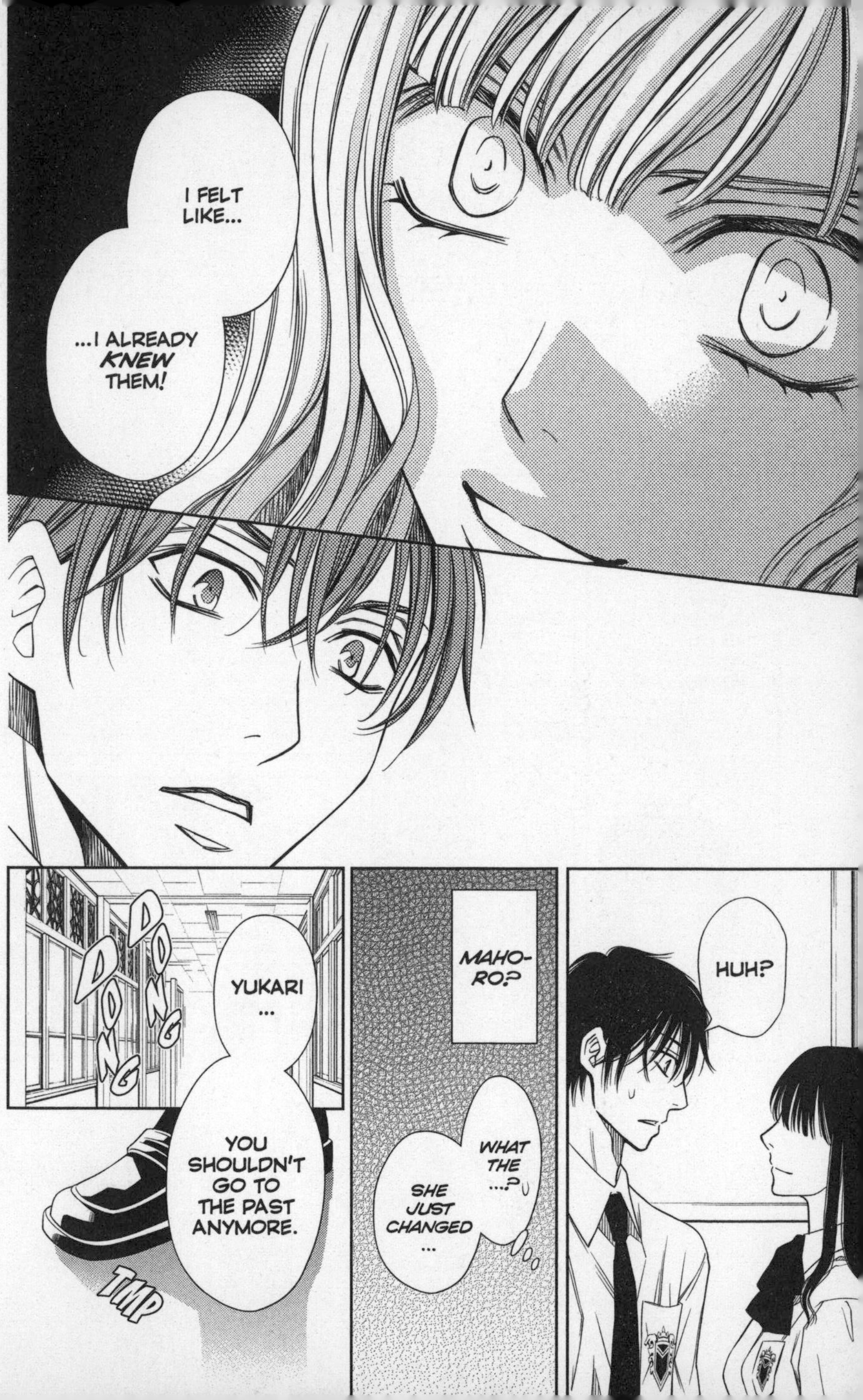
I FELT LIKE...
...I ALREADY *KNEW* THEM!
HUH?
MAHO-RO?
WHAT THE ...?
SHE JUST CHANGED ...
DONG DONG
YUKARI ...
YOU SHOULDN'T GO TO THE PAST ANYMORE.
TMP

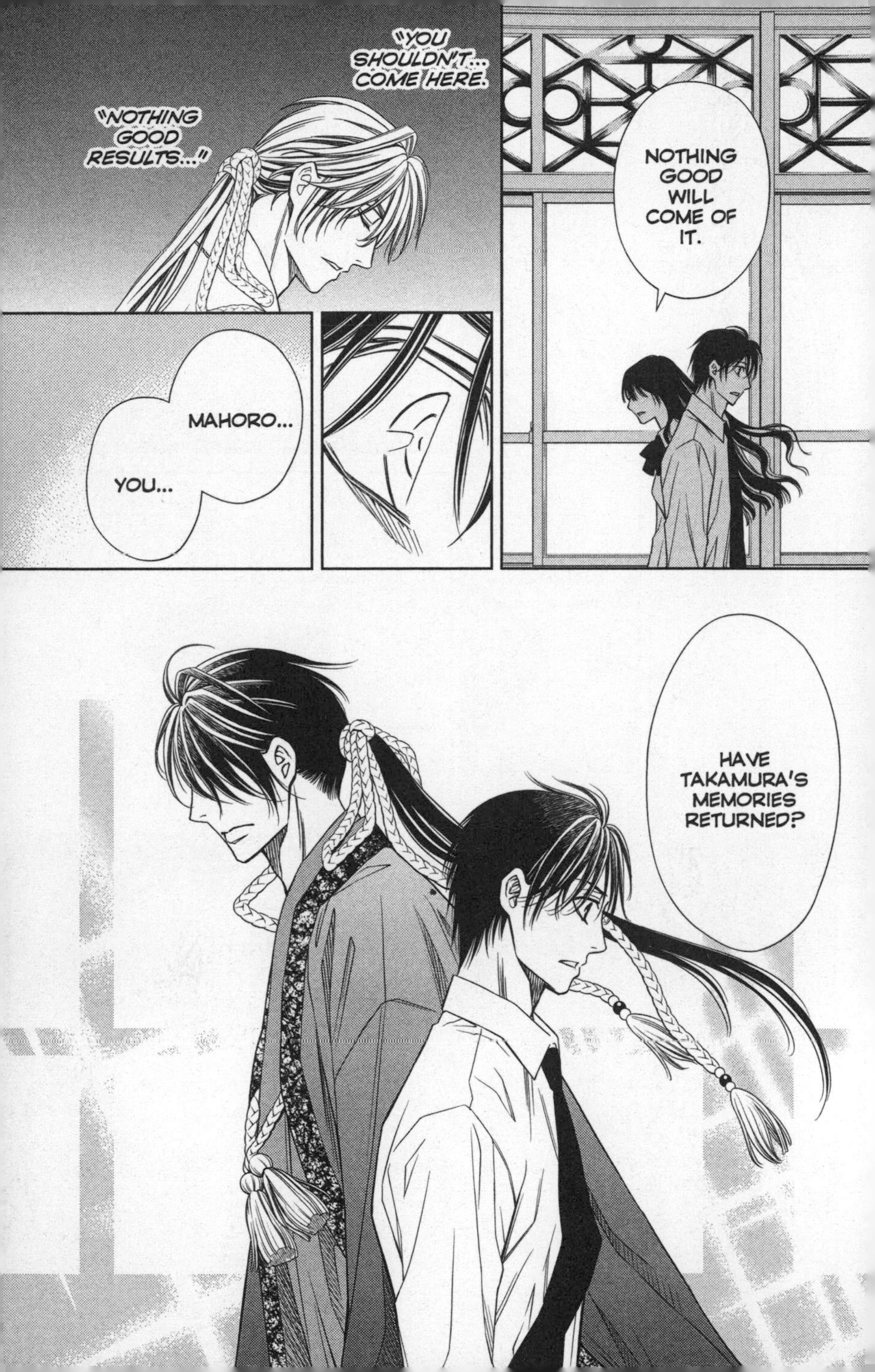
NOTHING GOOD WILL COME OF IT.
"YOU SHOULDN'T... COME HERE.
"NOTHING GOOD RESULTS..."
MAHORO... YOU...
HAVE TAKAMURA'S MEMORIES RETURNED?

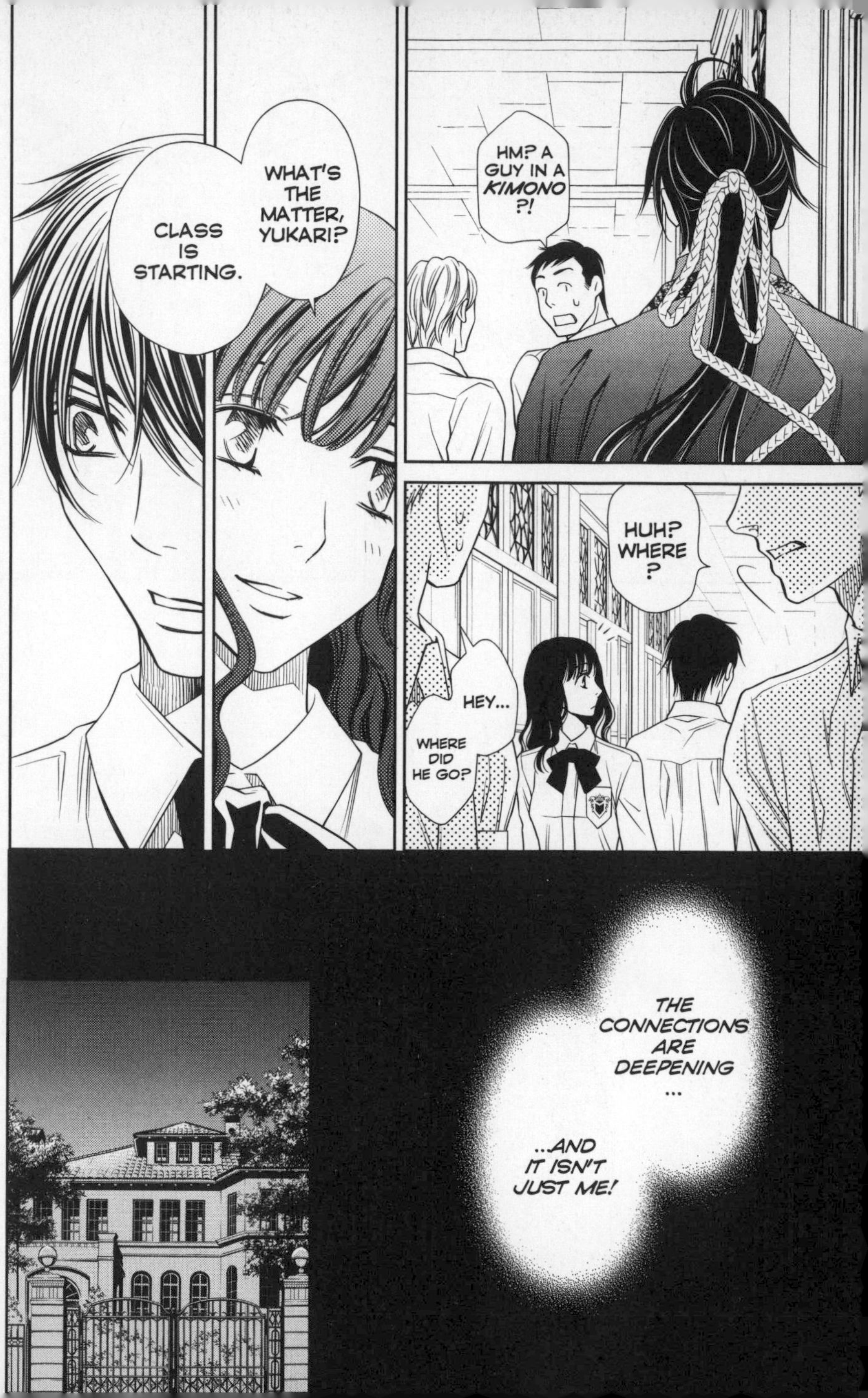
HM? A GUY IN A *KIMONO* ?!
HUH? WHERE ?
HEY...
WHERE DID HE GO?
WHAT'S THE MATTER, YUKARI?
CLASS IS STARTING.
THE CONNECTIONS ARE DEEPENING ...
...AND IT ISN'T JUST ME!

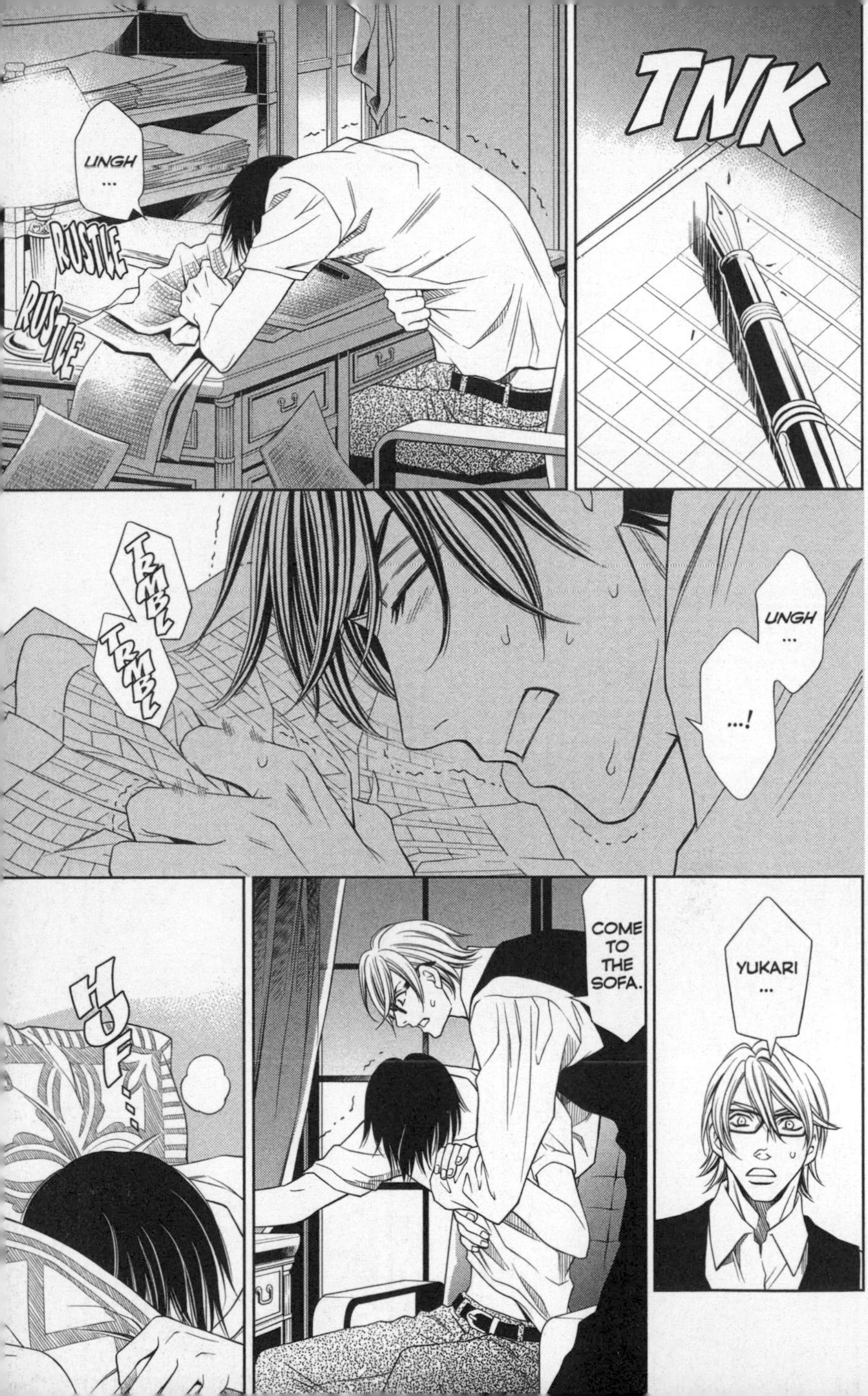
TNK
UNGH ...
RUSTLE
RUSTLE
UNGH ...
...!
TRMBL
TRMBL
YUKARI ...
COME TO THE SOFA.
HUF...

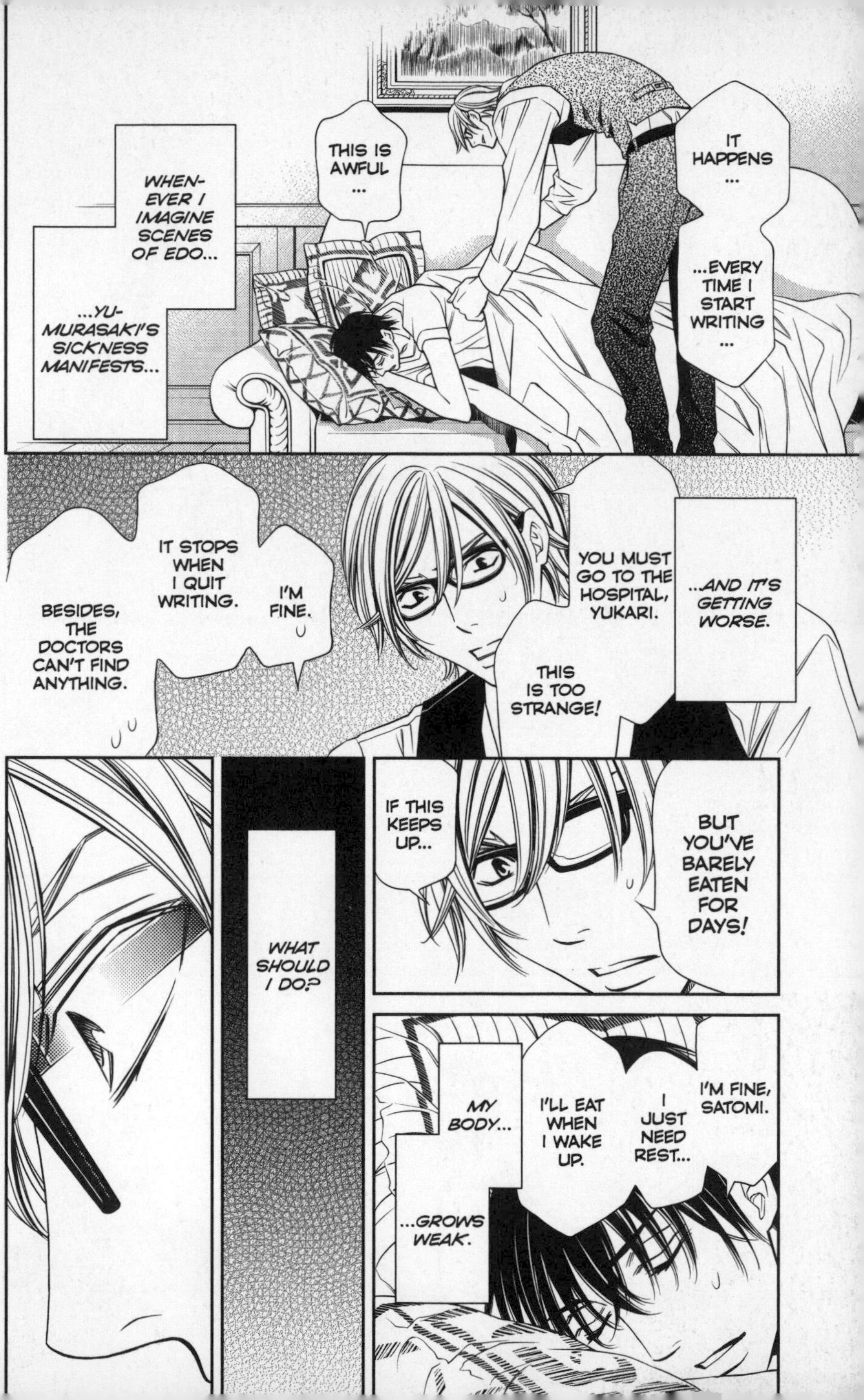
IT HAPPENS ...
...EVERY TIME I START WRITING ...
THIS IS AWFUL ...
WHENEVER I IMAGINE SCENES OF EDO...
...YUMURASAKI'S SICKNESS MANIFESTS...
...AND IT'S GETTING WORSE.
YOU MUST GO TO THE HOSPITAL, YUKARI.
THIS IS TOO STRANGE!
I'M FINE.
IT STOPS WHEN I QUIT WRITING.
BESIDES, THE DOCTORS CAN'T FIND ANYTHING.
BUT YOU'VE BARELY EATEN FOR DAYS!
IF THIS KEEPS UP...
I'M FINE, SATOMI.
I JUST NEED REST...
I'LL EAT WHEN I WAKE UP.
MY BODY...
...GROWS WEAK.
WHAT SHOULD I DO?

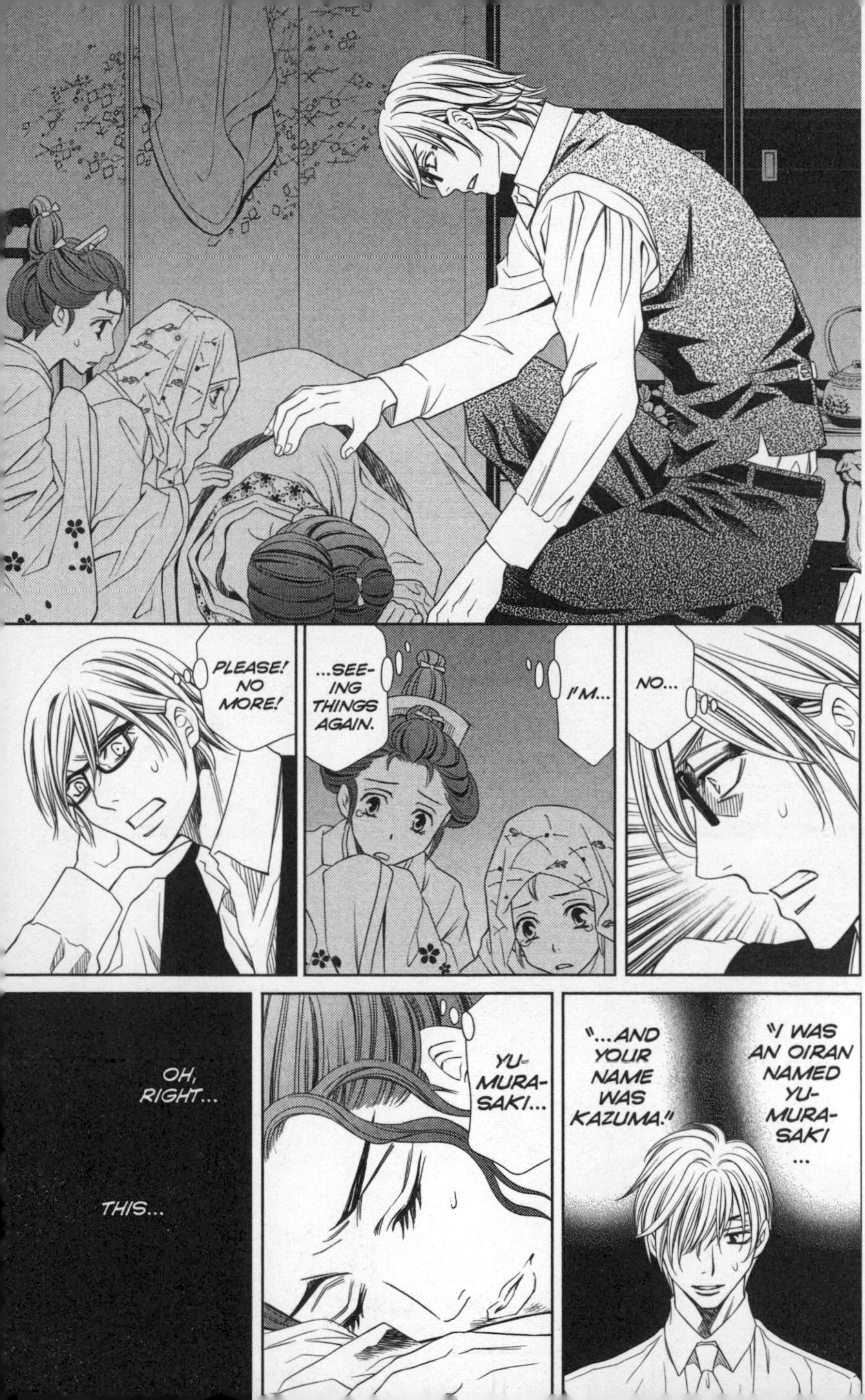
NO...
I'M...
...SEEING THINGS AGAIN.
PLEASE! NO MORE!
"I WAS AN OIRAN NAMED YUMURASAKI...
"...AND YOUR NAME WAS KAZUMA."
YUMURASAKI...
OH, RIGHT...
THIS...

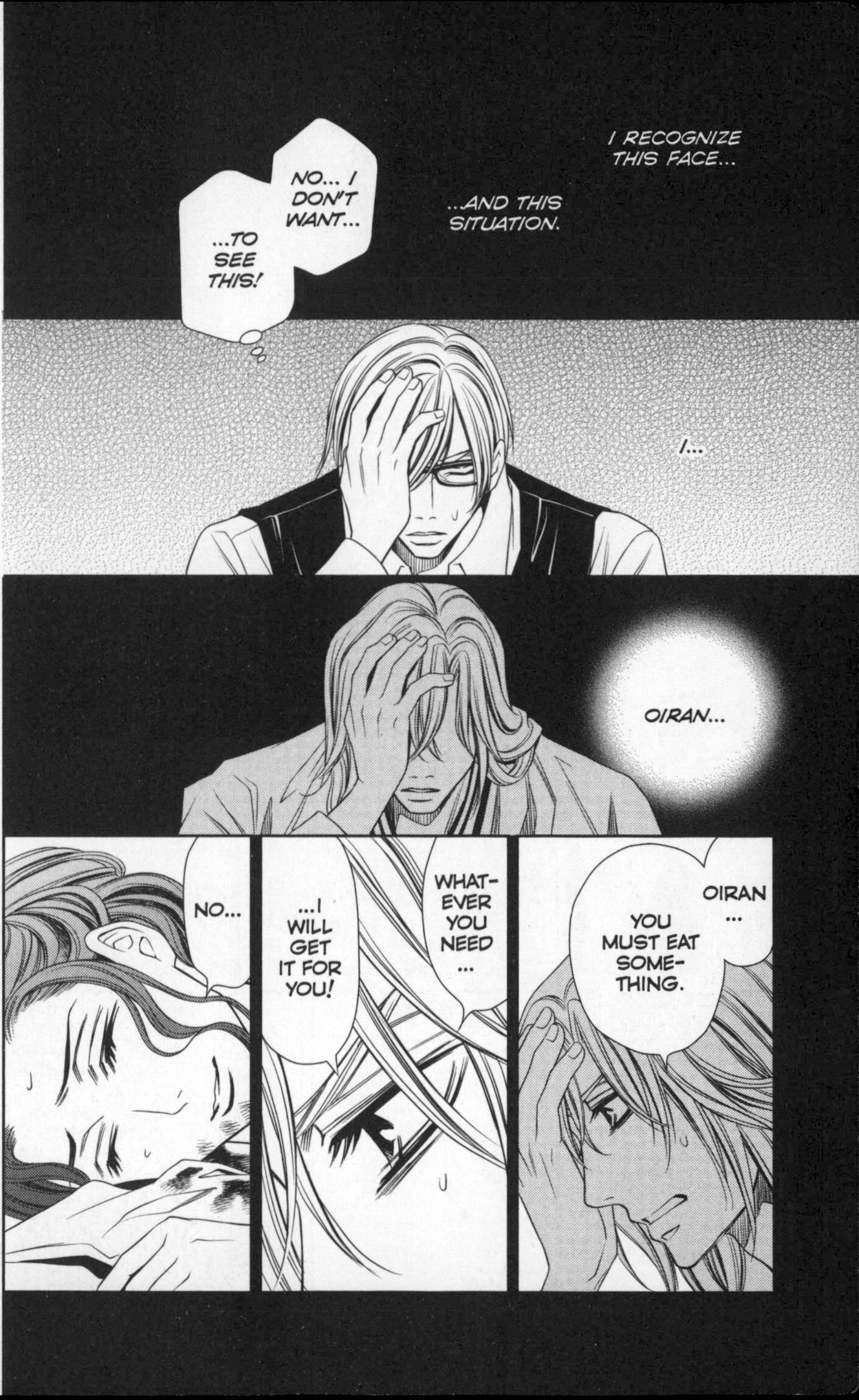
I RECOGNIZE THIS FACE...
...AND THIS SITUATION.
NO... I DON'T WANT... ...TO SEE THIS!
I...
OIRAN...
OIRAN ...
YOU MUST EAT SOMETHING.
WHATEVER YOU NEED ...
...I WILL GET IT FOR YOU!
NO...

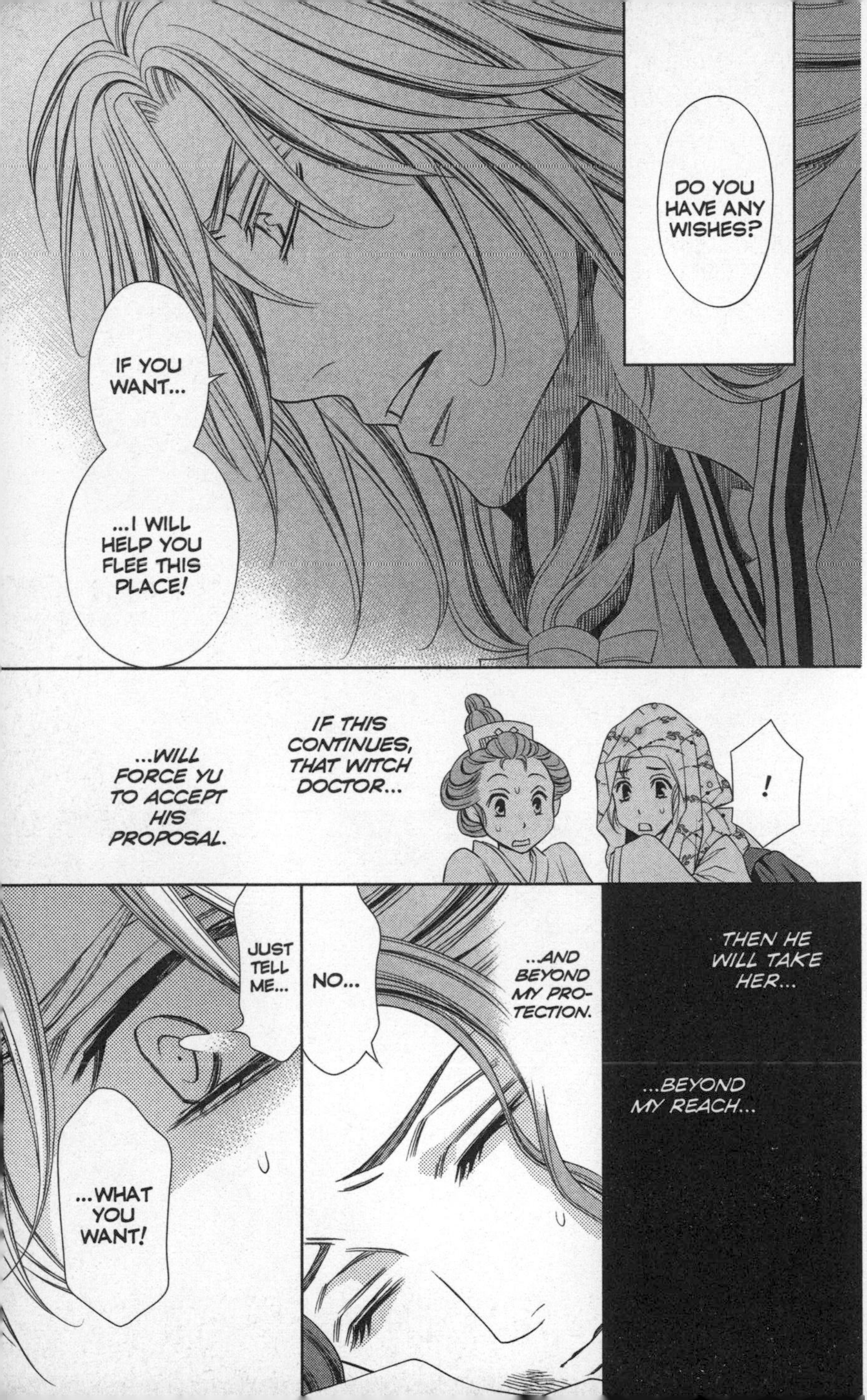
DO YOU HAVE ANY WISHES?
IF YOU WANT...
...I WILL HELP YOU FLEE THIS PLACE!
!
IF THIS CONTINUES, THAT WITCH DOCTOR...
...WILL FORCE YU TO ACCEPT HIS PROPOSAL.
THEN HE WILL TAKE HER...
...BEYOND MY REACH...
...AND BEYOND MY PRO-TECTION.
NO...
JUST TELL ME...
...WHAT YOU WANT!

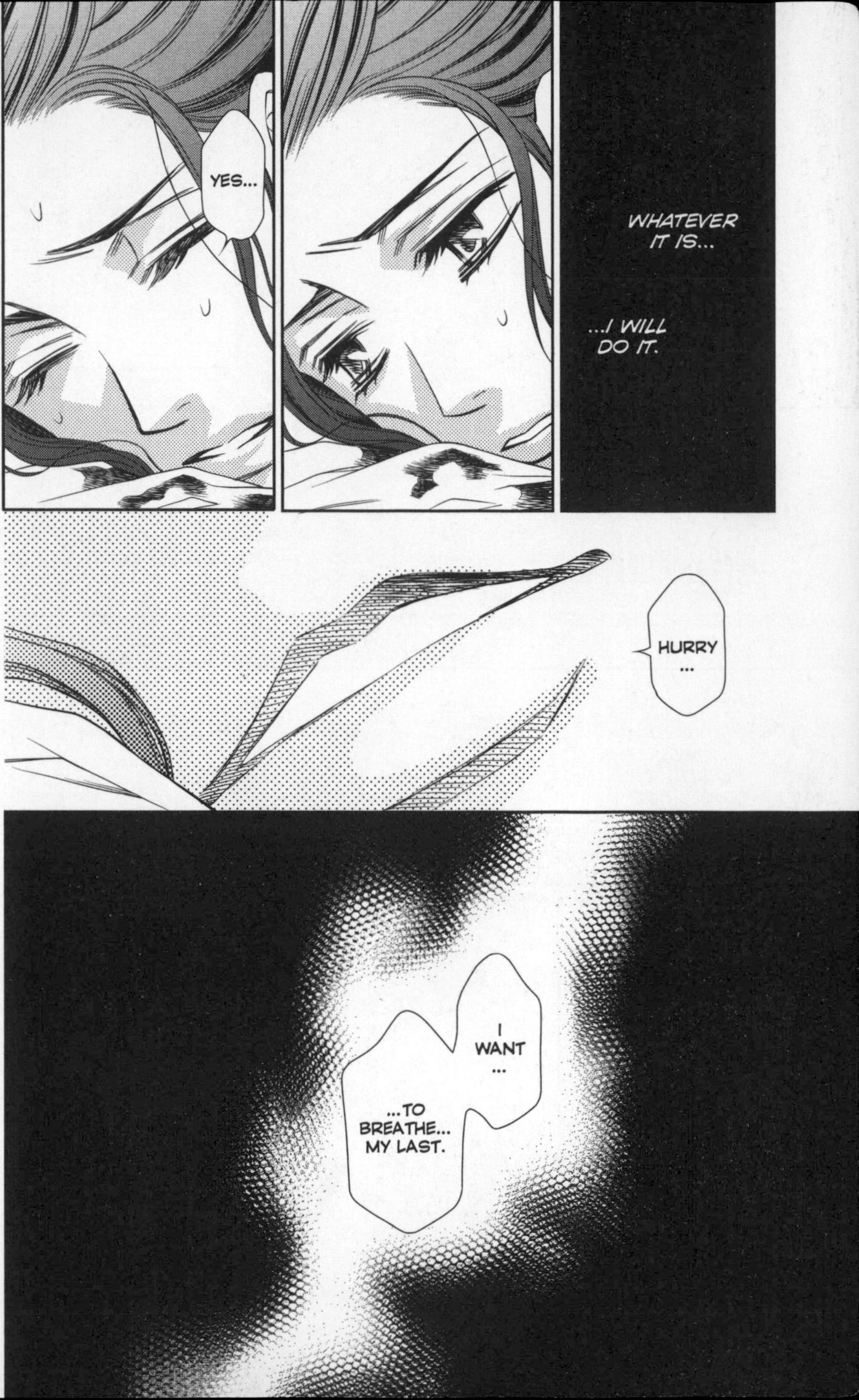
WHATEVER IT IS...
...I WILL DO IT.
YES...
HURRY ...
I WANT ...
...TO BREATHE... MY LAST.

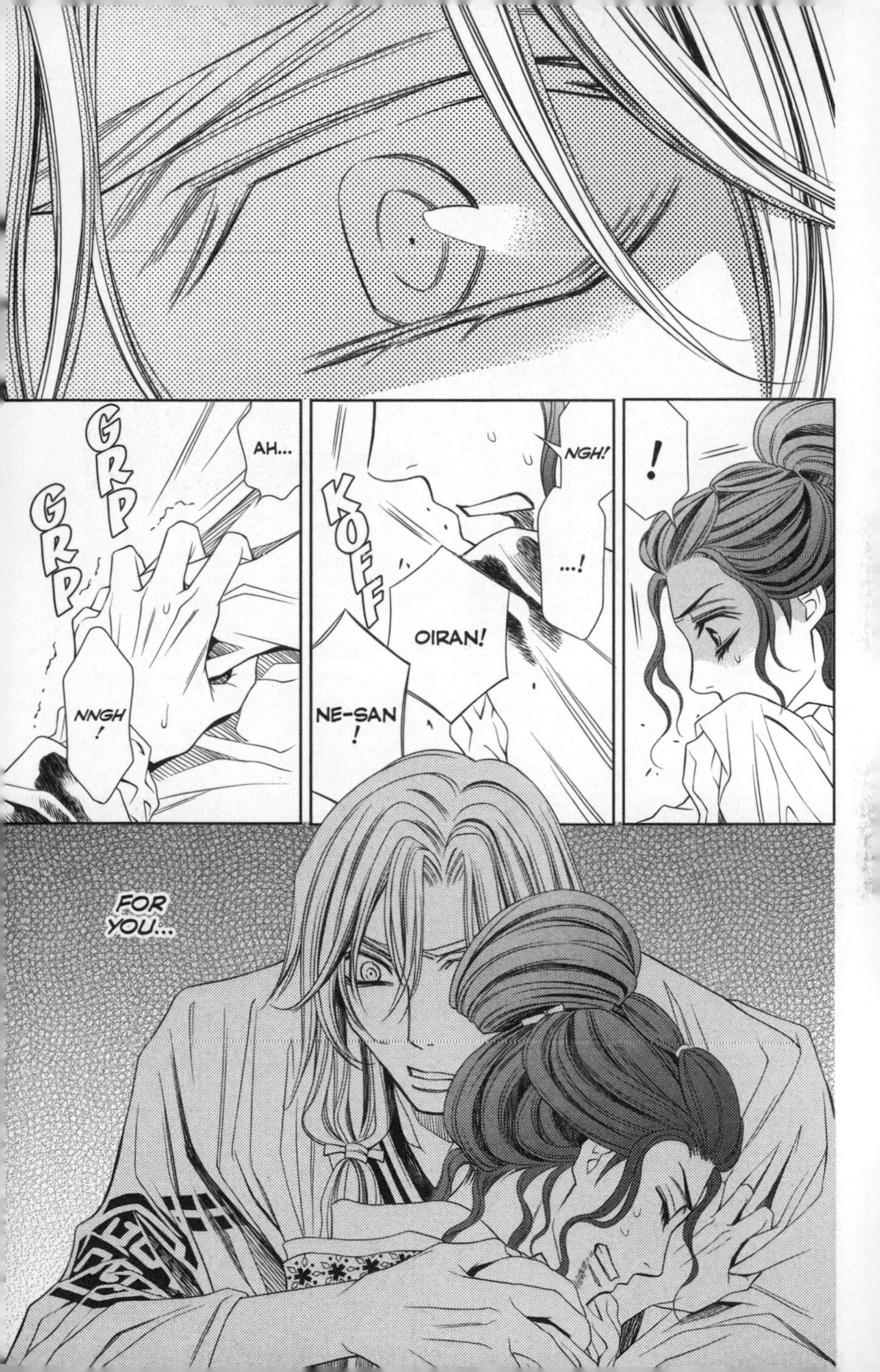
!
NGH!
...!
KOFF
OIRAN!
NE-SAN!
AH...
GRP
GRP
NNGH!
FOR YOU...

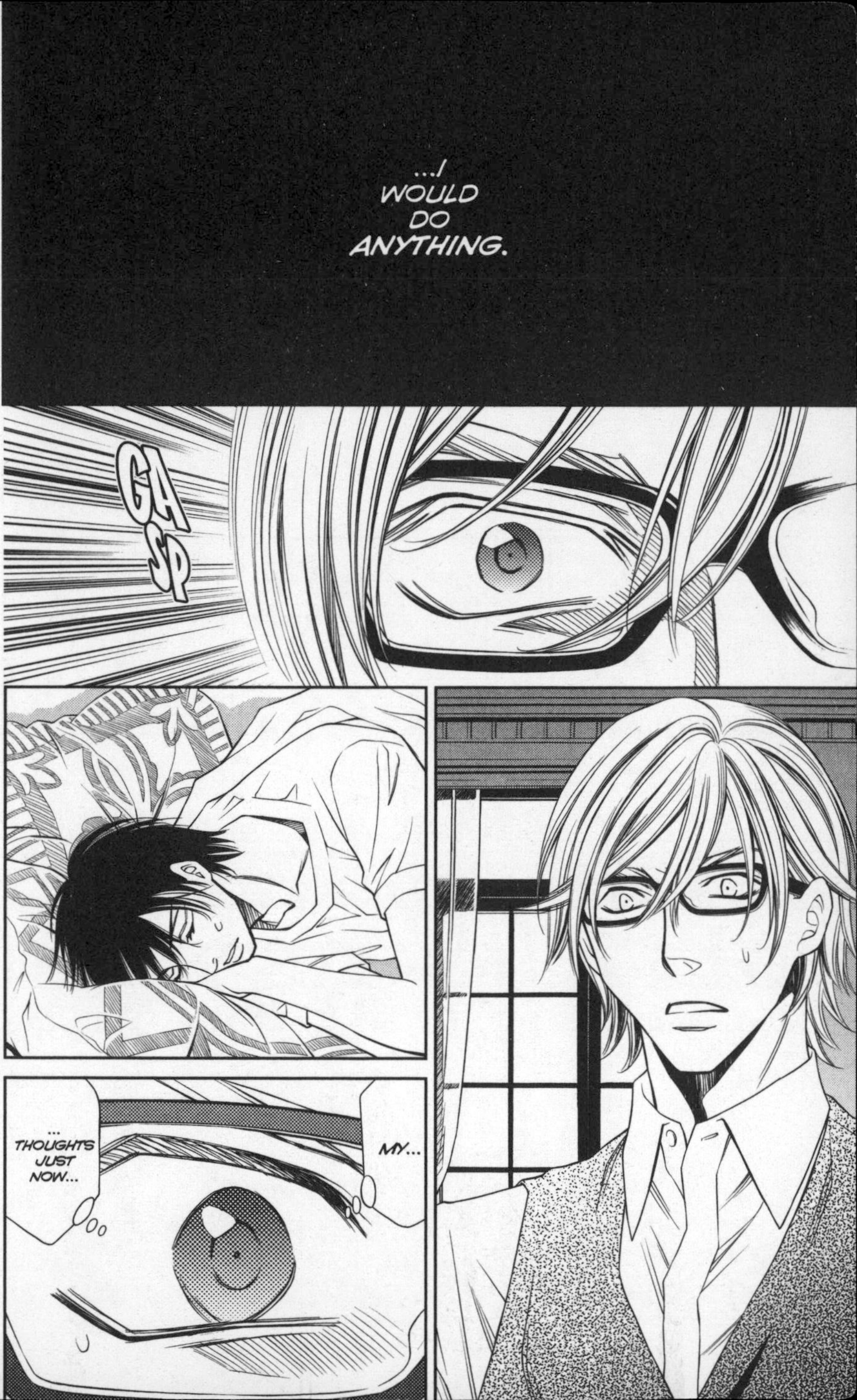
...I WOULD DO ANYTHING.
GASP
MY...
...THOUGHTS JUST NOW...

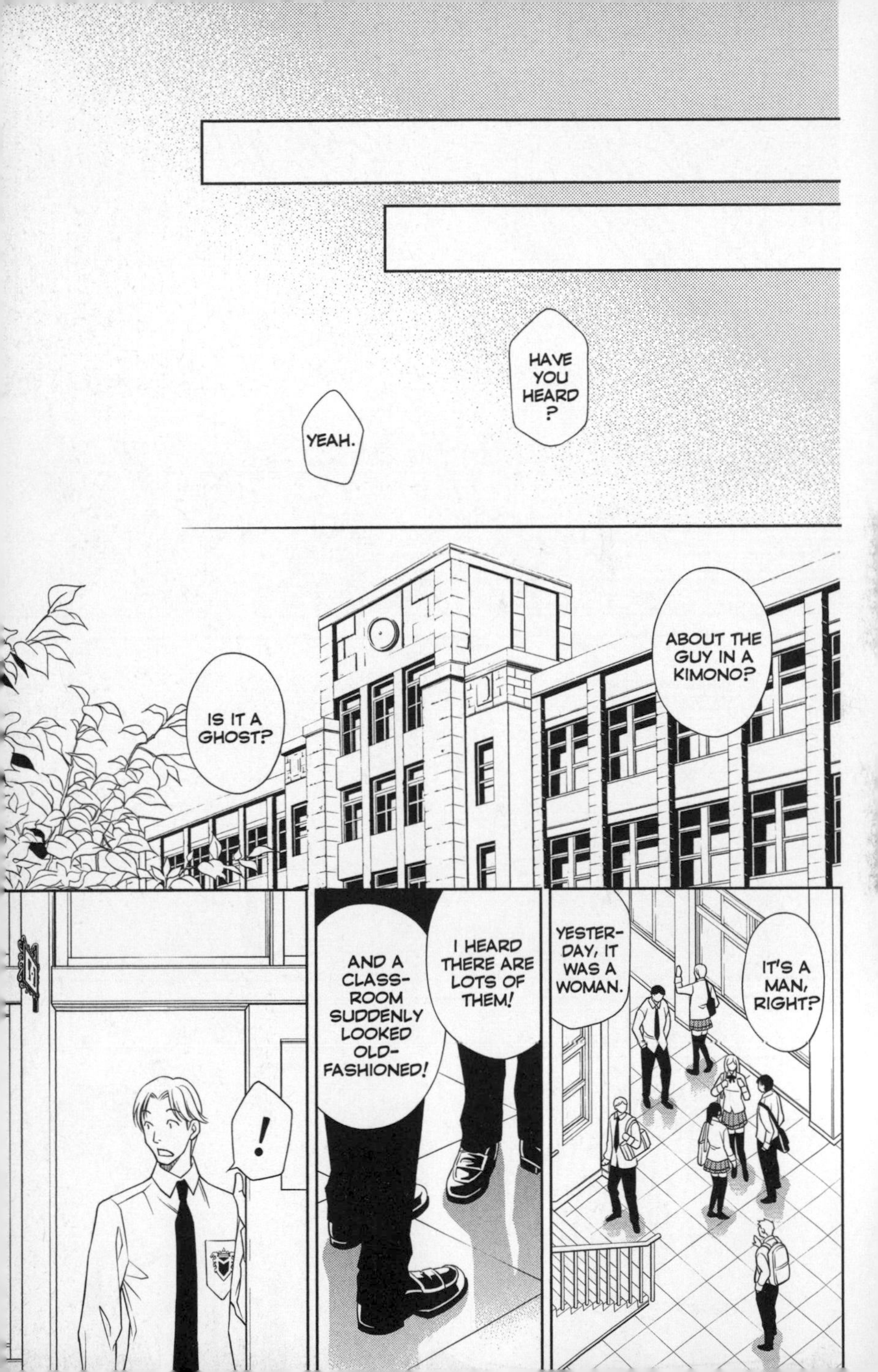
HAVE YOU HEARD?
YEAH.
ABOUT THE GUY IN A KIMONO?
IS IT A GHOST?
IT'S A MAN, RIGHT?
YESTER-DAY, IT WAS A WOMAN.
I HEARD THERE ARE LOTS OF THEM!
AND A CLASS-ROOM SUDDENLY LOOKED OLD-FASHIONED!
!

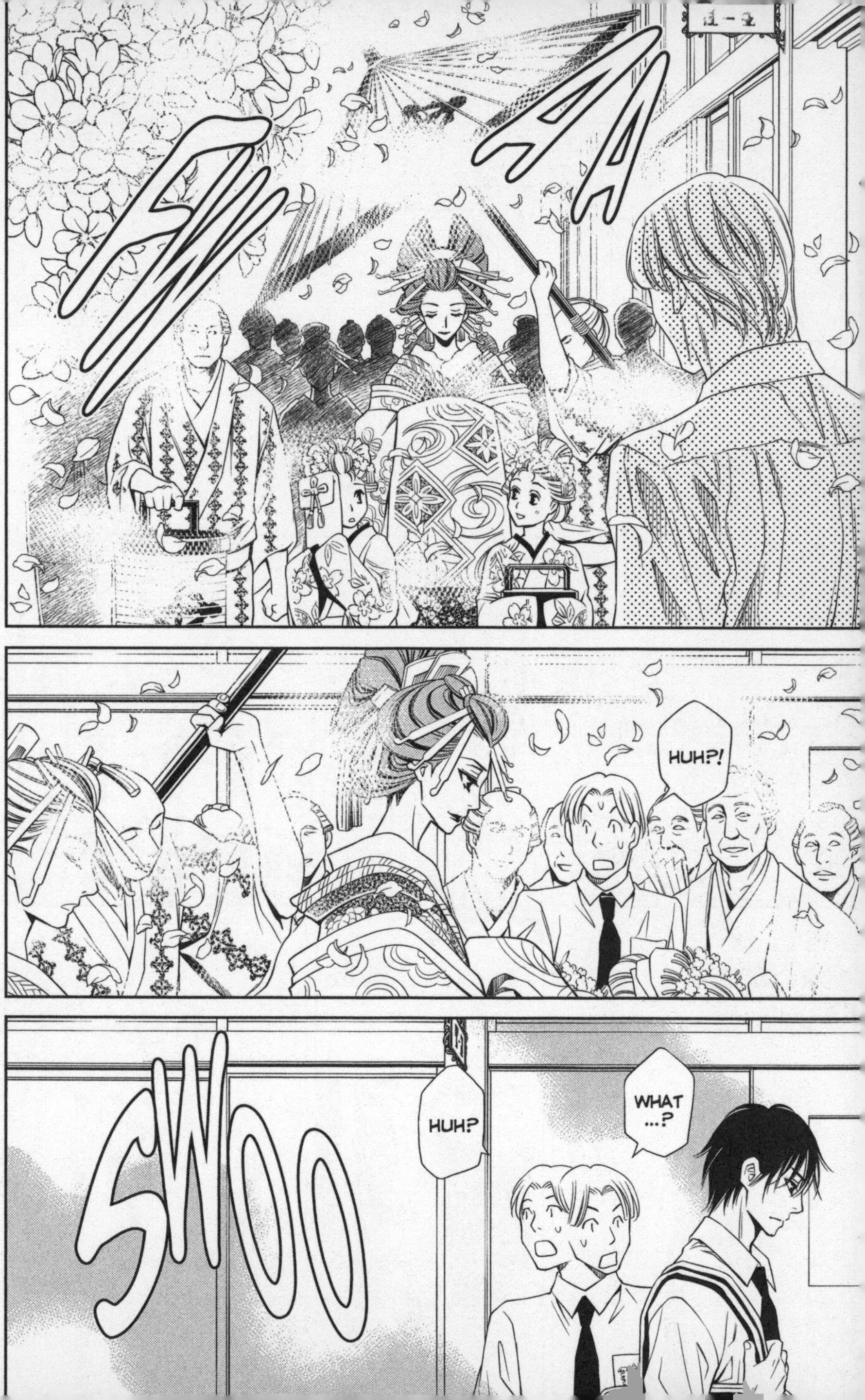
FWAA
HUH?!
WHAT ...?
HUH?
SWOO

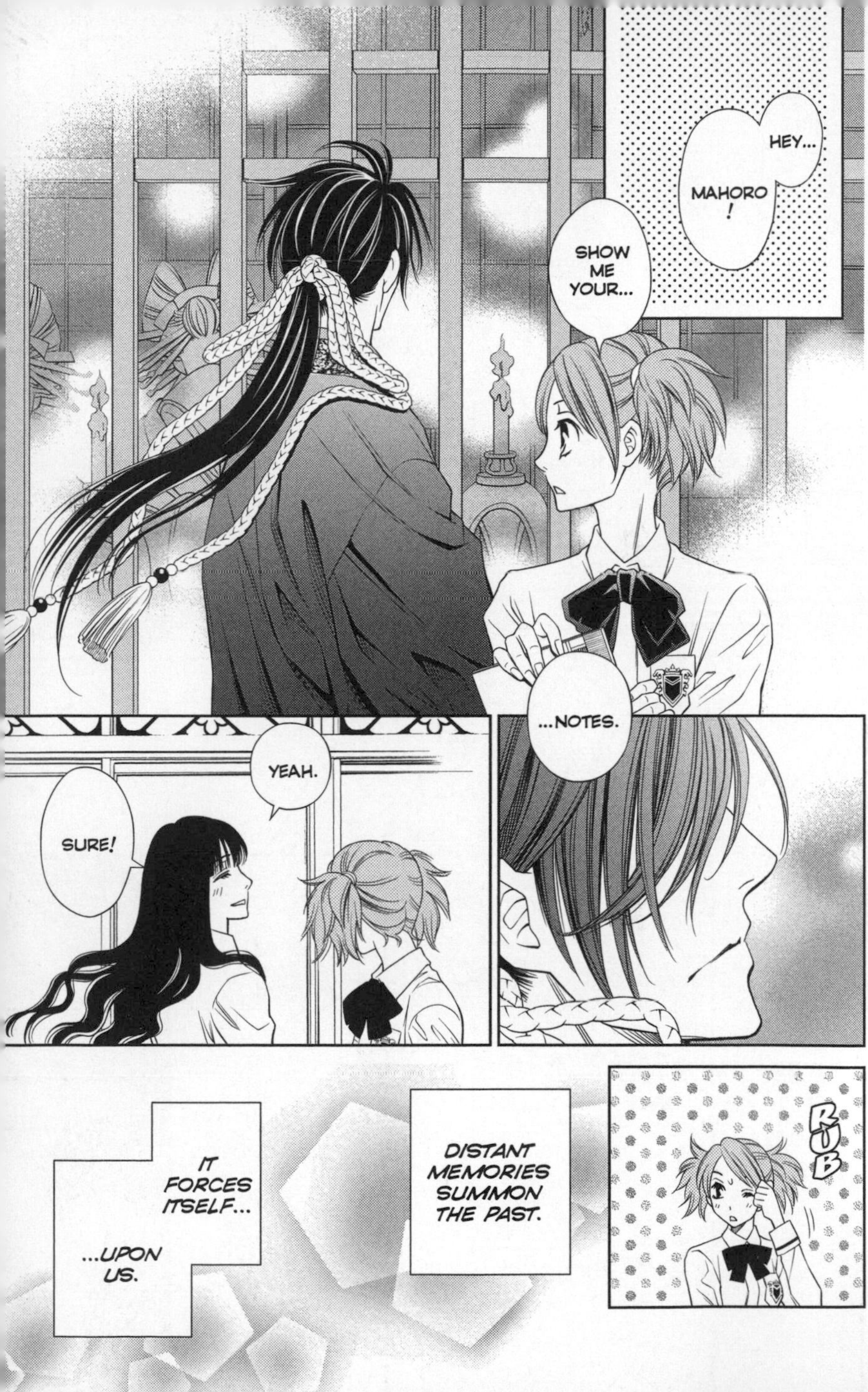
HEY... MAHORO!
SHOW ME YOUR...
...NOTES.
YEAH.
SURE!
RUB
DISTANT MEMORIES SUMMON THE PAST.
IT FORCES ITSELF...
...UPON US.

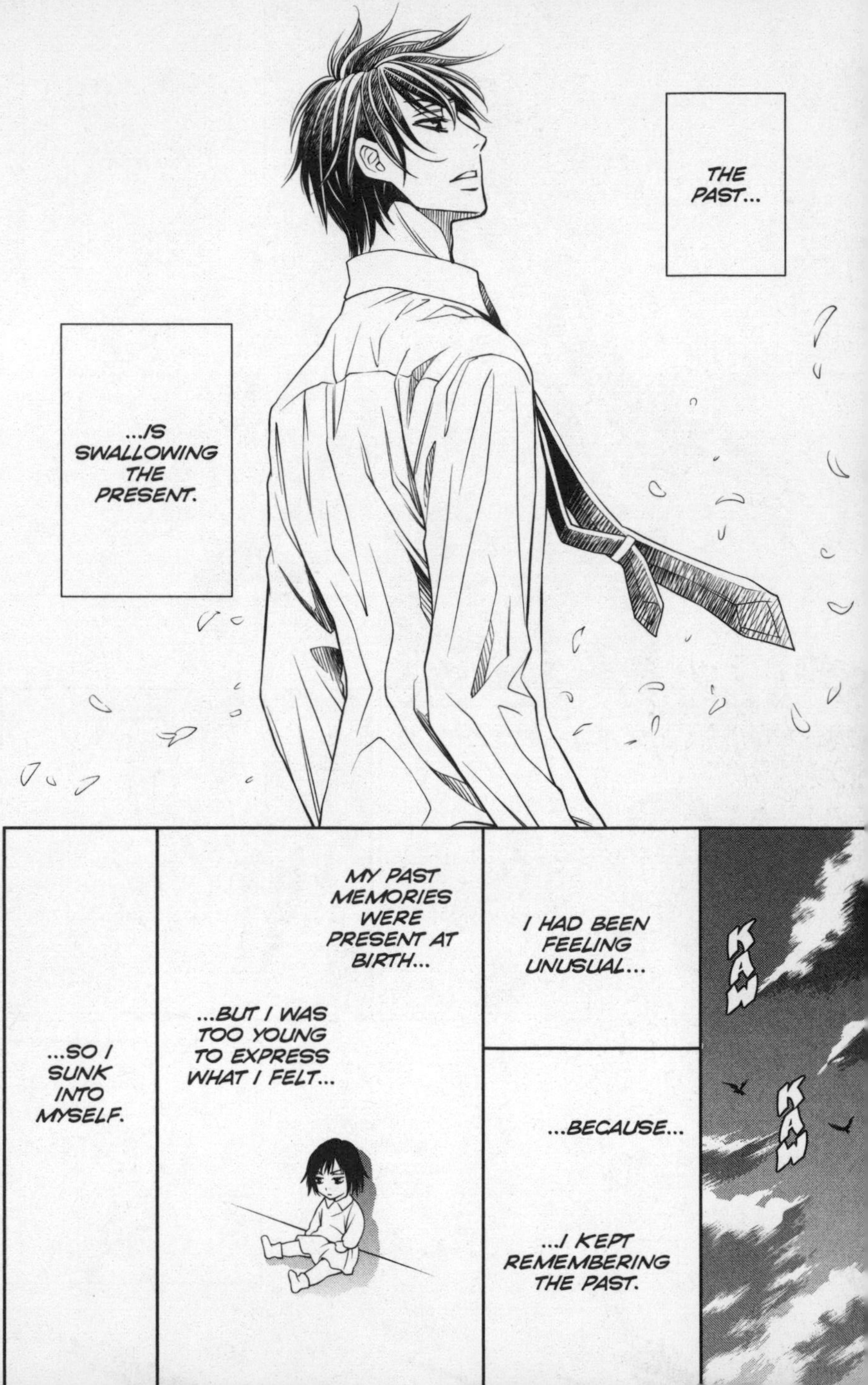
THE PAST...
...IS SWALLOWING THE PRESENT.
KAW
KAW
I HAD BEEN FEELING UNUSUAL...
...BECAUSE...
...I KEPT REMEMBERING THE PAST.
MY PAST MEMORIES WERE PRESENT AT BIRTH...
...BUT I WAS TOO YOUNG TO EXPRESS WHAT I FELT...
...SO I SUNK INTO MYSELF.

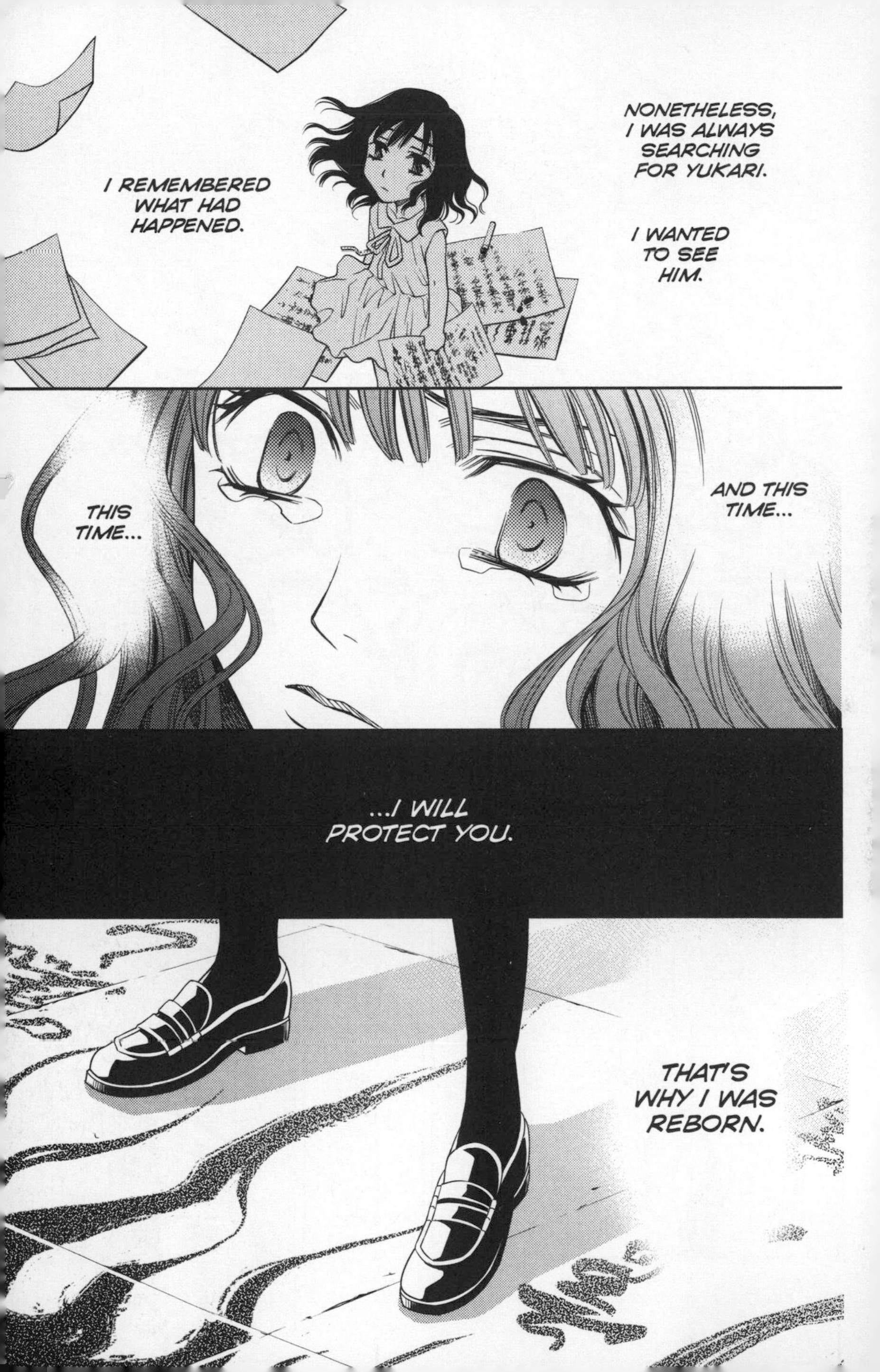
NONETHELESS, I WAS ALWAYS SEARCHING FOR YUKARI.
I WANTED TO SEE HIM.
I REMEMBERED WHAT HAD HAPPENED.
AND THIS TIME...
THIS TIME...
...I WILL PROTECT YOU.
THAT'S WHY I WAS REBORN.

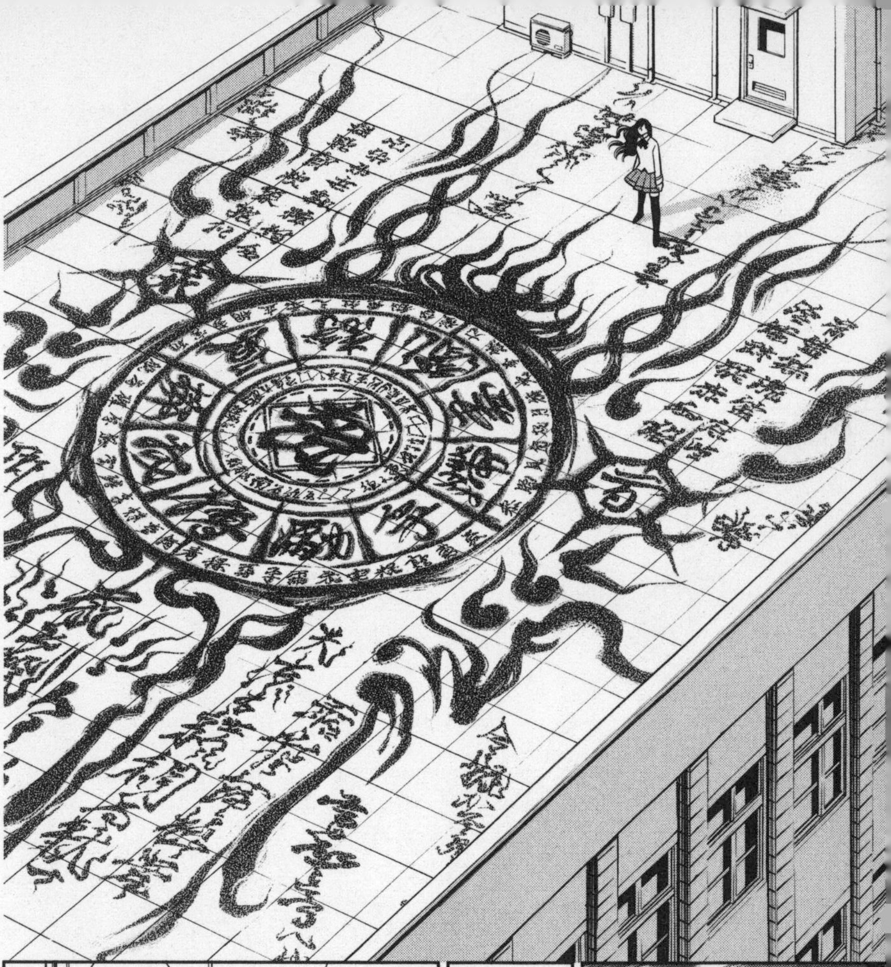
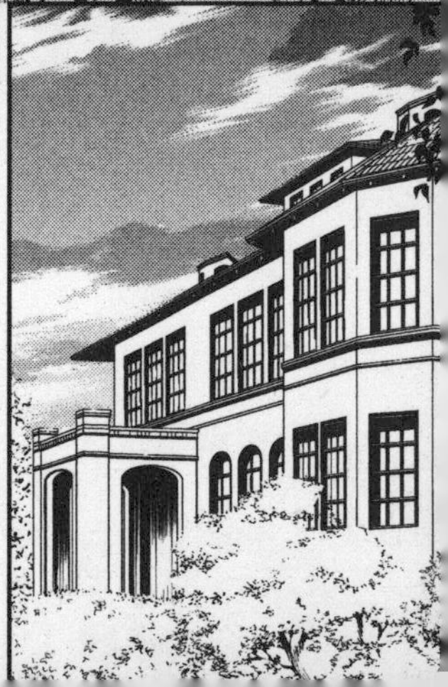
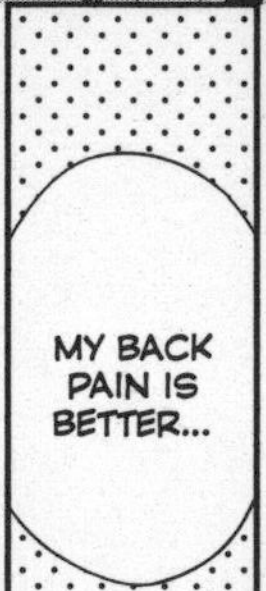
MY BACK PAIN IS BETTER...
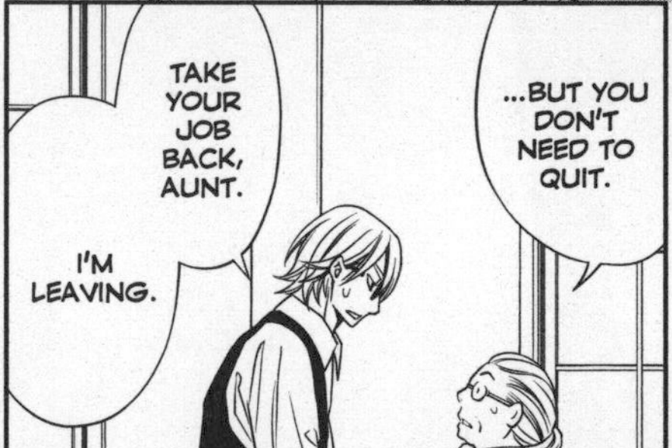
...BUT YOU DON'T NEED TO QUIT.
TAKE YOUR JOB BACK, AUNT.
I'M LEAVING.

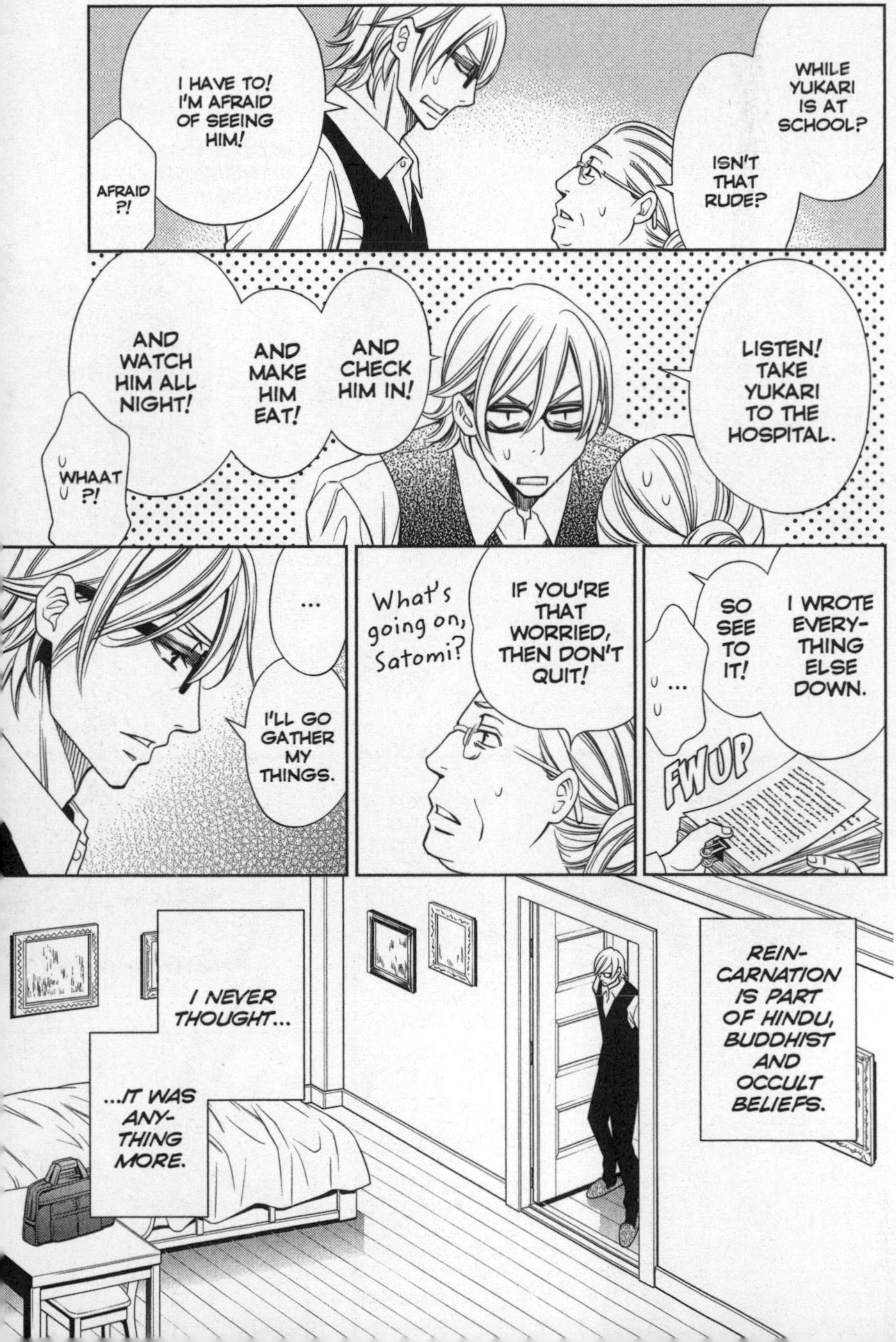
WHILE YUKARI IS AT SCHOOL?
ISN'T THAT RUDE?
I HAVE TO! I'M AFRAID OF SEEING HIM!
AFRAID?!
LISTEN! TAKE YUKARI TO THE HOSPITAL.
AND CHECK HIM IN!
AND MAKE HIM EAT!
AND WATCH HIM ALL NIGHT!
WHAAT?!
I WROTE EVERY-THING ELSE DOWN.
SO SEE TO IT!
...
FWUP
IF YOU'RE THAT WORRIED, THEN DON'T QUIT!
What's going on, Satomi?
...
I'LL GO GATHER MY THINGS.
REIN-CARNATION IS PART OF HINDU, BUDDHIST AND OCCULT BELIEFS.
I NEVER THOUGHT...
...IT WAS ANY-THING MORE.

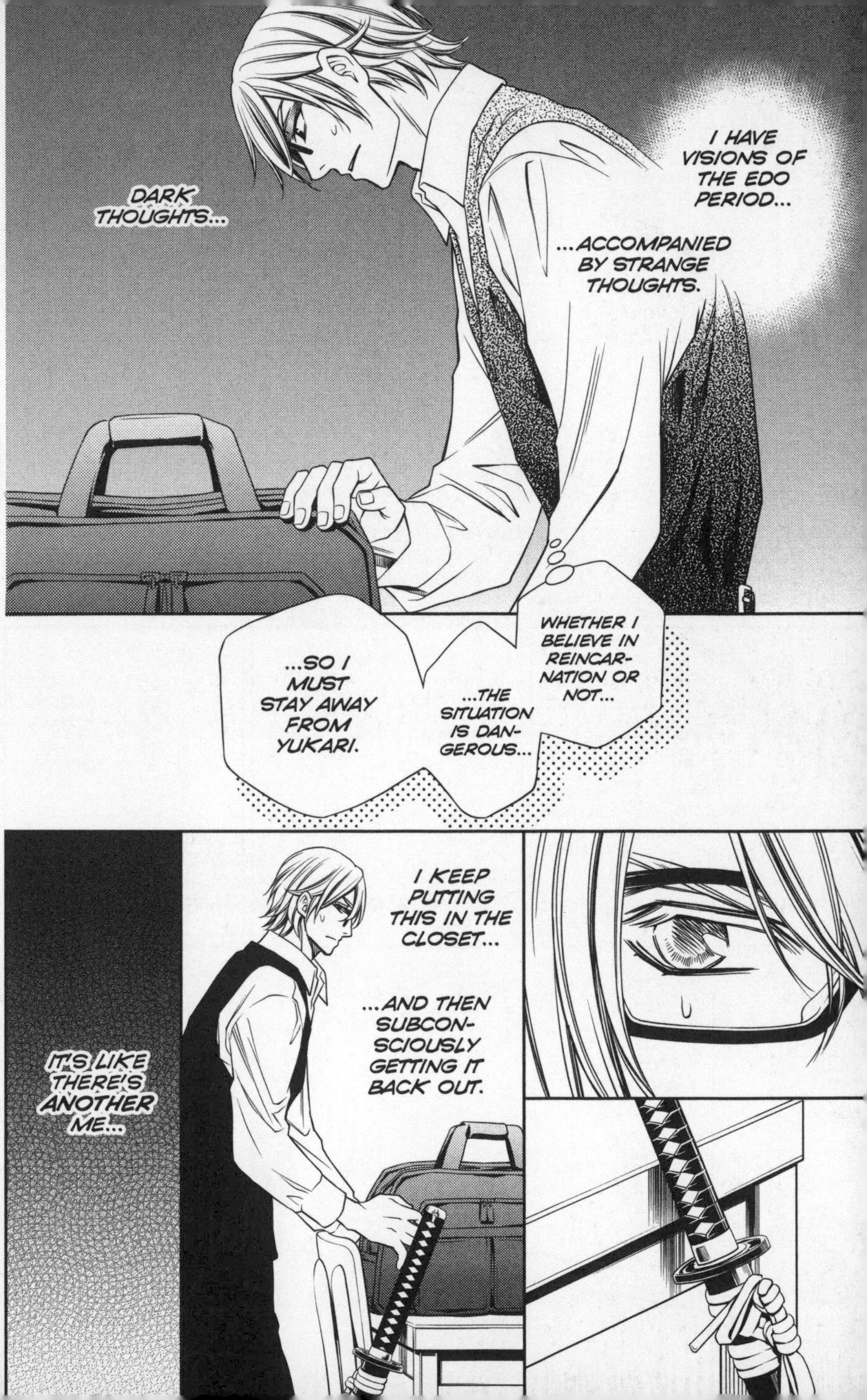
I HAVE VISIONS OF THE EDO PERIOD...
...ACCOMPANIED BY STRANGE THOUGHTS.
DARK THOUGHTS...
WHETHER I BELIEVE IN REINCAR-NATION OR NOT...
...THE SITUATION IS DAN-GEROUS...
...SO I MUST STAY AWAY FROM YUKARI.
I KEEP PUTTING THIS IN THE CLOSET...
...AND THEN SUBCON-SCIOUSLY GETTING IT BACK OUT.
IT'S LIKE THERE'S ANOTHER ME...

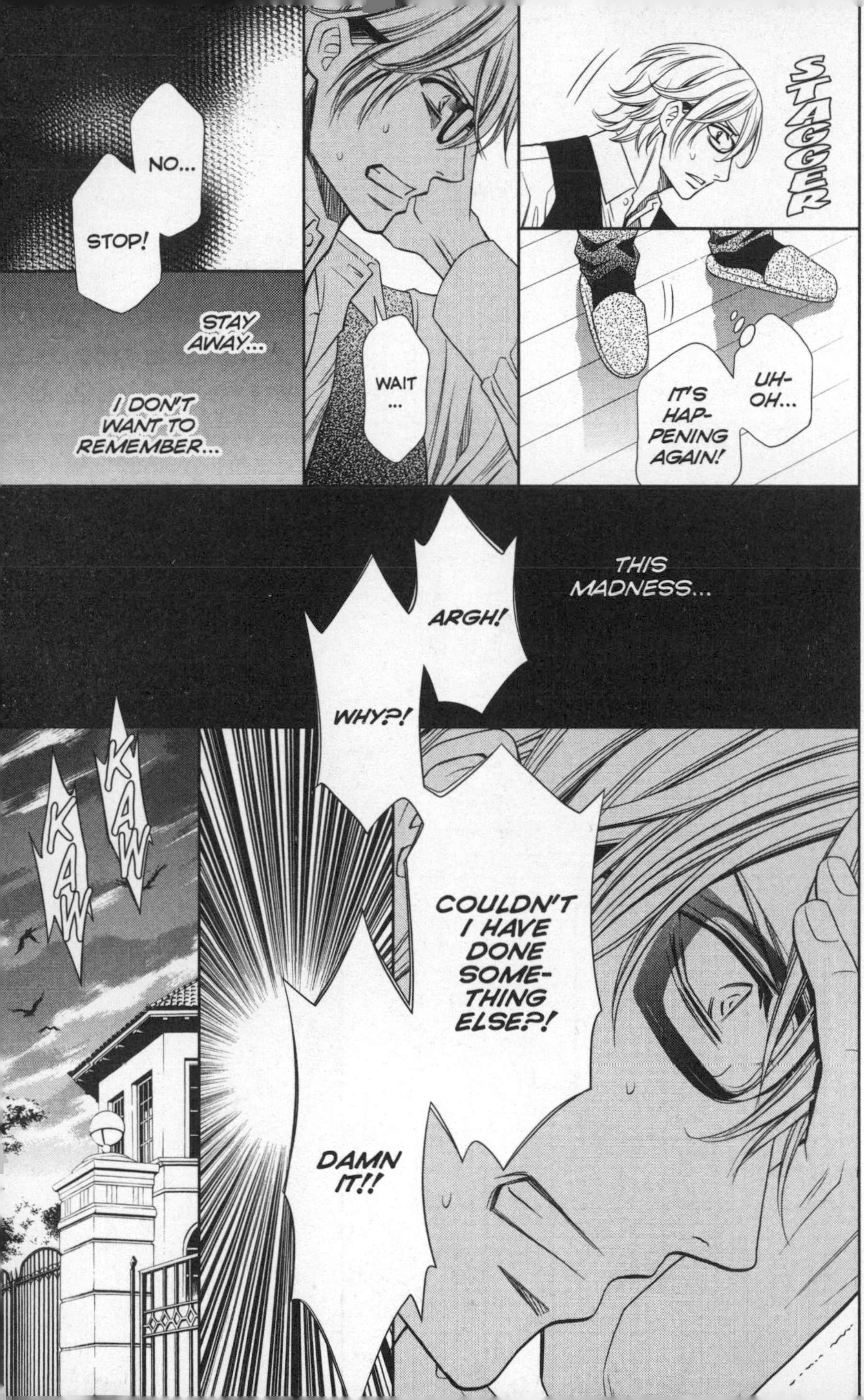
STAGGER
UH-OH... IT'S HAPPENING AGAIN!
WAIT ...
NO...
STOP!
STAY AWAY...
I DON'T WANT TO REMEMBER...
THIS MADNESS...
ARGH!
WHY?!
COULDN'T I HAVE DONE SOMETHING ELSE?!
DAMN IT!!
KAW
KAW

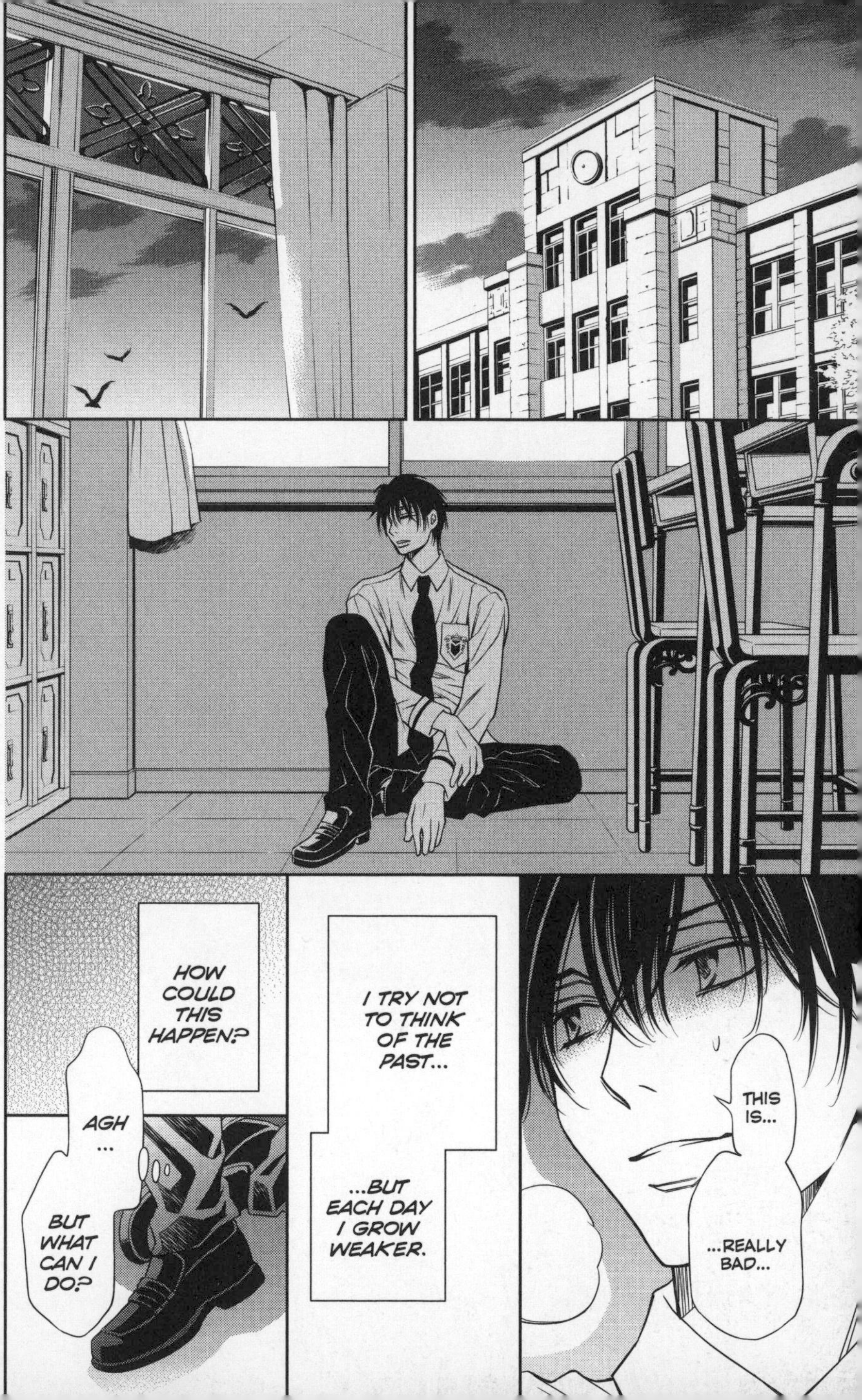
THIS IS...
...REALLY BAD...
I TRY NOT TO THINK OF THE PAST...
...BUT EACH DAY I GROW WEAKER.
HOW COULD THIS HAPPEN?
AGH...
BUT WHAT CAN I DO?

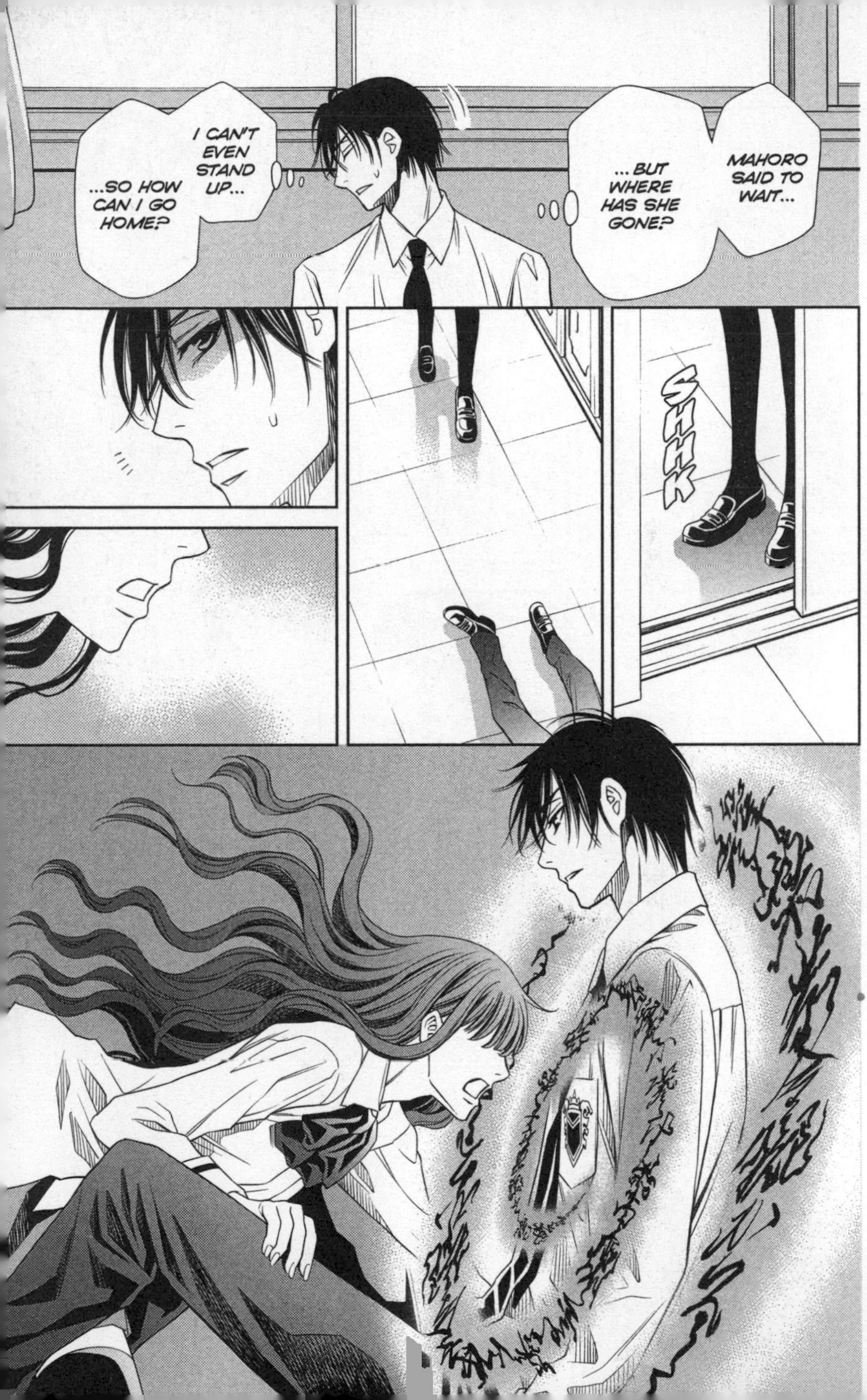
MAHORO SAID TO WAIT...
...BUT WHERE HAS SHE GONE?
I CAN'T EVEN STAND UP...
...SO HOW CAN I GO HOME?
SHHK

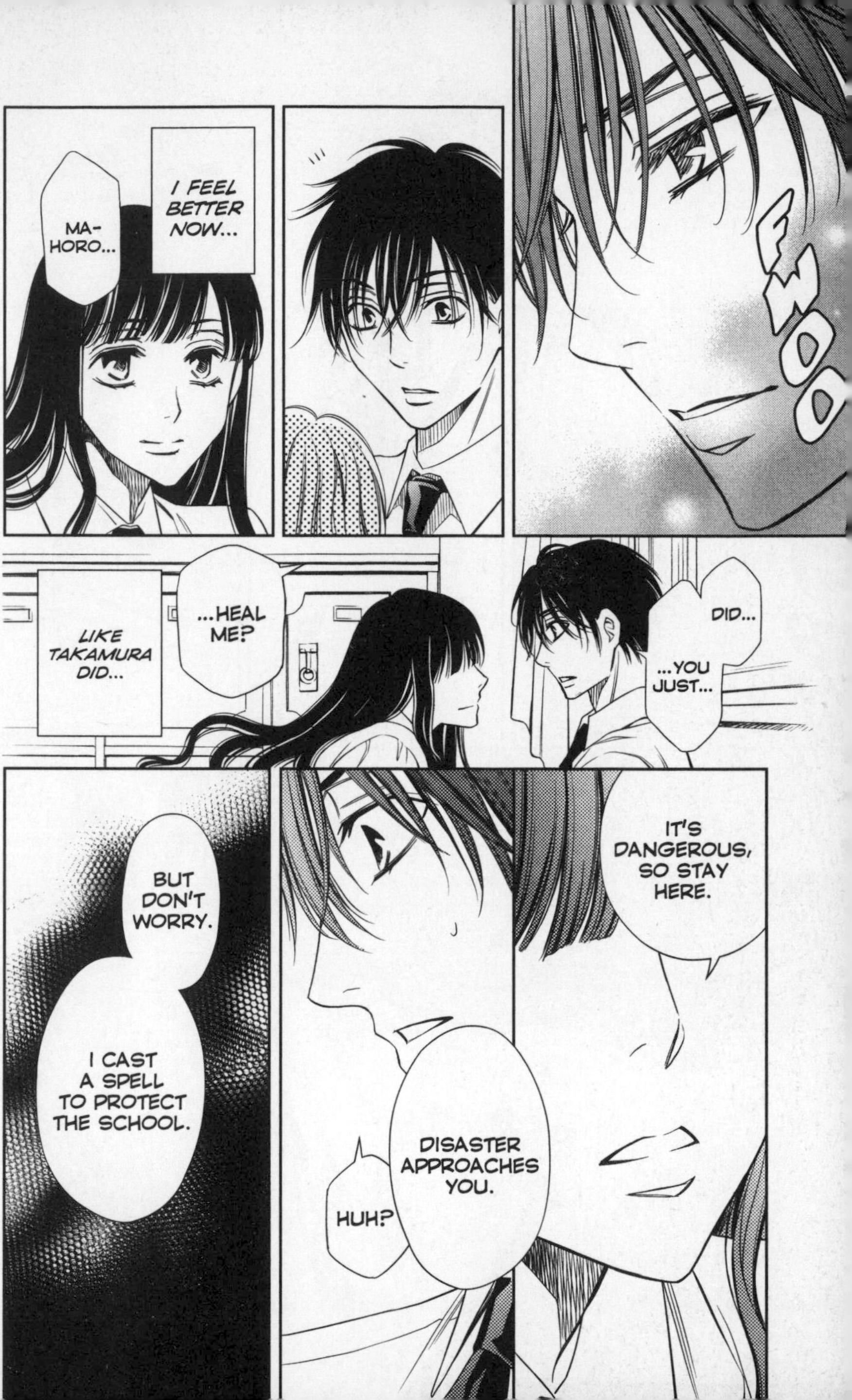
FWOO
I FEEL BETTER NOW...
MA-HORO...
DID...
...YOU JUST...
...HEAL ME?
LIKE TAKAMURA DID...
IT'S DANGEROUS, SO STAY HERE.
DISASTER APPROACHES YOU.
HUH?
BUT DON'T WORRY.
I CAST A SPELL TO PROTECT THE SCHOOL.

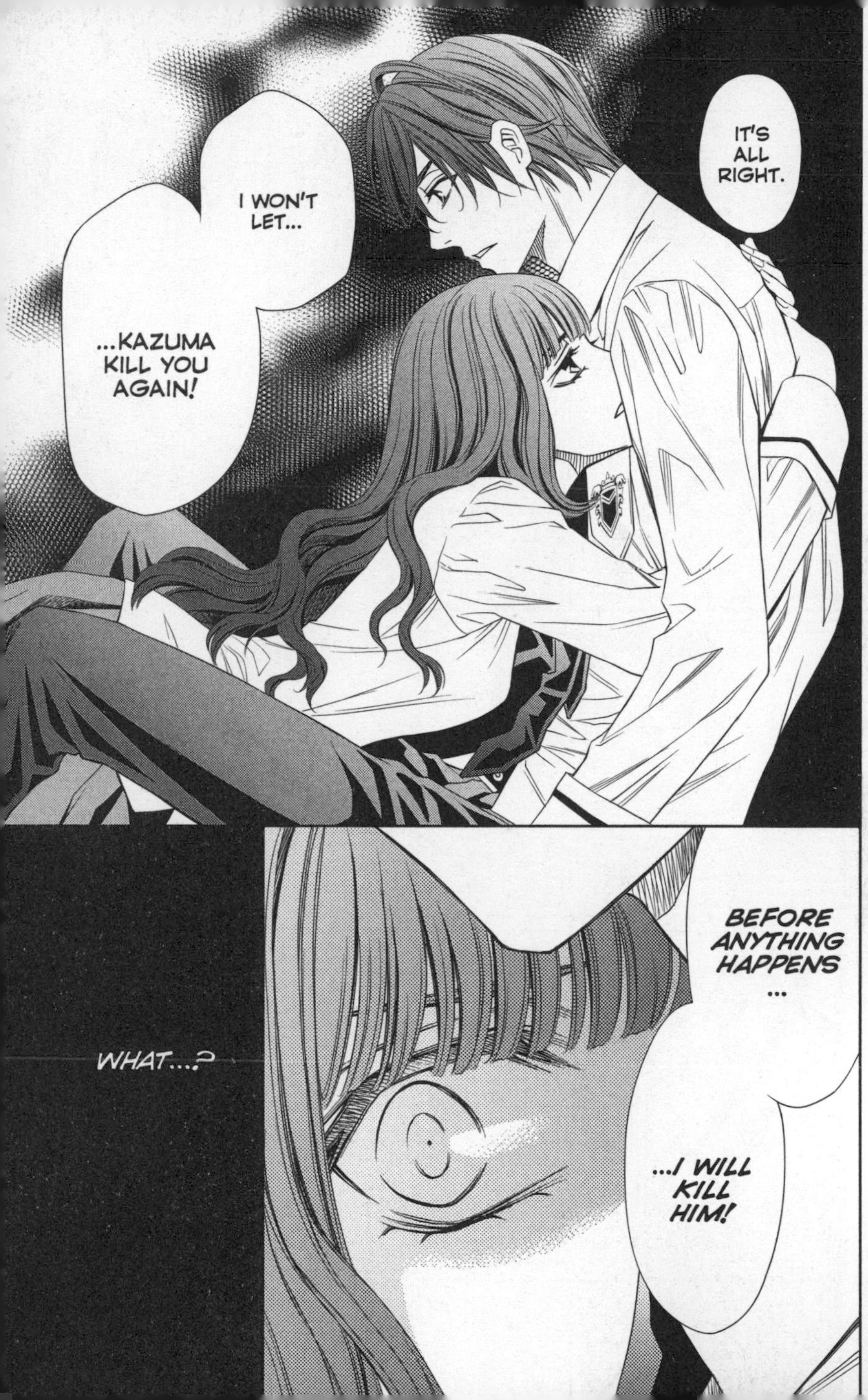
IT'S ALL RIGHT.
I WON'T LET...
...KAZUMA KILL YOU AGAIN!
BEFORE ANYTHING HAPPENS...
...I WILL KILL HIM!
WHAT...?

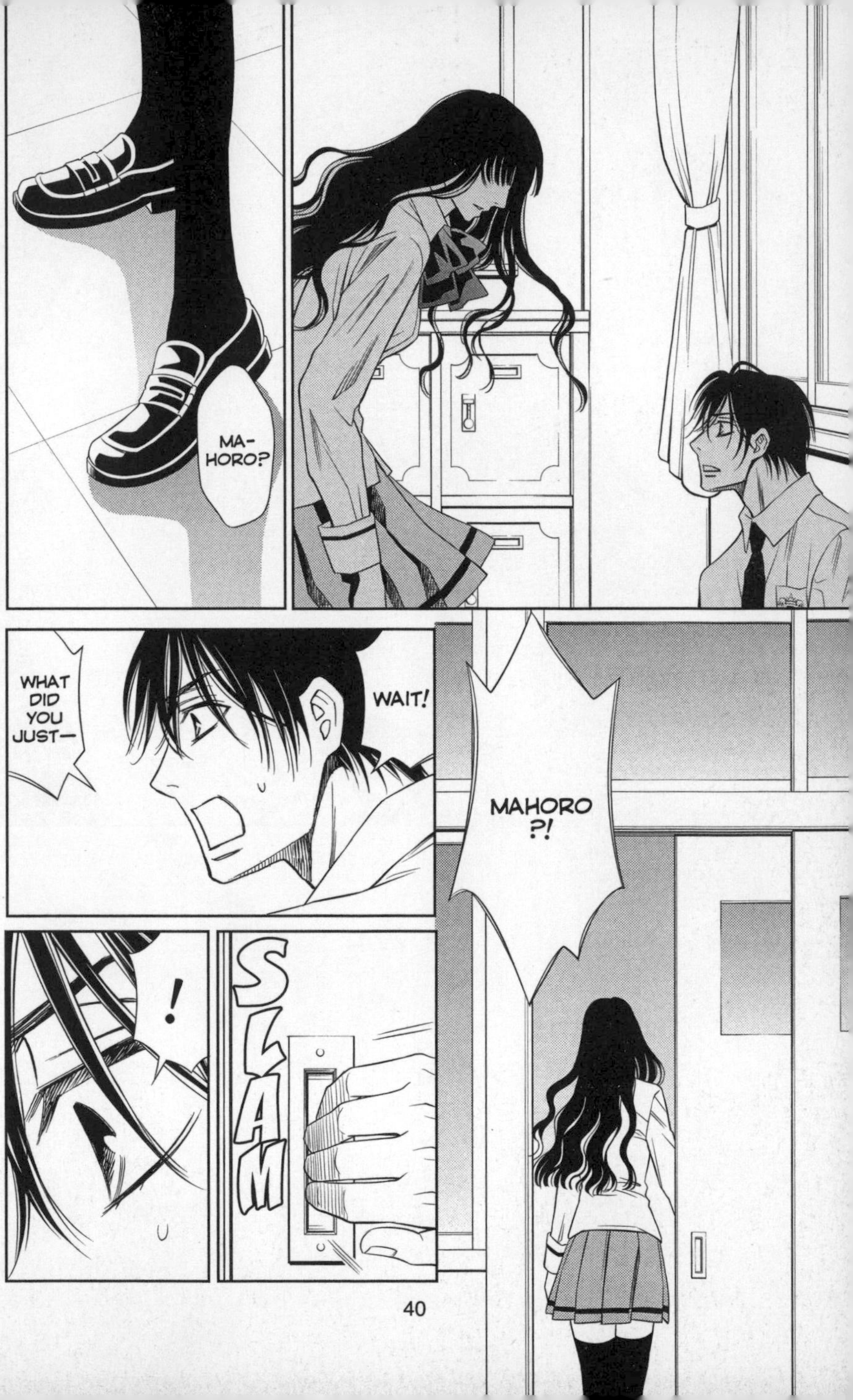
MA-HORO?
MAHORO ?!
WAIT!
WHAT DID YOU JUST—
SLAM
!

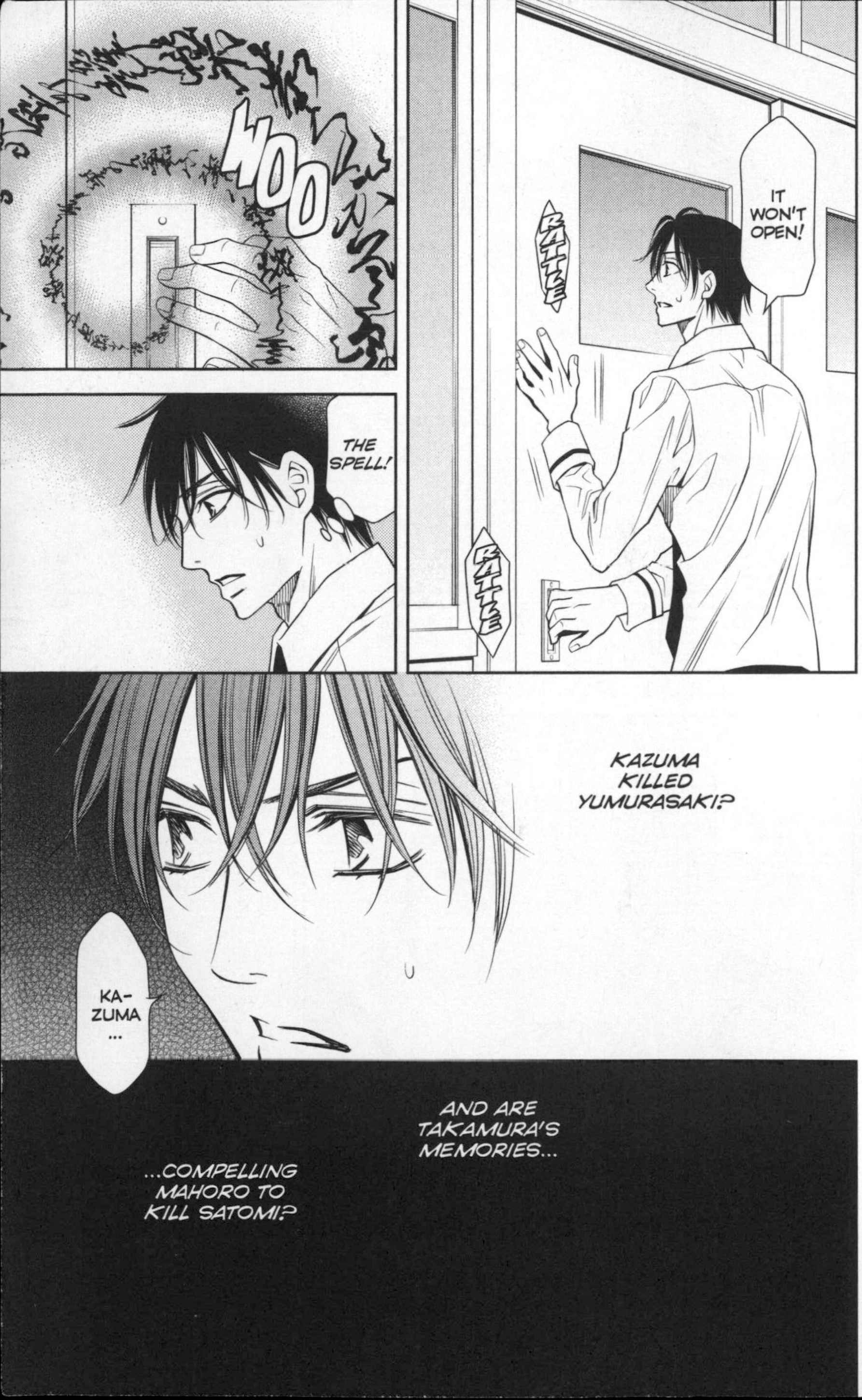
IT WON'T OPEN!
RATTLE
RATTLE
WOO
THE SPELL!
KAZUMA KILLED YUMURASAKI?
KA-ZUMA ...
AND ARE TAKAMURA'S MEMORIES...
...COMPELLING MAHORO TO KILL SATOMI?

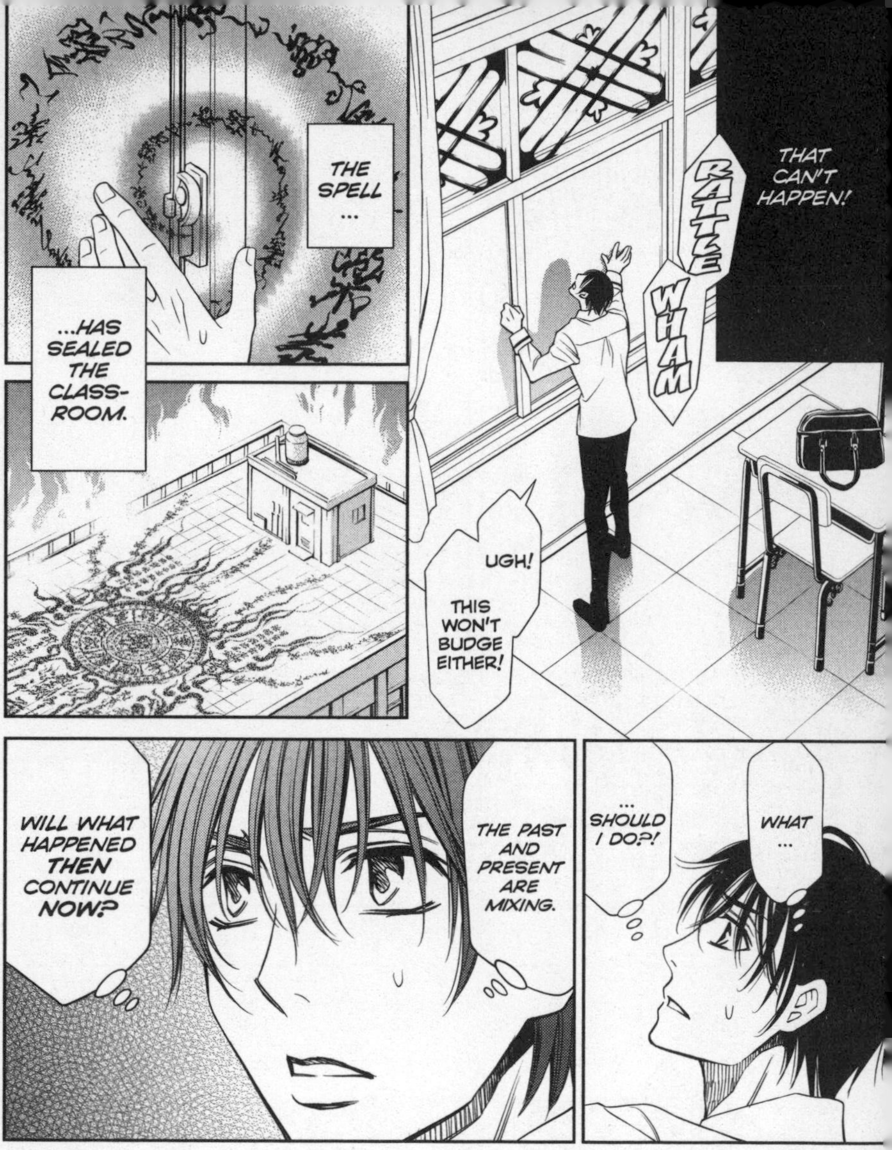
THAT CAN'T HAPPEN!
RATTLE
WHAM
UGH!
THIS WON'T BUDGE EITHER!
THE SPELL...
...HAS SEALED THE CLASSROOM.
WHAT...
...SHOULD I DO?!
THE PAST AND PRESENT ARE MIXING.
WILL WHAT HAPPENED THEN CONTINUE NOW?

ON THE DAY YUMURASAKI DIED...

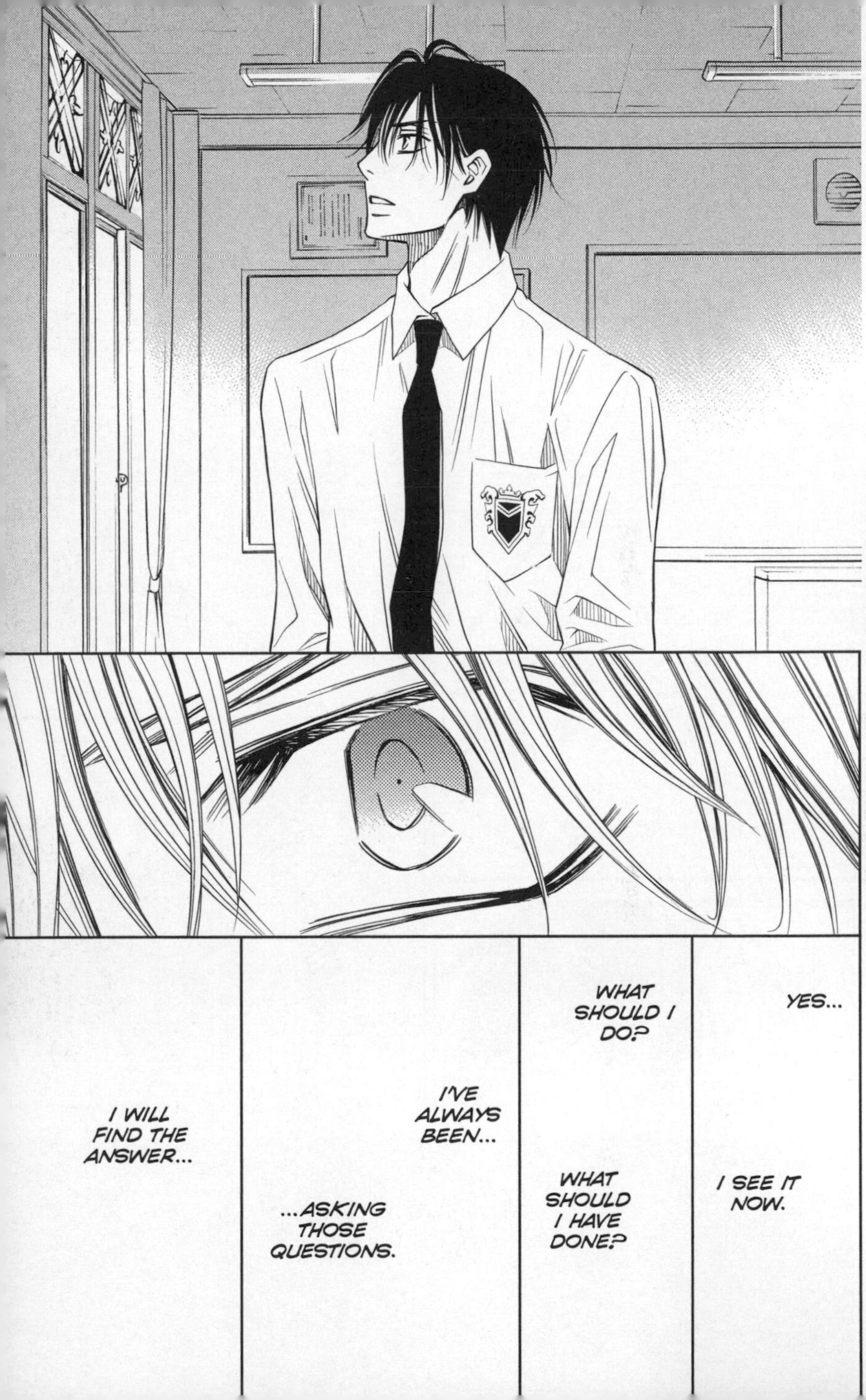
YES...
I SEE IT NOW.
WHAT SHOULD I DO?
WHAT SHOULD I HAVE DONE?
I'VE ALWAYS BEEN...
...ASKING THOSE QUESTIONS.
I WILL FIND THE ANSWER...

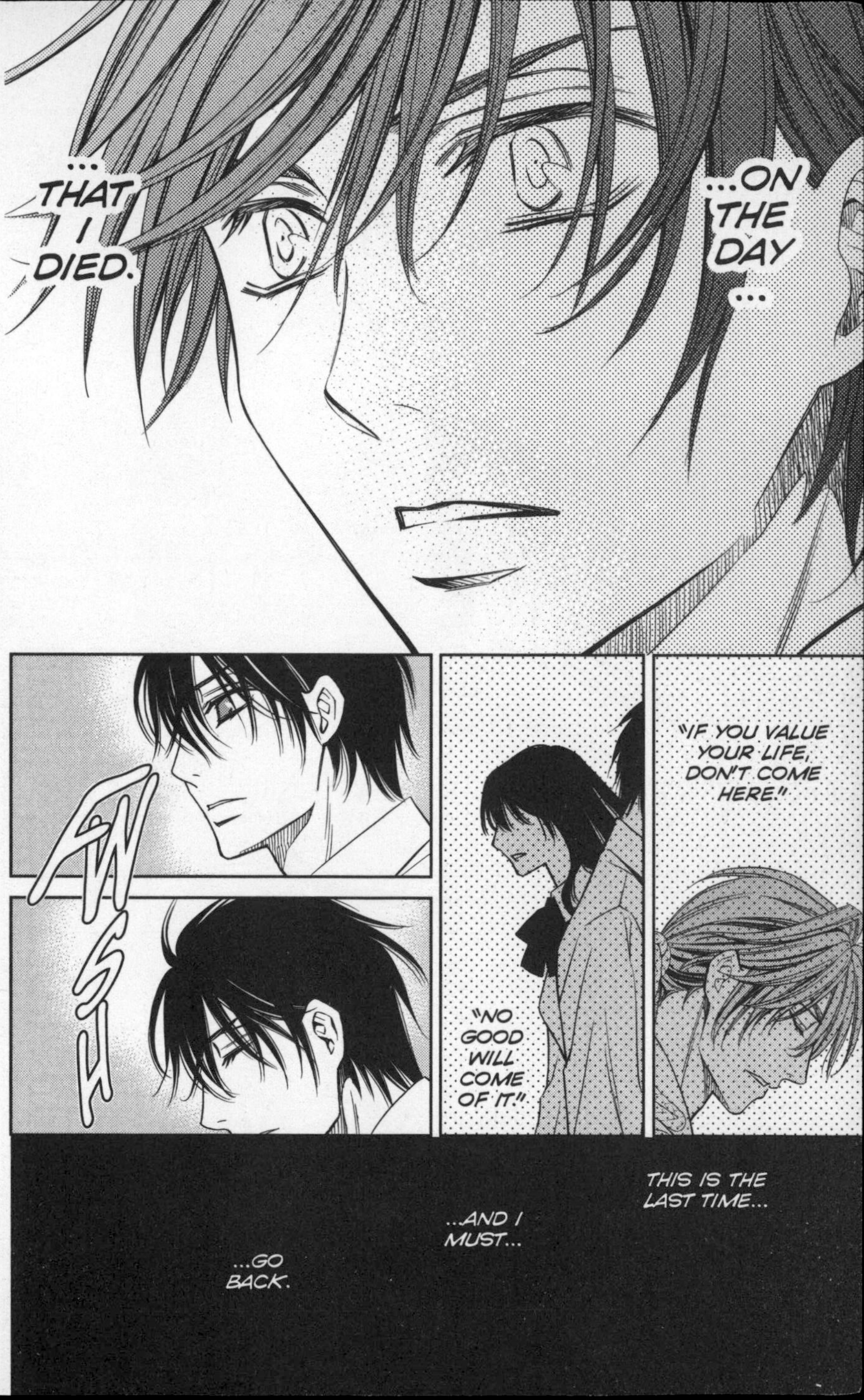
...ON THE DAY...
...THAT I DIED.
FWSH
"IF YOU VALUE YOUR LIFE, DON'T COME HERE."
"NO GOOD WILL COME OF IT."
THIS IS THE LAST TIME...
...AND I MUST...
...GO BACK.

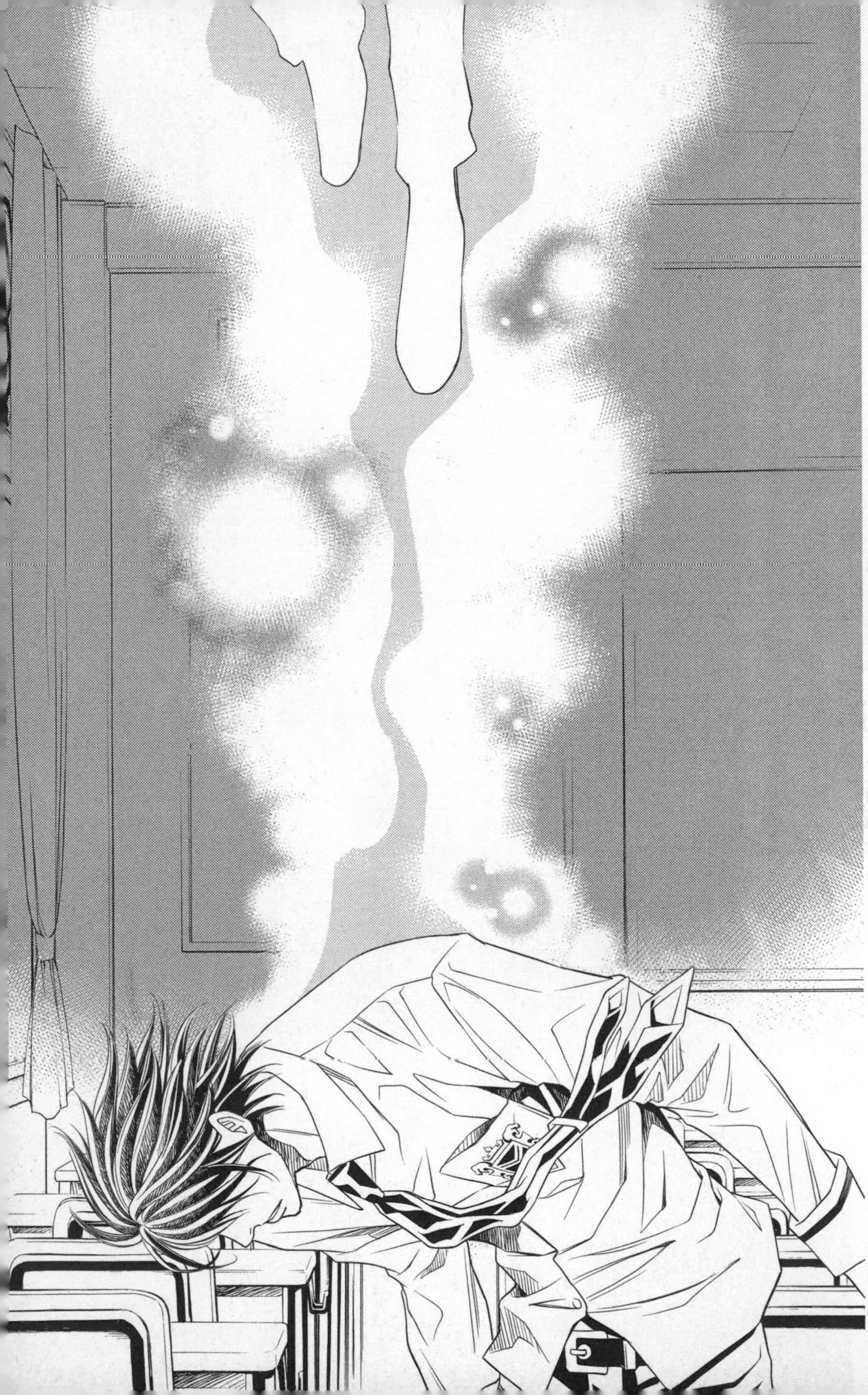

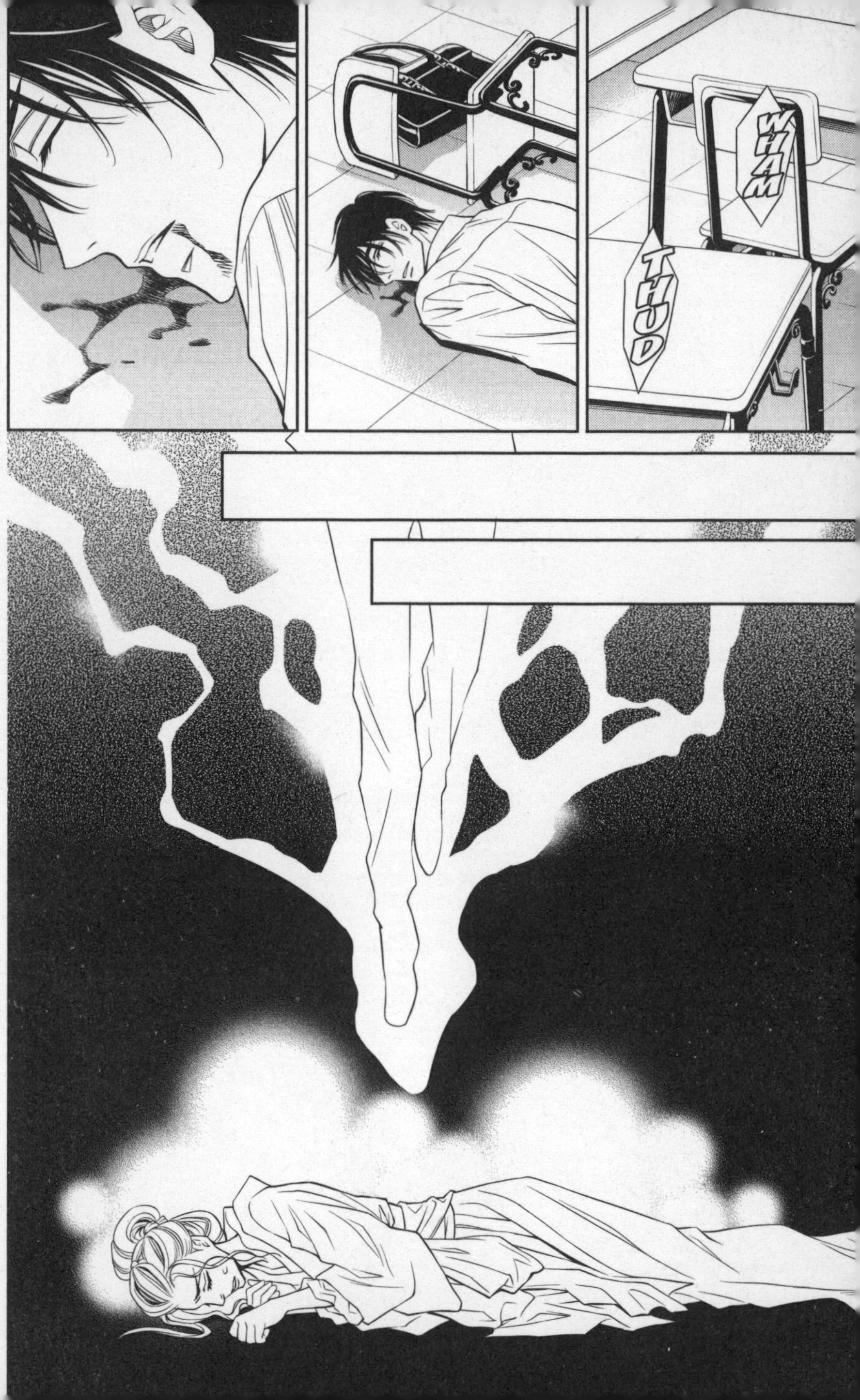
WHAM
THUD

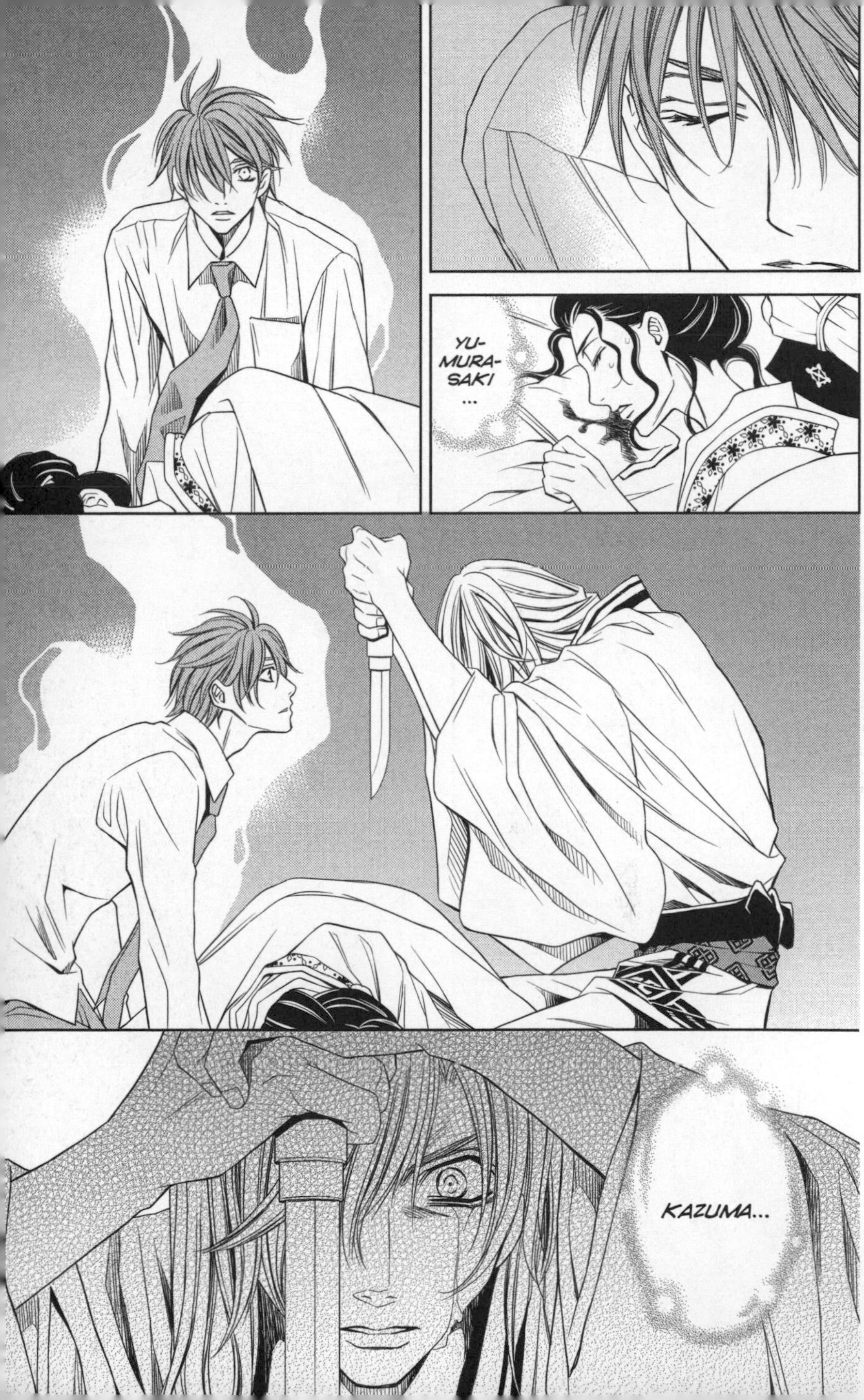
YU-
MURA-
SAKI
...
KAZUMA...

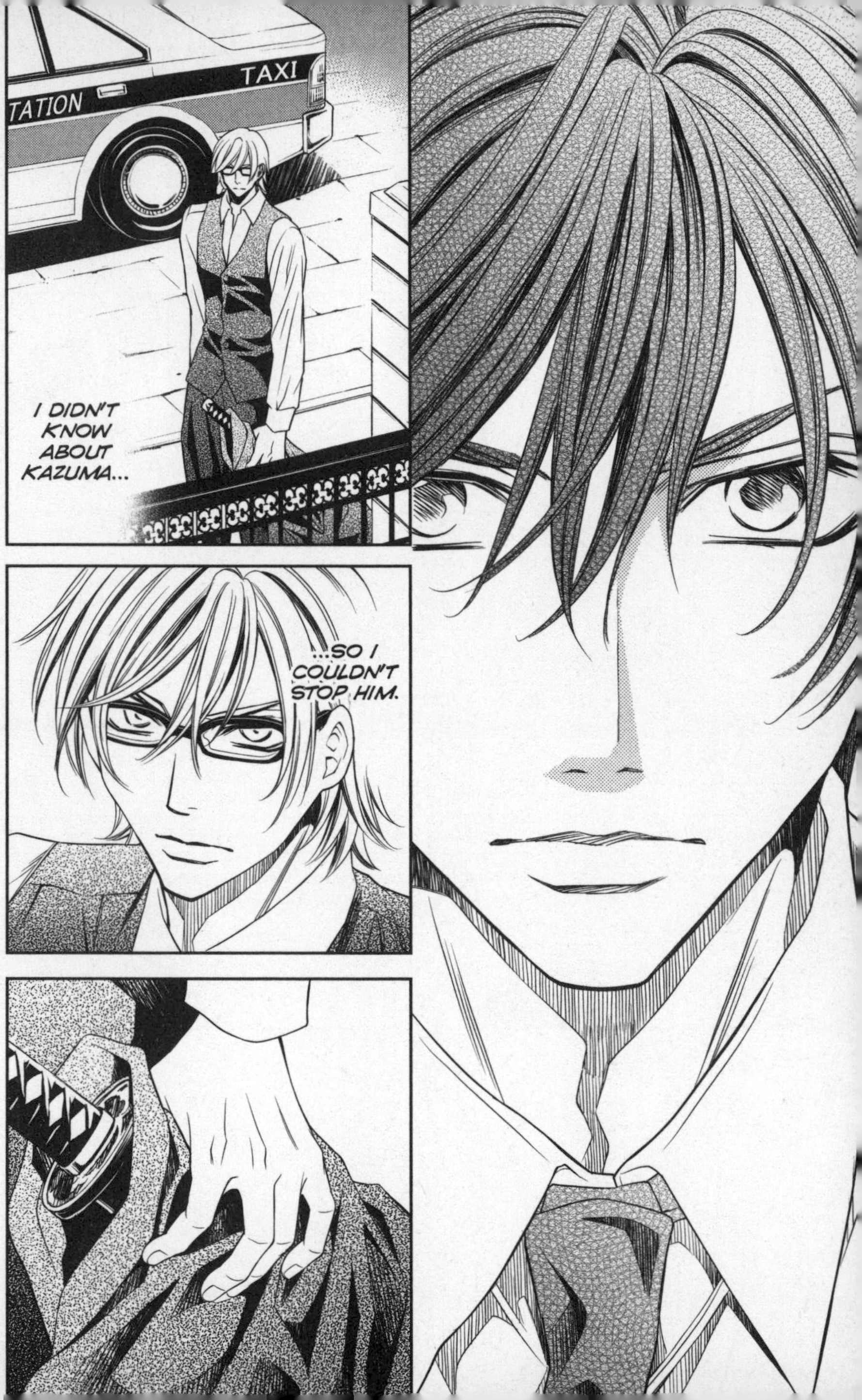
TAXI
TATION
I DIDN'T KNOW ABOUT KAZUMA...
...SO I COULDN'T STOP HIM.

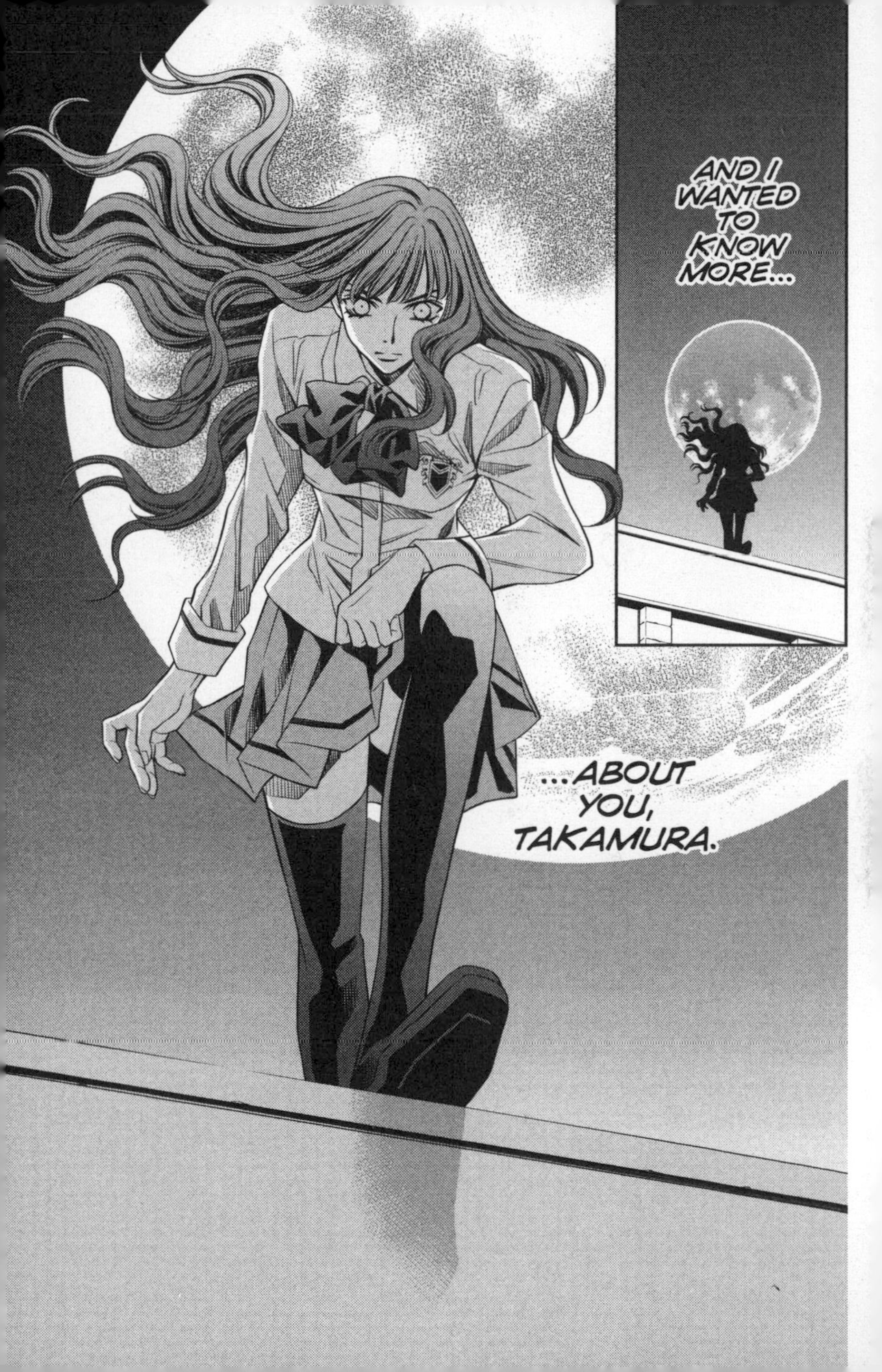
AND I WANTED TO KNOW MORE...
...ABOUT YOU, TAKAMURA.

Chapter 15

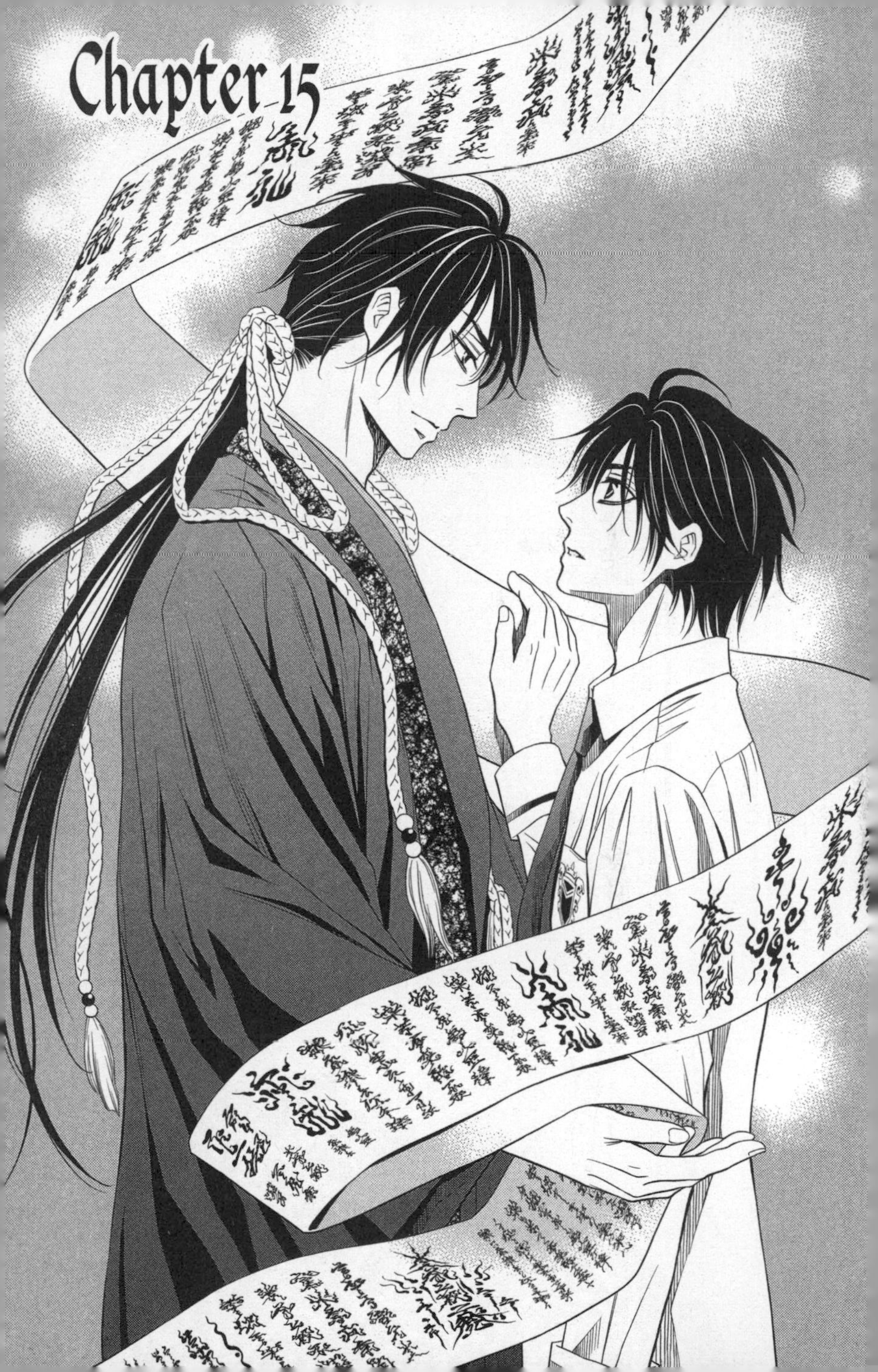

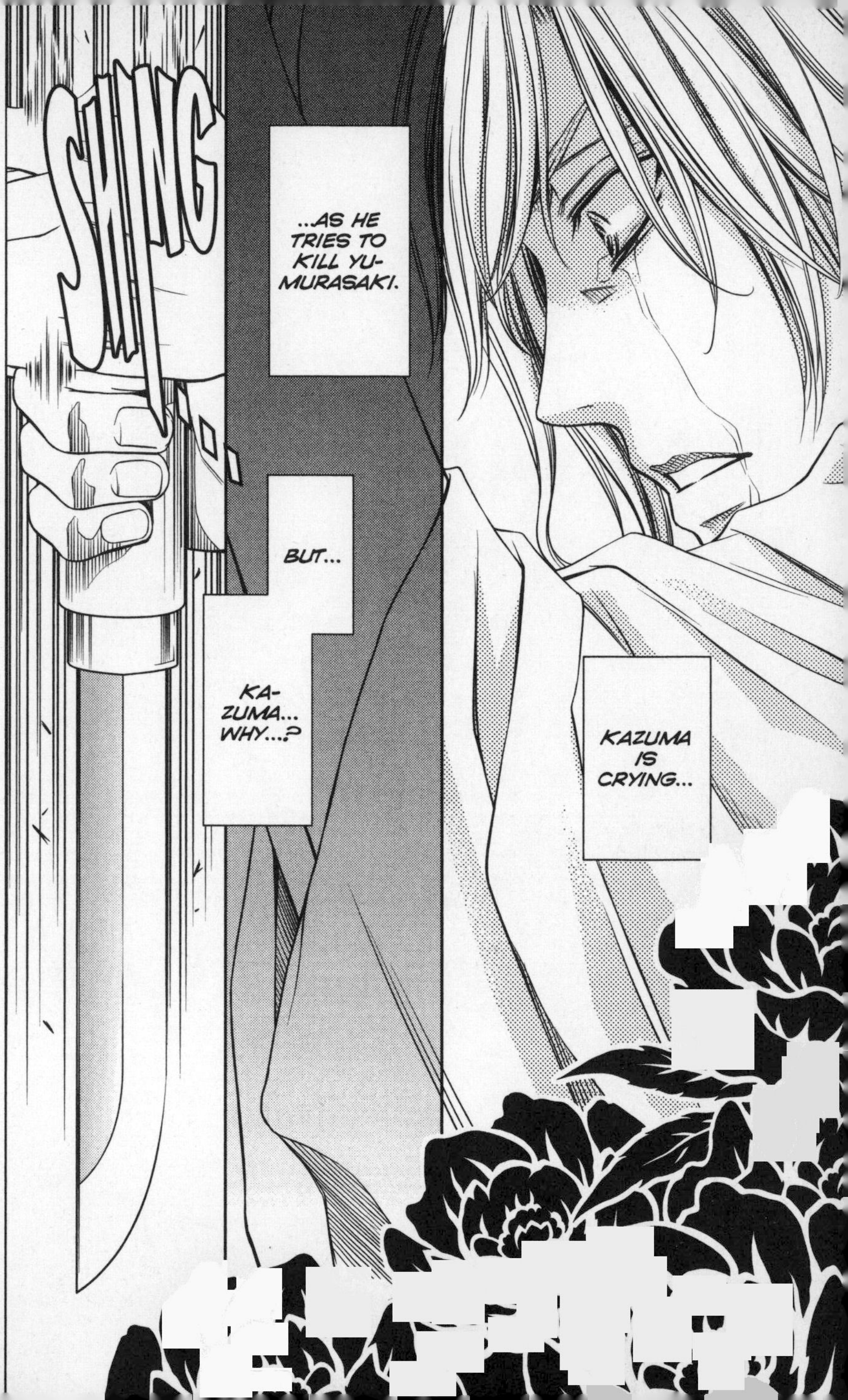
KAZUMA IS CRYING...
...AS HE TRIES TO KILL YU-MURASAKI.
BUT...
KA-ZUMA... WHY...?
SHING

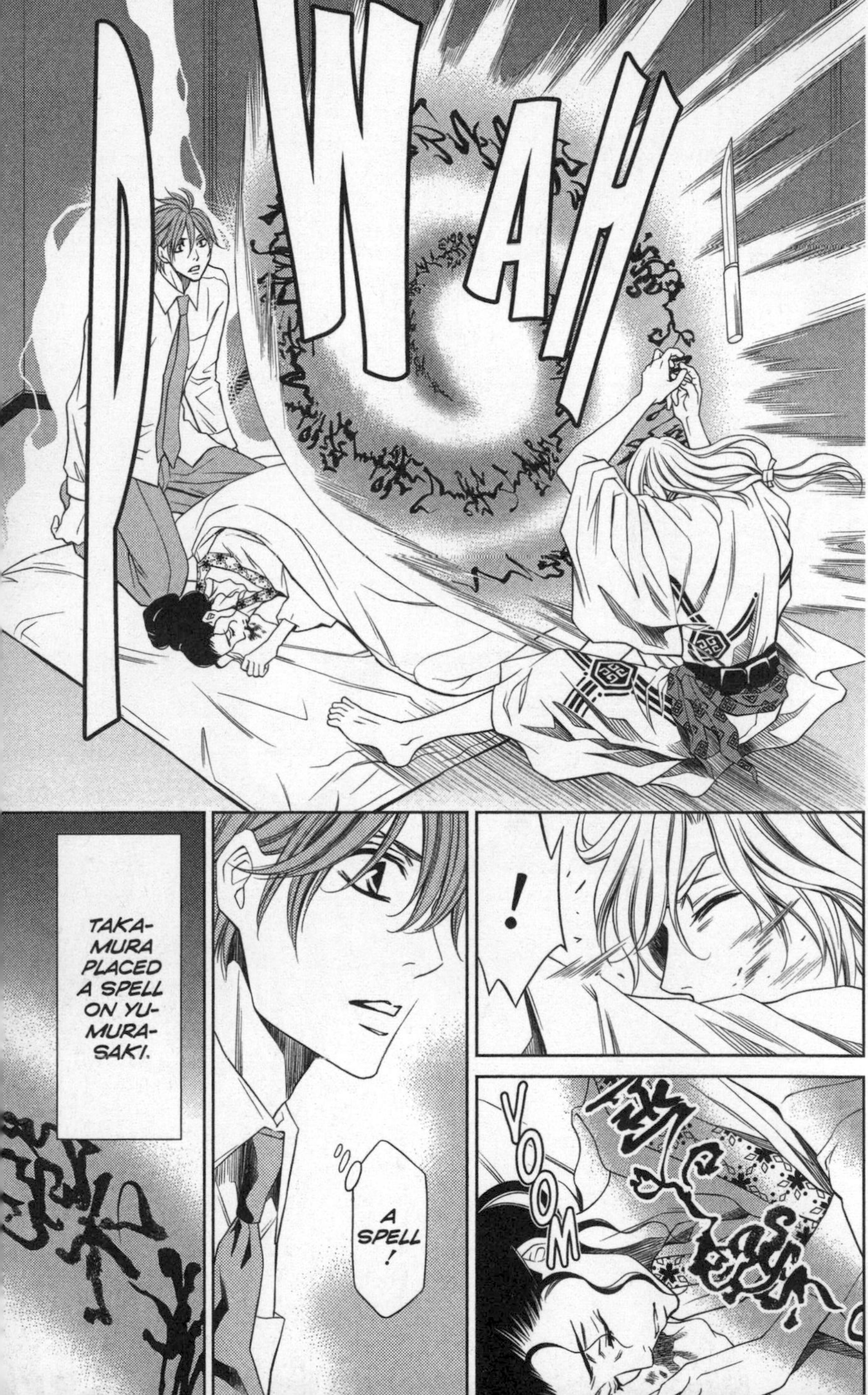
DWAH
!
VOOM
A SPELL!
TAKAMURA PLACED A SPELL ON YUMURASAKI.

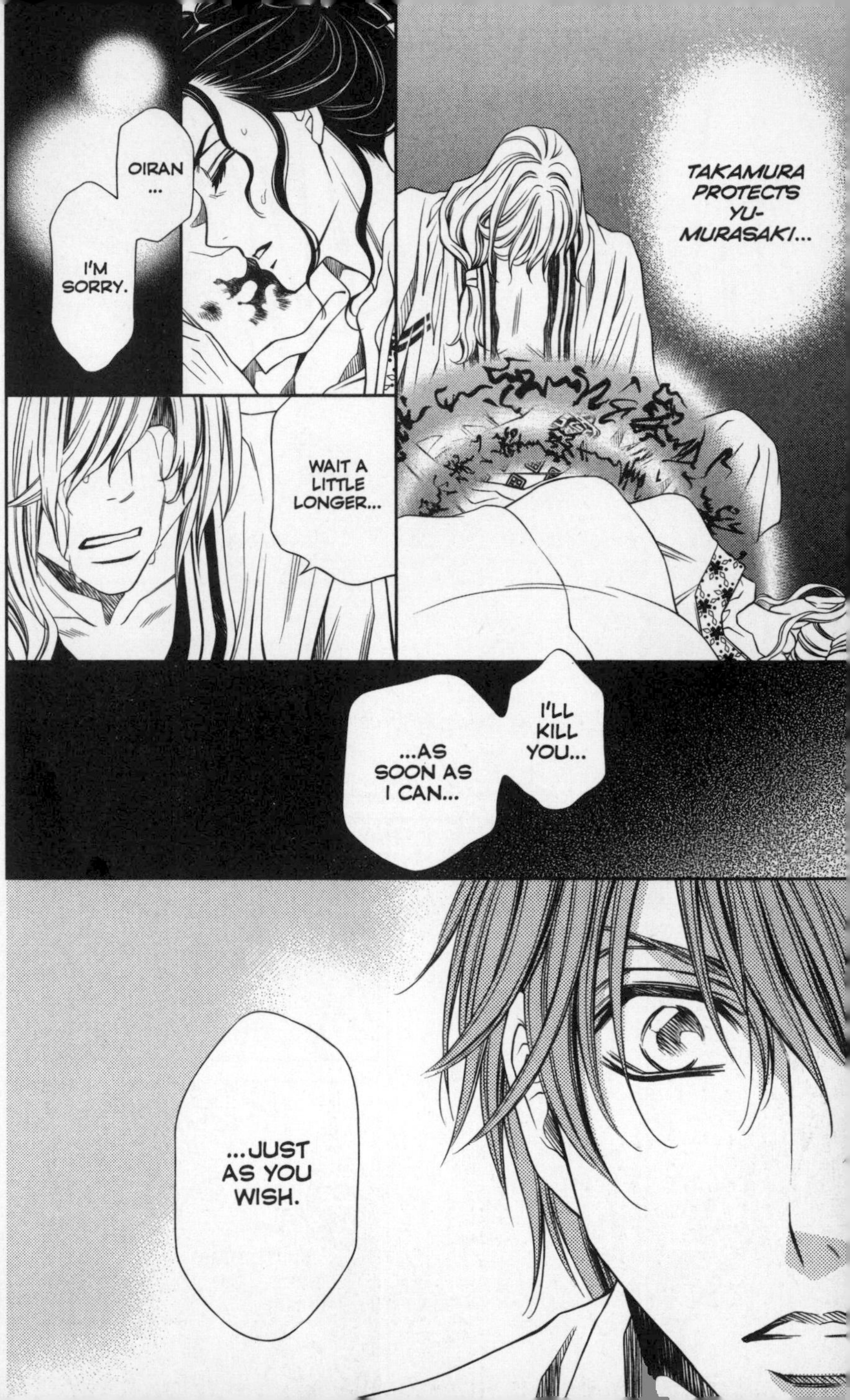
TAKAMURA PROTECTS YU-MURASAKI...
OIRAN...
I'M SORRY.
WAIT A LITTLE LONGER...
I'LL KILL YOU...
...AS SOON AS I CAN...
...JUST AS YOU WISH.

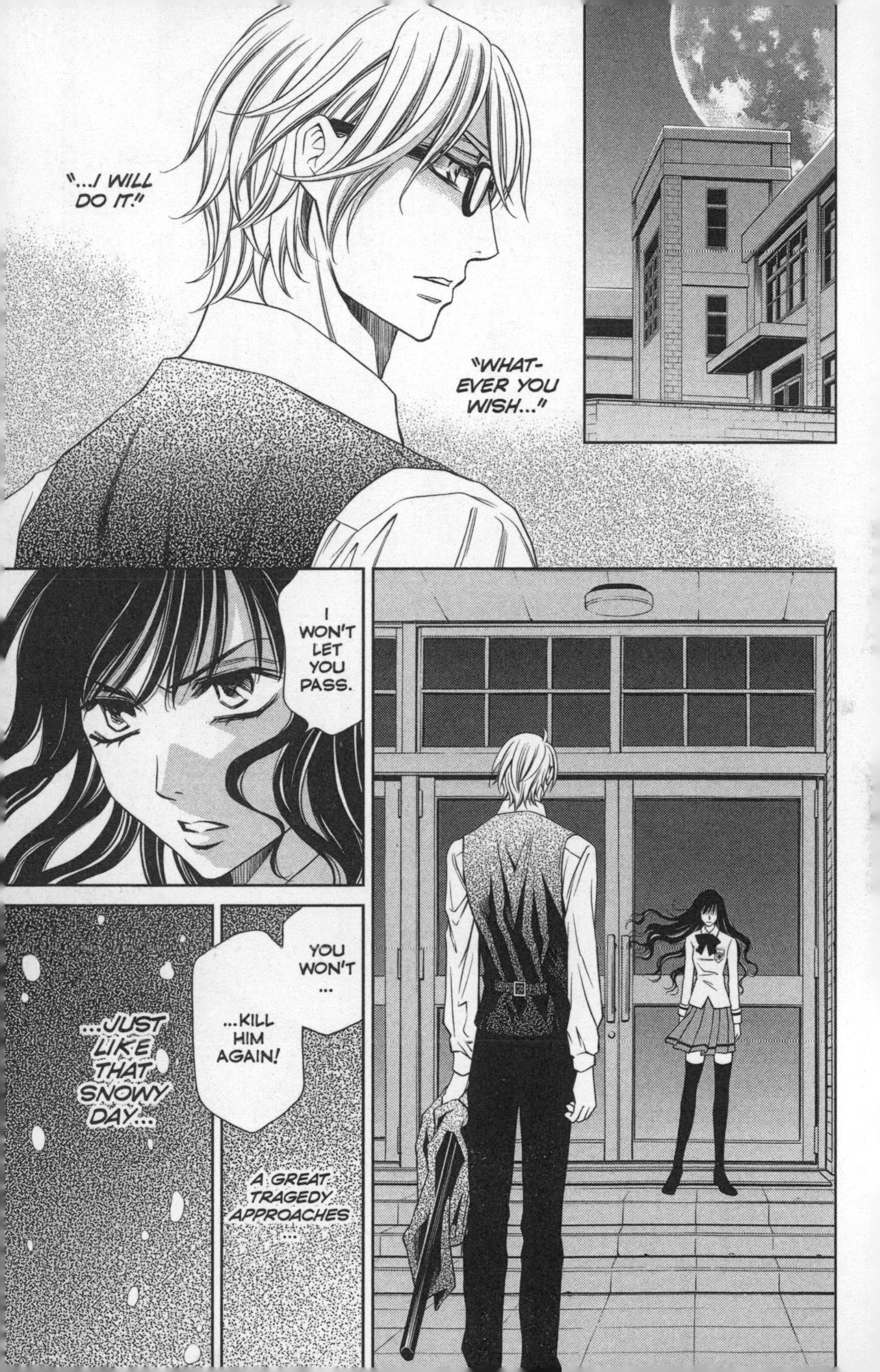
"WHAT-EVER YOU WISH..."
"...I WILL DO IT."
I WON'T LET YOU PASS.
YOU WON'T ...
...KILL HIM AGAIN!
A GREAT TRAGEDY APPROACHES ...
...JUST LIKE THAT SNOWY DAY...

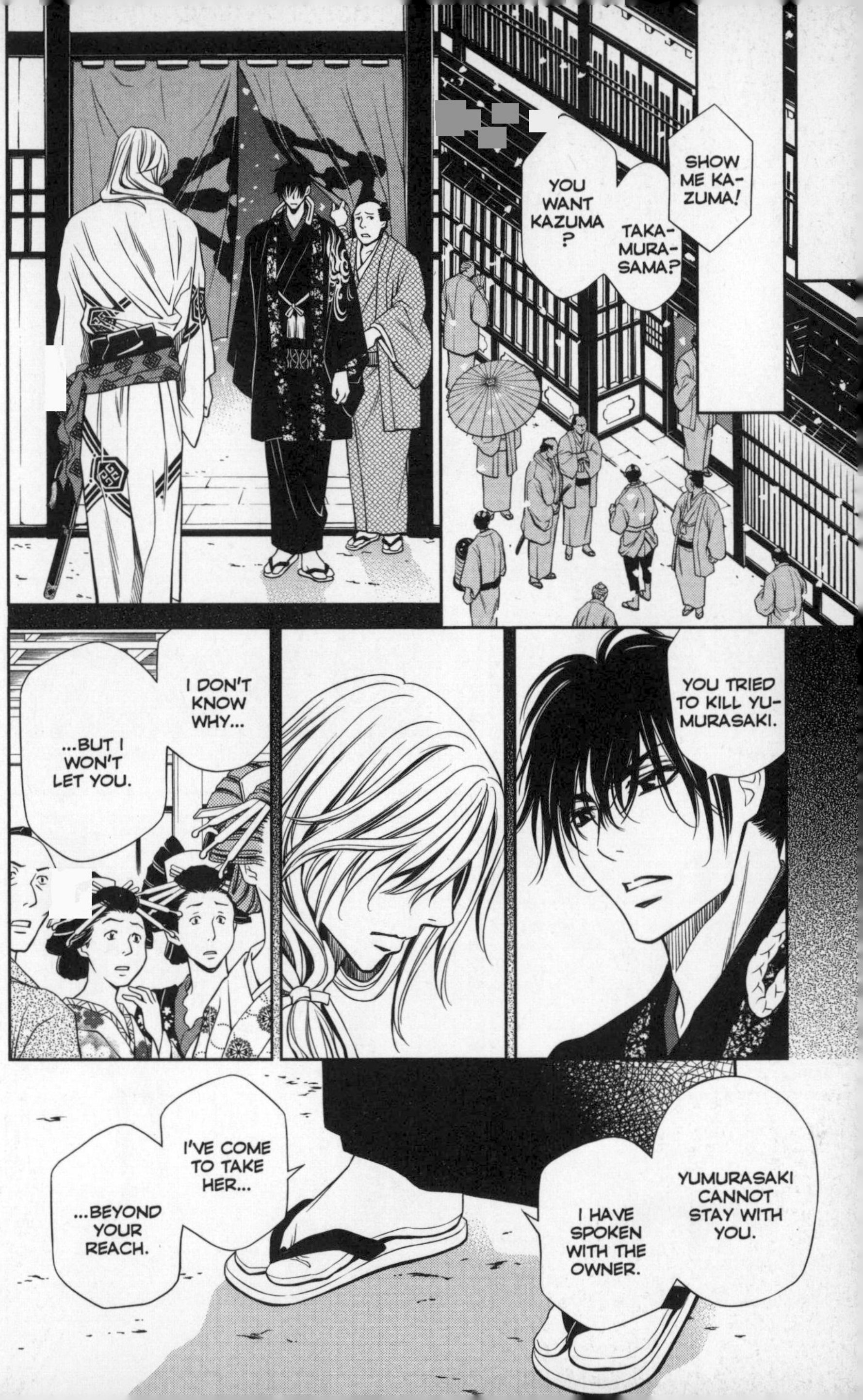
SHOW ME KA-ZUMA!
YOU WANT KAZUMA?
TAKA-MURA-SAMA?
YOU TRIED TO KILL YU-MURASAKI.
I DON'T KNOW WHY...
...BUT I WON'T LET YOU.
YUMURASAKI CANNOT STAY WITH YOU.
I HAVE SPOKEN WITH THE OWNER.
I'VE COME TO TAKE HER...
...BEYOND YOUR REACH.

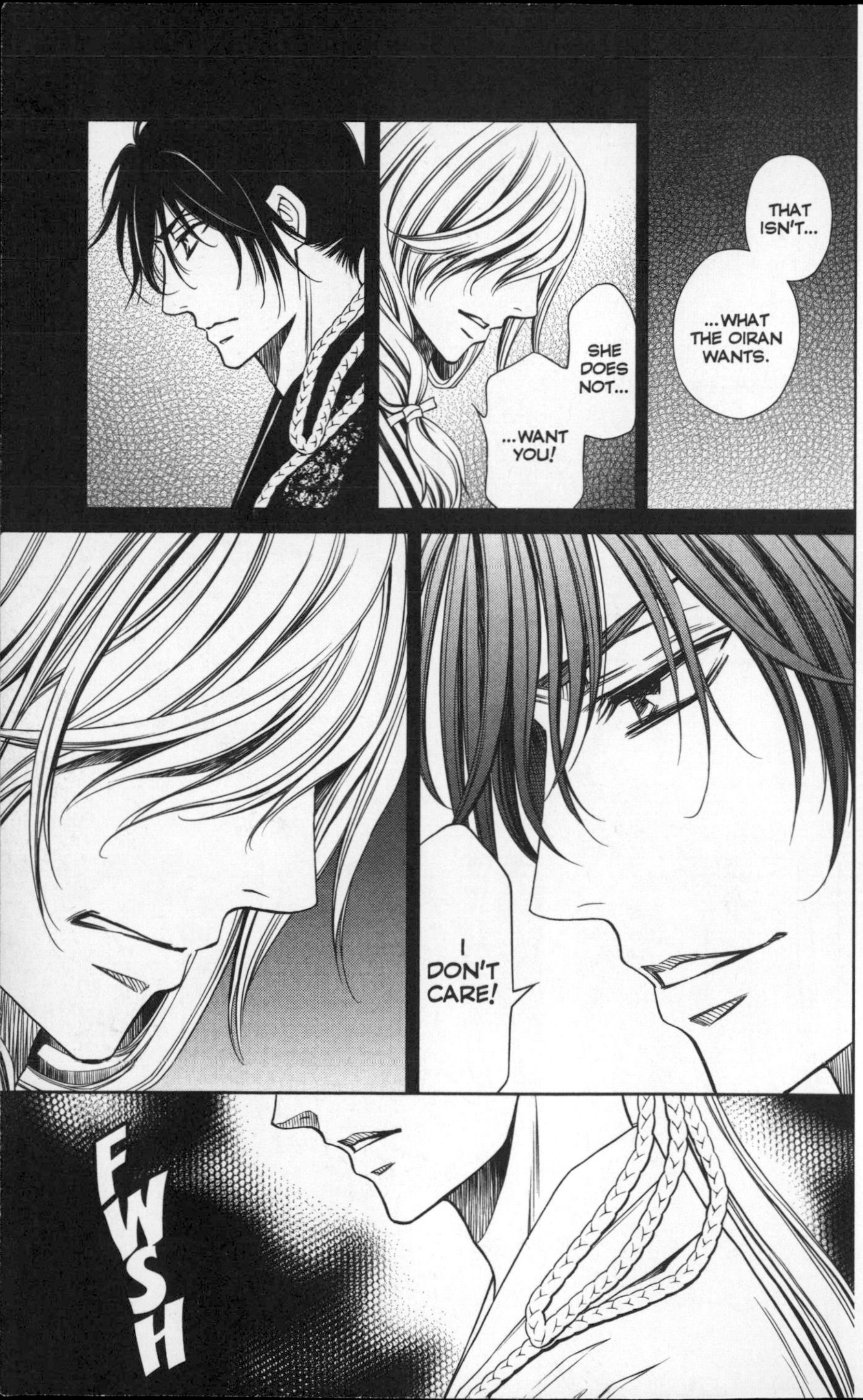
THAT ISN'T...
...WHAT THE OIRAN WANTS.
SHE DOES NOT...
...WANT YOU!
I DON'T CARE!
FWSH

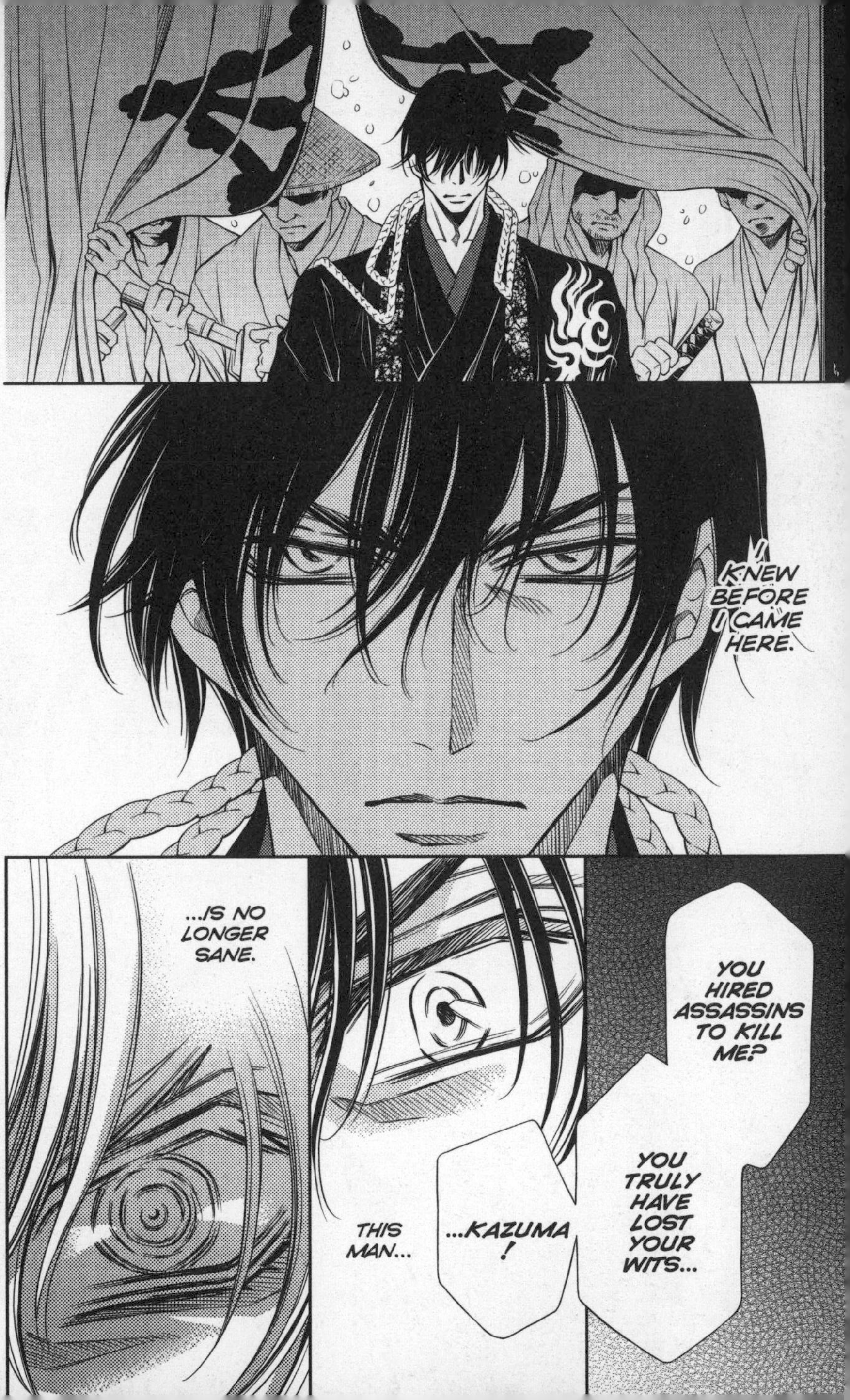
I KNEW BEFORE I CAME HERE.
YOU HIRED ASSASSINS TO KILL ME?
YOU TRULY HAVE LOST YOUR WITS...
...KAZUMA!
THIS MAN...
...IS NO LONGER SANE.

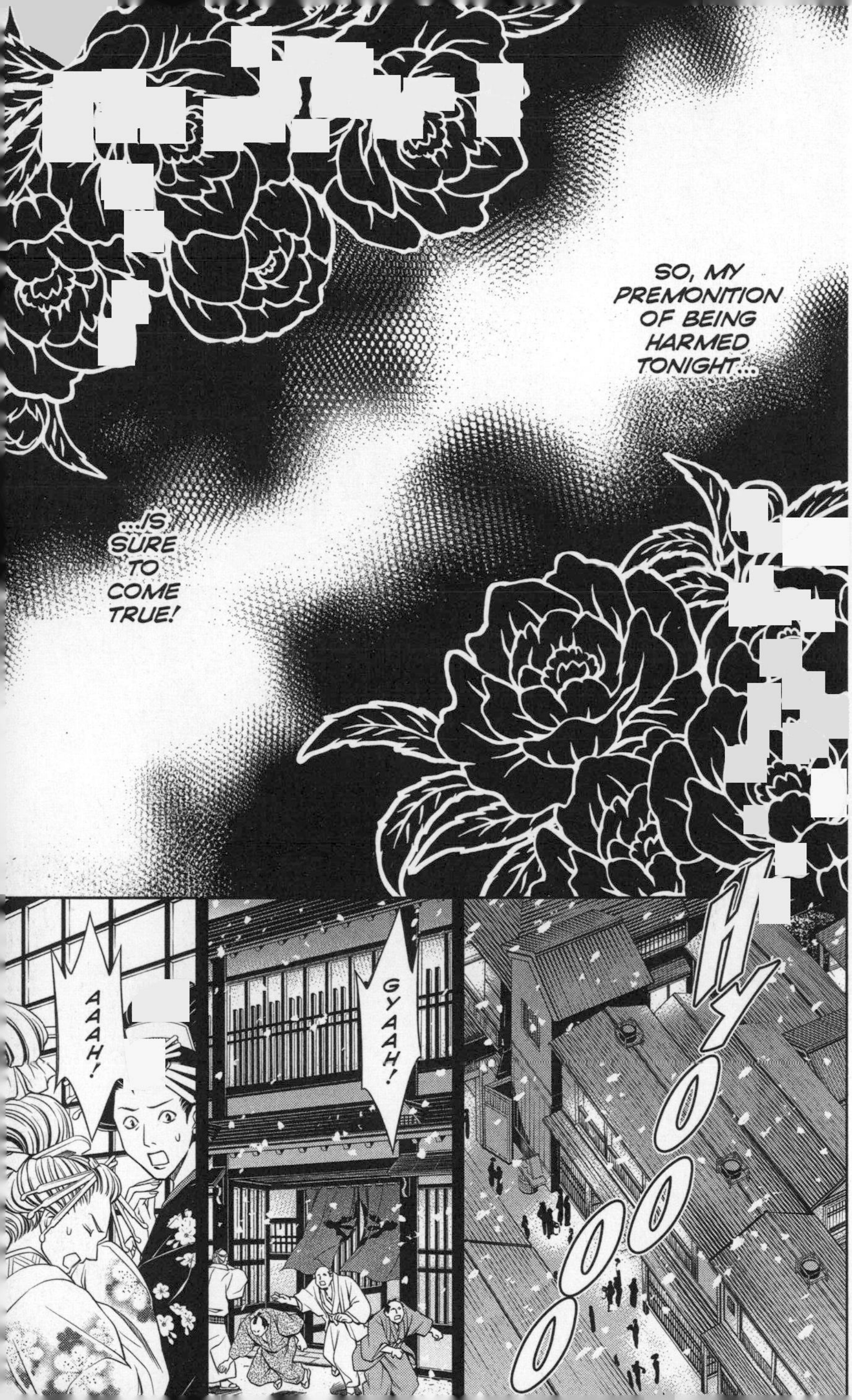
SO, MY PREMONITION OF BEING HARMED TONIGHT...
...IS SURE TO COME TRUE!
HYOOOO
GYAAAH!
AAAH!

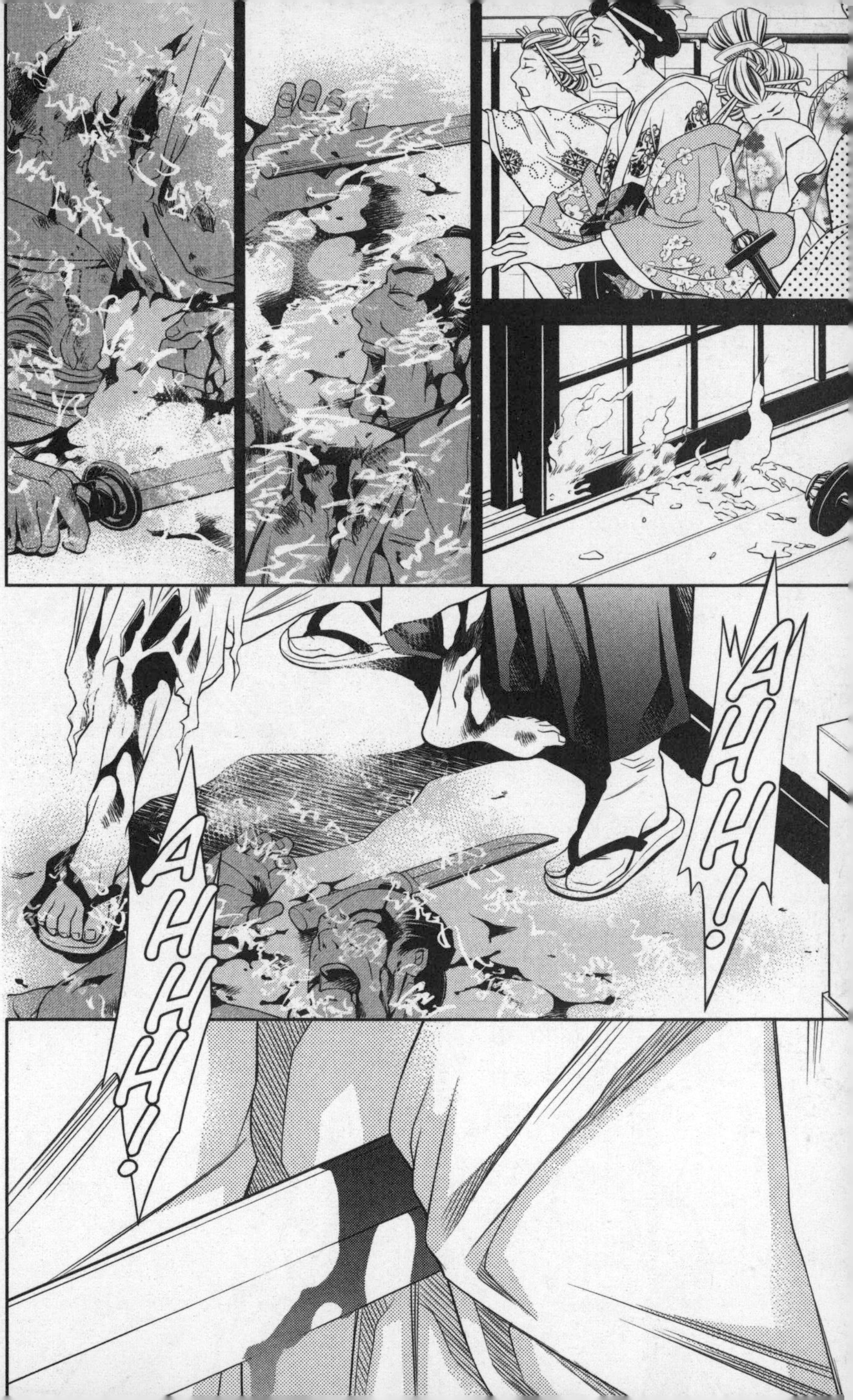
AHH!
AHHH!

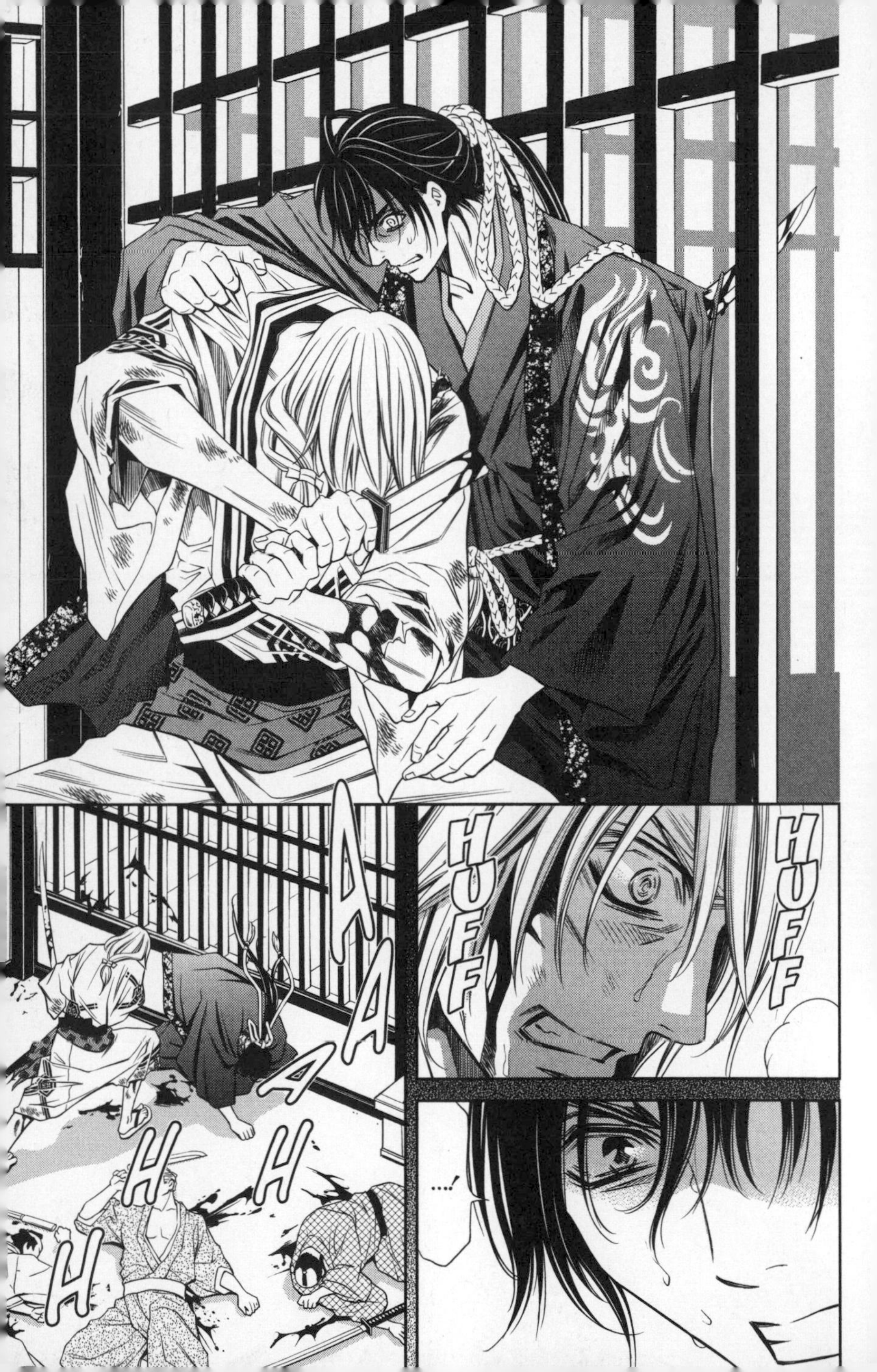
HUFF HUFF
HUFF HUFF
...!
AAAHHH

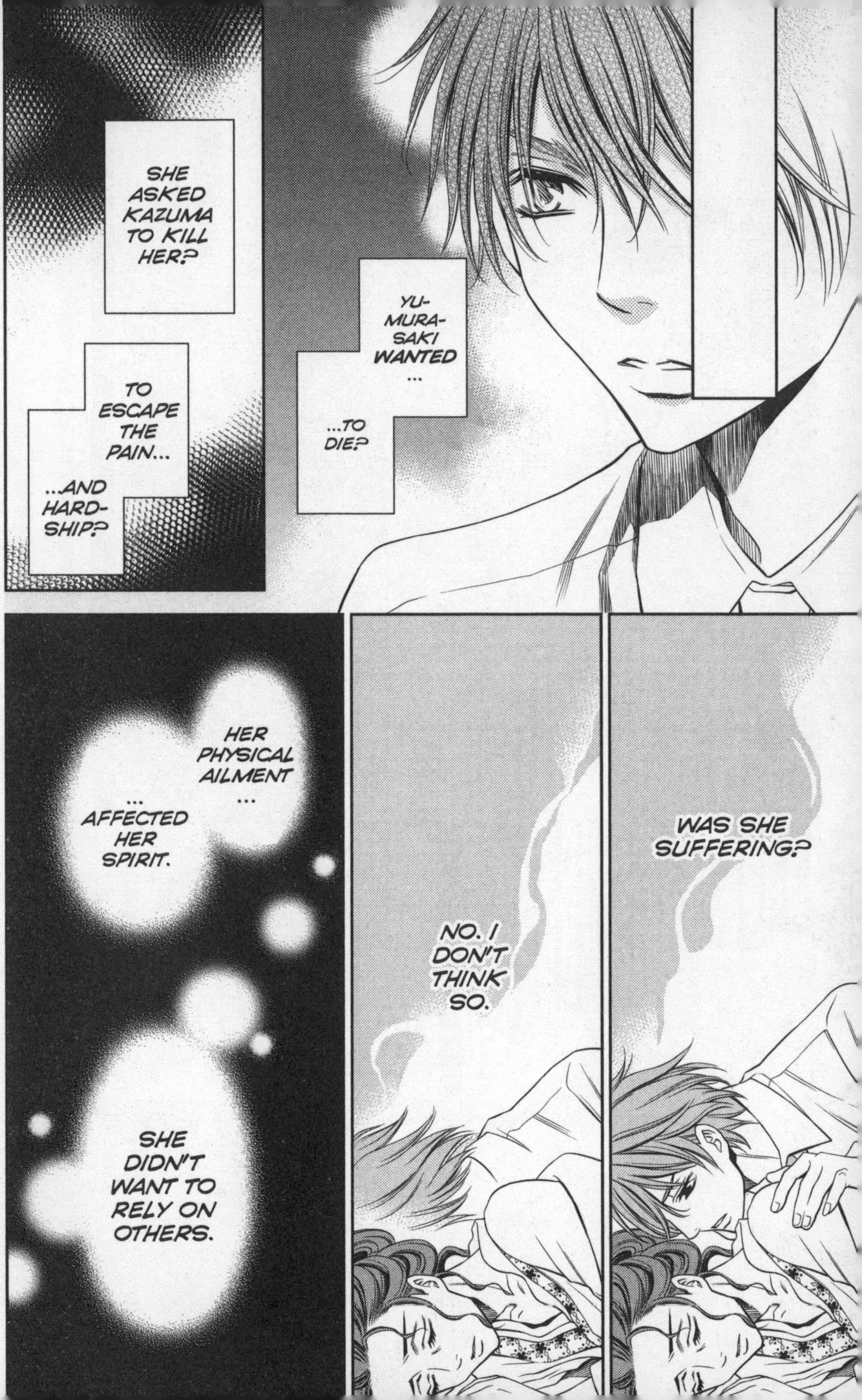
YU-MURA-SAKI WANTED ...
...TO DIE?
SHE ASKED KAZUMA TO KILL HER?
TO ESCAPE THE PAIN...
...AND HARD-SHIP?
WAS SHE SUFFERING?
NO. I DON'T THINK SO.
HER PHYSICAL AILMENT ...
... AFFECTED HER SPIRIT.
SHE DIDN'T WANT TO RELY ON OTHERS.

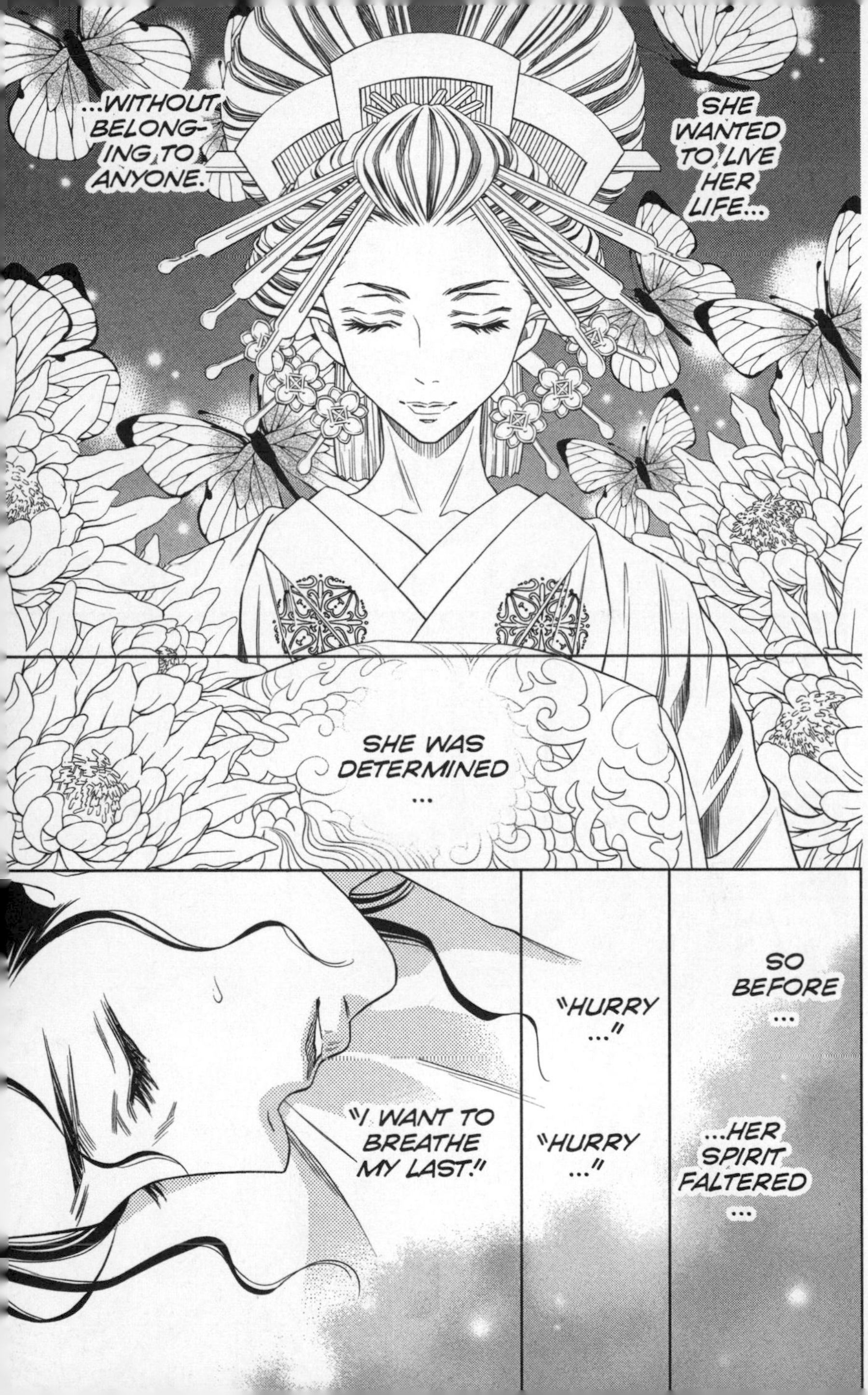
SHE WANTED TO LIVE HER LIFE...
...WITHOUT BELONG-ING TO ANYONE.
SHE WAS DETERMINED ...
SO BEFORE ...
...HER SPIRIT FALTERED ...
"HURRY ..."
"HURRY ..."
"I WANT TO BREATHE MY LAST!"

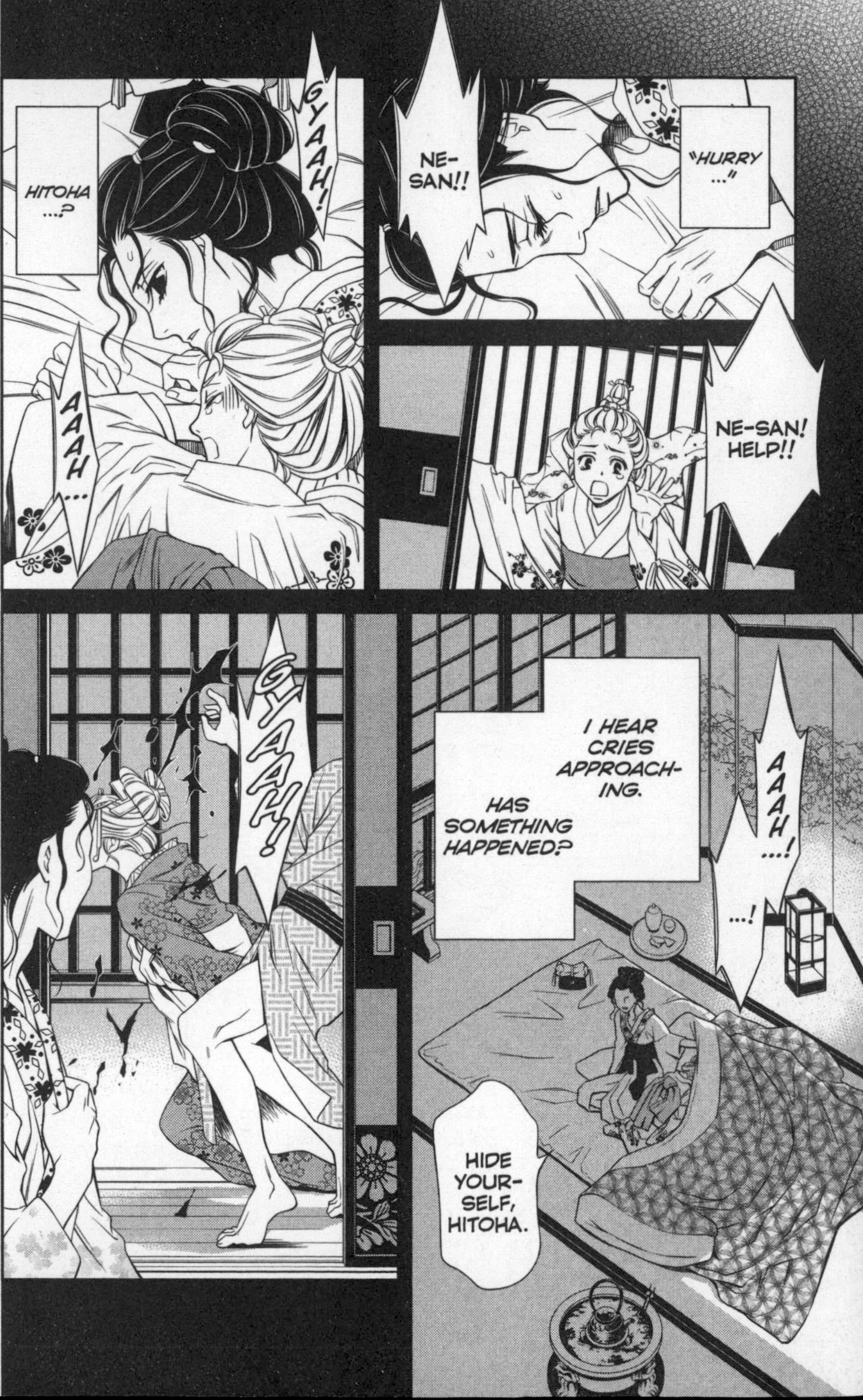
"HURRY ..."
NE-SAN!!
NE-SAN! HELP!!
GYAAAH!
HITOHA ...?
AAAAH ...
AAAAH ...!
I HEAR CRIES APPROACHING.
HAS SOMETHING HAPPENED?
...!
HIDE YOURSELF, HITOHA.
GYAAAH!

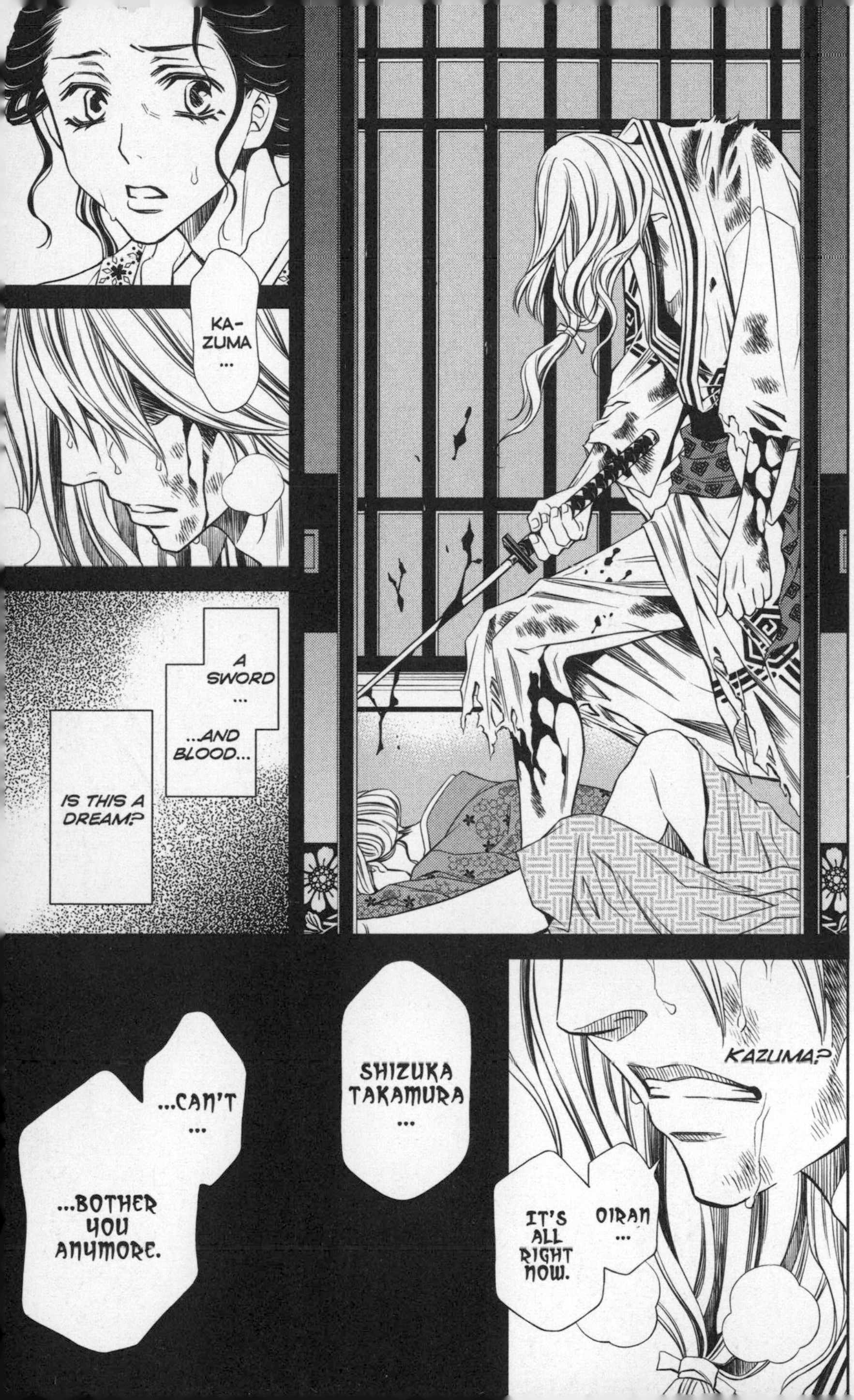
KA-ZUMA...
A SWORD...
...AND BLOOD...
IS THIS A DREAM?
KAZUMA?
OIRAN...
IT'S ALL RIGHT NOW.
SHIZUKA TAKAMURA...
...CAN'T...
...BOTHER YOU ANYMORE.

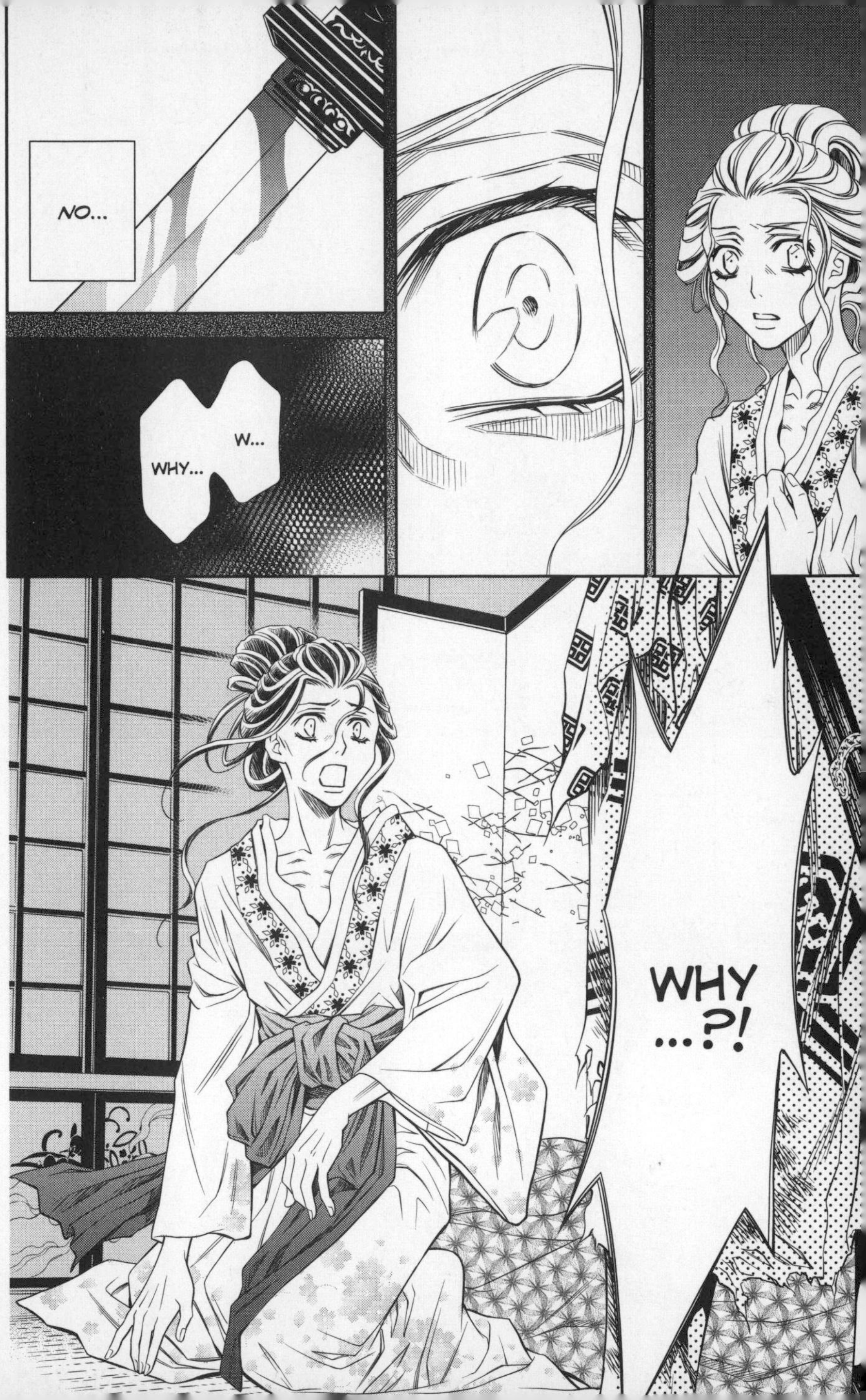
NO...
W... WHY...
WHY ...?!

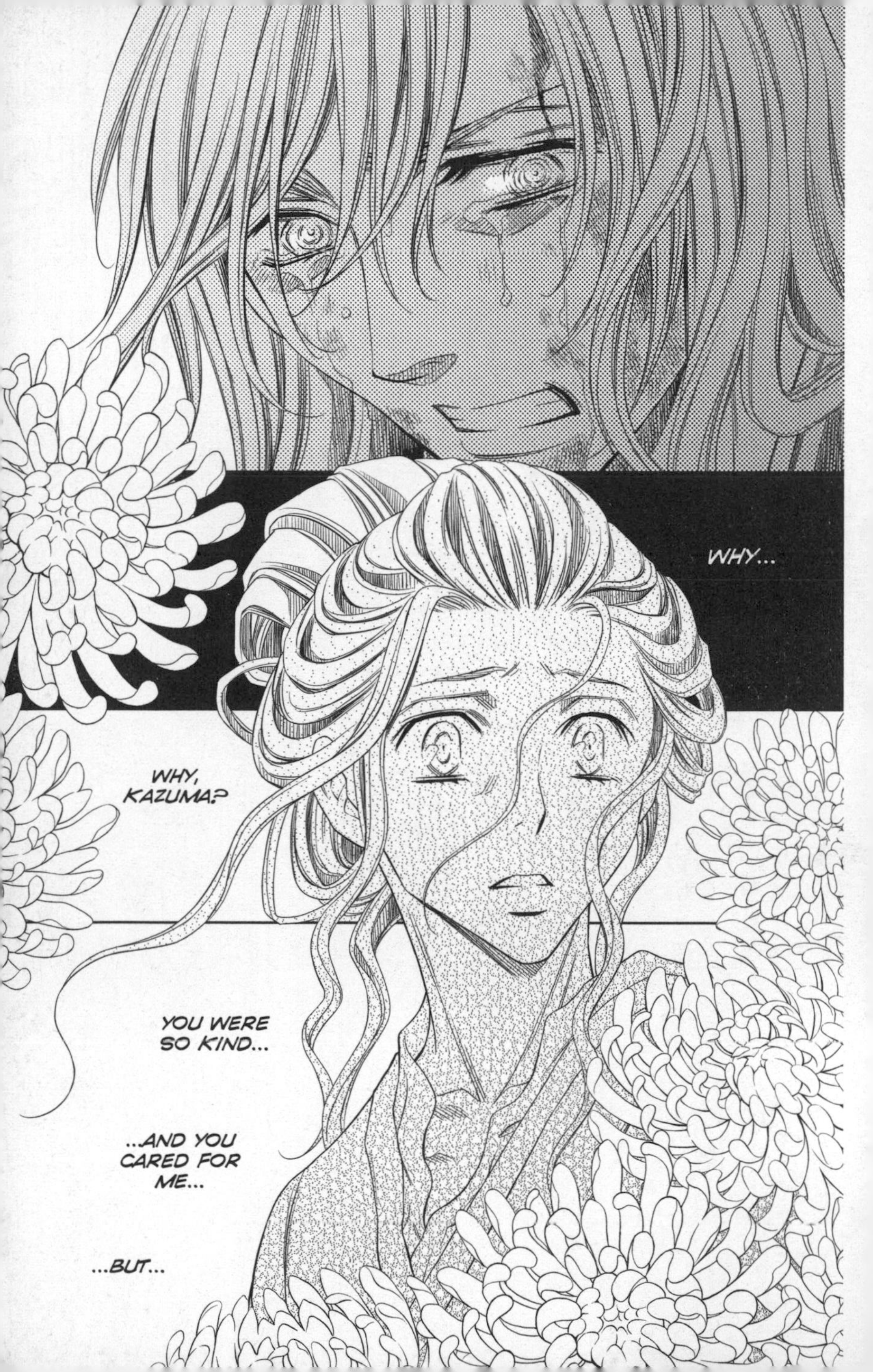
WHY...
WHY, KAZUMA?
YOU WERE SO KIND...
...AND YOU CARED FOR ME...
...BUT...

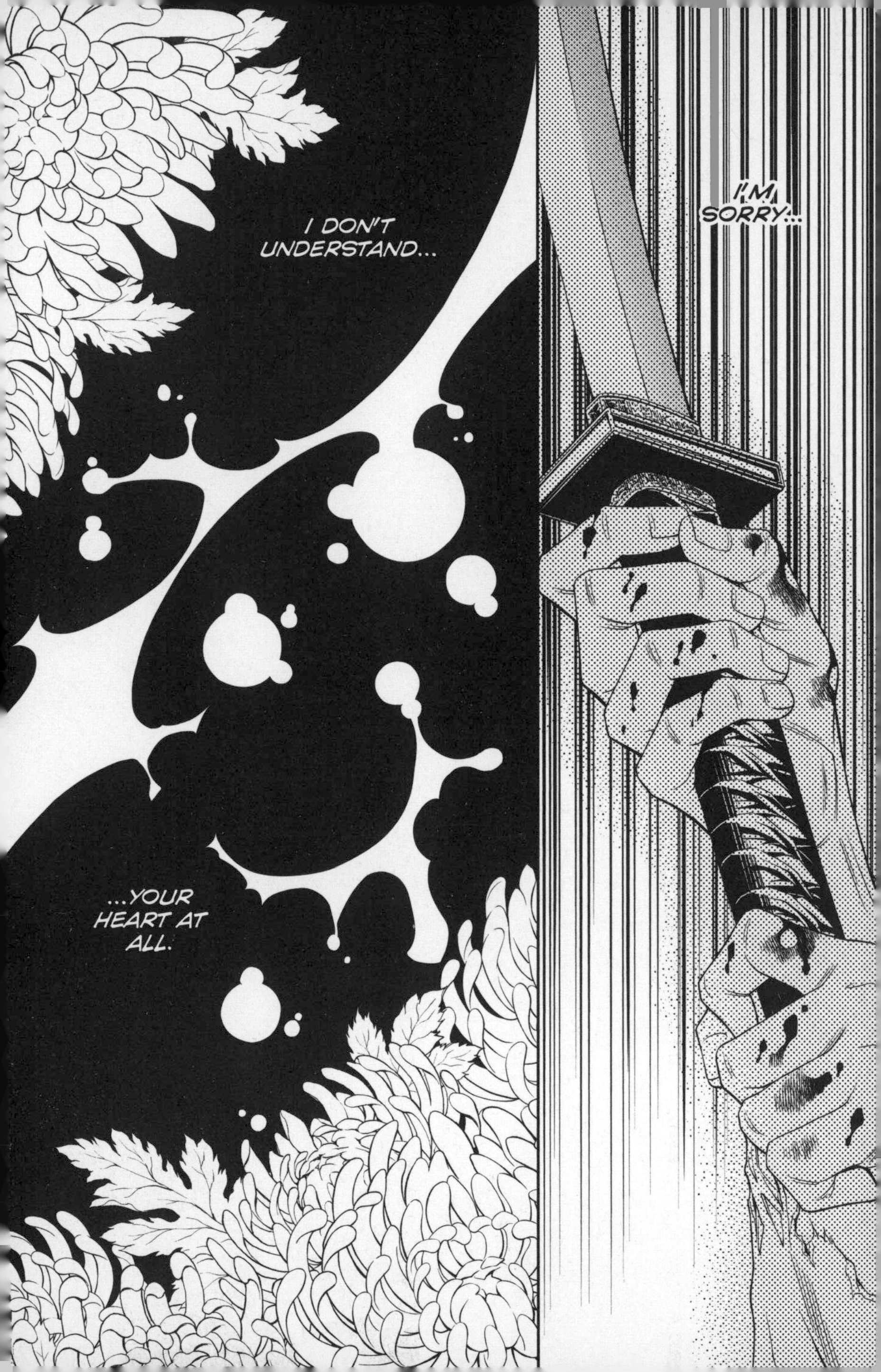
I'M SORRY...
I DON'T UNDERSTAND...
...YOUR HEART AT ALL.

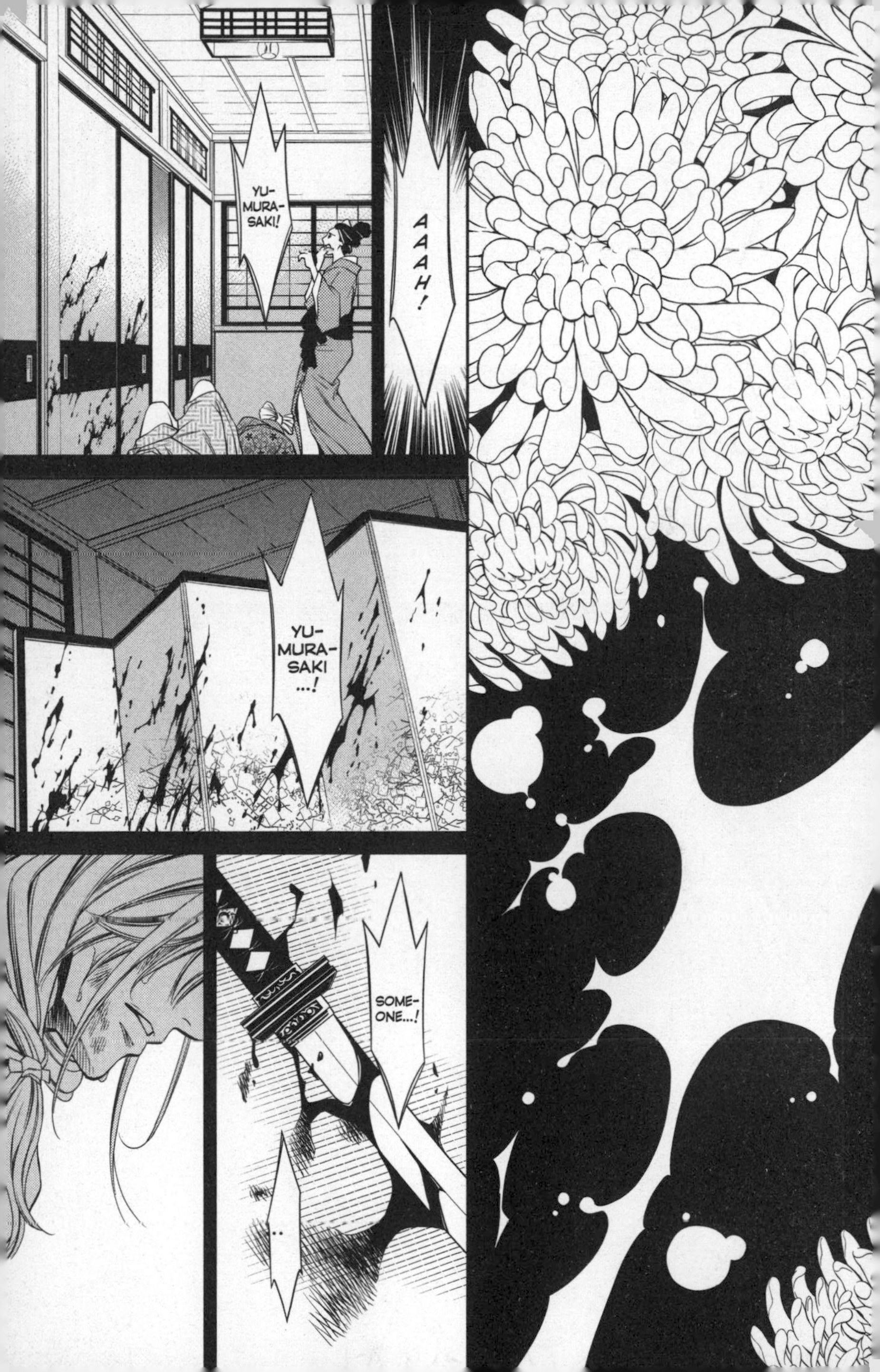
AAAH!
YU-MURA-SAKI!
YU-MURA-SAKI...!
SOME-ONE...!
..

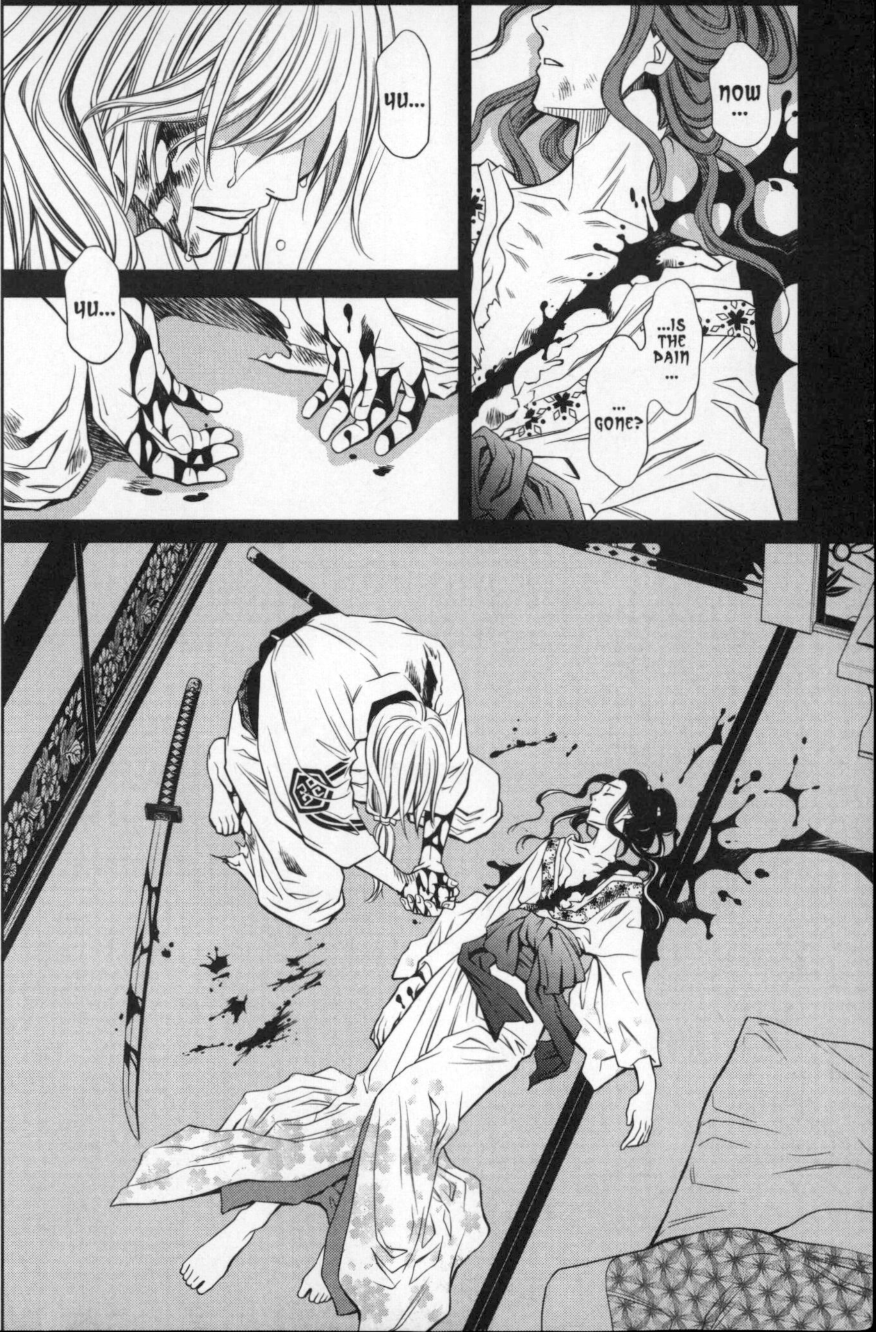
NOW ...
...IS THE PAIN ...
... GONE?
YU...
YU...

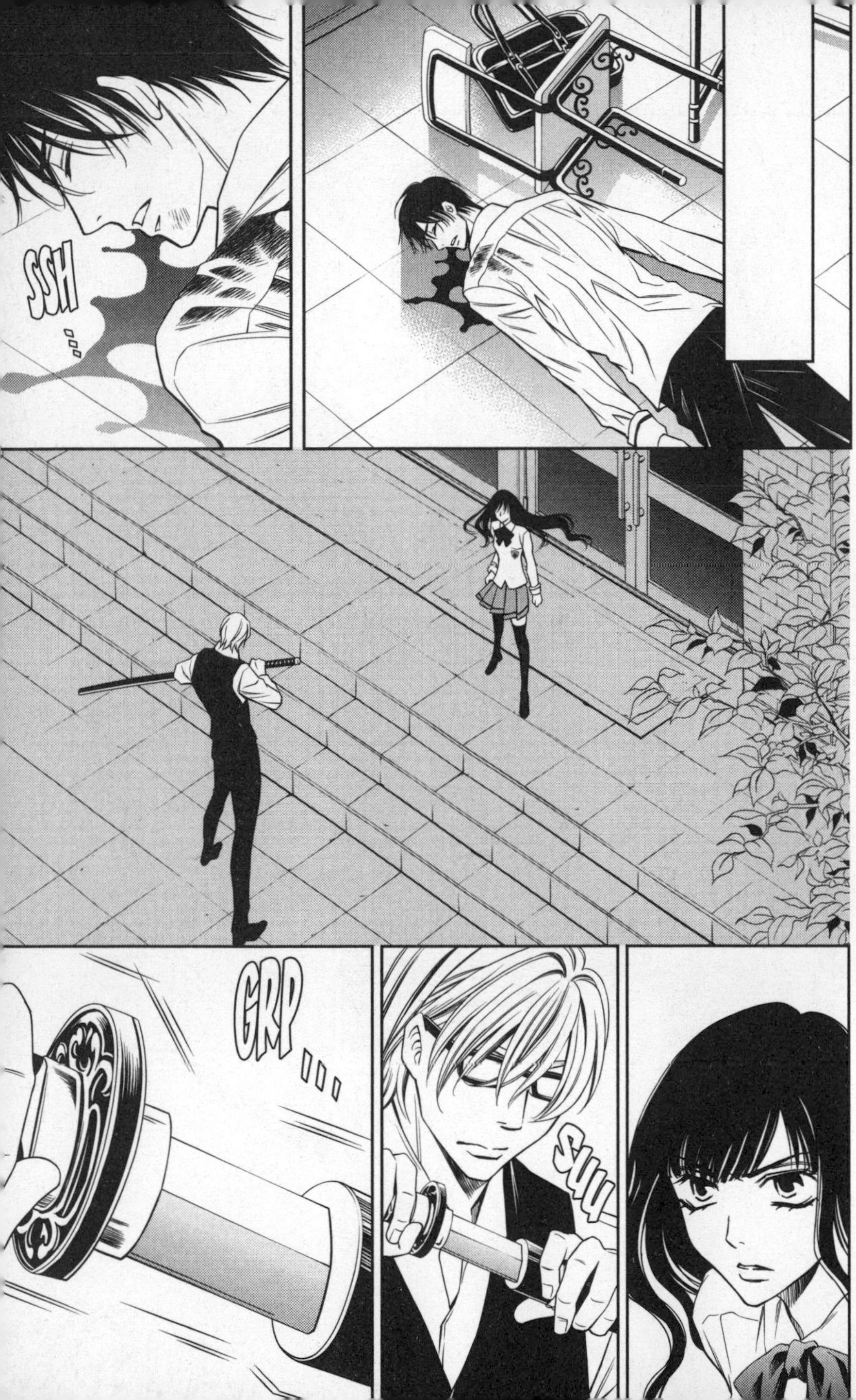
SSH...
SUU
GRP...

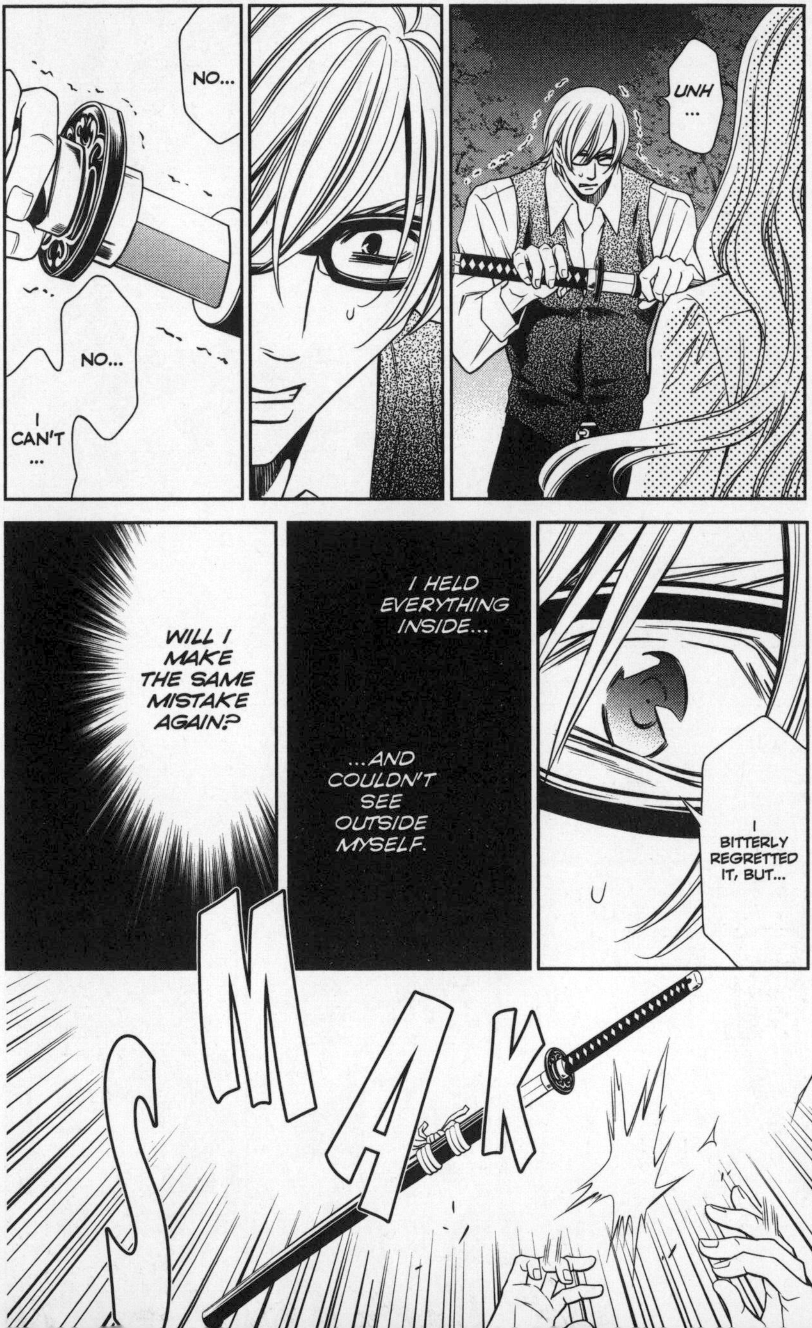
UNH ...
NO...
NO...
I CAN'T ...
I BITTERLY REGRETTED IT, BUT...
I HELD EVERYTHING INSIDE...
...AND COULDN'T SEE OUTSIDE MYSELF.
WILL I MAKE THE SAME MISTAKE AGAIN?
SMAK

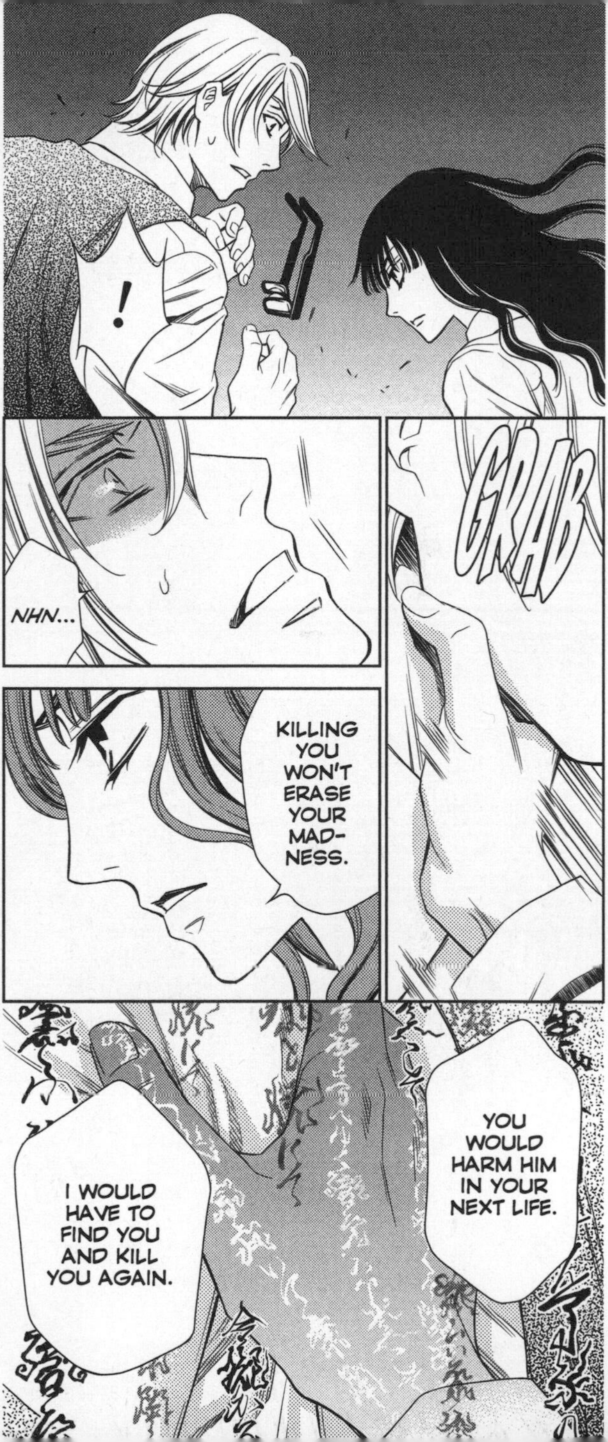
!
GRAB
NHN...
KILLING YOU WON'T ERASE YOUR MADNESS.
YOU WOULD HARM HIM IN YOUR NEXT LIFE.
I WOULD HAVE TO FIND YOU AND KILL YOU AGAIN.

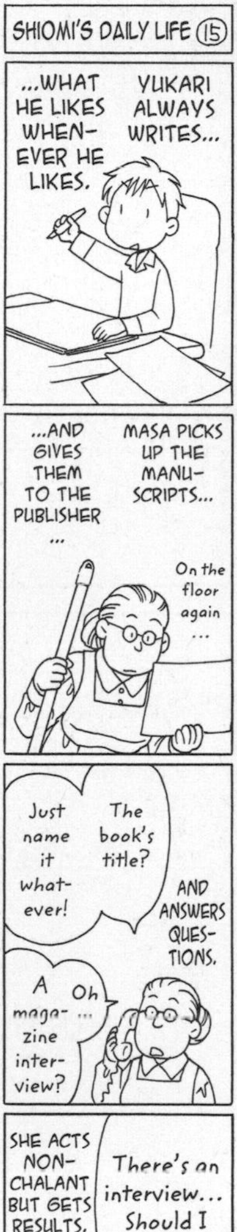
SHIOMI'S DAILY LIFE 15
YUKARI ALWAYS WRITES...
...WHAT HE LIKES WHENEVER HE LIKES.
MASA PICKS UP THE MANUSCRIPTS...
...AND GIVES THEM TO THE PUBLISHER...
On the floor again...
The book's title?
Just name it whatever!
AND ANSWERS QUESTIONS.
A magazine interview?
Oh...
SHE ACTS NONCHALANT BUT GETS RESULTS.
There's an interview... Should I plug the book?
Sure.
Have a good day.
See ya!

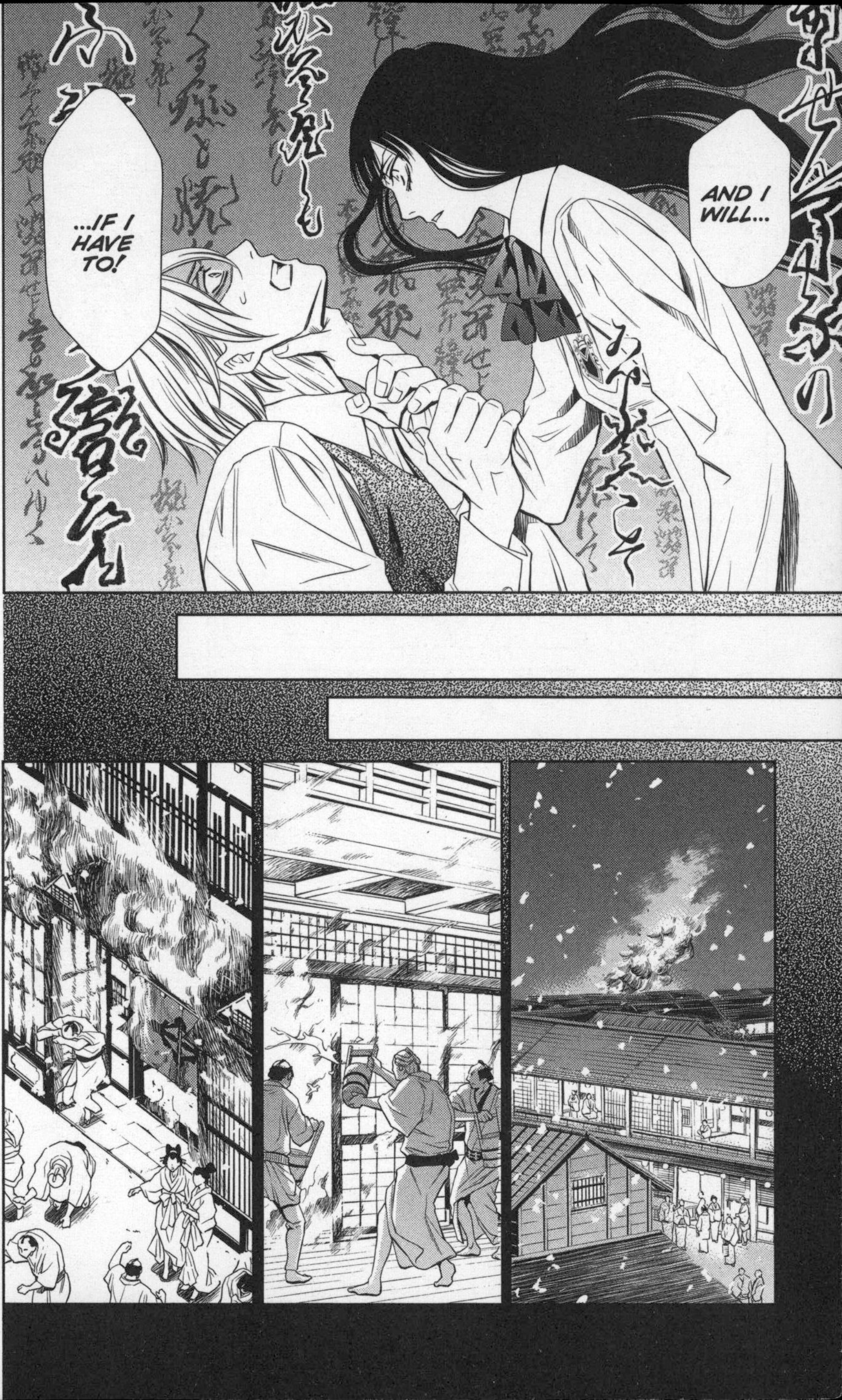
AND I WILL...
...IF I HAVE TO!

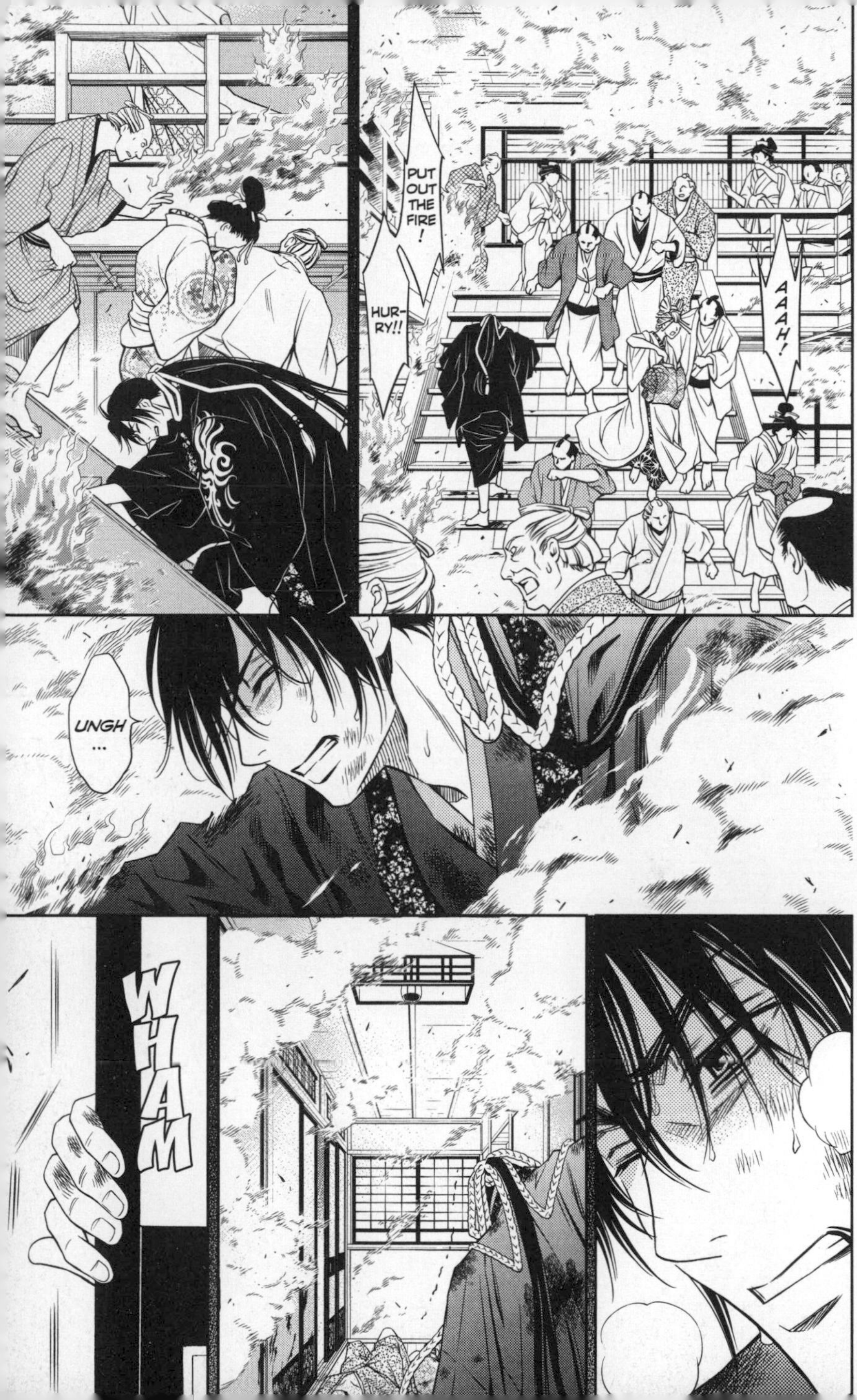
AAAH!
PUT OUT THE FIRE!
HURRY!!
UNGH...
WHAM

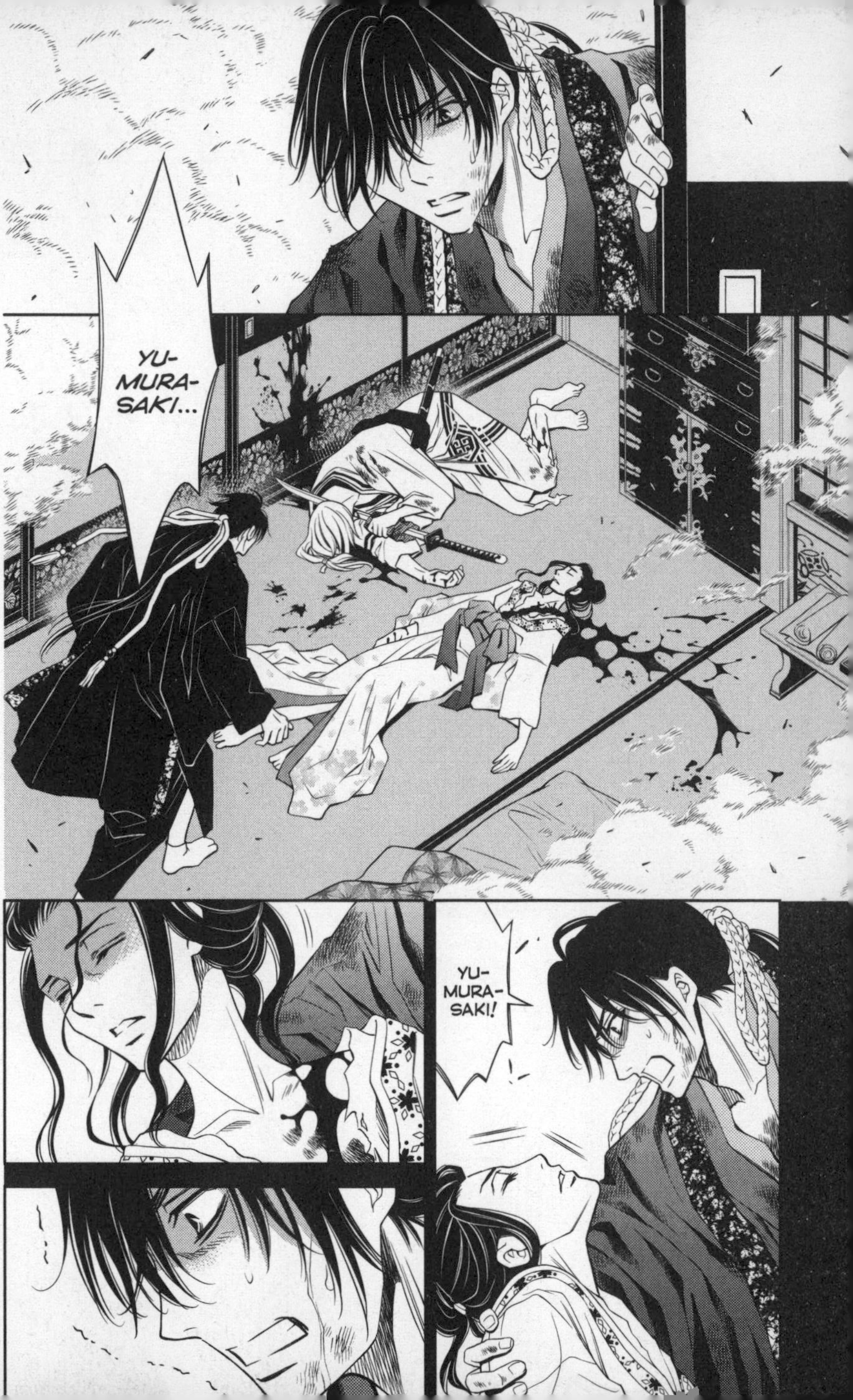
YU-MURA-SAKI...
YU-MURA-SAKI!

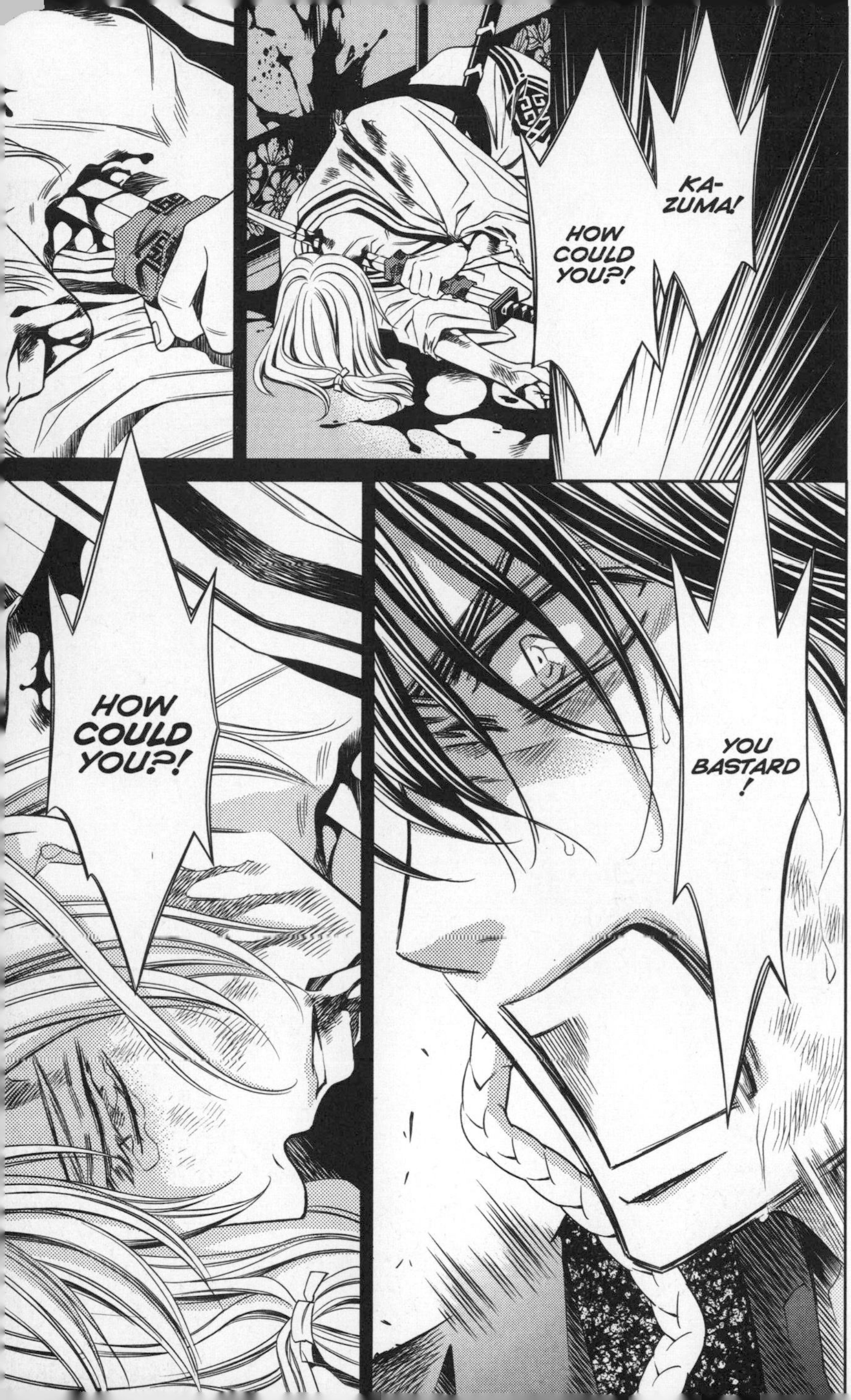
KA-ZUMA!
HOW COULD YOU?!
YOU BASTARD!
HOW COULD YOU?!

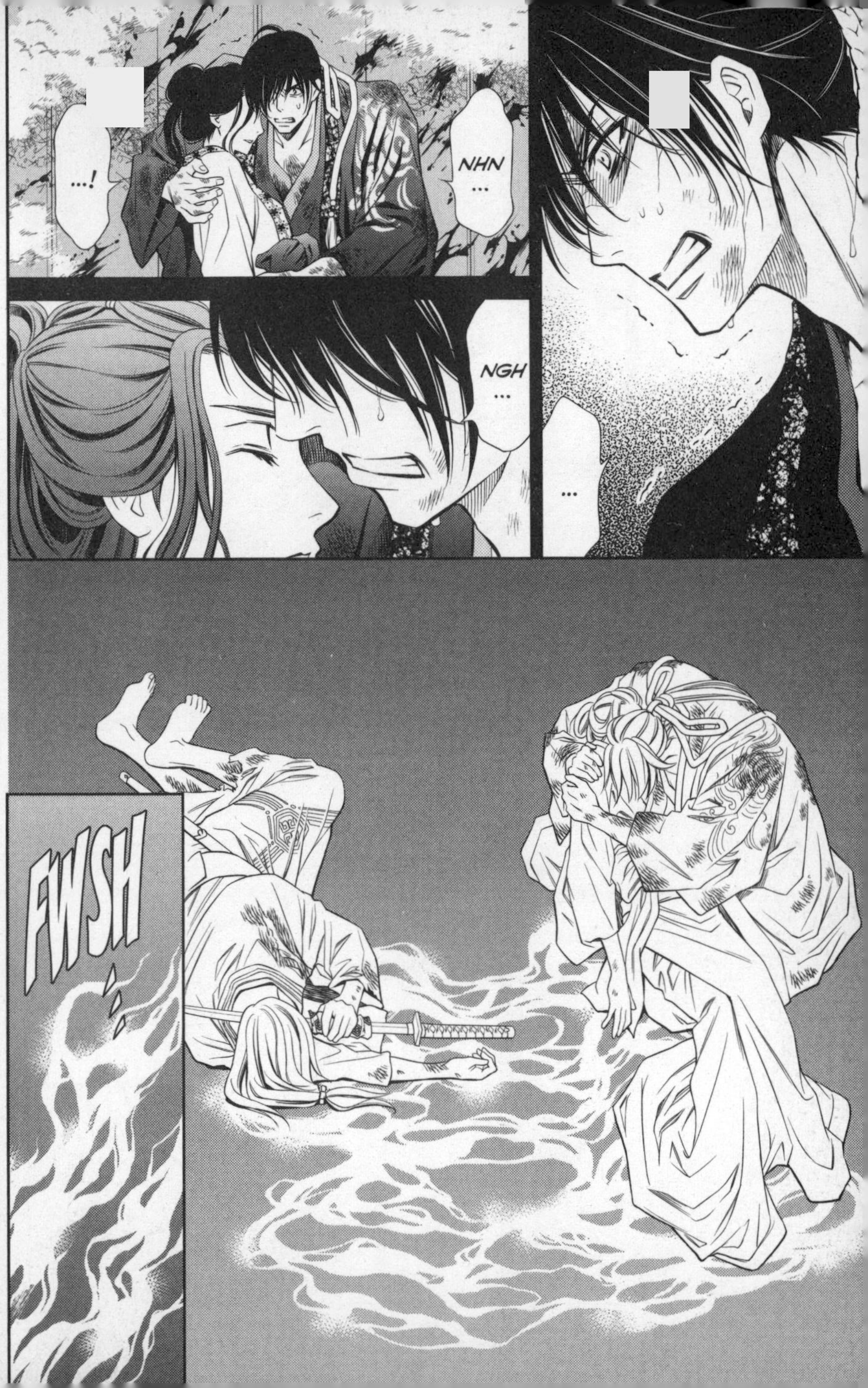
...
NHN ...
...!
NGH ...
FWSH

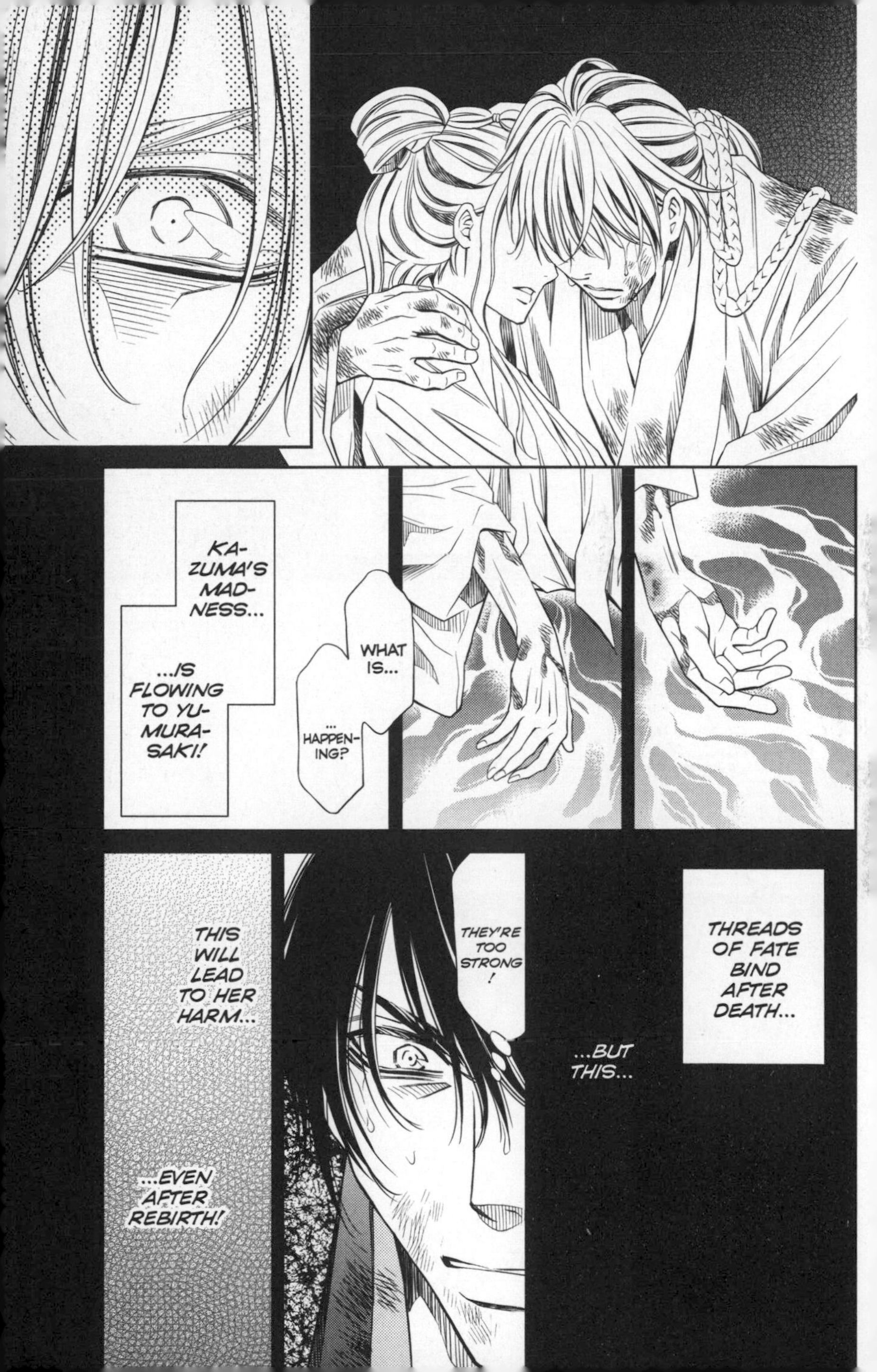
WHAT IS...
...HAPPENING?
KAZUMA'S MADNESS...
...IS FLOWING TO YUMURASAKI!
THREADS OF FATE BIND AFTER DEATH...
...BUT THIS...
THEY'RE TOO STRONG!
THIS WILL LEAD TO HER HARM...
...EVEN AFTER REBIRTH!

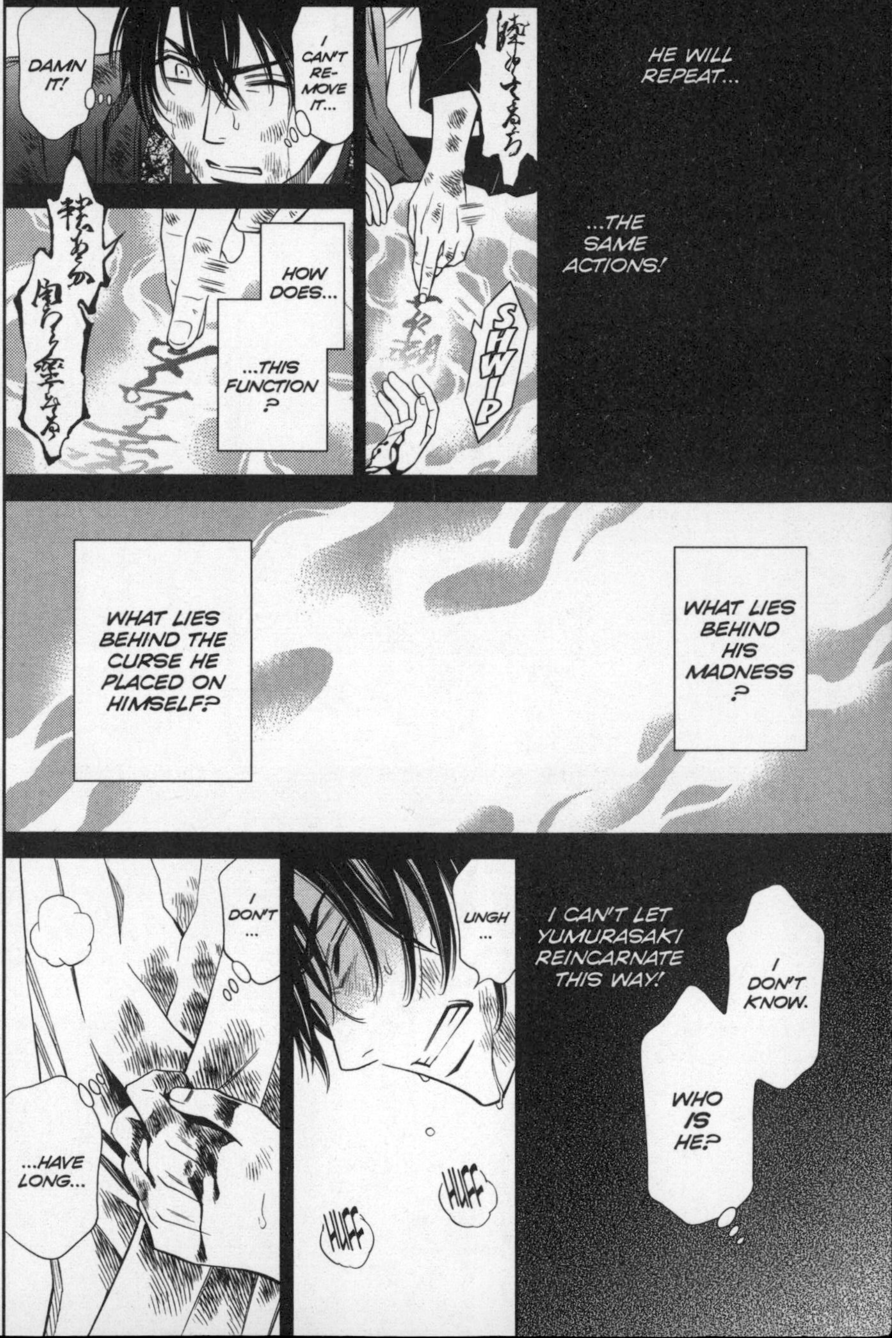
HE WILL REPEAT...
...THE SAME ACTIONS!
SHWIP
I CAN'T RE-MOVE IT...
DAMN IT!
HOW DOES...
...THIS FUNCTION?
WHAT LIES BEHIND HIS MADNESS?
WHAT LIES BEHIND THE CURSE HE PLACED ON HIMSELF?
I CAN'T LET YUMURASAKI REINCARNATE THIS WAY!
I DON'T KNOW.
WHO IS HE?
UNGH...
HUFF
HUFF
I DON'T...
...HAVE LONG...

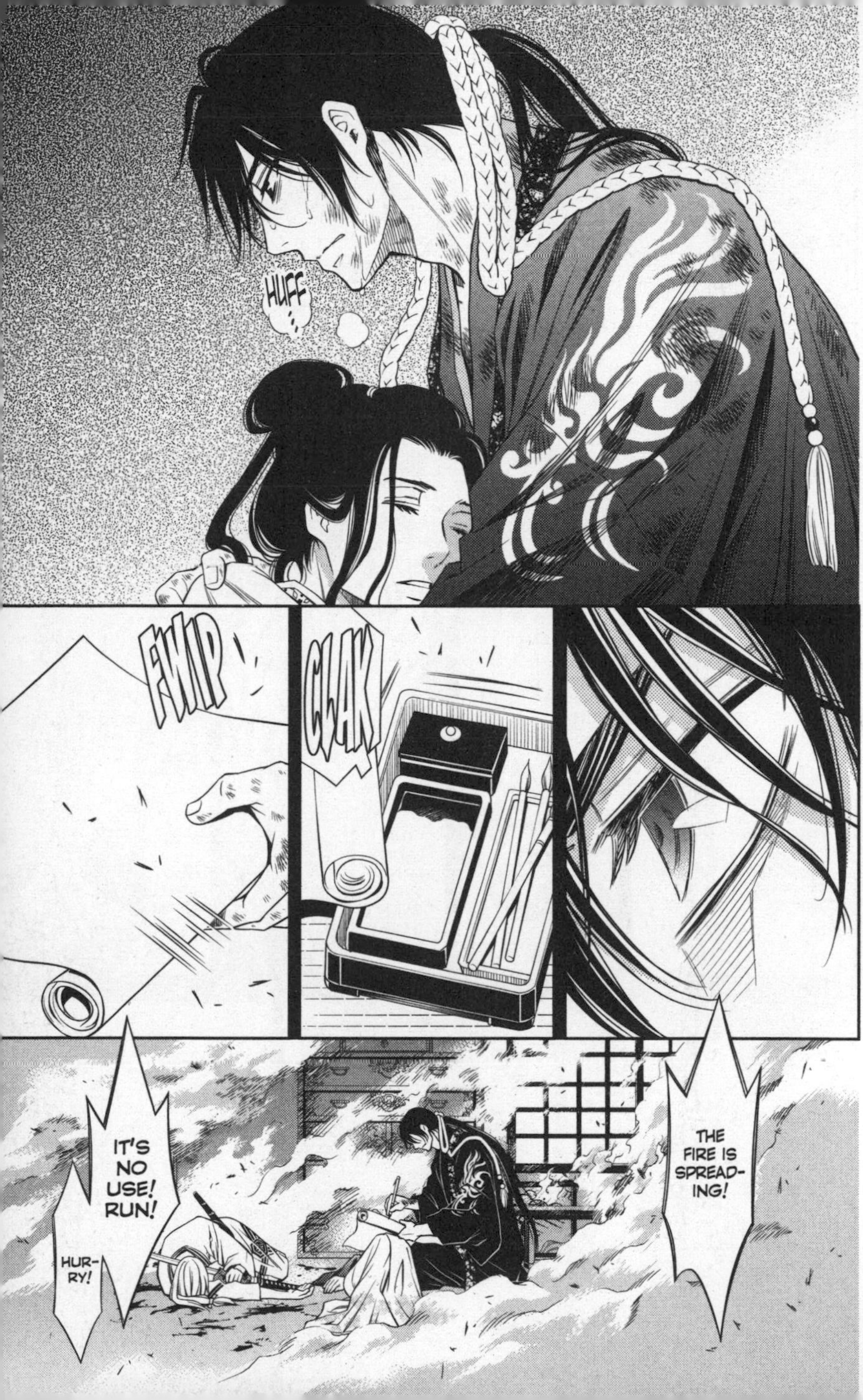
HUFF
CLAK
FWIP
THE FIRE IS SPREAD-ING!
IT'S NO USE! RUN!
HUR-RY!

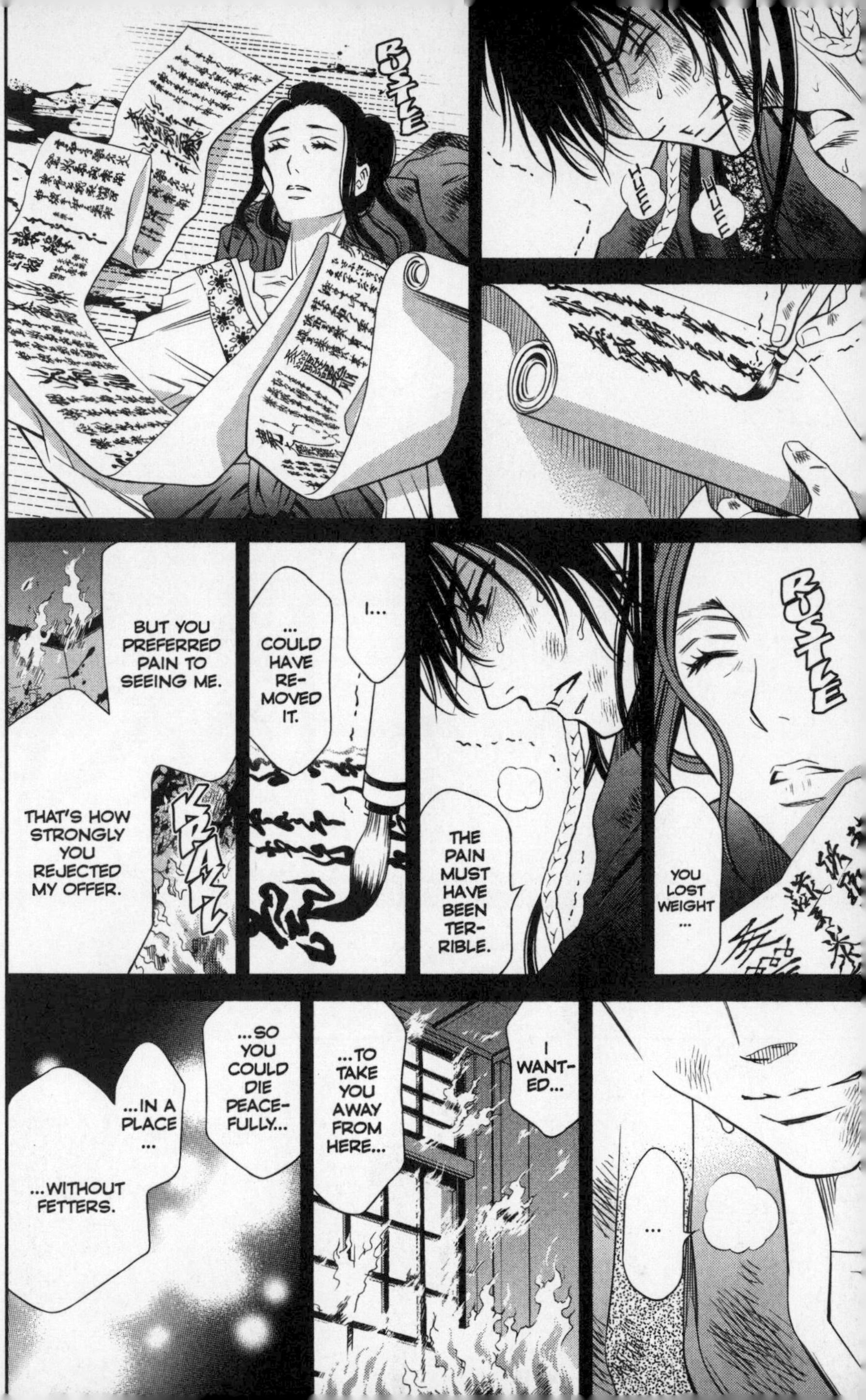
HUFF
HUFF
RUSTLE
RUSTLE
YOU LOST WEIGHT...
THE PAIN MUST HAVE BEEN TER-RIBLE.
I...
...COULD HAVE RE-MOVED IT.
BUT YOU PREFERRED PAIN TO SEEING ME.
THAT'S HOW STRONGLY YOU REJECTED MY OFFER.
...
I WANT-ED...
...TO TAKE YOU AWAY FROM HERE...
...SO YOU COULD DIE PEACE-FULLY...
...IN A PLACE...
...WITHOUT FETTERS.

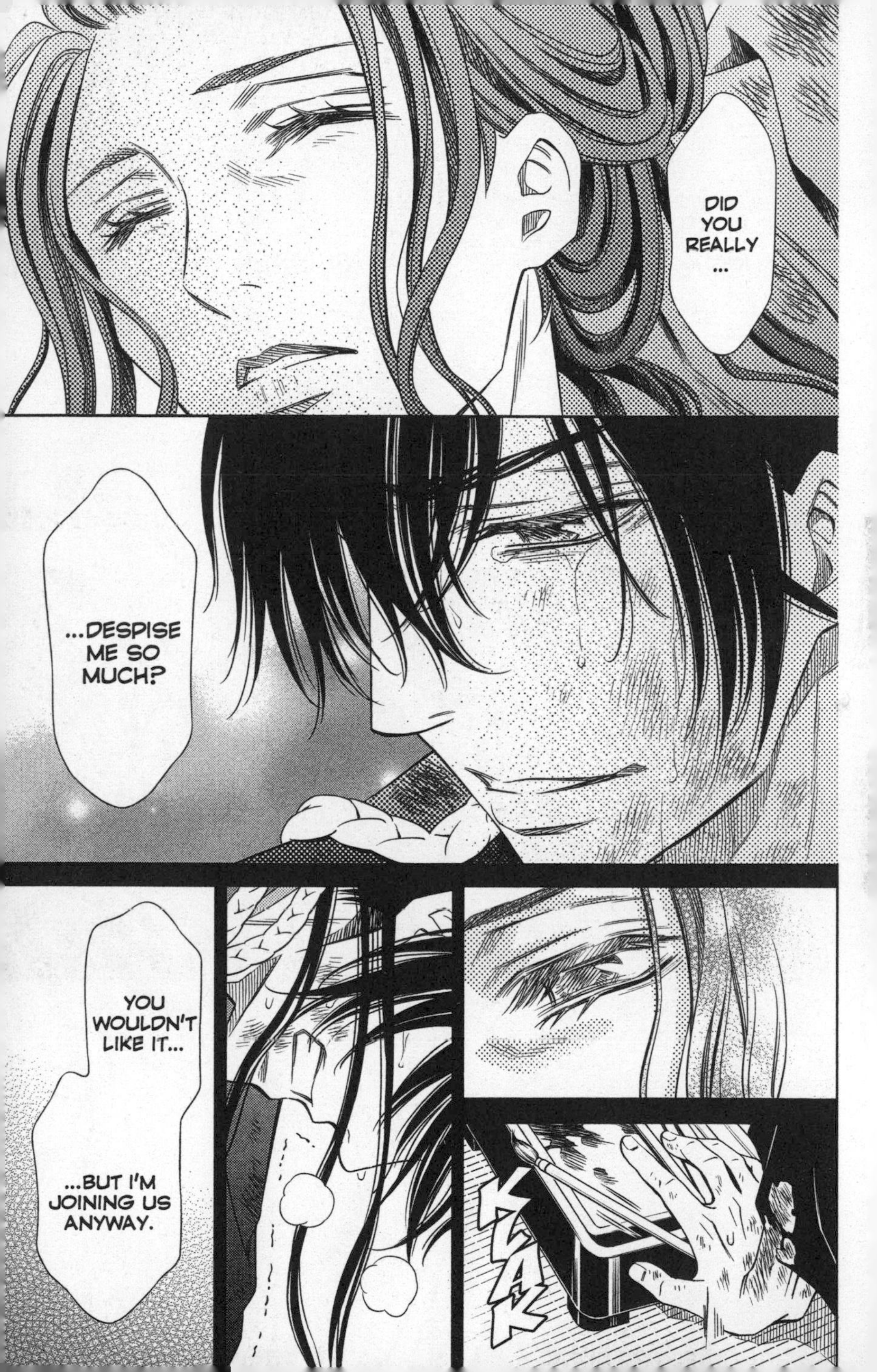
DID YOU REALLY ...
...DESPISE ME SO MUCH?
KLAK
YOU WOULDN'T LIKE IT...
...BUT I'M JOINING US ANYWAY.

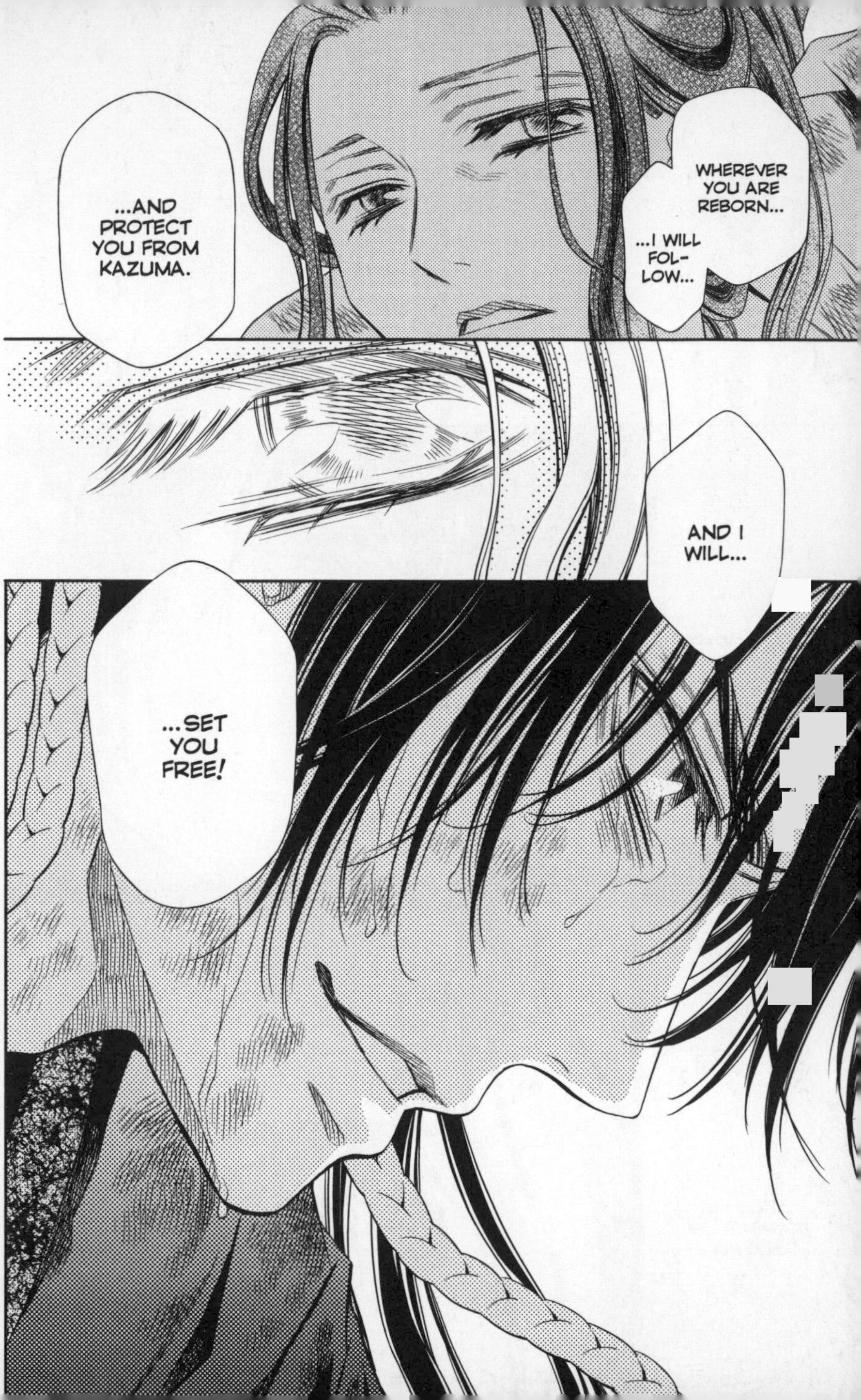
WHEREVER YOU ARE REBORN...
...I WILL FOL-LOW...
...AND PROTECT YOU FROM KAZUMA.
AND I WILL...
...SET YOU FREE!

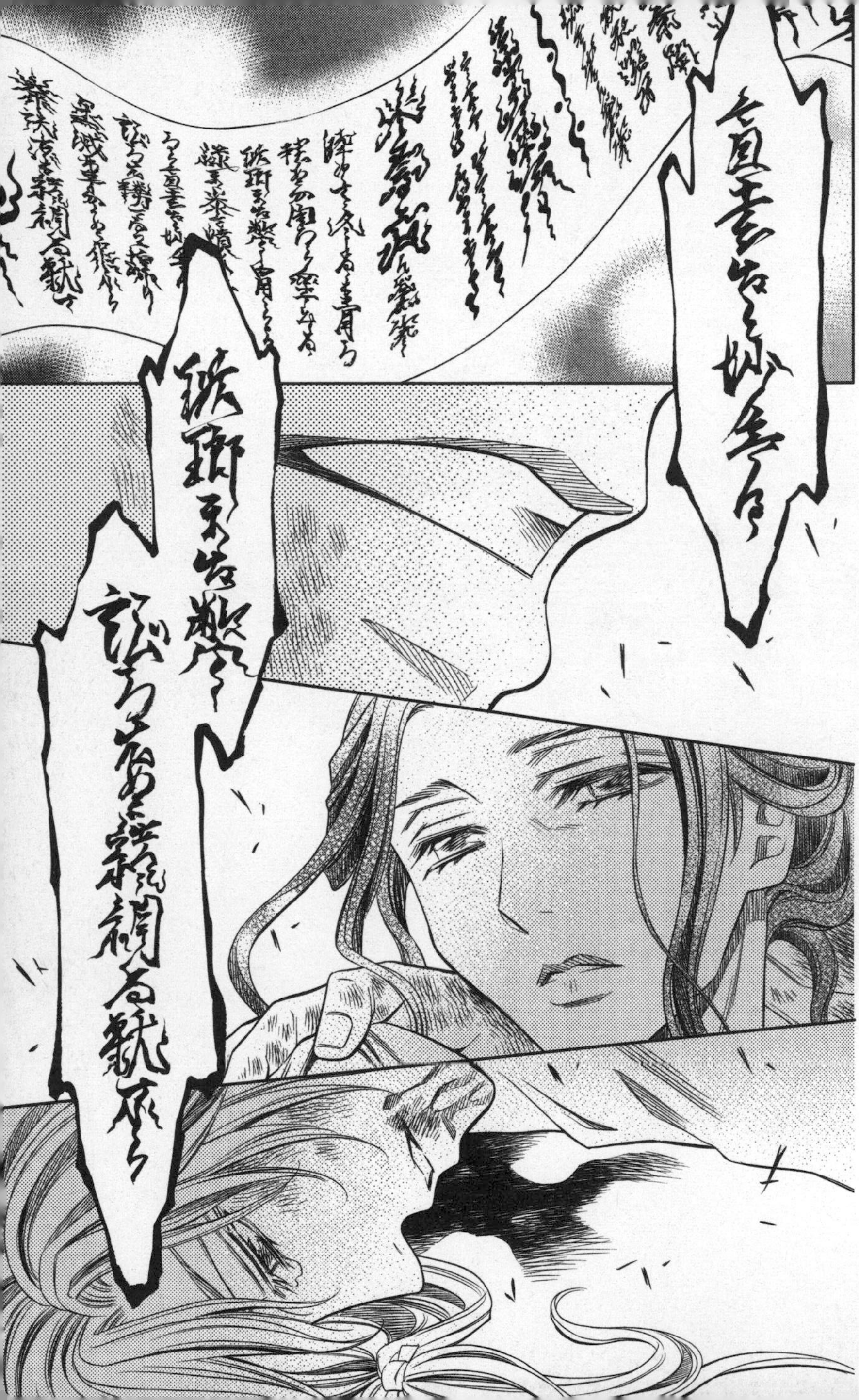

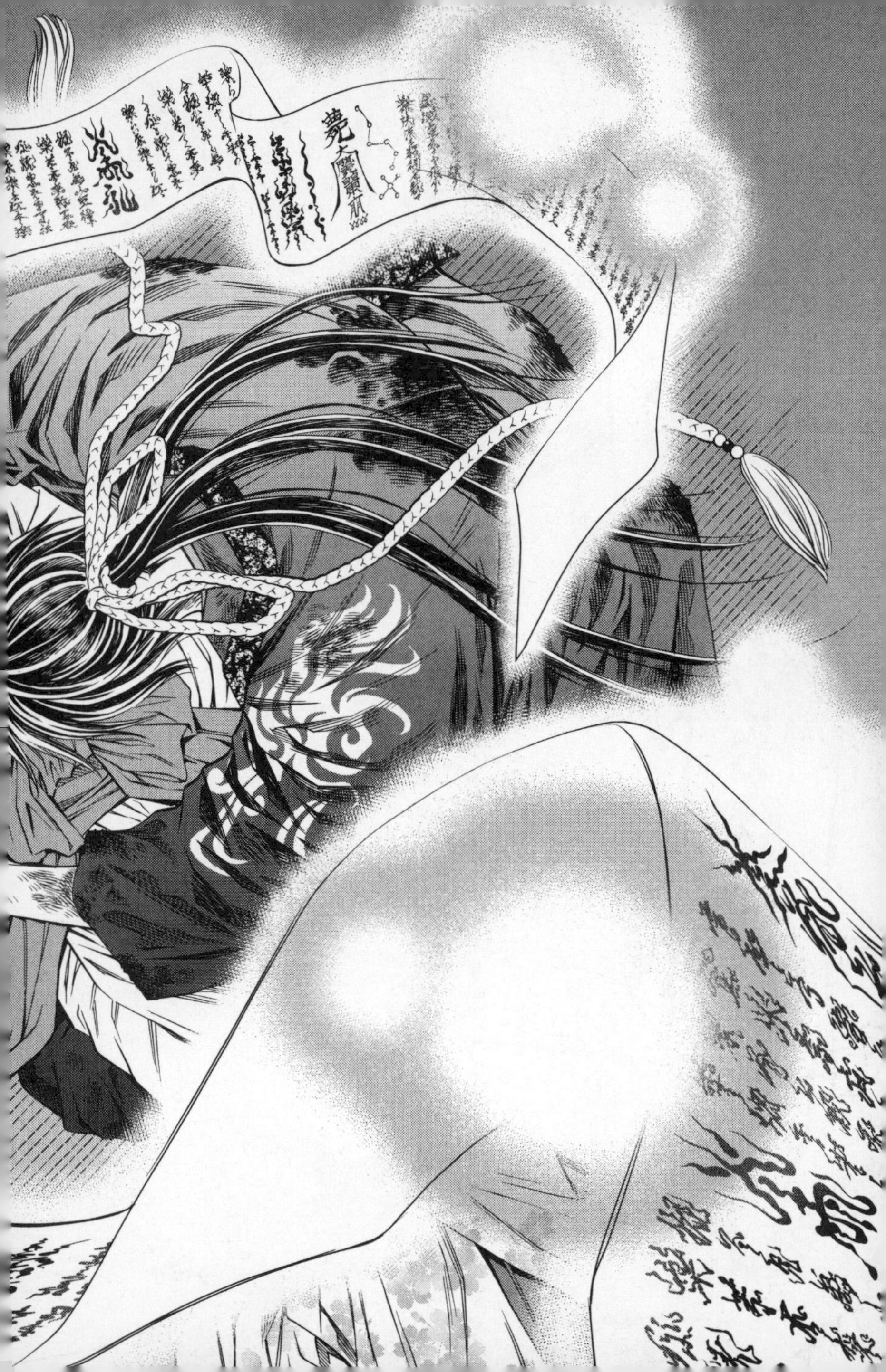

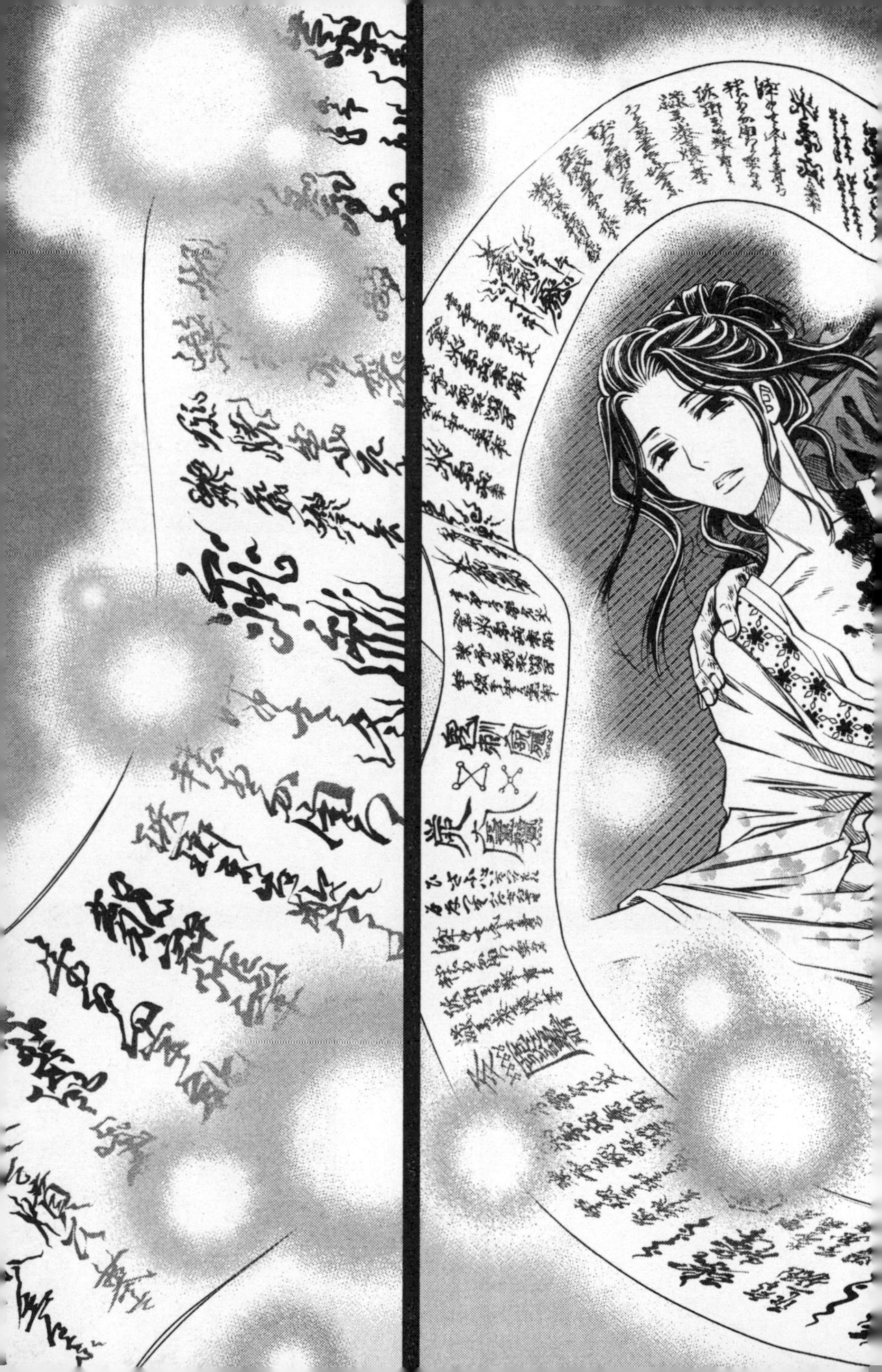

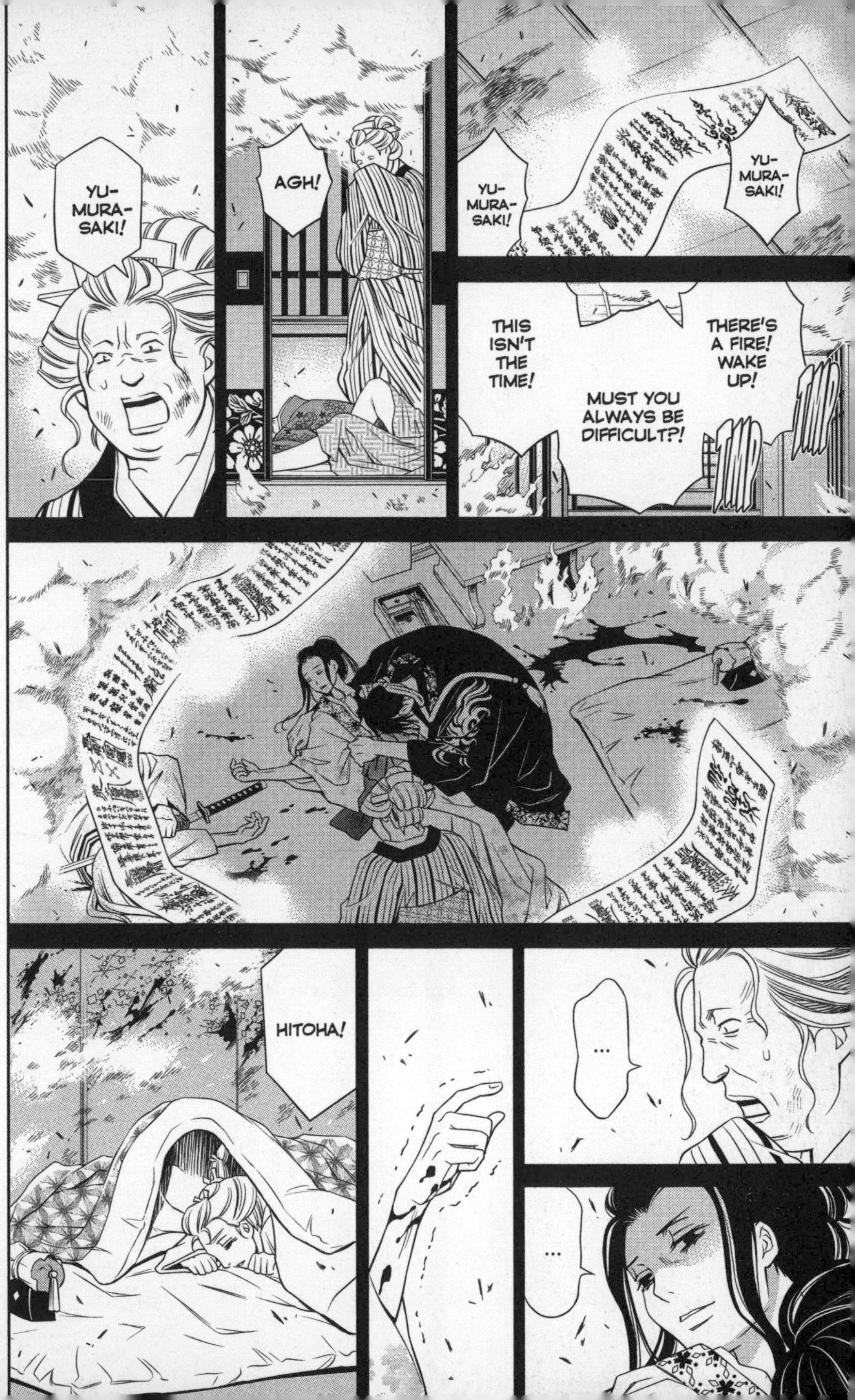
YU-MURA-SAKI!
YU-MURA-SAKI!
THERE'S A FIRE! WAKE UP!
THIS ISN'T THE TIME!
MUST YOU ALWAYS BE DIFFICULT?!
AGH!
YU-MURA-SAKI!
...
...
HITOHA!

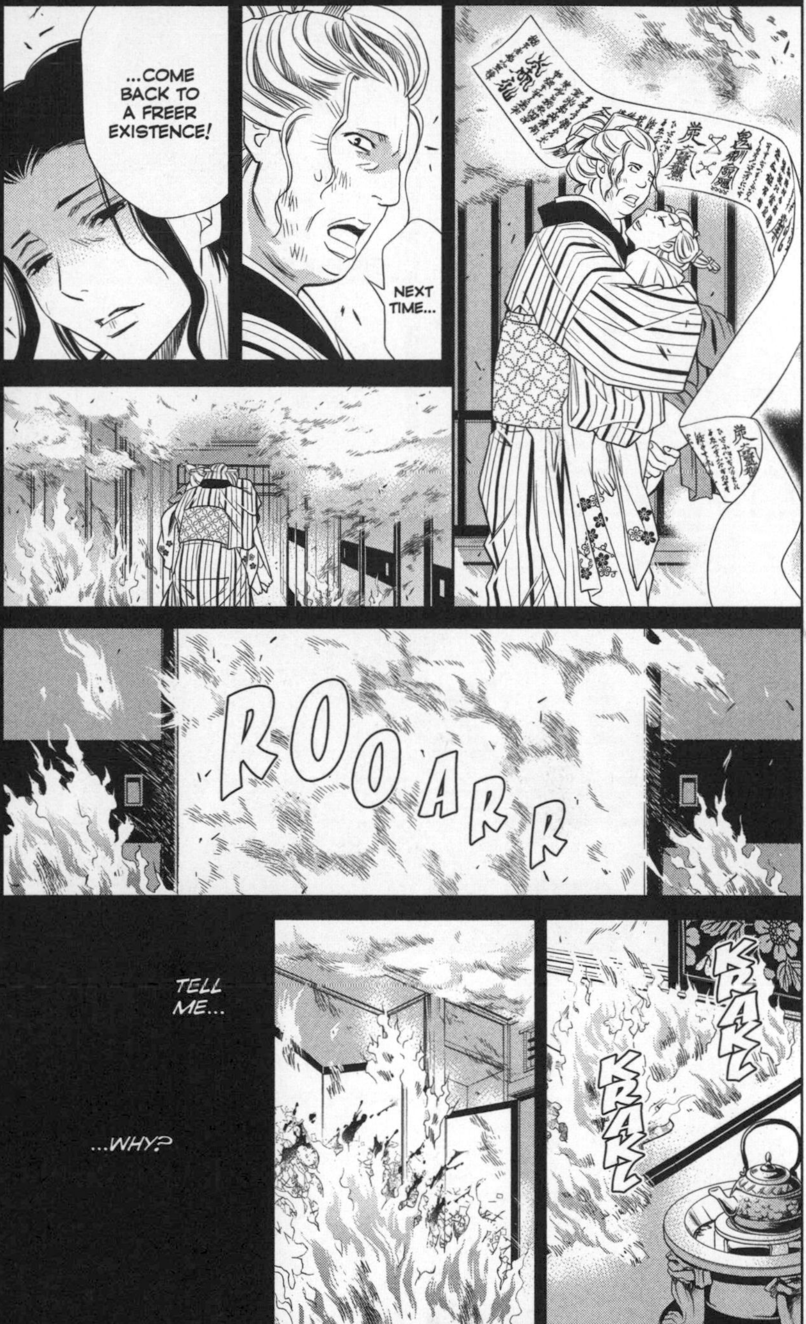
NEXT TIME...
...COME BACK TO A FREER EXISTENCE!
ROOARRR
KRAK
KRAK
TELL ME...
...WHY?

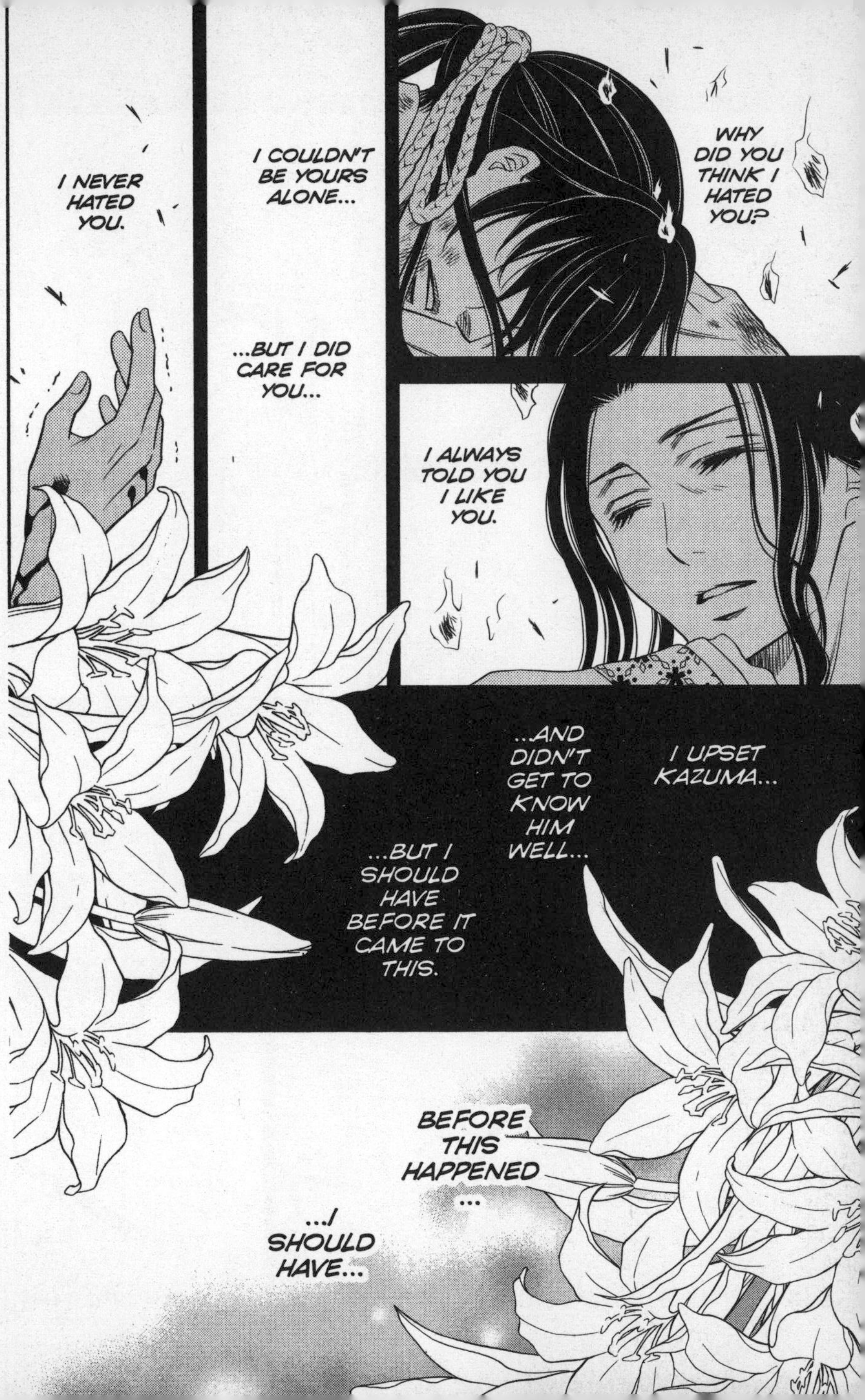
WHY DID YOU THINK I HATED YOU?
I ALWAYS TOLD YOU I LIKE YOU.
I COULDN'T BE YOURS ALONE...
...BUT I DID CARE FOR YOU...
I NEVER HATED YOU.
I UPSET KAZUMA...
...AND DIDN'T GET TO KNOW HIM WELL...
...BUT I SHOULD HAVE BEFORE IT CAME TO THIS.
BEFORE THIS HAPPENED...
...I SHOULD HAVE...

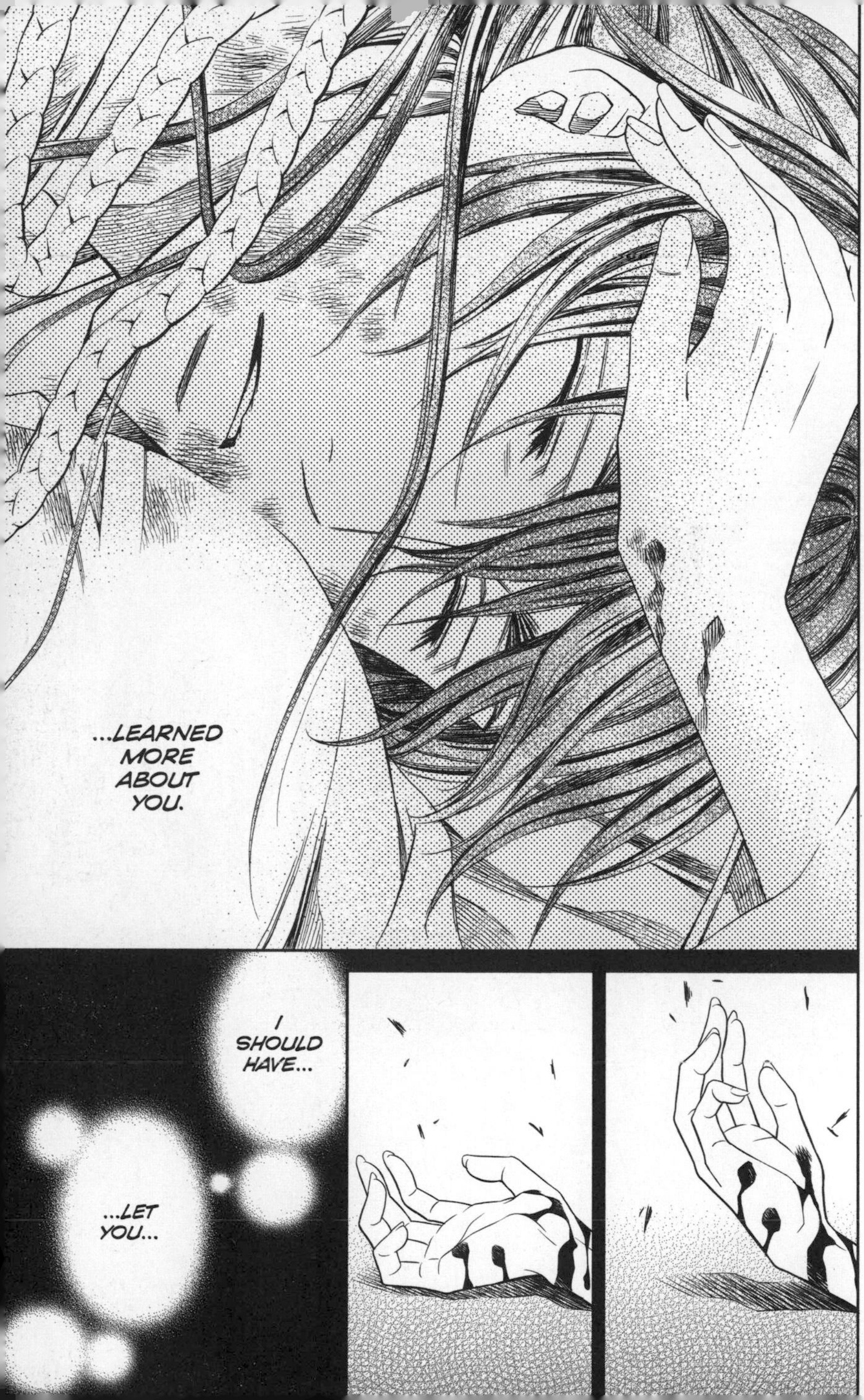
...LEARNED MORE ABOUT YOU.
I SHOULD HAVE...
...LET YOU...

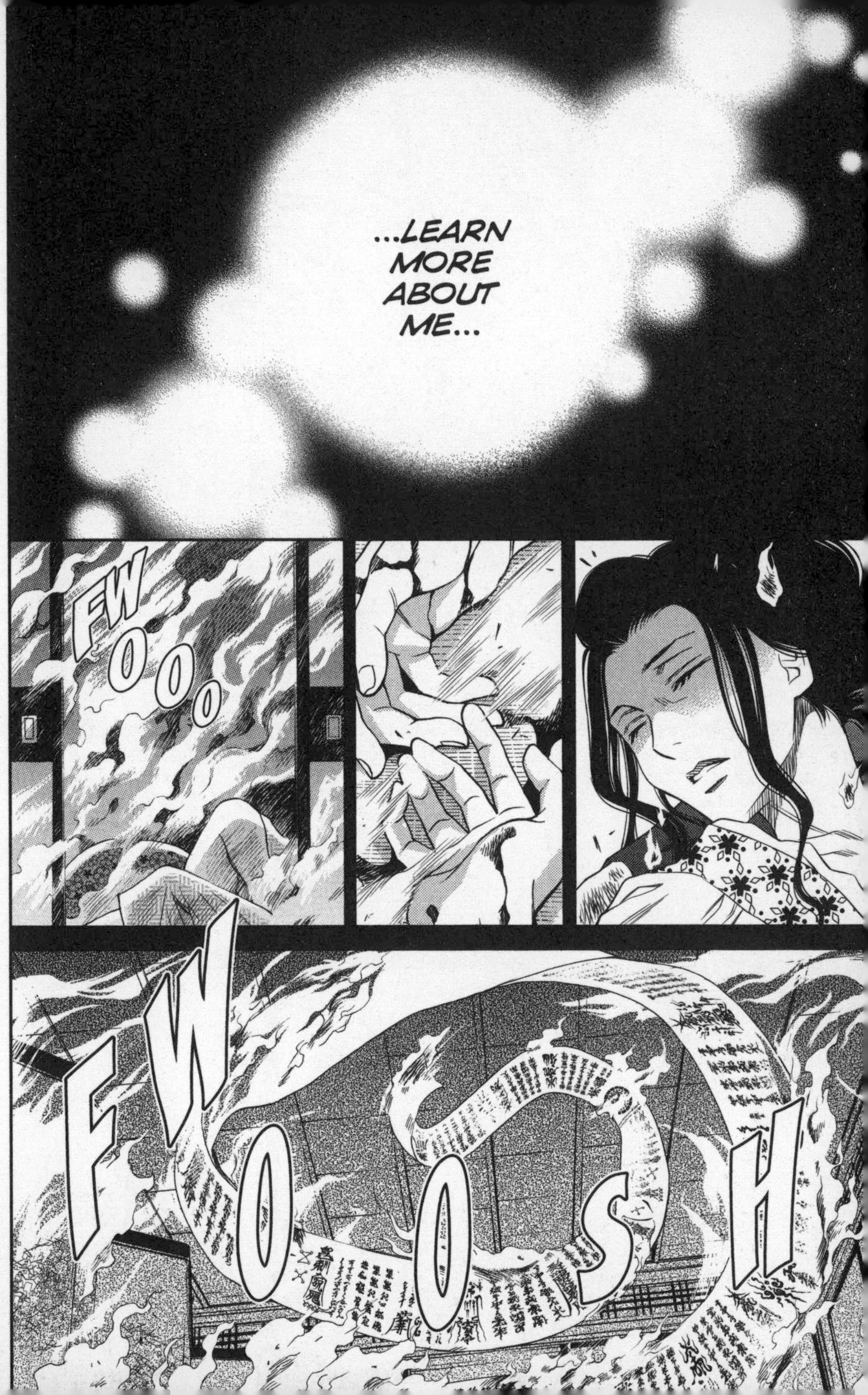
...LEARN MORE ABOUT ME...
FWOOO
FWOOSH

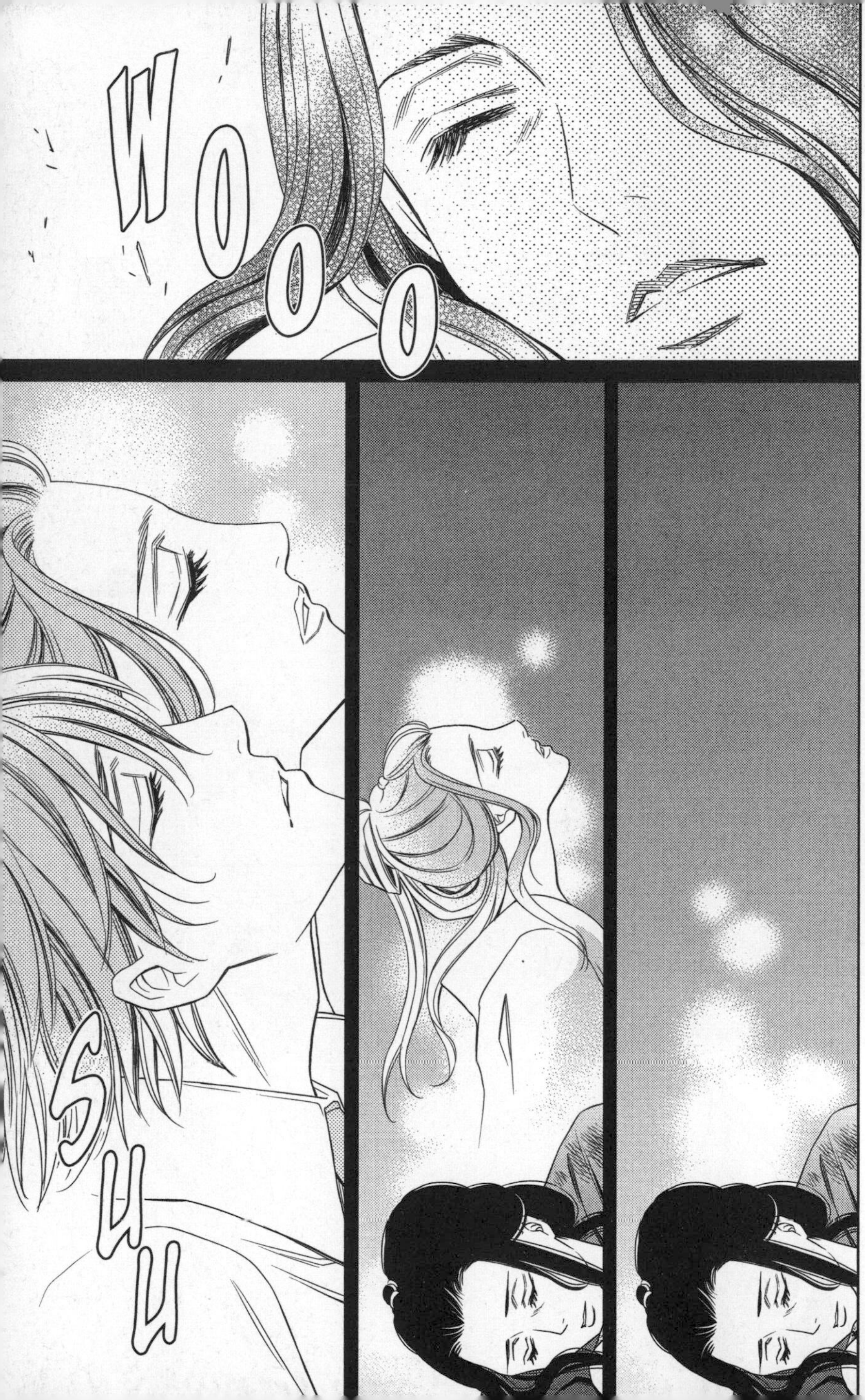
WOOOO
SUUU

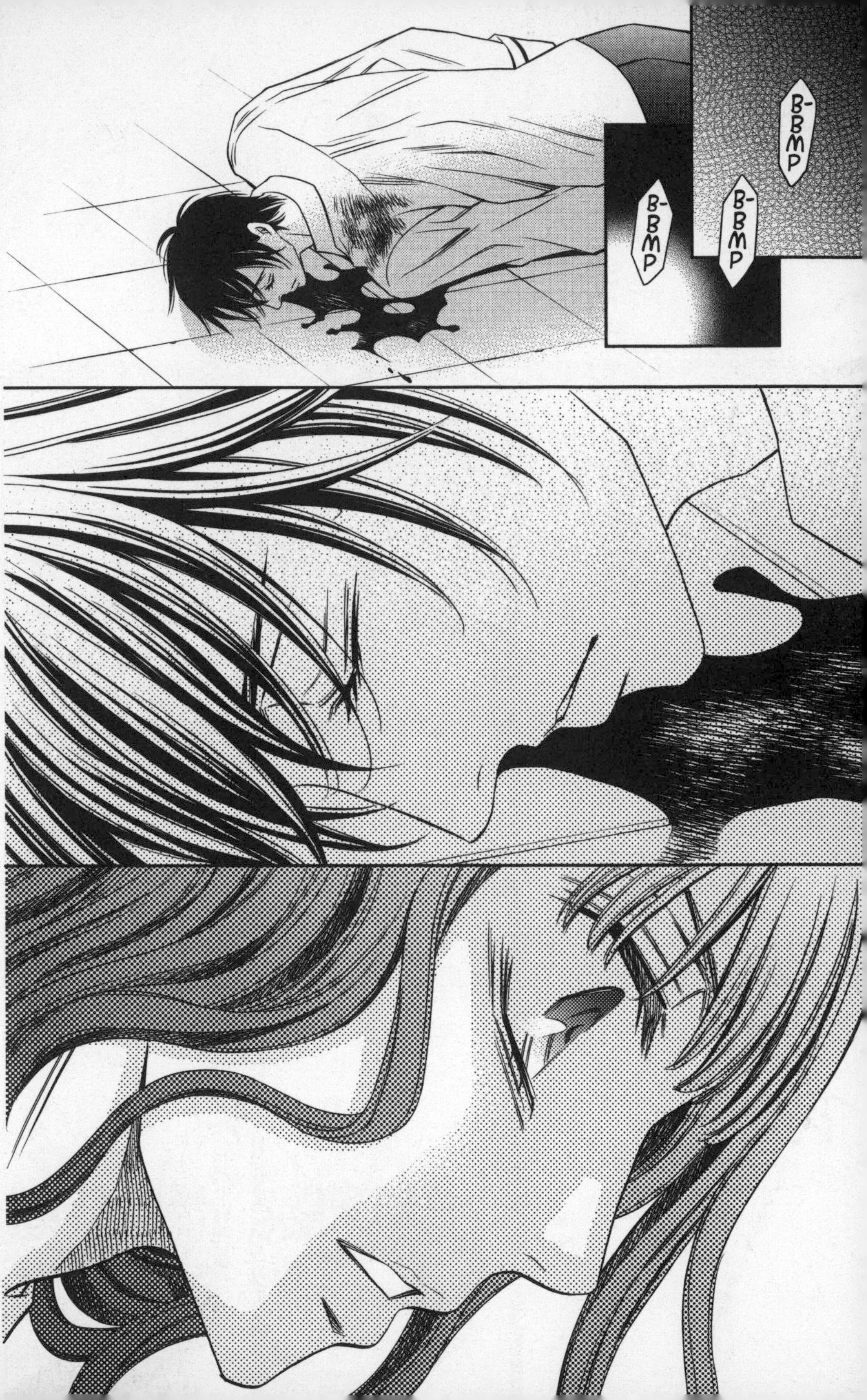
B-BBMP
B-BBMP
B-BBMP

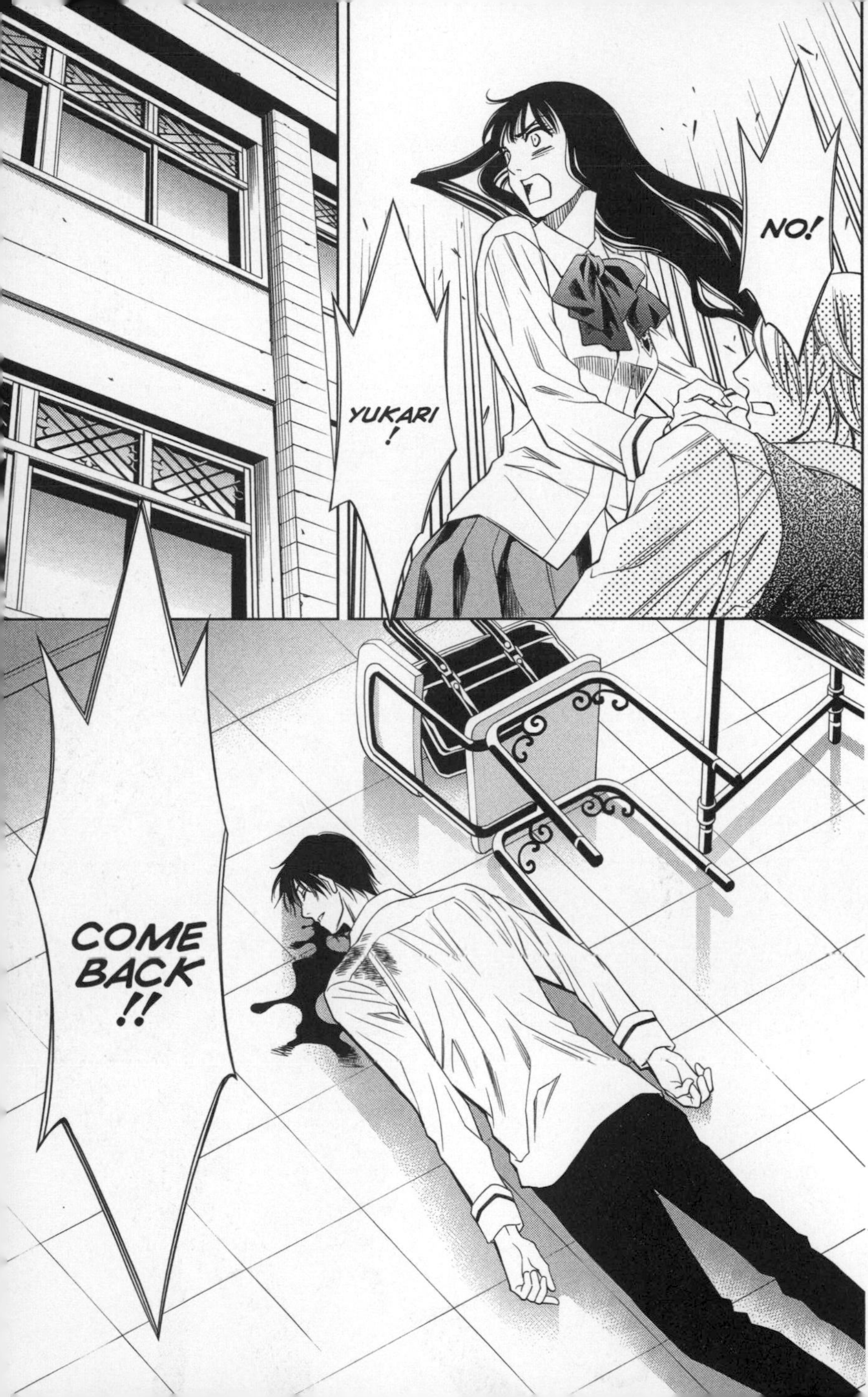
NO!
YUKARI!
COME BACK!!

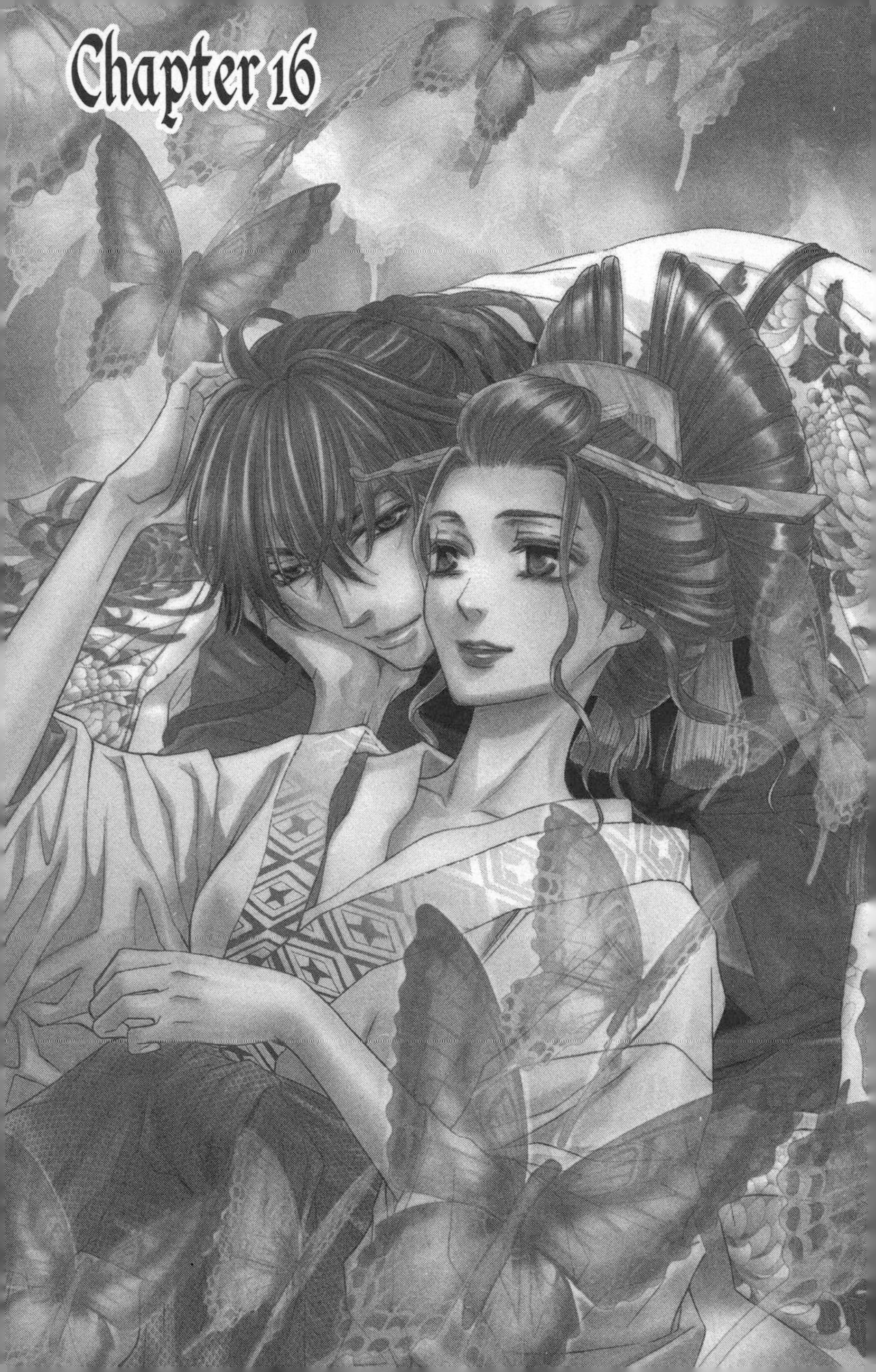
Chapter 16

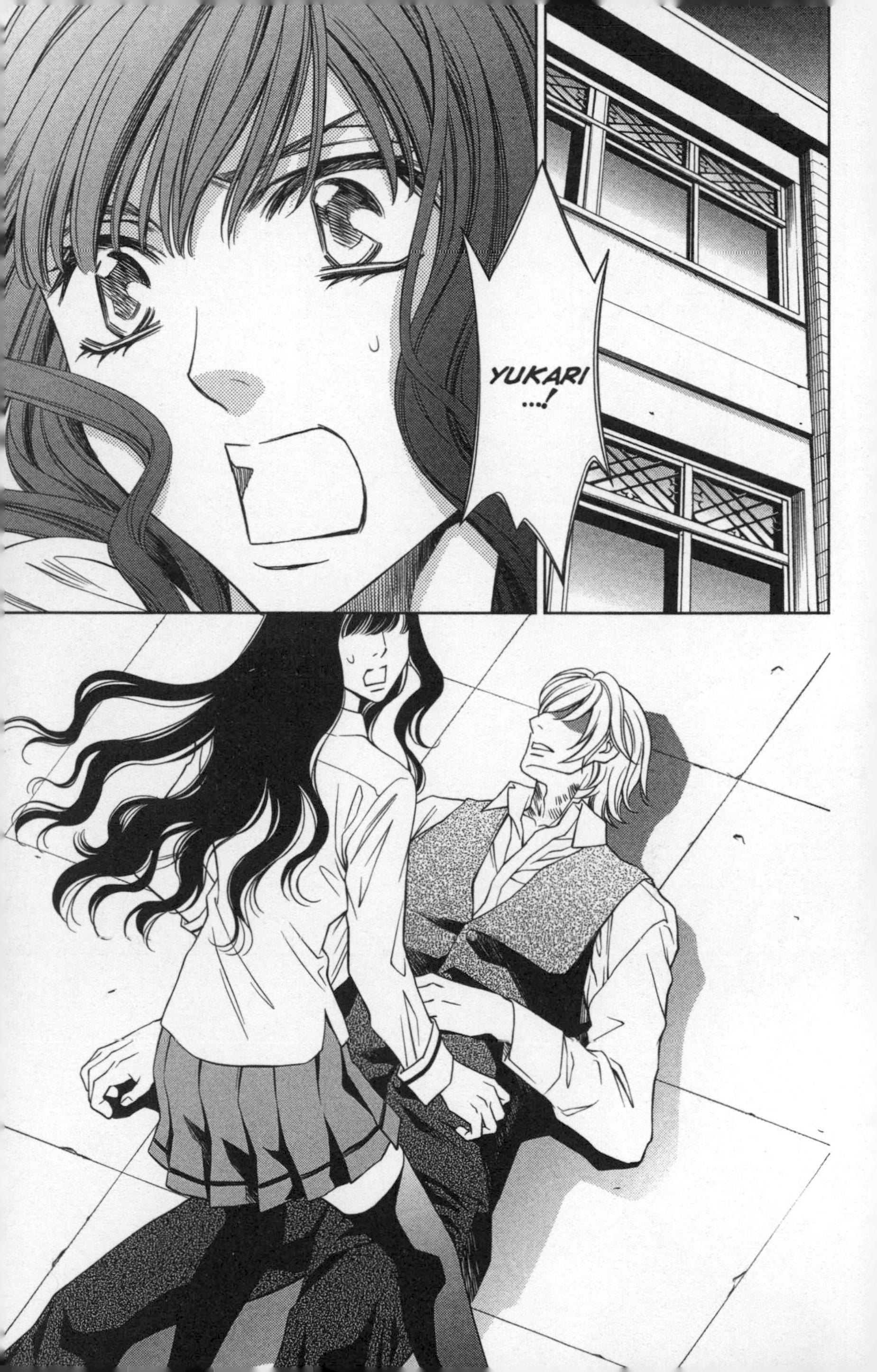
YUKARI ...!

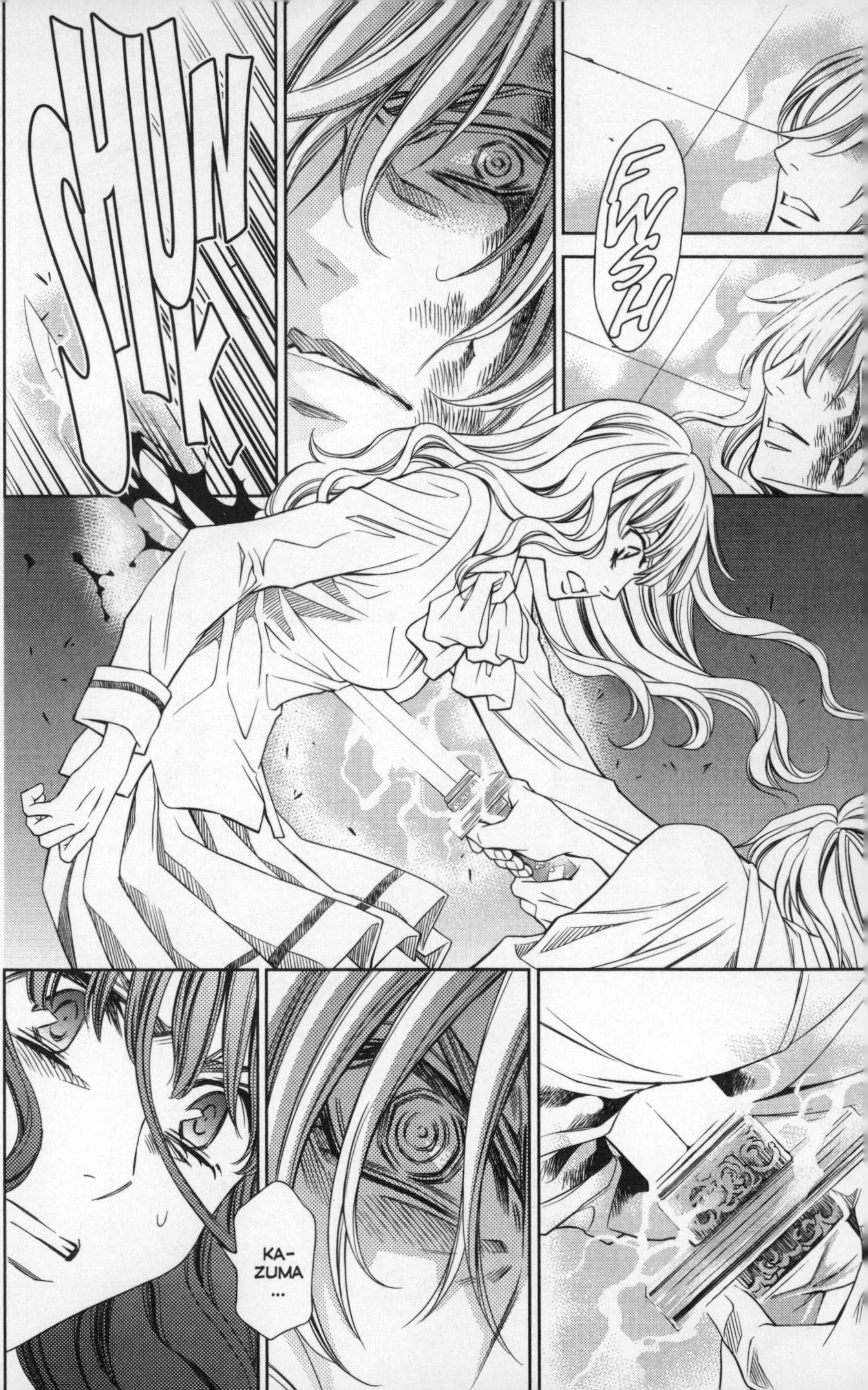
FWSH
CHUNK
KA-
ZUMA
...

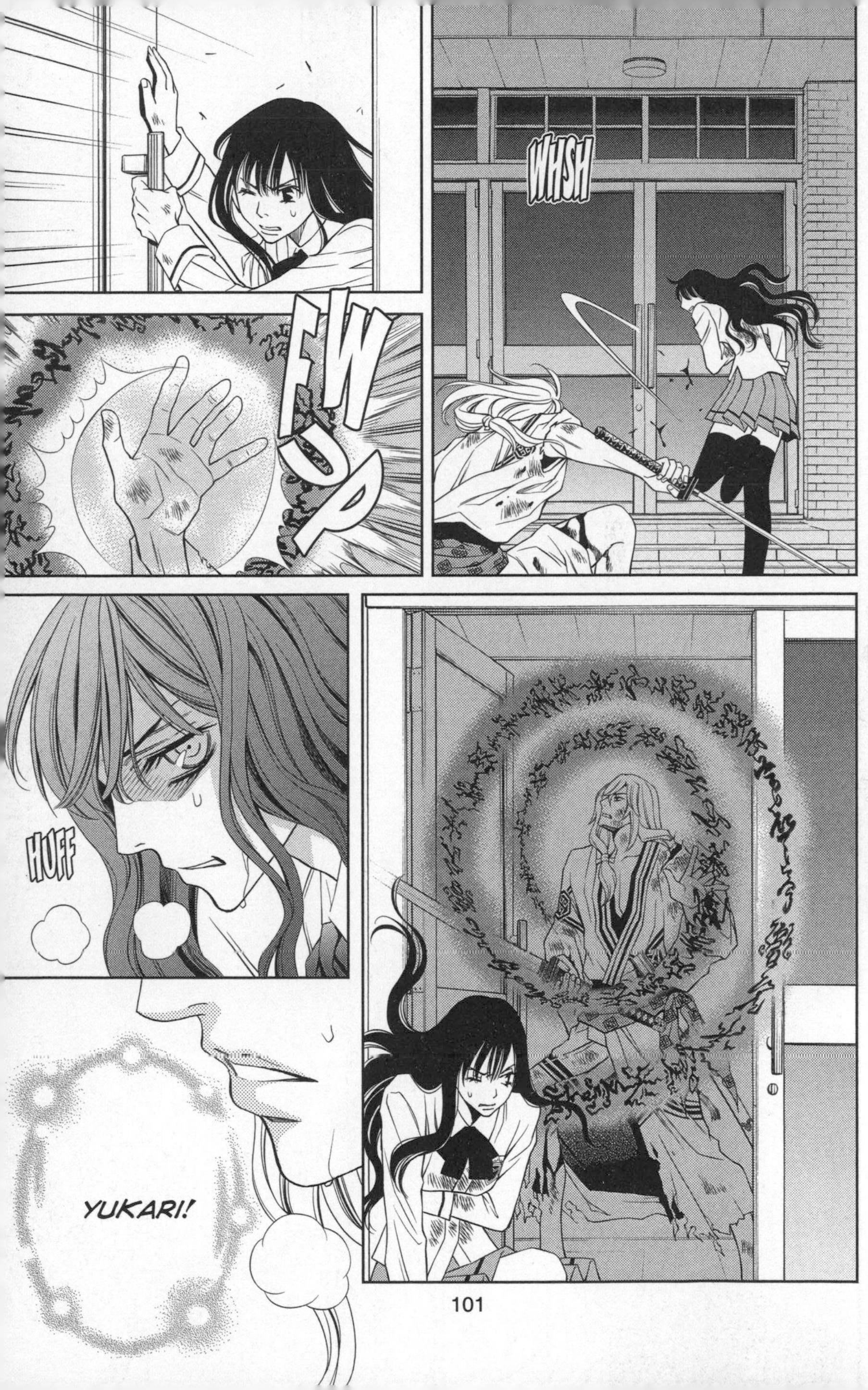
WHSH
FWUP
HUFF
YUKARI!

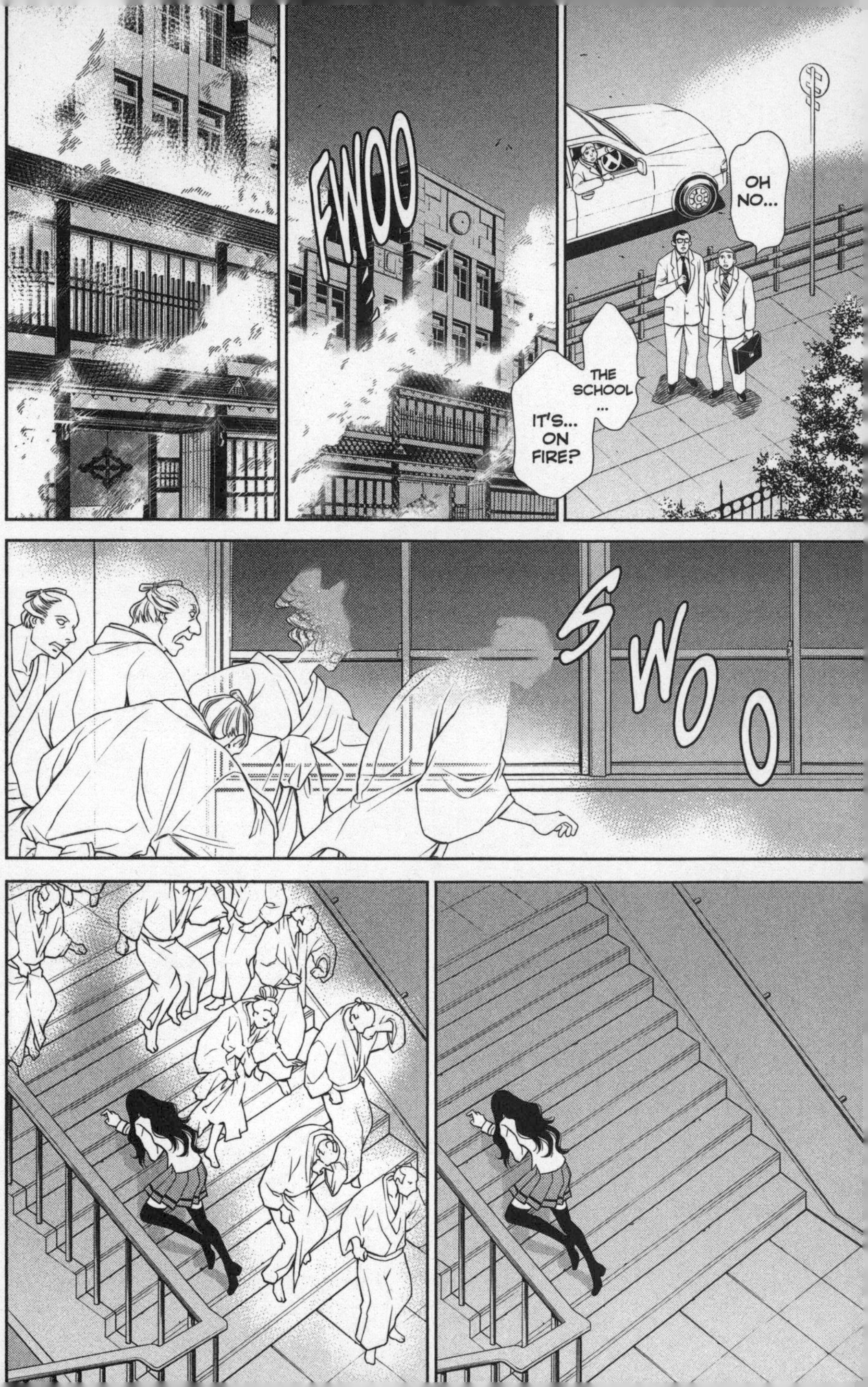
OH NO...
THE SCHOOL ...
IT'S... ON FIRE?
FWOO
SWOO

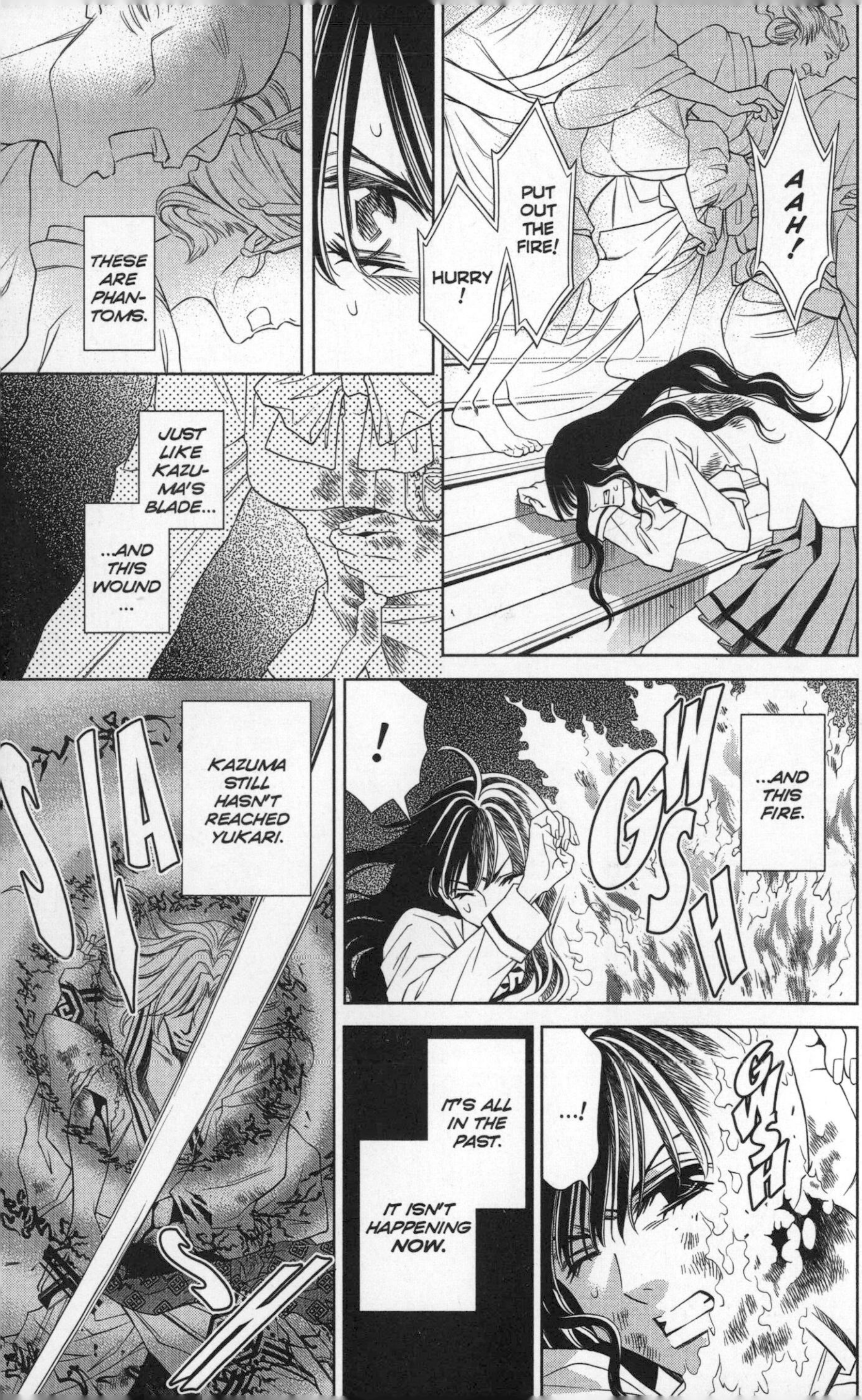
AAH!
PUT OUT THE FIRE!
HURRY!
THESE ARE PHANTOMS.
JUST LIKE KAZUMA'S BLADE...
...AND THIS WOUND...
...AND THIS FIRE.
GWSH
!
GUSH
...!
IT'S ALL IN THE PAST.
IT ISN'T HAPPENING NOW.
KAZUMA STILL HASN'T REACHED YUKARI.
SLASH

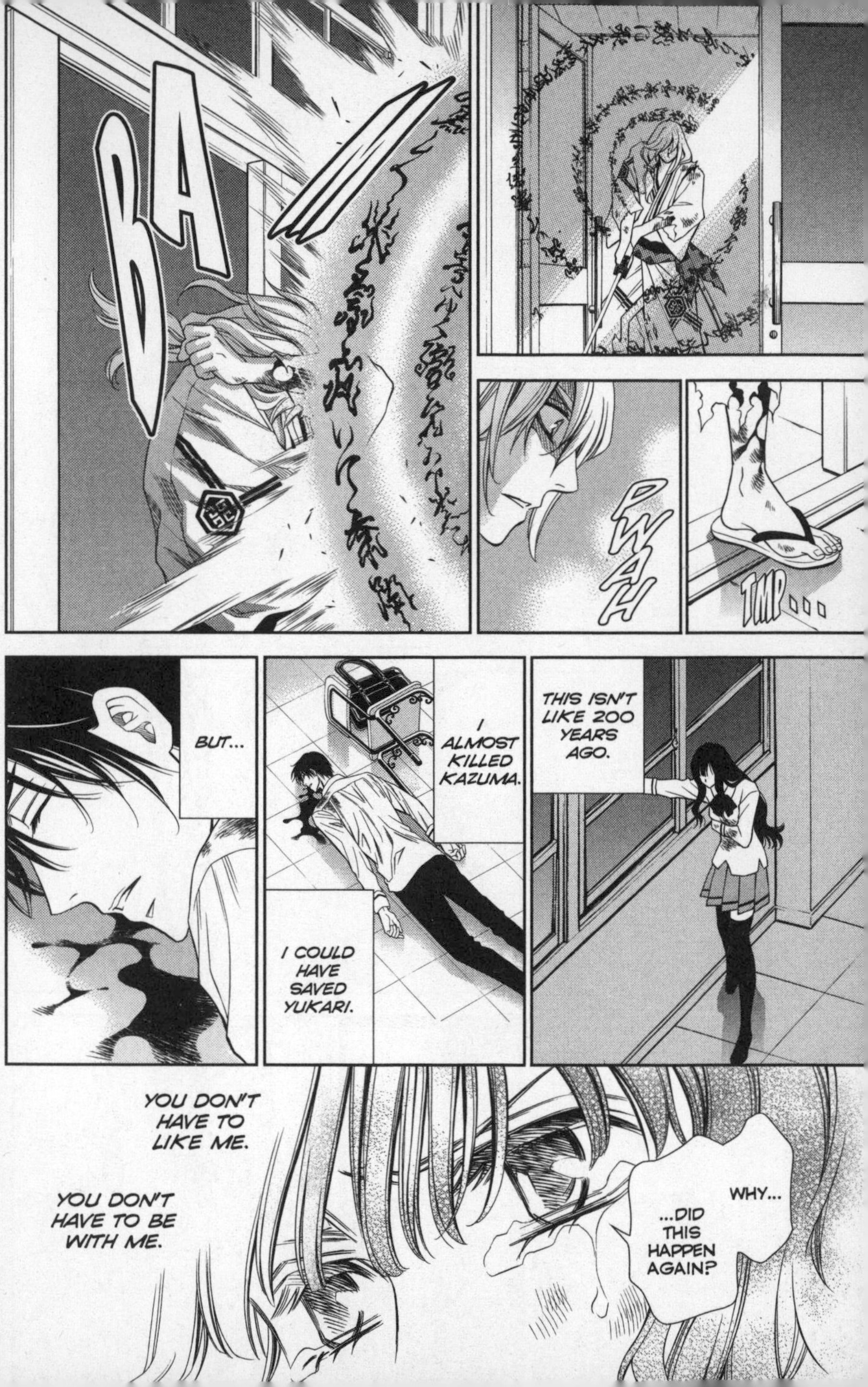
TMP...
PWAH
BA
THIS ISN'T LIKE 200 YEARS AGO.
I ALMOST KILLED KAZUMA.
I COULD HAVE SAVED YUKARI.
BUT...
WHY...
...DID THIS HAPPEN AGAIN?
YOU DON'T HAVE TO LIKE ME.
YOU DON'T HAVE TO BE WITH ME.

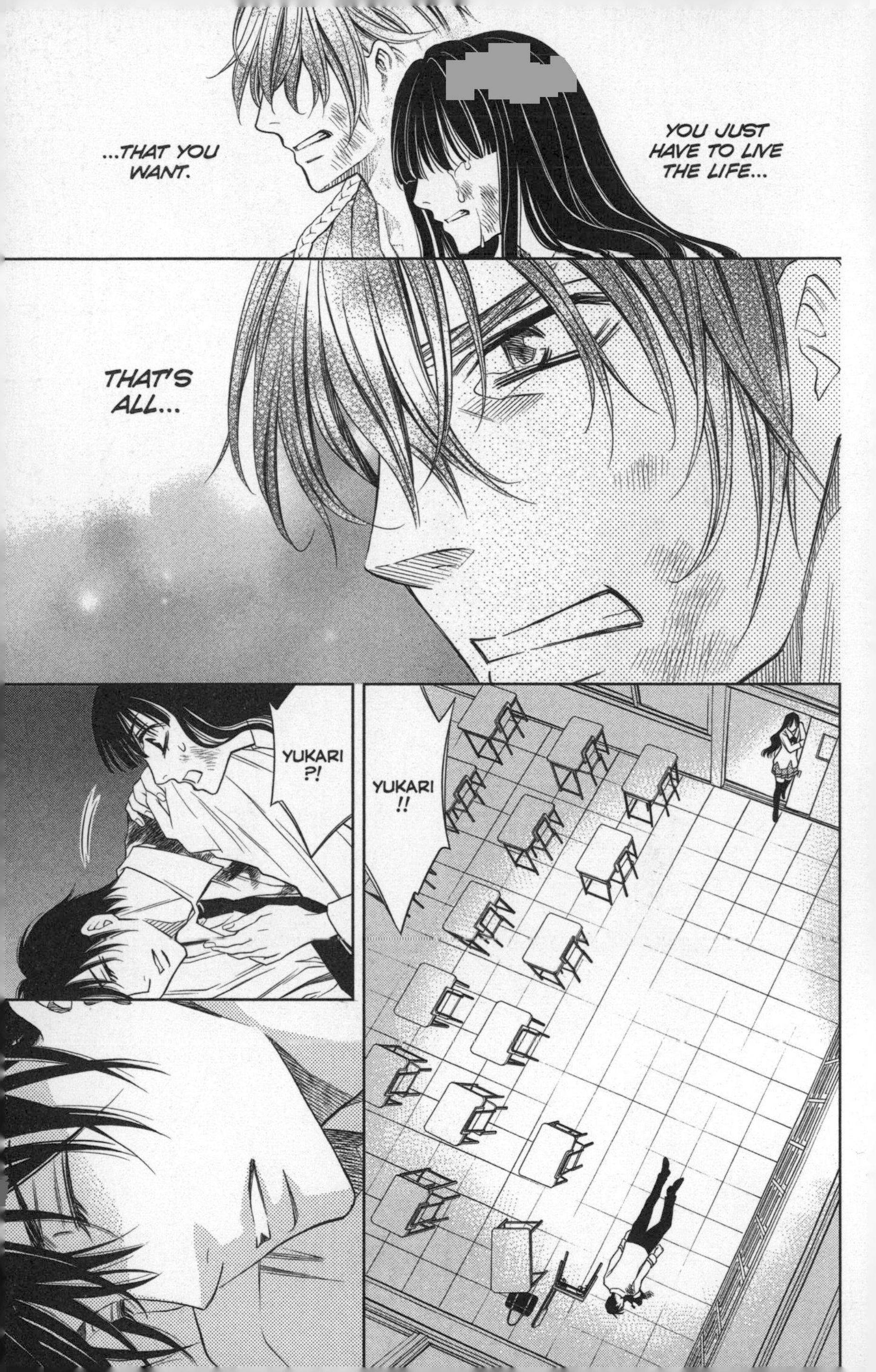
YOU JUST HAVE TO LIVE THE LIFE...
...THAT YOU WANT.
THAT'S ALL...
YUKARI !!
YUKARI ?!

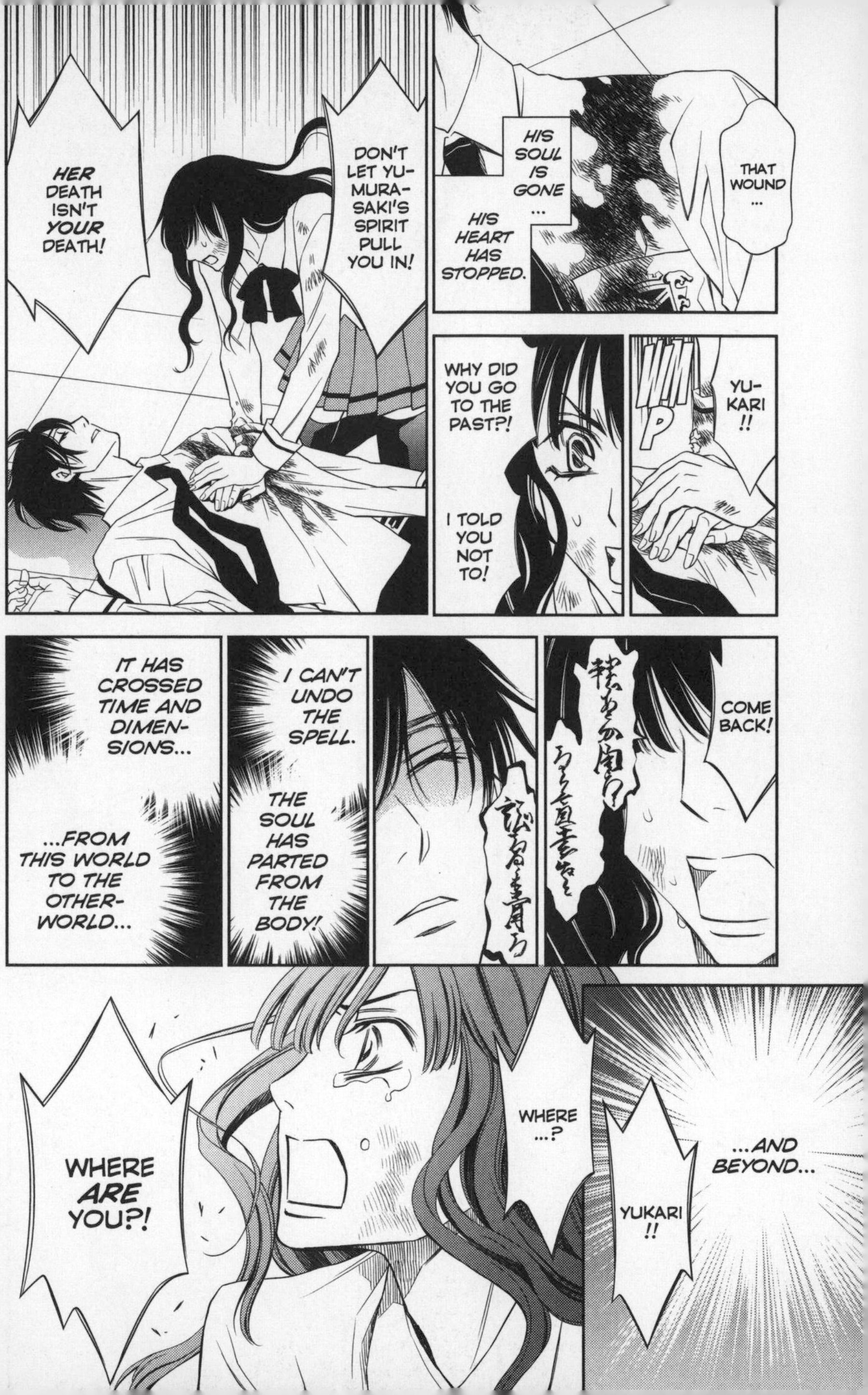
THAT WOUND ...
HIS SOUL IS GONE ...
HIS HEART HAS STOPPED.
WMP
YU-KARI !!
WHY DID YOU GO TO THE PAST?!
I TOLD YOU NOT TO!
DON'T LET YU-MURA-SAKI'S SPIRIT PULL YOU IN!
HER DEATH ISN'T YOUR DEATH!
COME BACK!
I CAN'T UNDO THE SPELL.
THE SOUL HAS PARTED FROM THE BODY!
IT HAS CROSSED TIME AND DIMEN-SIONS...
...FROM THIS WORLD TO THE OTHER-WORLD...
...AND BEYOND...
YUKARI !!
WHERE ...?
WHERE ARE YOU?!

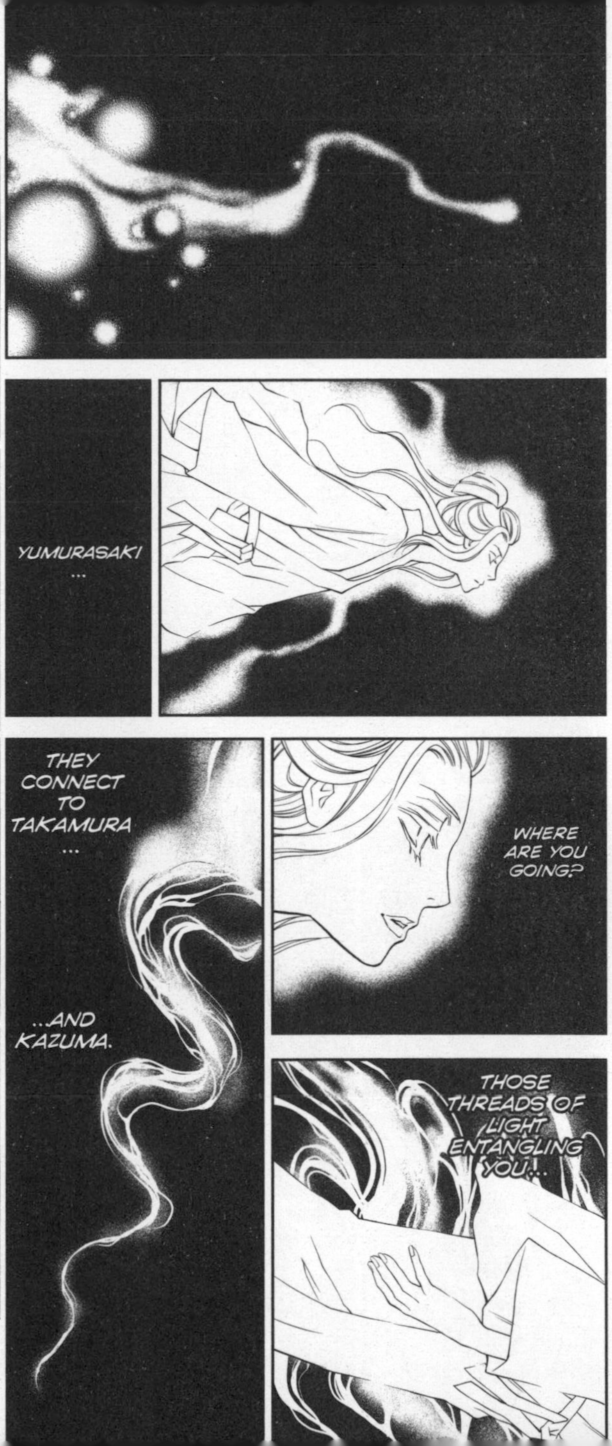
YUMURASAKI ...
WHERE ARE YOU GOING?
THOSE THREADS OF LIGHT ENTANGLING YOU...
THEY CONNECT TO TAKAMURA ...
...AND KAZUMA.

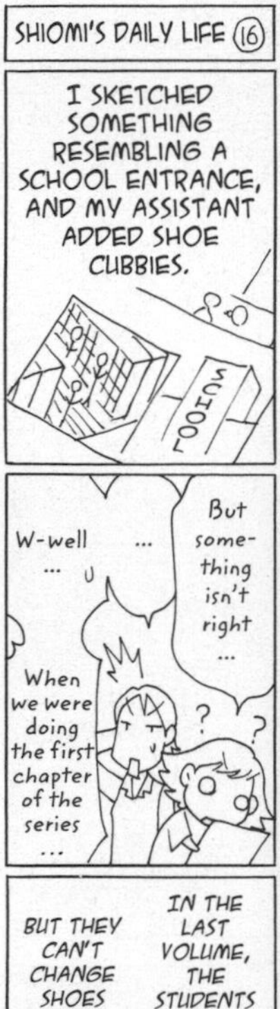
SHIOMI'S DAILY LIFE 16
I SKETCHED SOMETHING RESEMBLING A SCHOOL ENTRANCE, AND MY ASSISTANT ADDED SHOE CUBBIES.
SCHOOL
But something isn't right ...
...
W-well ...
When we were doing the first chapter of the series ...
IN THE LAST VOLUME, THE STUDENTS GO IN AND OUT OF THE COURTYARD ...
BUT THEY CAN'T CHANGE SHOES EVERY TIME.
SO...
THEY'LL WEAR SHOES INSIDE AND OUTSIDE THE SCHOOL.
That's what happened!
Which means ...
...this school doesn't need shoe cubbies!
SO I HAD HER REDRAW IT...

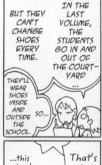

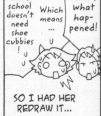

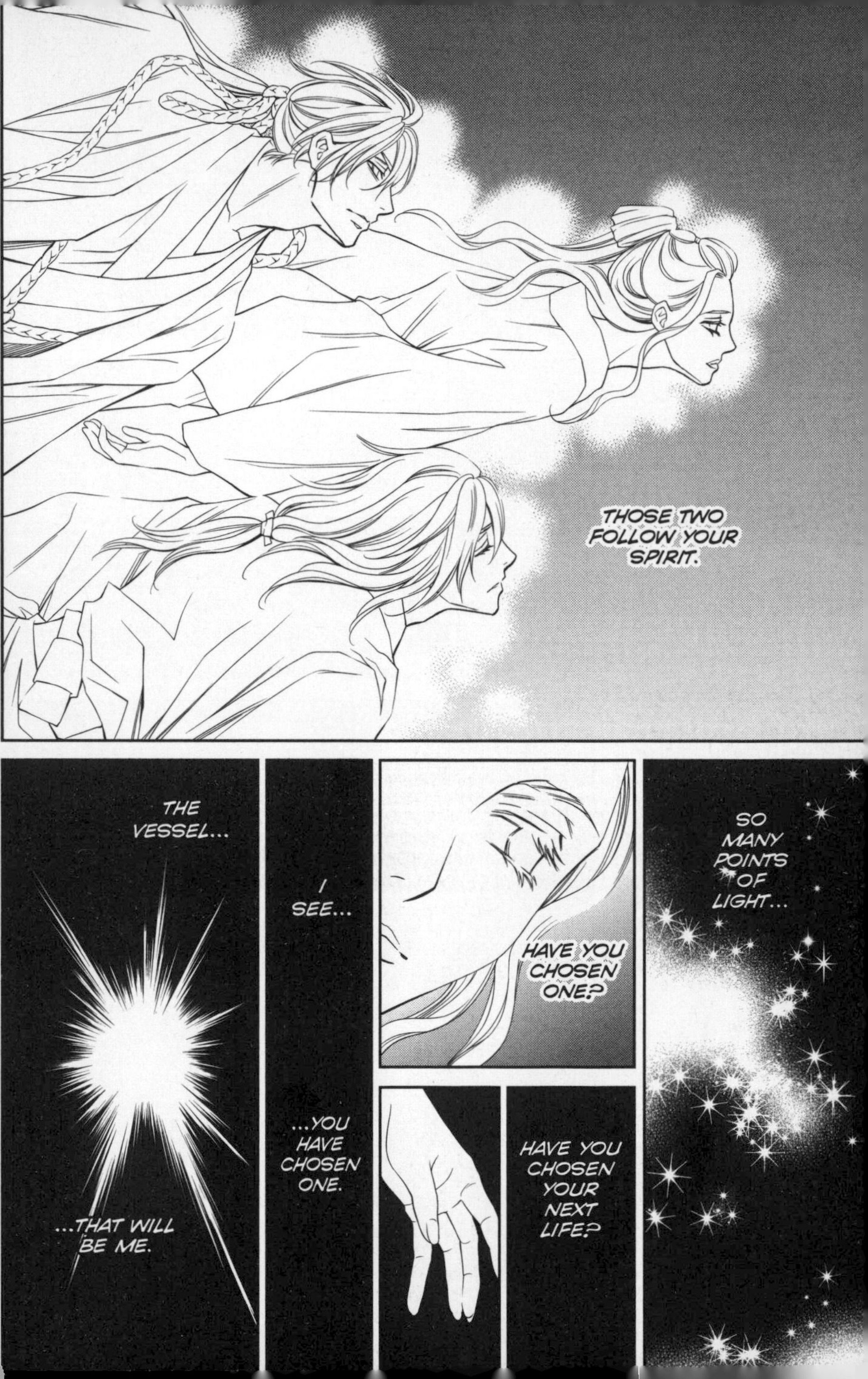
THOSE TWO FOLLOW YOUR SPIRIT.
SO MANY POINTS OF LIGHT...
HAVE YOU CHOSEN ONE?
HAVE YOU CHOSEN YOUR NEXT LIFE?
I SEE...
...YOU HAVE CHOSEN ONE.
THE VESSEL...
...THAT WILL BE ME.

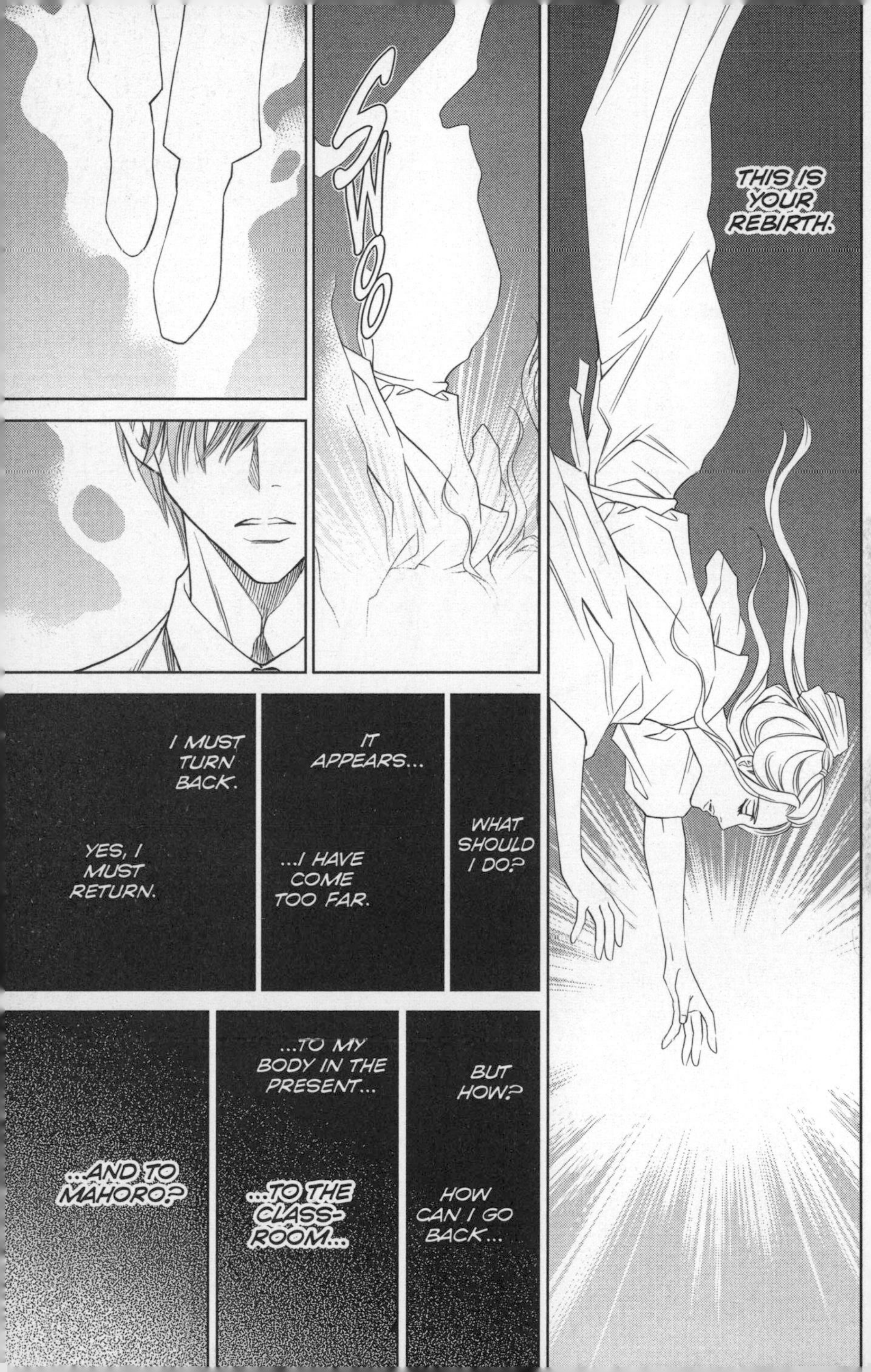
THIS IS YOUR REBIRTH.
SWOO
WHAT SHOULD I DO?
IT APPEARS...
...I HAVE COME TOO FAR.
I MUST TURN BACK.
YES, I MUST RETURN.
BUT HOW?
HOW CAN I GO BACK...
...TO MY BODY IN THE PRESENT...
...TO THE CLASS-ROOM...
...AND TO MAHORO?

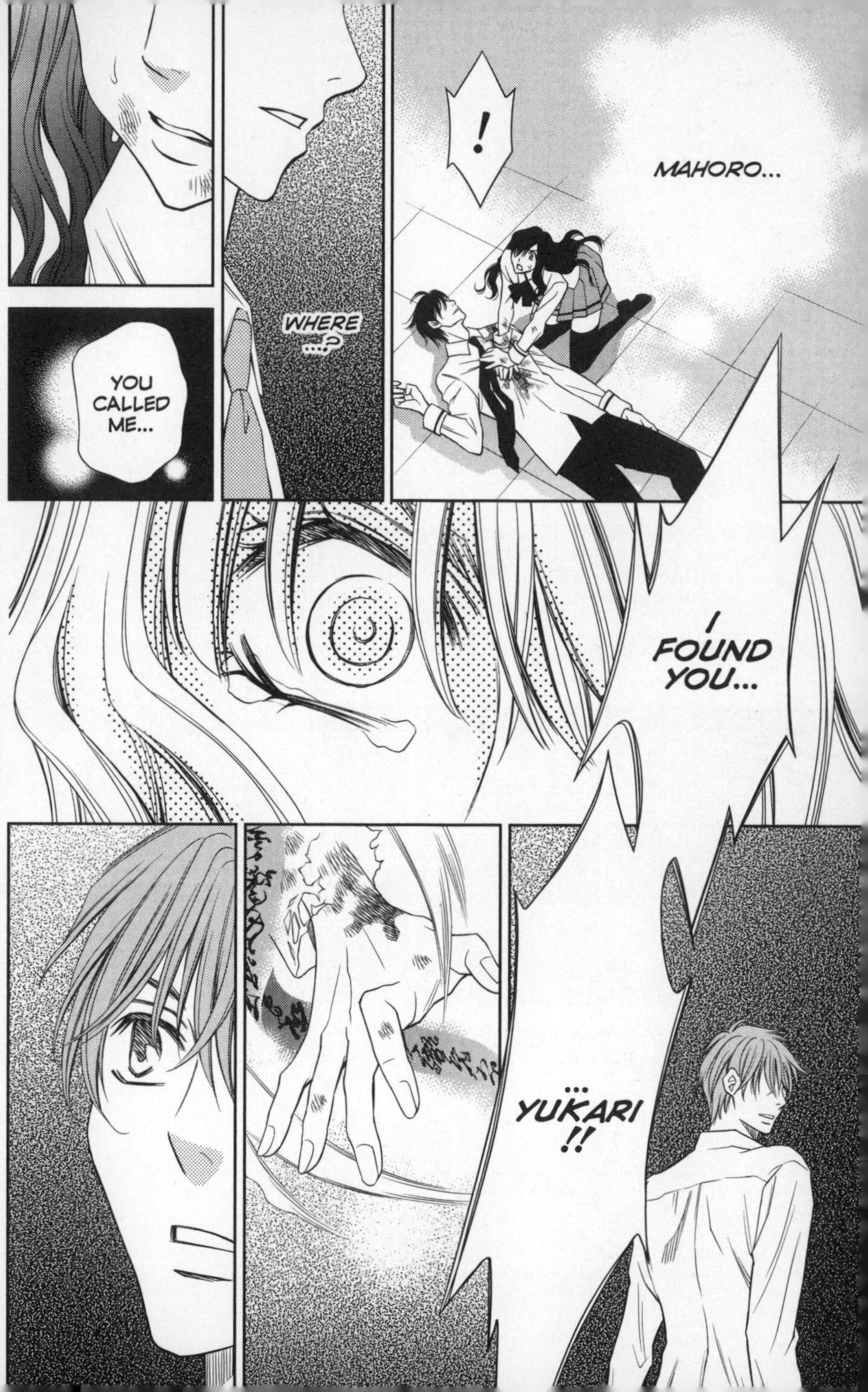
MAHORO...
!
WHERE ...?
YOU CALLED ME...
I FOUND YOU...
... YUKARI !!

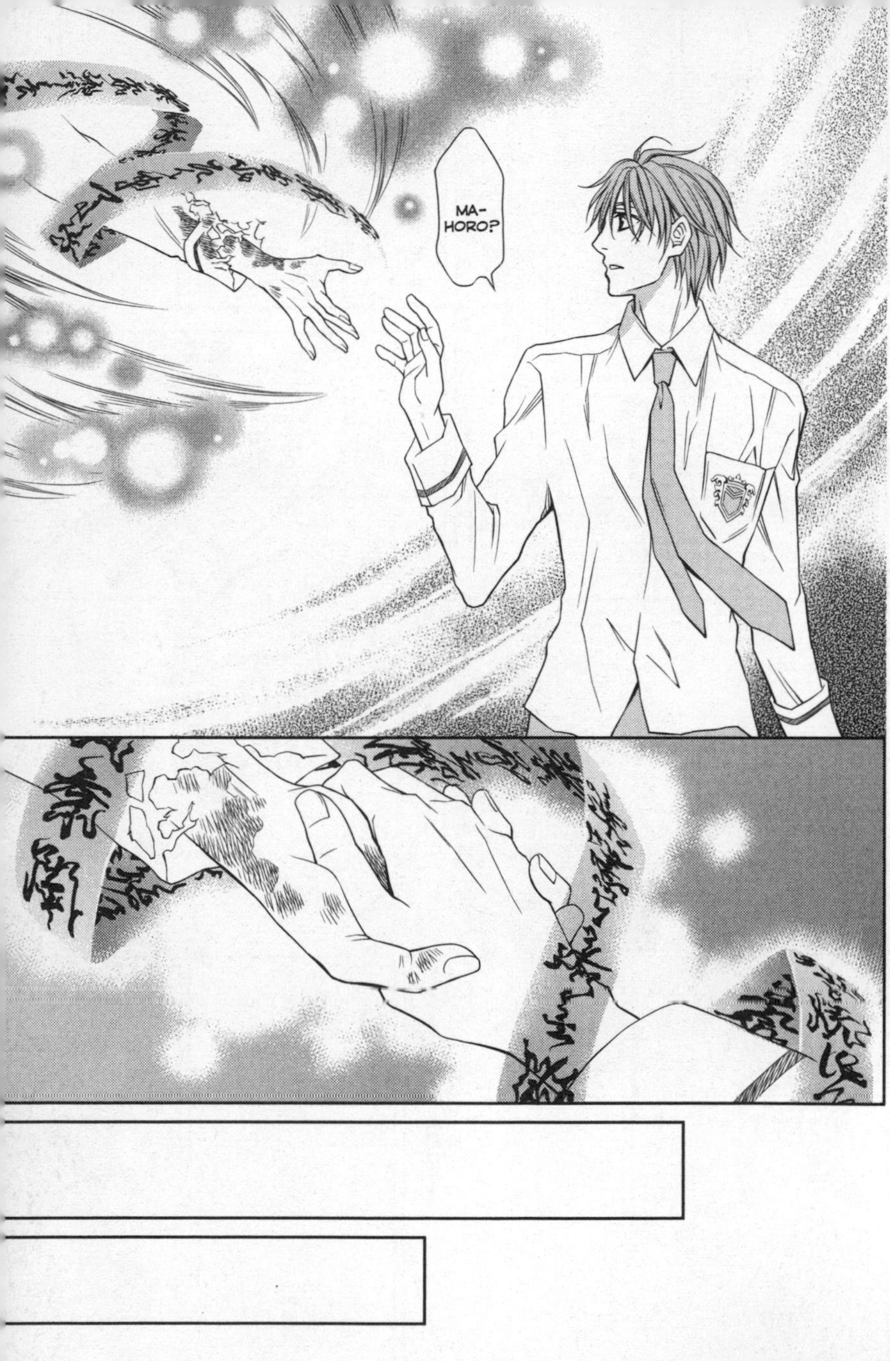
MA-HORO?

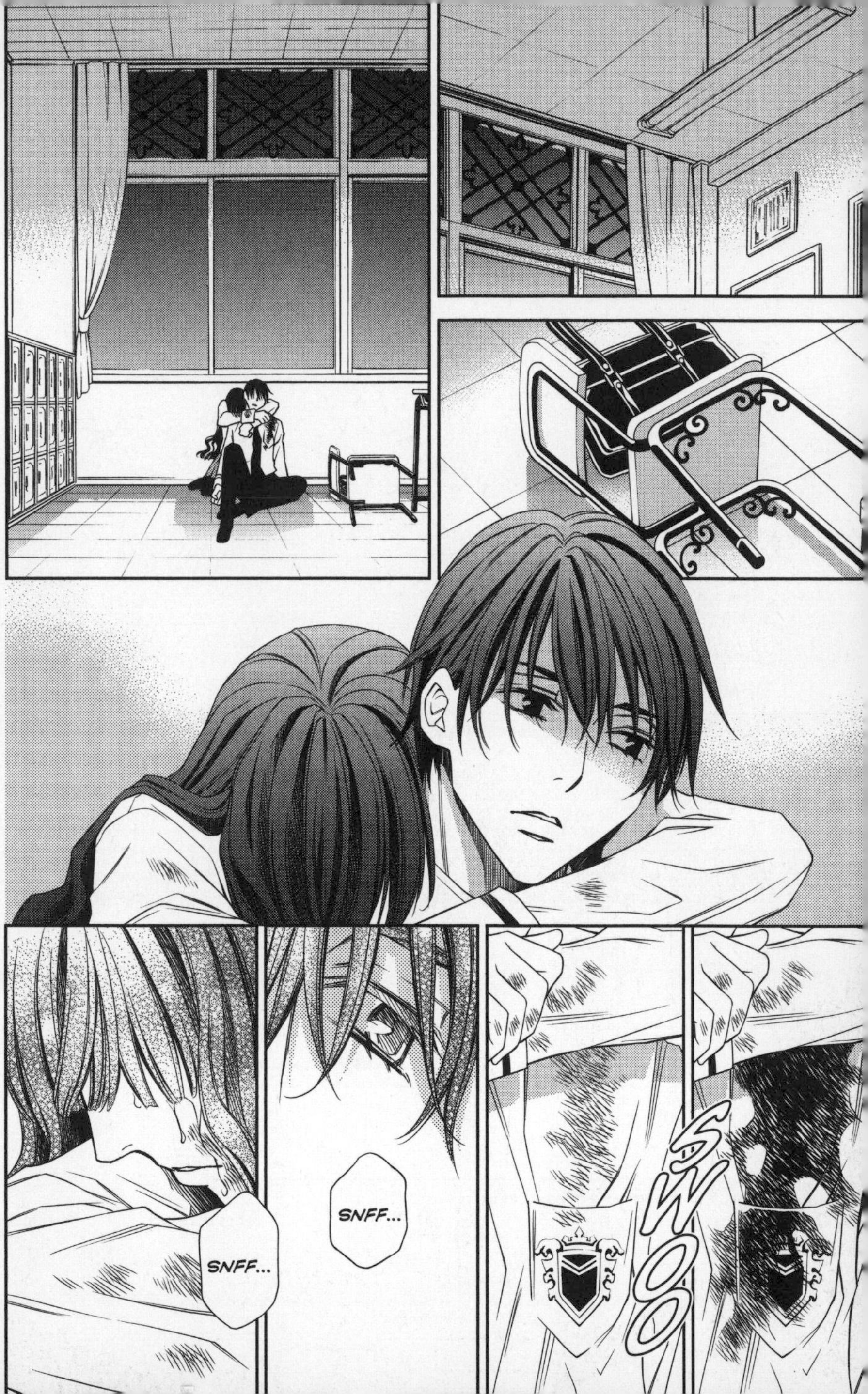
SWOO
SNFF...
SNFF...

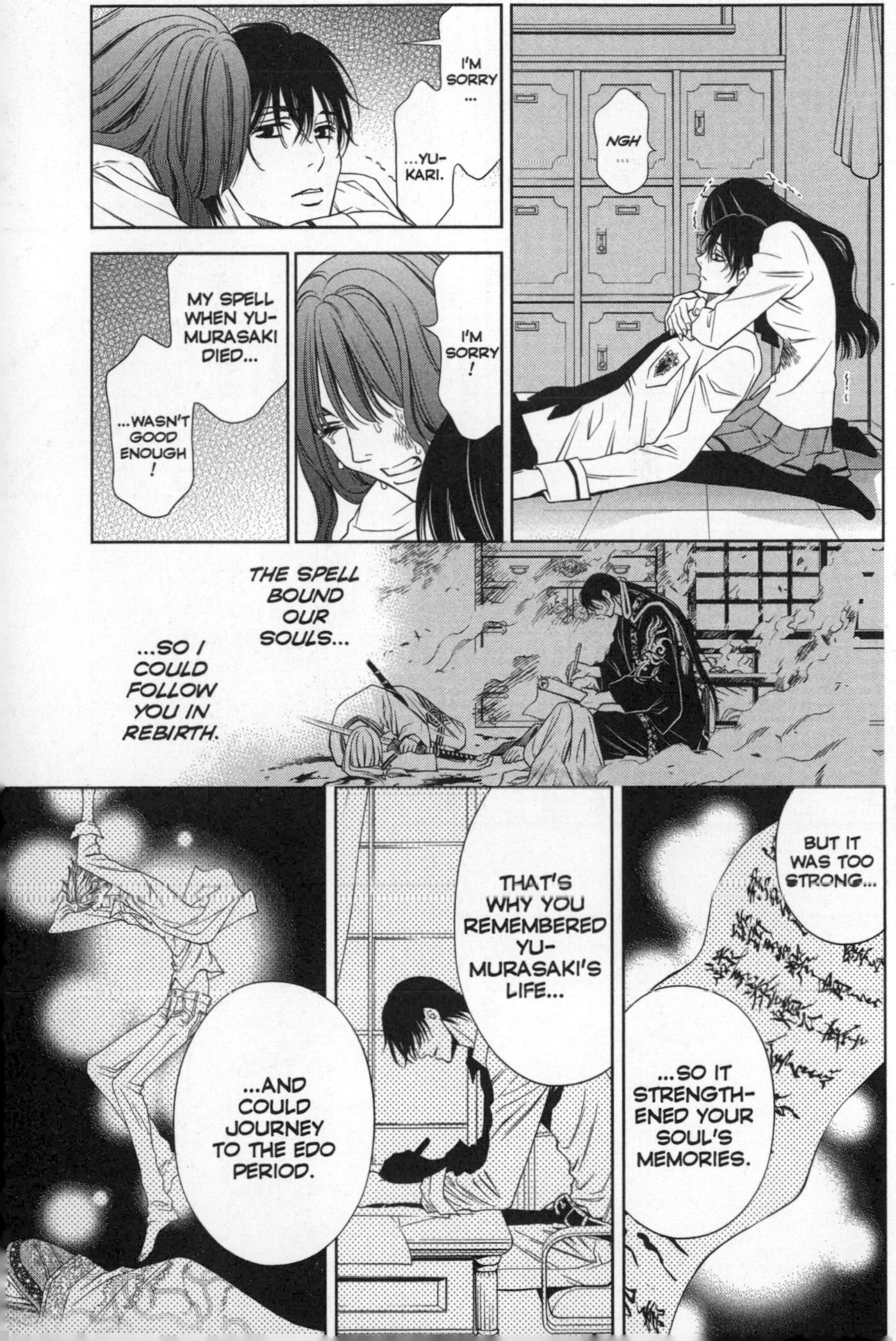
NGH ...
I'M SORRY ...
...YU-KARI.
I'M SORRY!
MY SPELL WHEN YU-MURASAKI DIED...
...WASN'T GOOD ENOUGH!
THE SPELL BOUND OUR SOULS...
...SO I COULD FOLLOW YOU IN REBIRTH.
BUT IT WAS TOO STRONG...
...SO IT STRENGTH-ENED YOUR SOUL'S MEMORIES.
THAT'S WHY YOU REMEMBERED YU-MURASAKI'S LIFE...
...AND COULD JOURNEY TO THE EDO PERIOD.

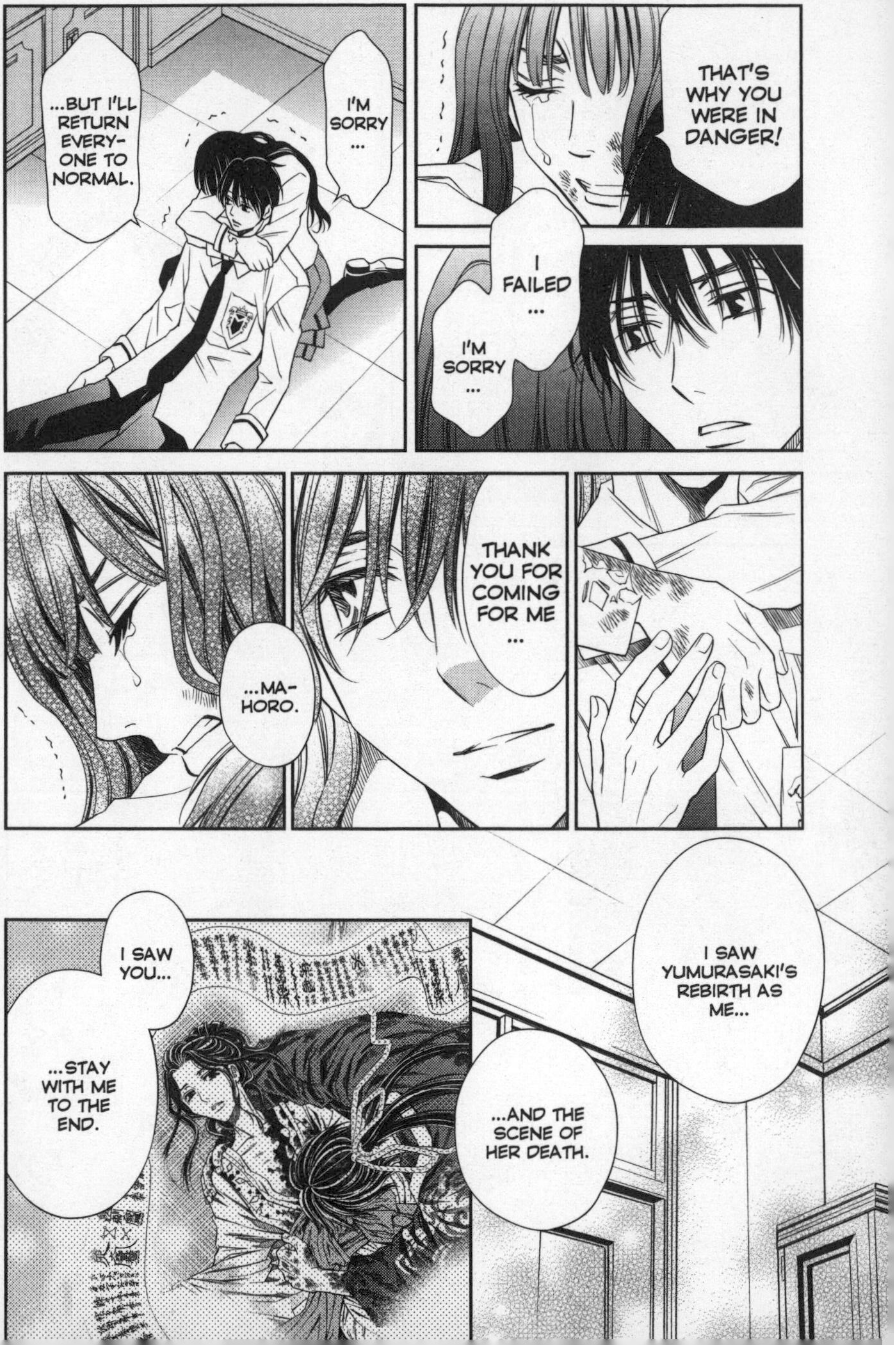
THAT'S WHY YOU WERE IN DANGER!
I FAILED ...
I'M SORRY ...
I'M SORRY ...
...BUT I'LL RETURN EVERY-ONE TO NORMAL.
THANK YOU FOR COMING FOR ME ...
...MA-HORO.
I SAW YUMURASAKI'S REBIRTH AS ME...
...AND THE SCENE OF HER DEATH.
I SAW YOU...
...STAY WITH ME TO THE END.

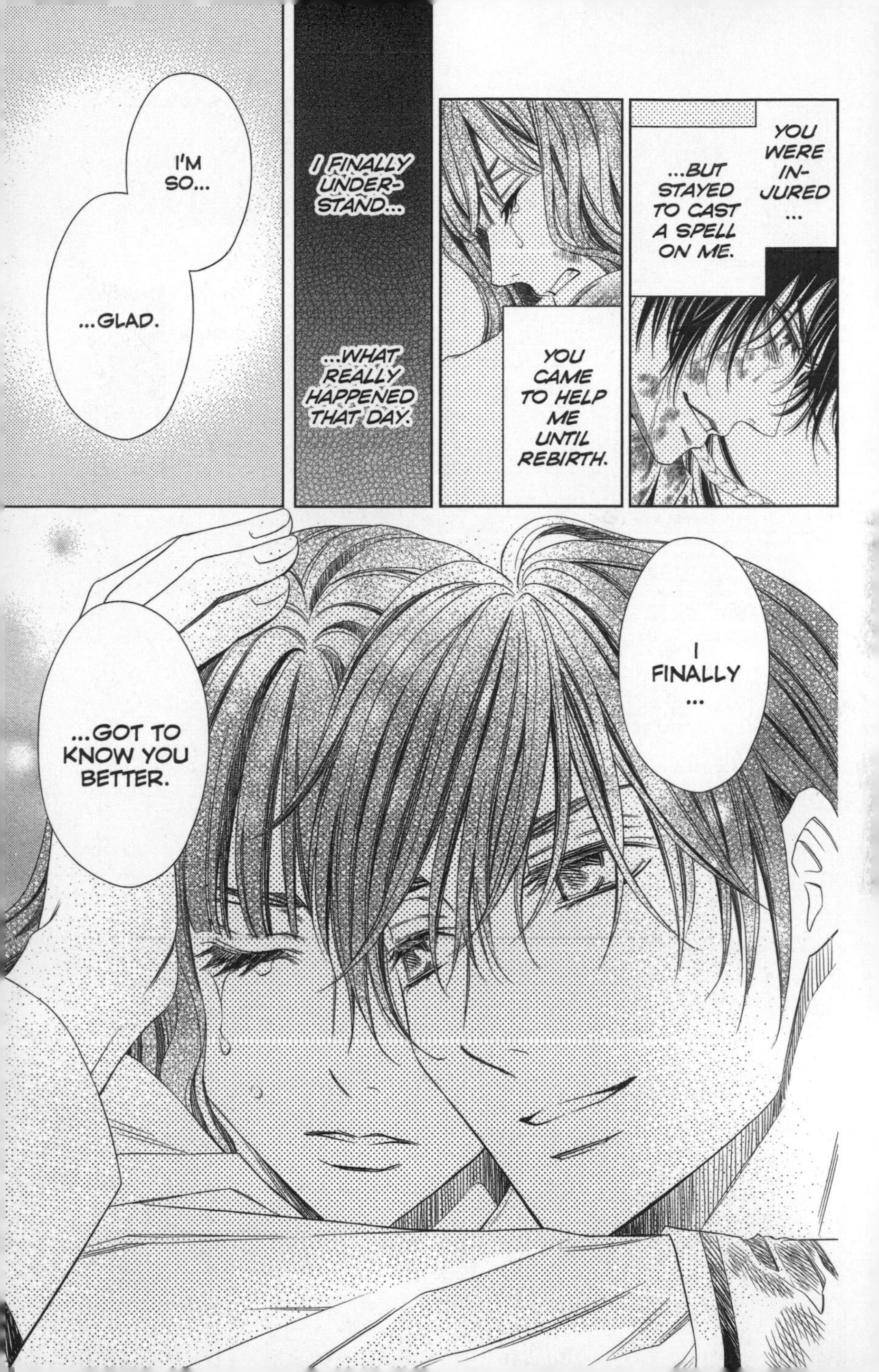
YOU WERE IN-JURED...
...BUT STAYED TO CAST A SPELL ON ME.
YOU CAME TO HELP ME UNTIL REBIRTH.
I FINALLY UNDER-STAND...
...WHAT REALLY HAPPENED THAT DAY.
I'M SO...
...GLAD.
I FINALLY...
...GOT TO KNOW YOU BETTER.

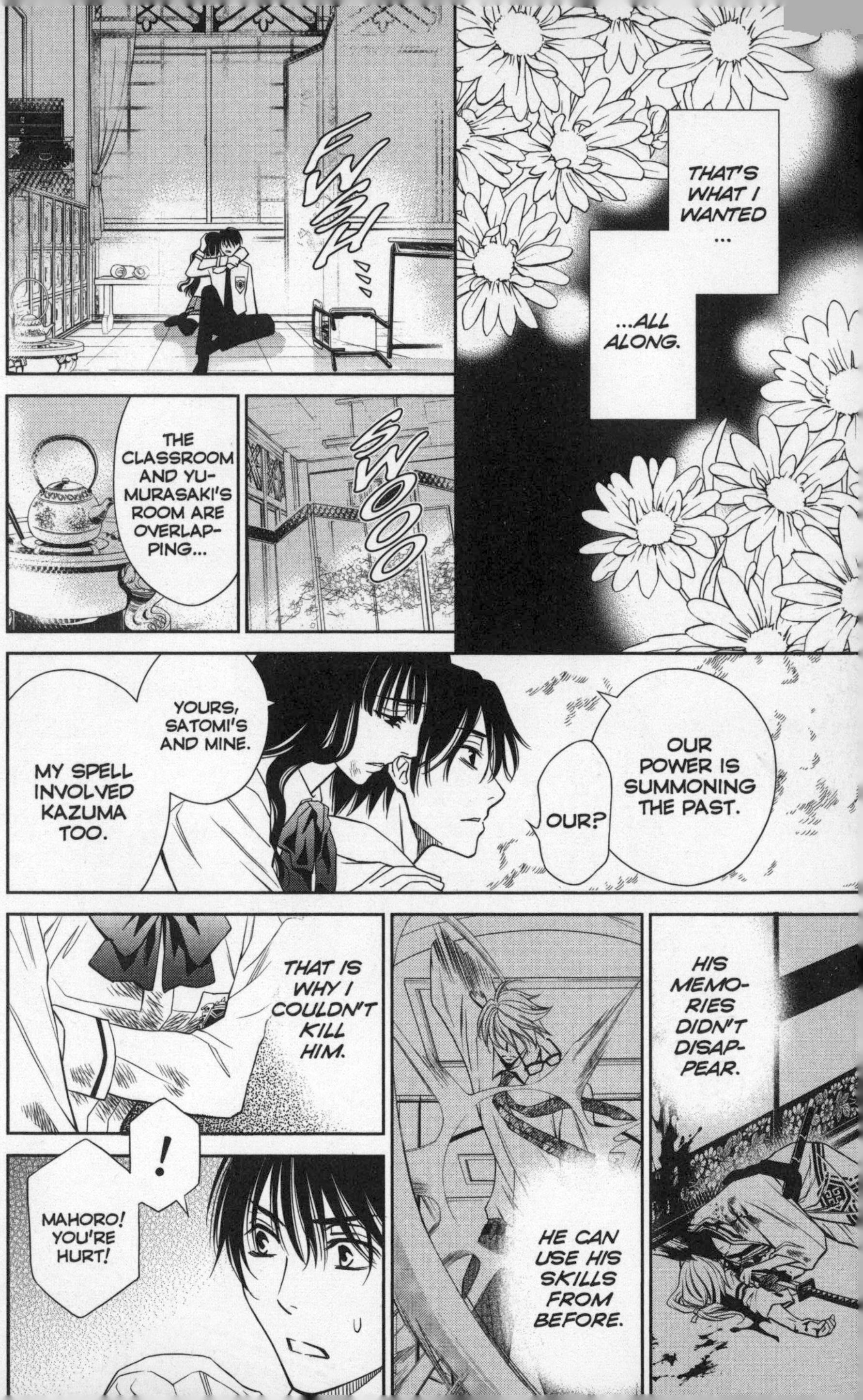
THAT'S WHAT I WANTED ...
...ALL ALONG.
FWSH
SWOOO
THE CLASSROOM AND YU-MURASAKI'S ROOM ARE OVERLAP-PING...
OUR POWER IS SUMMONING THE PAST.
OUR?
YOURS, SATOMI'S AND MINE.
MY SPELL INVOLVED KAZUMA TOO.
HIS MEMO-RIES DIDN'T DISAP-PEAR.
HE CAN USE HIS SKILLS FROM BEFORE.
THAT IS WHY I COULDN'T KILL HIM.
!
MAHORO! YOU'RE HURT!

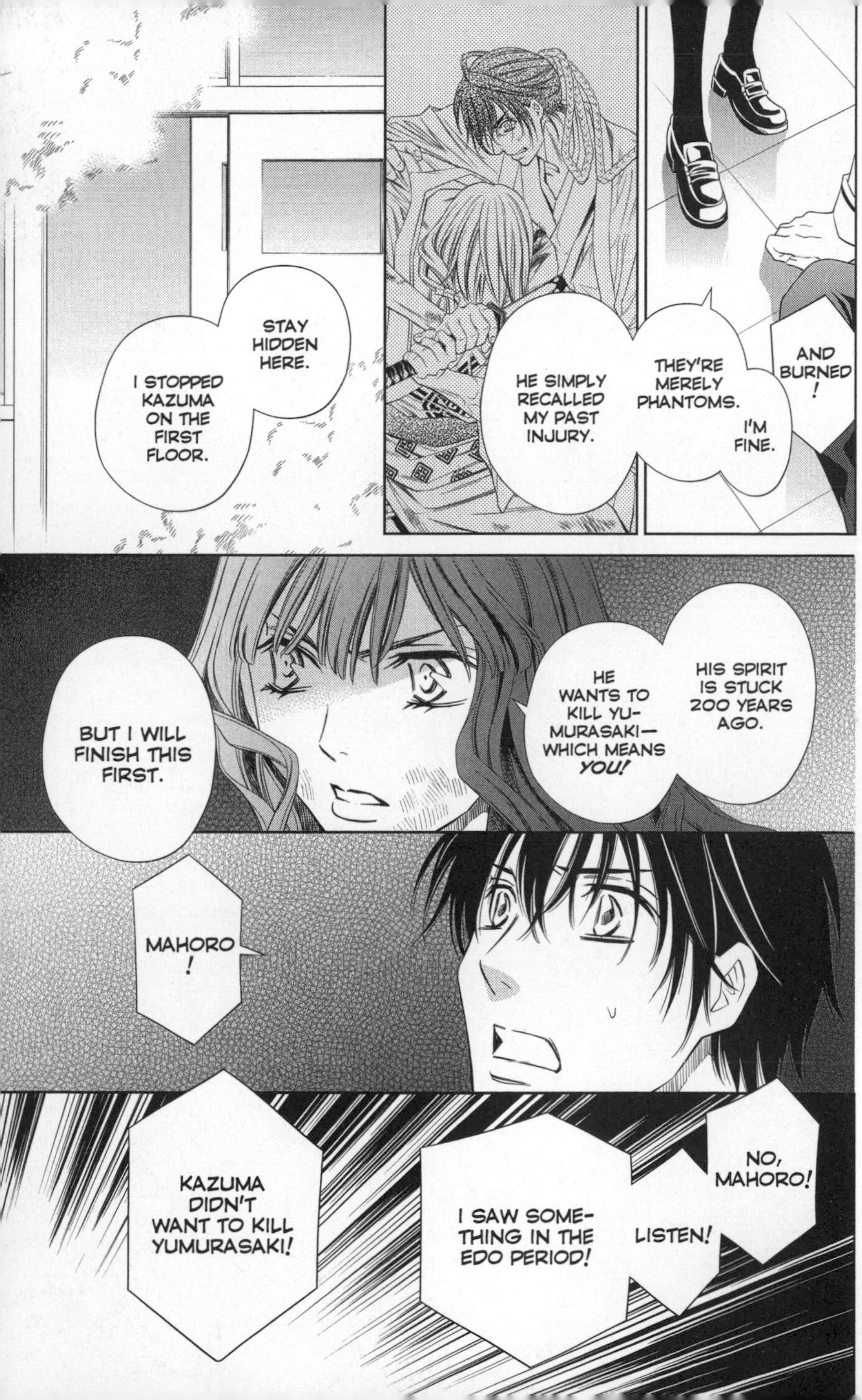
AND BURNED!
I'M FINE.
THEY'RE MERELY PHANTOMS.
HE SIMPLY RECALLED MY PAST INJURY.
STAY HIDDEN HERE.
I STOPPED KAZUMA ON THE FIRST FLOOR.
HIS SPIRIT IS STUCK 200 YEARS AGO.
HE WANTS TO KILL YU-MURASAKI—WHICH MEANS *YOU!*
BUT I WILL FINISH THIS FIRST.
MAHORO!
NO, MAHORO!
LISTEN!
I SAW SOME-THING IN THE EDO PERIOD!
KAZUMA DIDN'T WANT TO KILL YUMURASAKI!

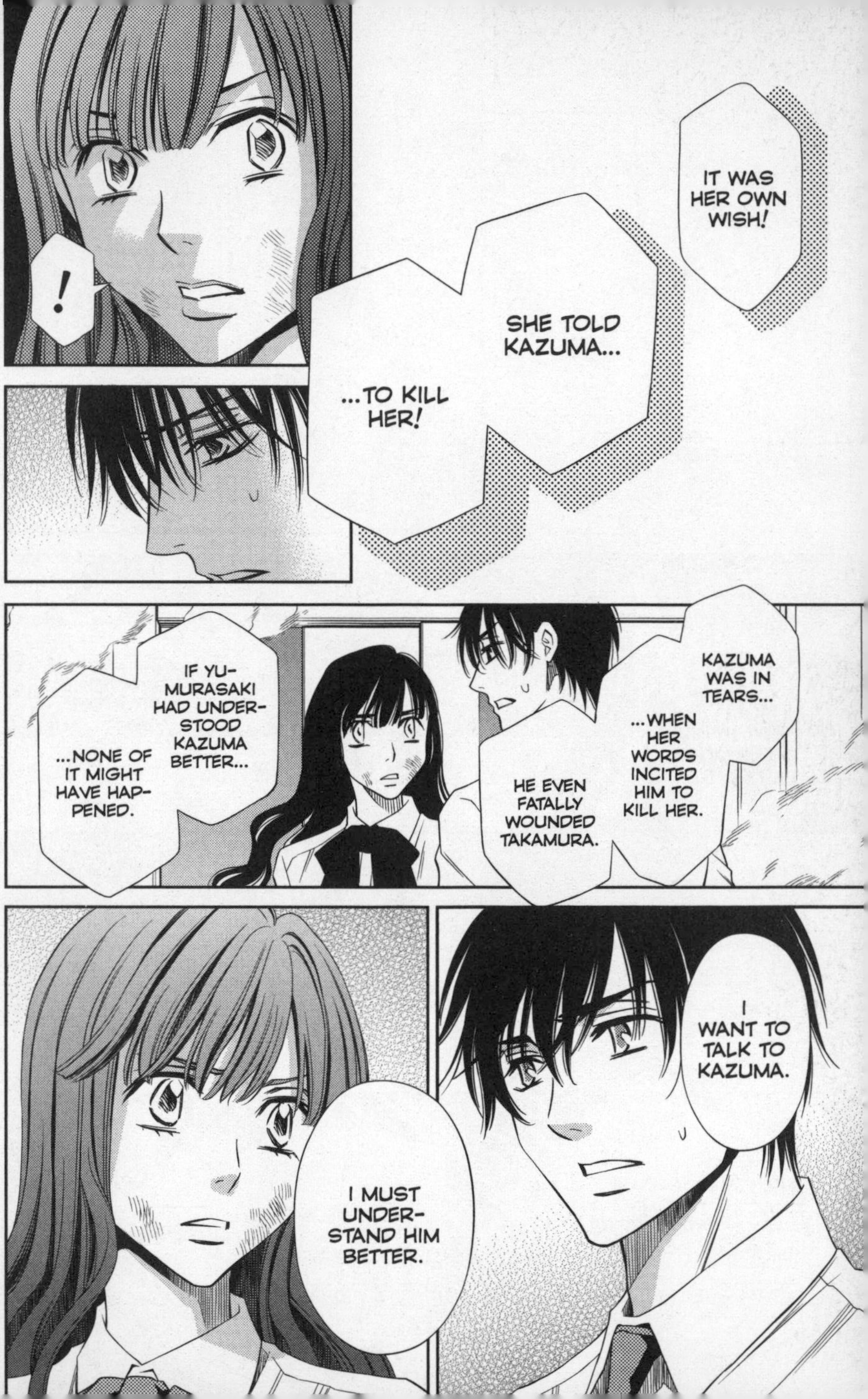
IT WAS HER OWN WISH!
SHE TOLD KAZUMA...
...TO KILL HER!
!
KAZUMA WAS IN TEARS...
...WHEN HER WORDS INCITED HIM TO KILL HER.
HE EVEN FATALLY WOUNDED TAKAMURA.
IF YU-MURASAKI HAD UNDER-STOOD KAZUMA BETTER...
...NONE OF IT MIGHT HAVE HAP-PENED.
I WANT TO TALK TO KAZUMA.
I MUST UNDER-STAND HIM BETTER.

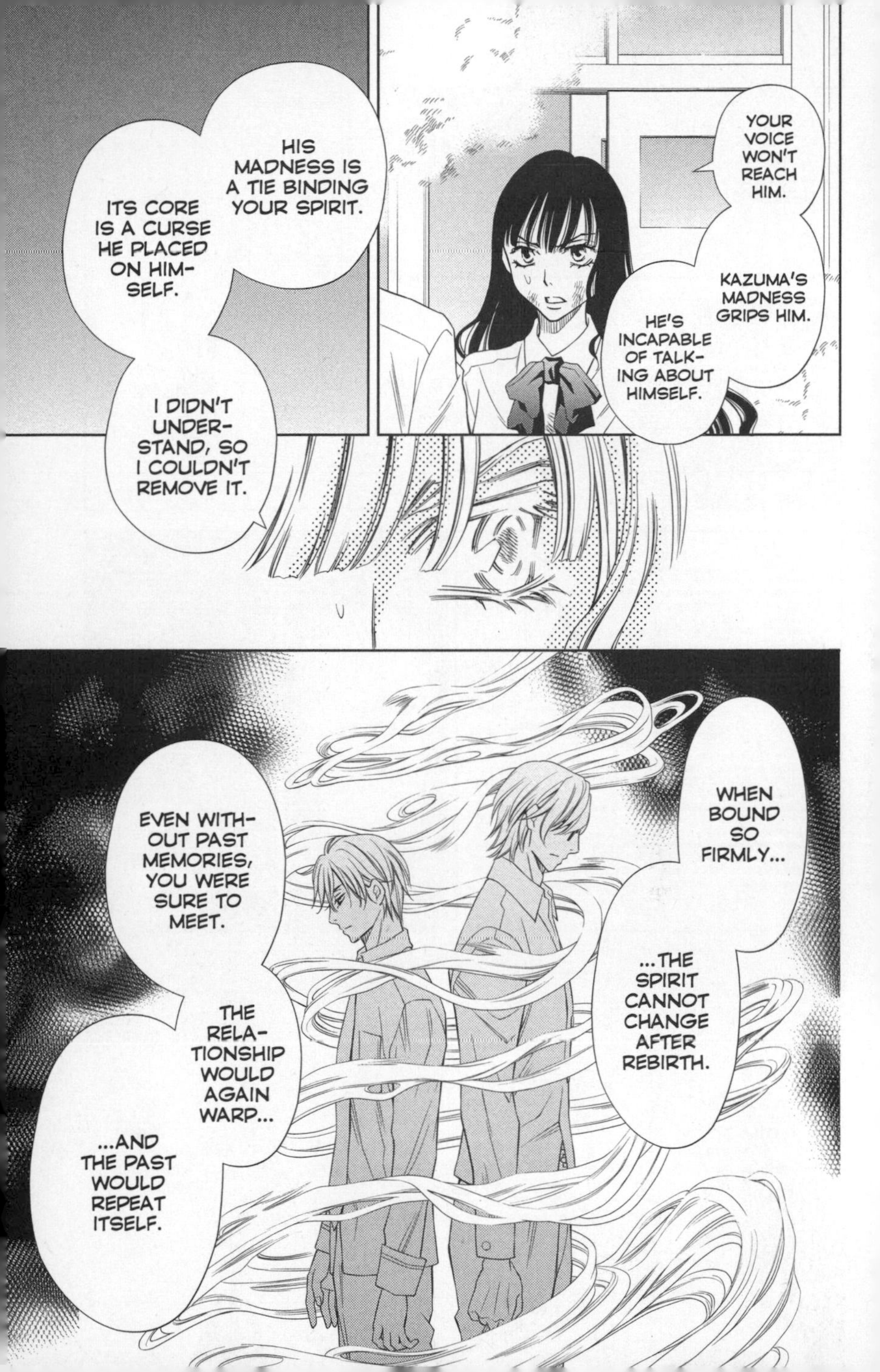
YOUR VOICE WON'T REACH HIM.
KAZUMA'S MADNESS GRIPS HIM.
HE'S INCAPABLE OF TALKING ABOUT HIMSELF.
HIS MADNESS IS A TIE BINDING YOUR SPIRIT.
ITS CORE IS A CURSE HE PLACED ON HIMSELF.
I DIDN'T UNDERSTAND, SO I COULDN'T REMOVE IT.
WHEN BOUND SO FIRMLY...
...THE SPIRIT CANNOT CHANGE AFTER REBIRTH.
EVEN WITHOUT PAST MEMORIES, YOU WERE SURE TO MEET.
THE RELATIONSHIP WOULD AGAIN WARP...
...AND THE PAST WOULD REPEAT ITSELF.

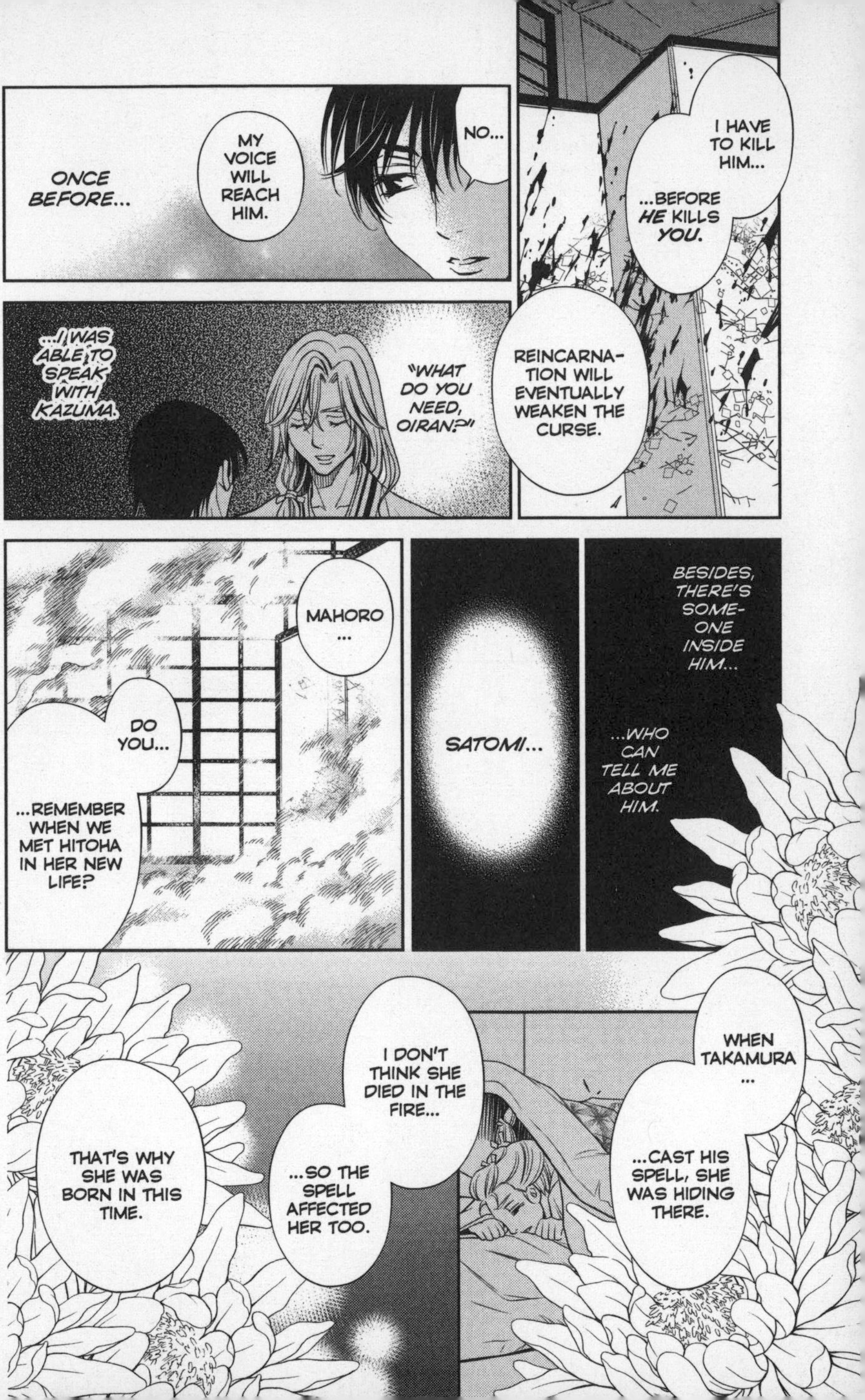
I HAVE TO KILL HIM...
...BEFORE HE KILLS YOU.
REINCARNATION WILL EVENTUALLY WEAKEN THE CURSE.
NO...
MY VOICE WILL REACH HIM.
ONCE BEFORE...
"WHAT DO YOU NEED, OIRAN?"
...I WAS ABLE TO SPEAK WITH KAZUMA.
BESIDES, THERE'S SOMEONE INSIDE HIM...
...WHO CAN TELL ME ABOUT HIM.
SATOMI...
MAHORO...
DO YOU...
...REMEMBER WHEN WE MET HITOHA IN HER NEW LIFE?
WHEN TAKAMURA...
...CAST HIS SPELL, SHE WAS HIDING THERE.
I DON'T THINK SHE DIED IN THE FIRE...
...SO THE SPELL AFFECTED HER TOO.
THAT'S WHY SHE WAS BORN IN THIS TIME.

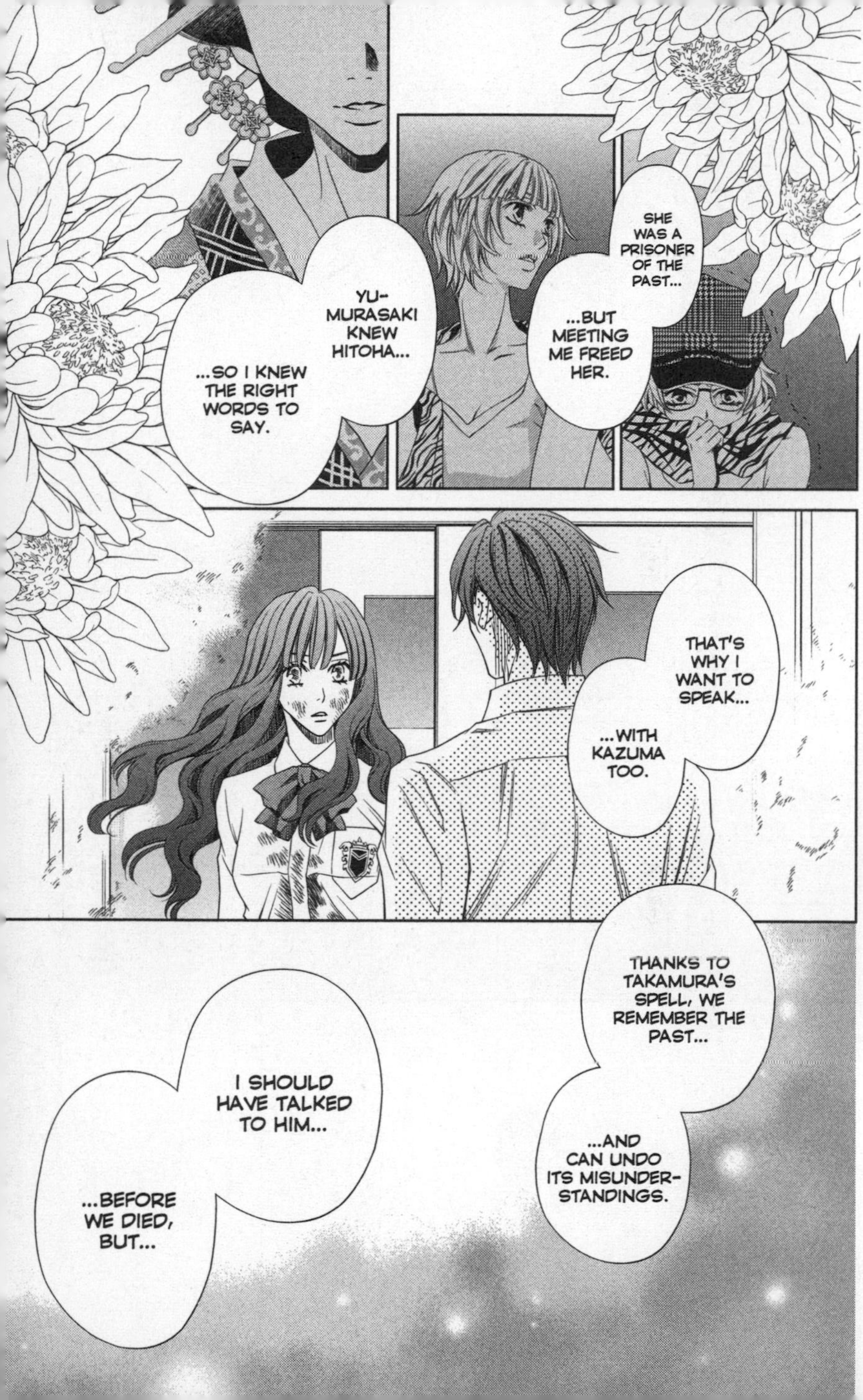
SHE WAS A PRISONER OF THE PAST...
...BUT MEETING ME FREED HER.
YU-MURASAKI KNEW HITOHA...
...SO I KNEW THE RIGHT WORDS TO SAY.
THAT'S WHY I WANT TO SPEAK...
...WITH KAZUMA TOO.
THANKS TO TAKAMURA'S SPELL, WE REMEMBER THE PAST...
...AND CAN UNDO ITS MISUNDER-STANDINGS.
I SHOULD HAVE TALKED TO HIM...
...BEFORE WE DIED, BUT...

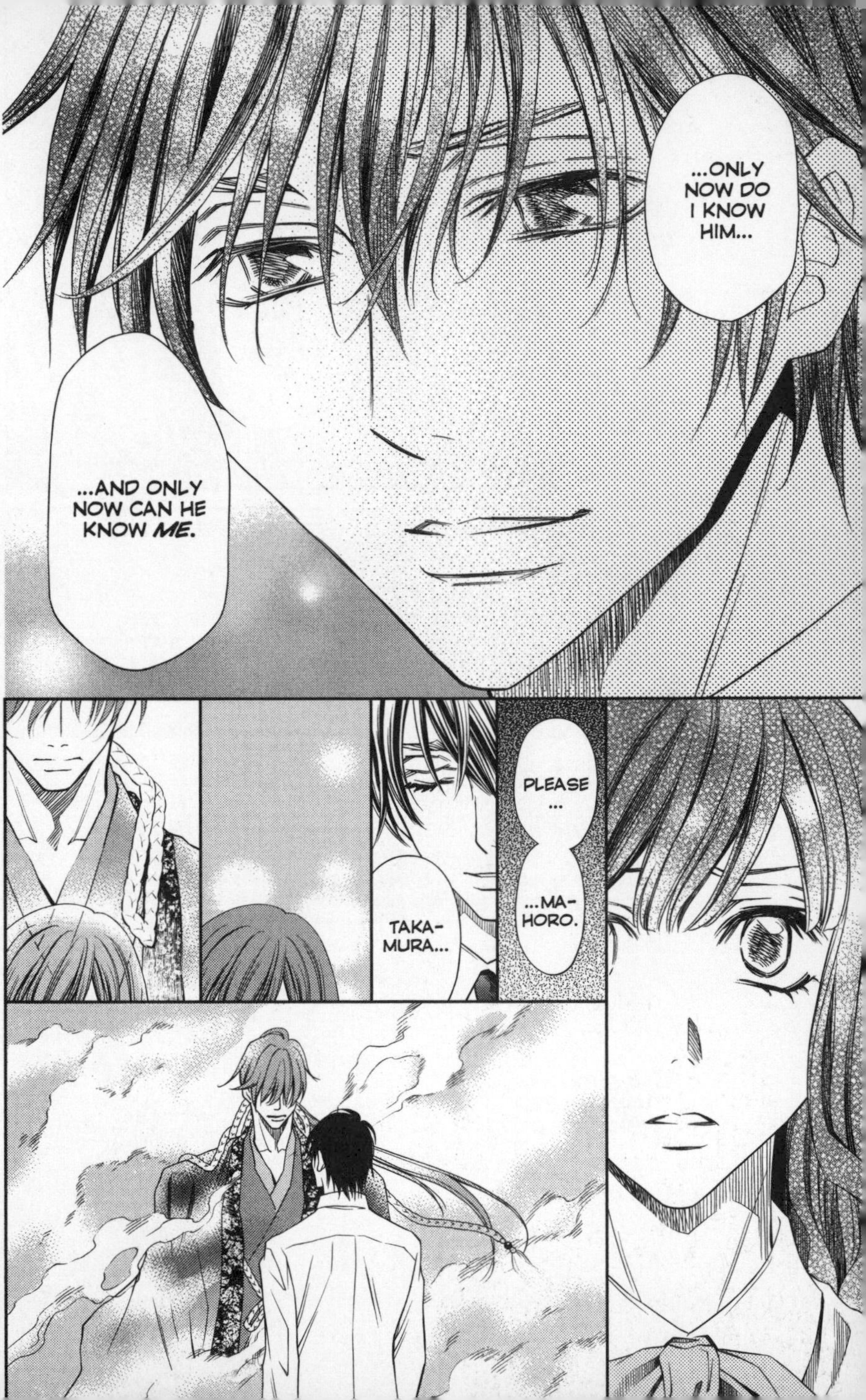
...ONLY NOW DO I KNOW HIM...
...AND ONLY NOW CAN HE KNOW *ME*.
PLEASE...
...MA-HORO.
TAKA-MURA...

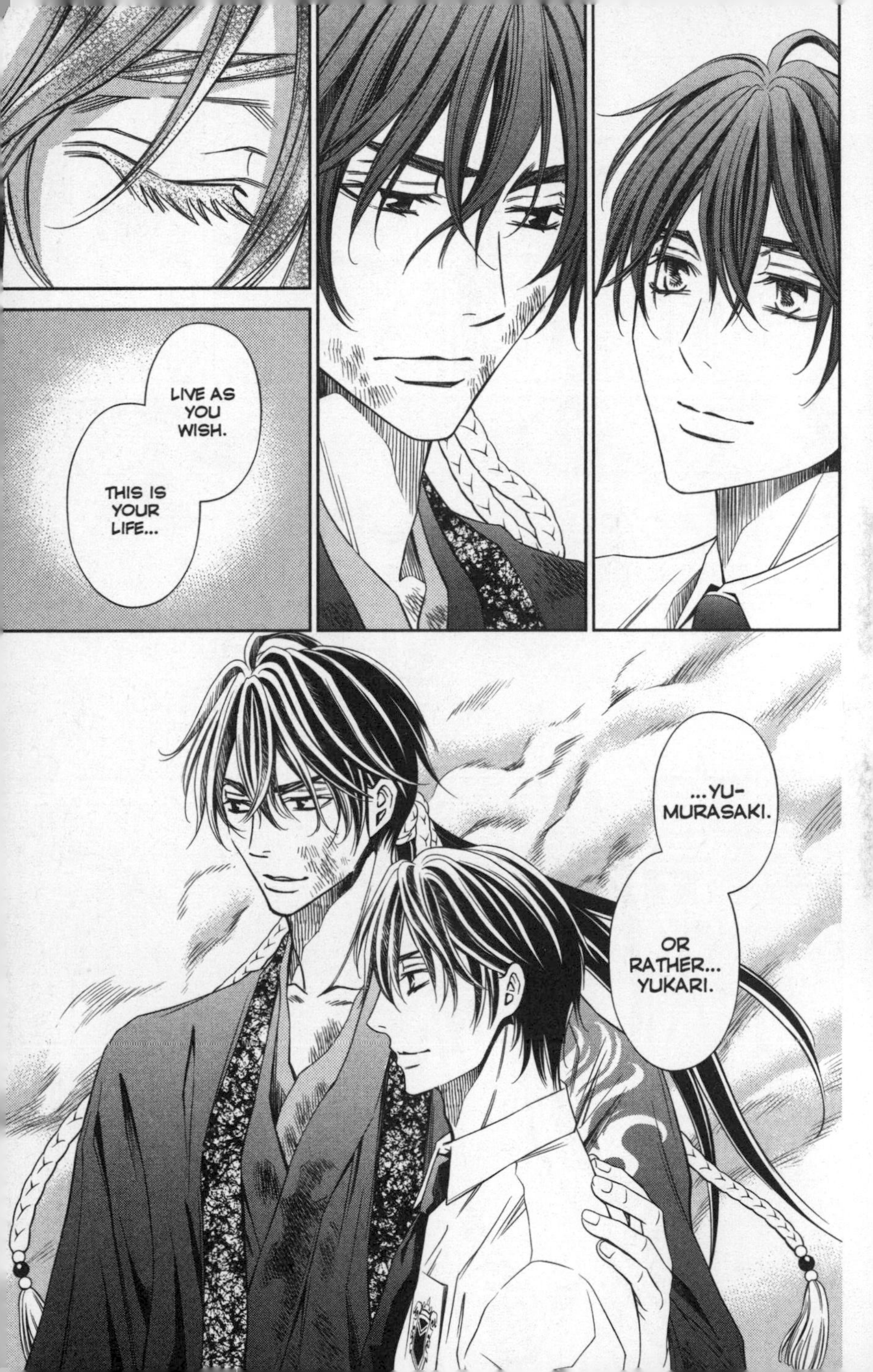
LIVE AS YOU WISH.
THIS IS YOUR LIFE...
...YU-MURASAKI.
OR RATHER... YUKARI.

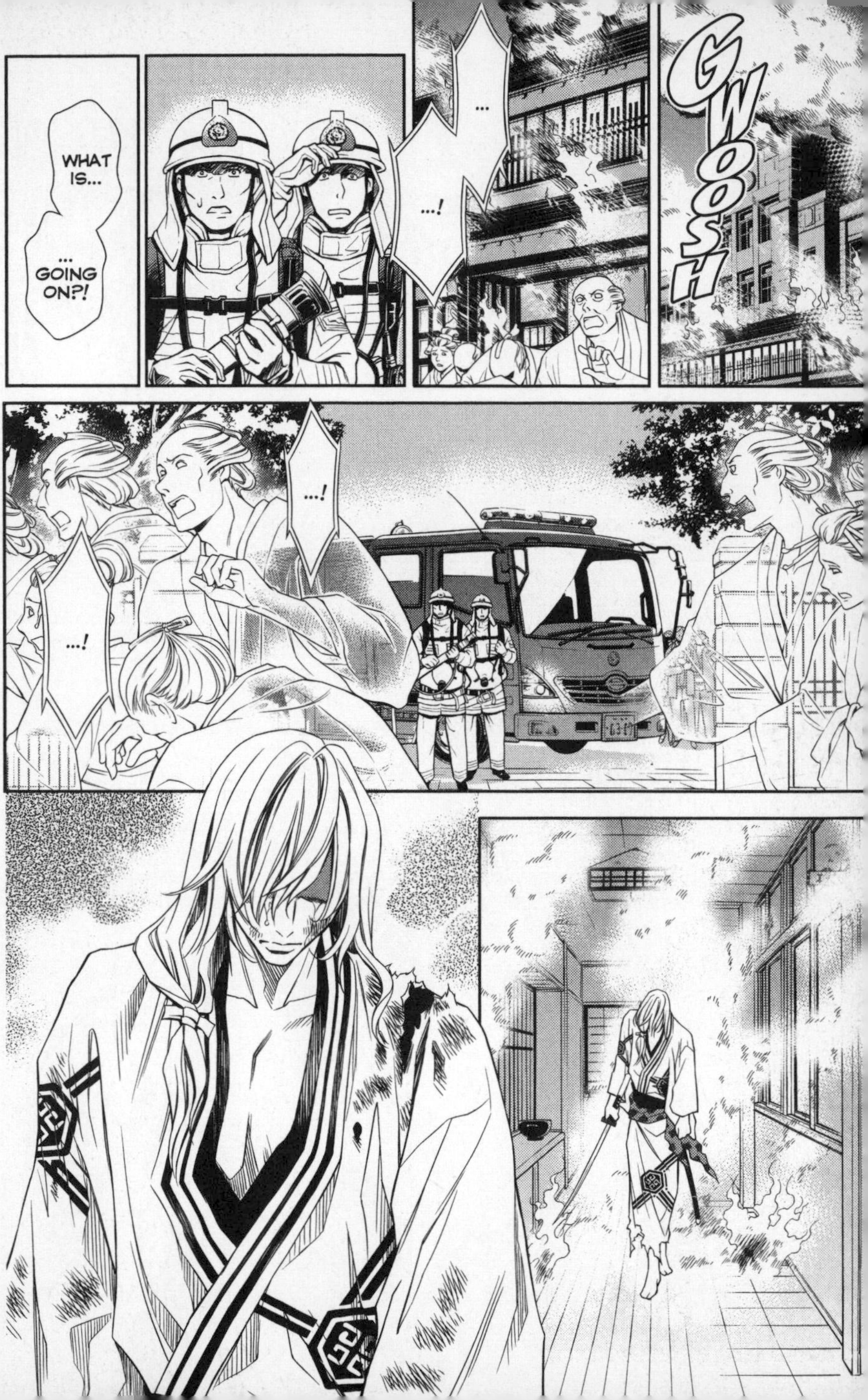
GWOOSH
...
...!
WHAT IS...
... GOING ON?!
...!
...!

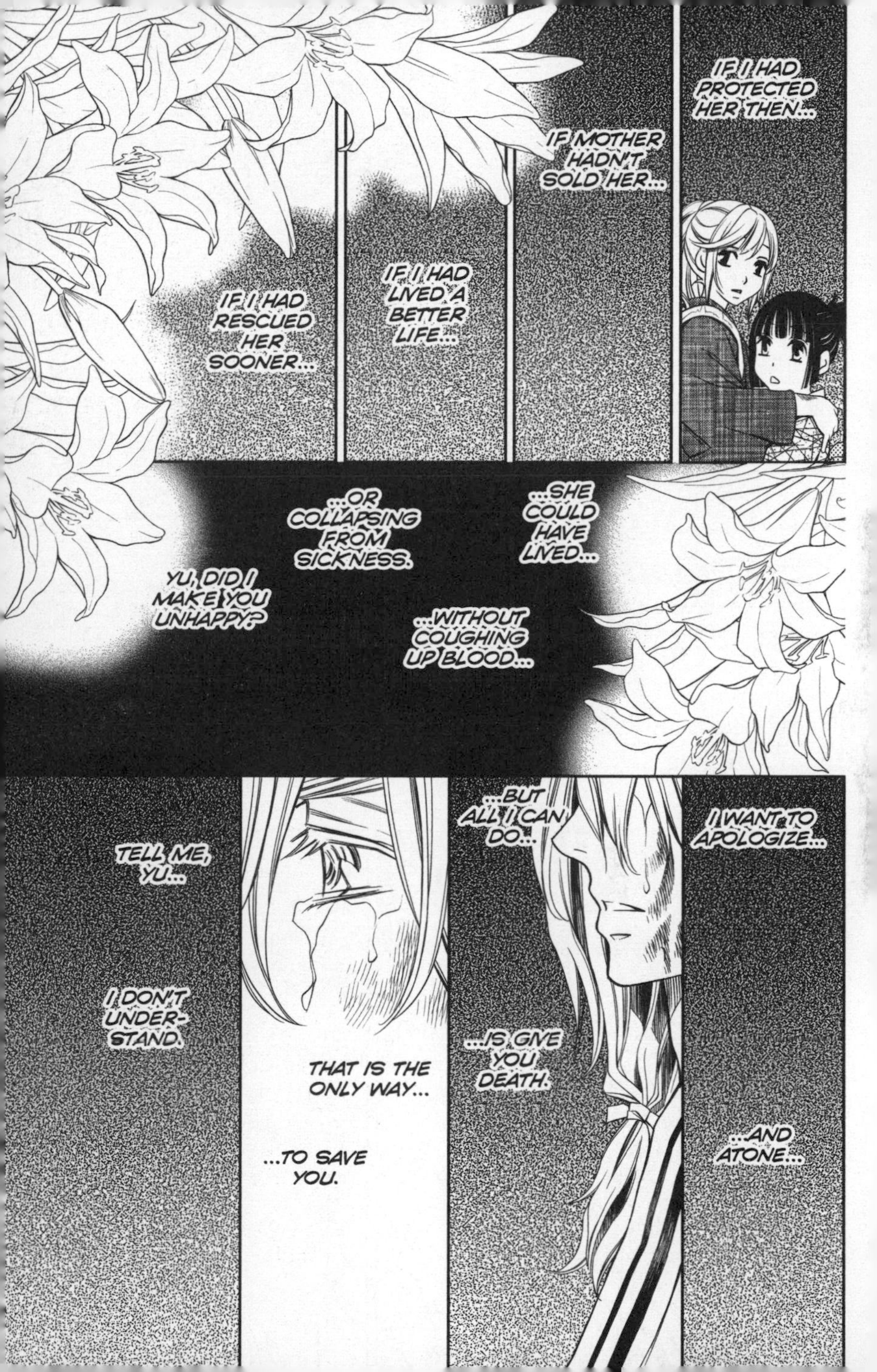
IF I HAD PROTECTED HER THEN...
IF MOTHER HADN'T SOLD HER...
IF I HAD LIVED A BETTER LIFE...
IF I HAD RESCUED HER SOONER...
...SHE COULD HAVE LIVED...
...WITHOUT COUGHING UP BLOOD...
...OR COLLAPSING FROM SICKNESS.
YU, DID I MAKE YOU UNHAPPY?
I WANT TO APOLOGIZE...
...AND ATONE...
...BUT ALL I CAN DO...
...IS GIVE YOU DEATH.
THAT IS THE ONLY WAY...
...TO SAVE YOU.
TELL ME, YU...
I DON'T UNDER-STAND.

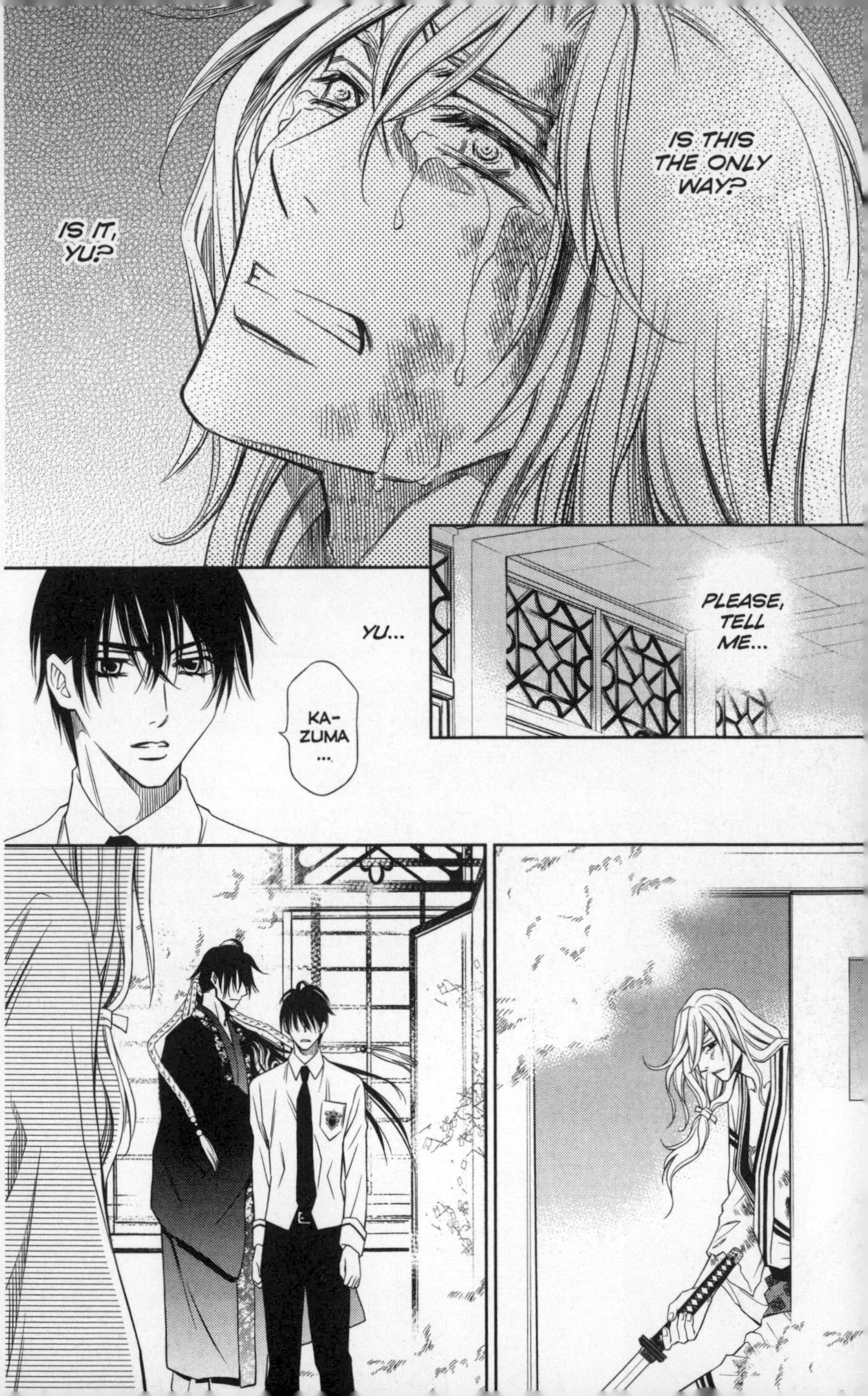
IS THIS THE ONLY WAY?
IS IT, YU?
PLEASE, TELL ME...
YU...
KA-ZUMA...

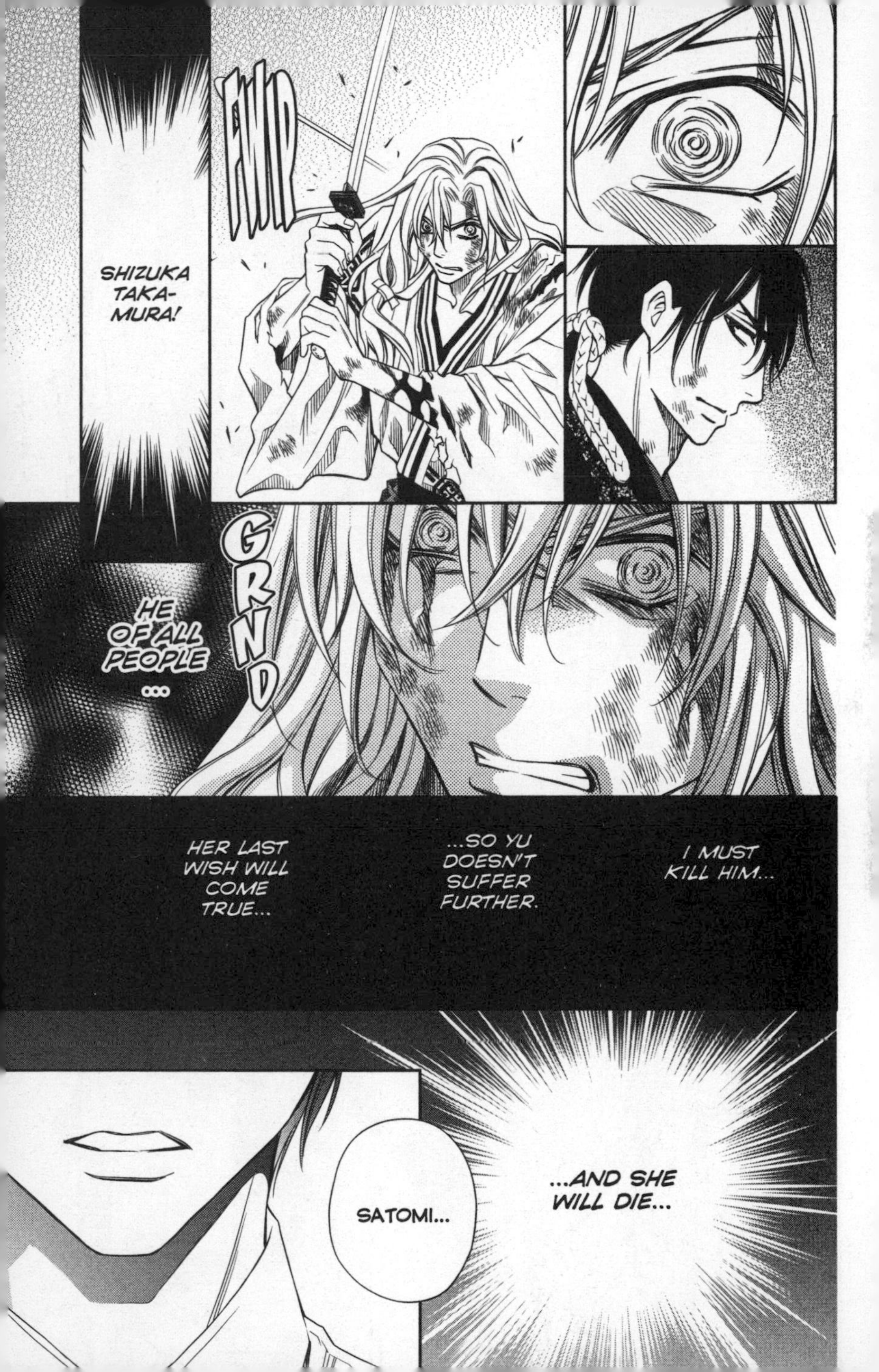
FWIP
SHIZUKA TAKAMURA!
GRND
HE OF ALL PEOPLE...
I MUST KILL HIM...
...SO YU DOESN'T SUFFER FURTHER.
HER LAST WISH WILL COME TRUE...
...AND SHE WILL DIE...
SATOMI...

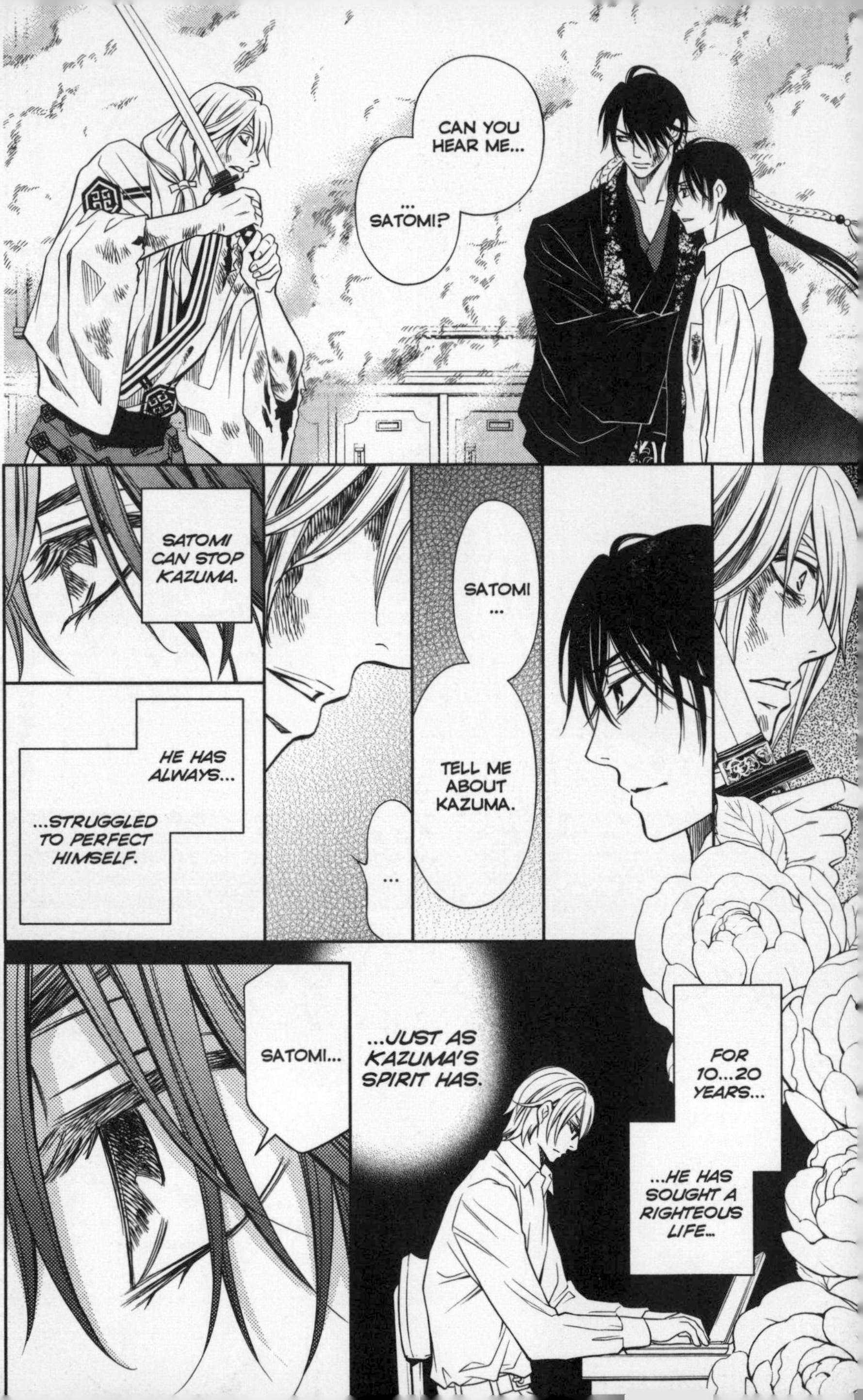
CAN YOU HEAR ME...
...SATOMI?
SATOMI...
TELL ME ABOUT KAZUMA.
...
SATOMI CAN STOP KAZUMA.
HE HAS ALWAYS...
...STRUGGLED TO PERFECT HIMSELF.
FOR 10...20 YEARS...
...HE HAS SOUGHT A RIGHTEOUS LIFE...
...JUST AS KAZUMA'S SPIRIT HAS.
SATOMI...

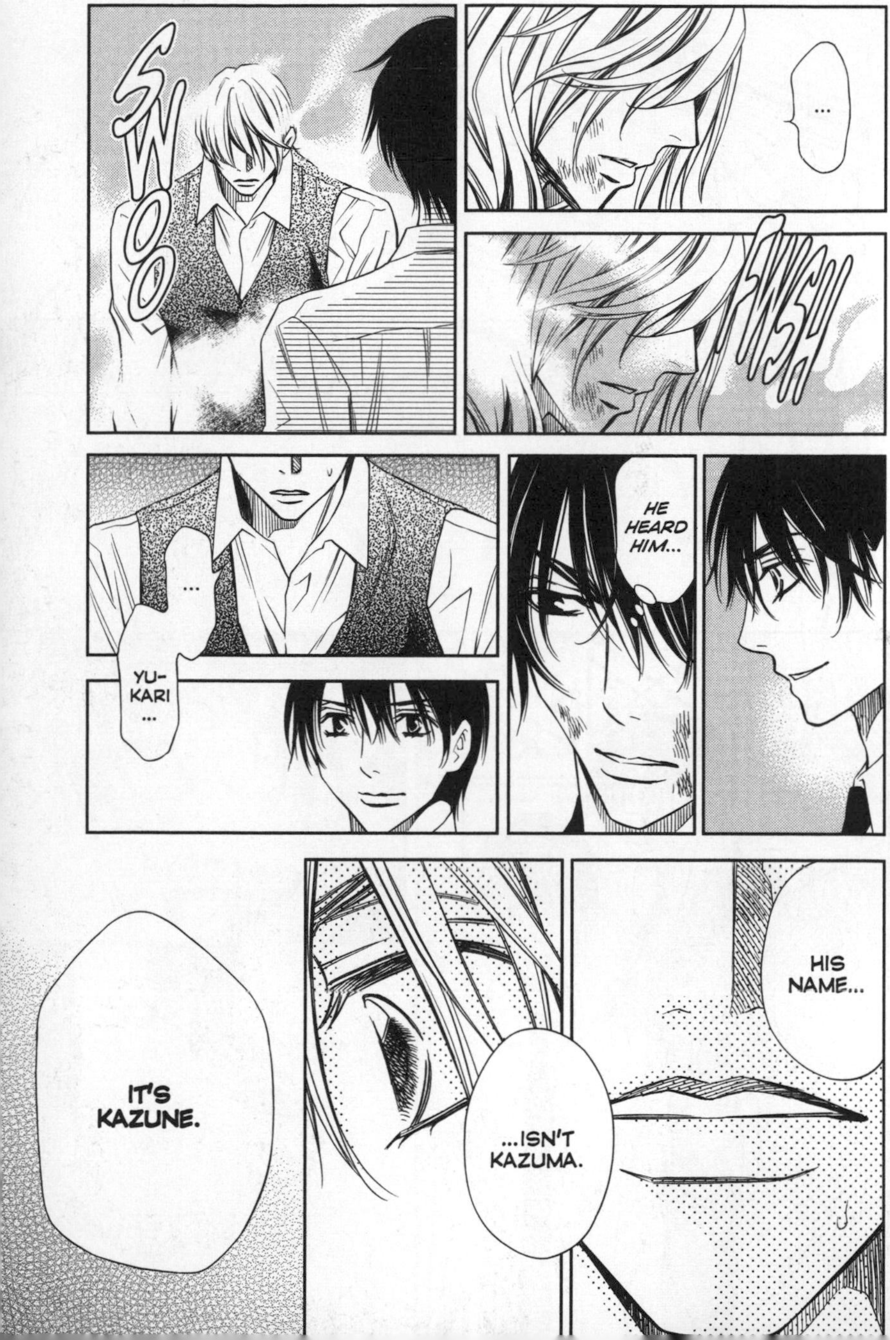
...
FWSH
SWOOSH
HE HEARD HIM...
...
YU-KARI ...
HIS NAME...
...ISN'T KAZUMA.
IT'S KAZUNE.

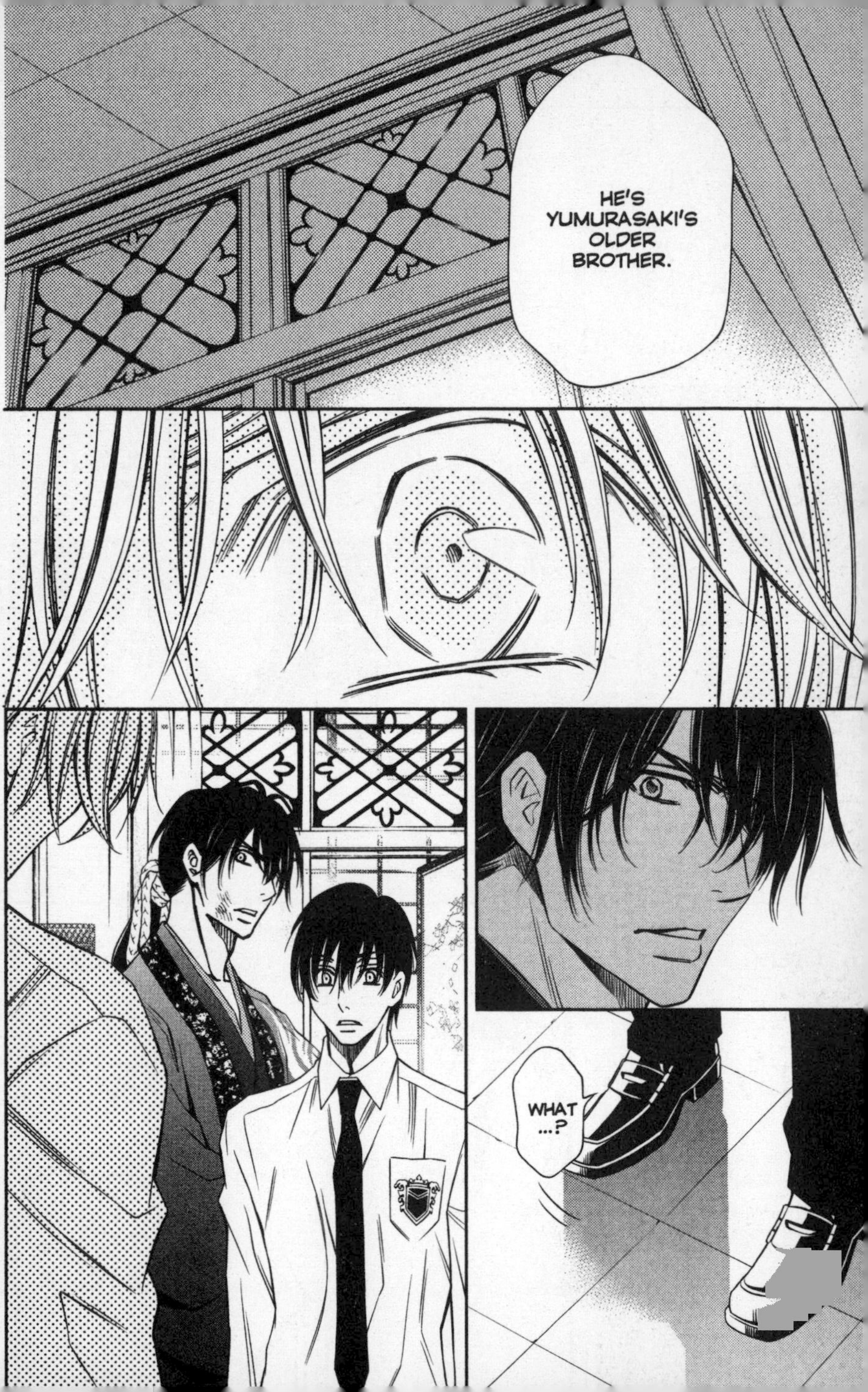
HE'S YUMURASAKI'S OLDER BROTHER.
WHAT ...?

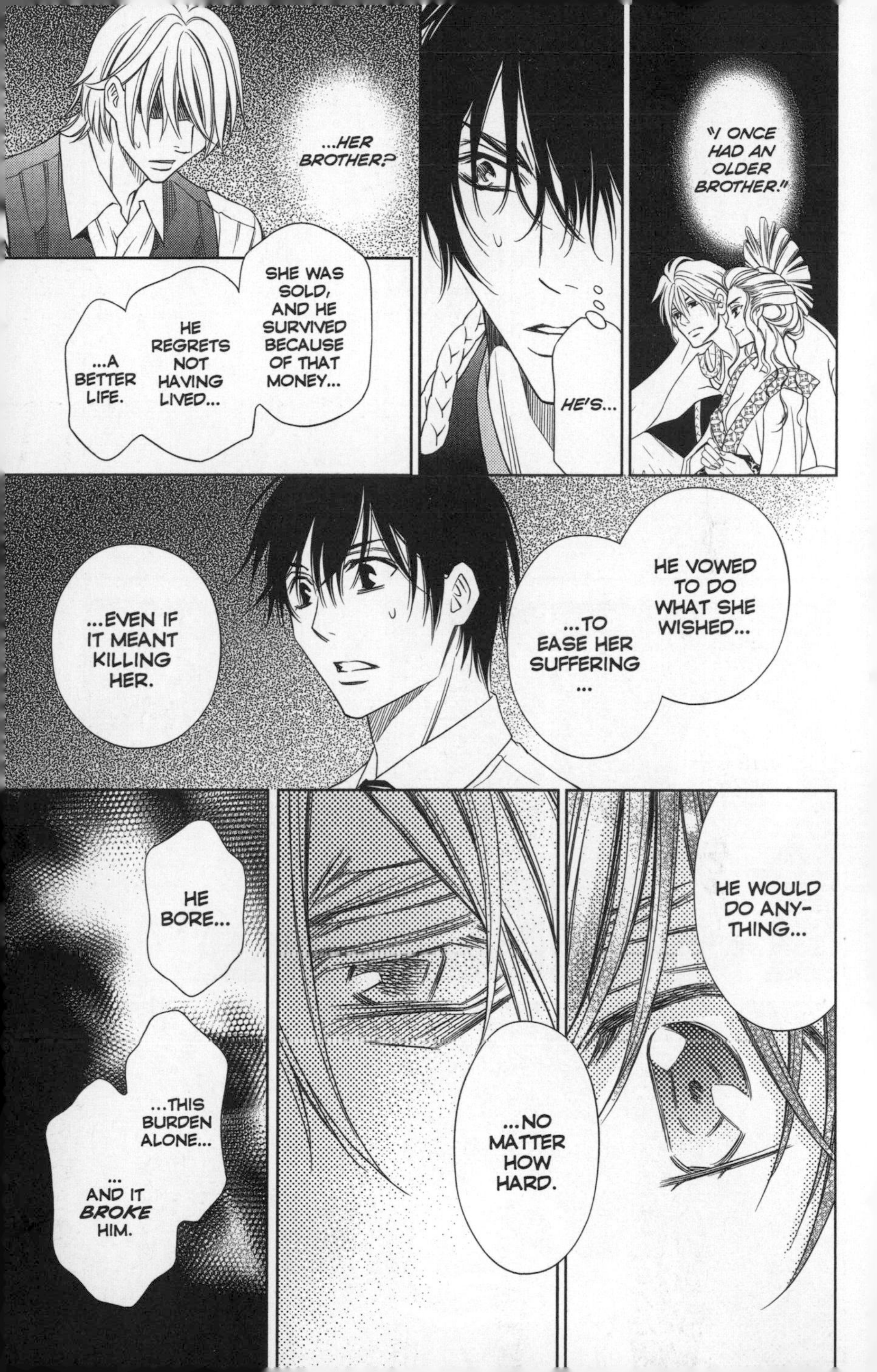
"I ONCE HAD AN OLDER BROTHER."
HE'S...
...HER BROTHER?
SHE WAS SOLD, AND HE SURVIVED BECAUSE OF THAT MONEY...
HE REGRETS NOT HAVING LIVED...
...A BETTER LIFE.
HE VOWED TO DO WHAT SHE WISHED...
...TO EASE HER SUFFERING...
...EVEN IF IT MEANT KILLING HER.
HE WOULD DO ANY-THING...
...NO MATTER HOW HARD.
HE BORE...
...THIS BURDEN ALONE...
...AND IT *BROKE* HIM.

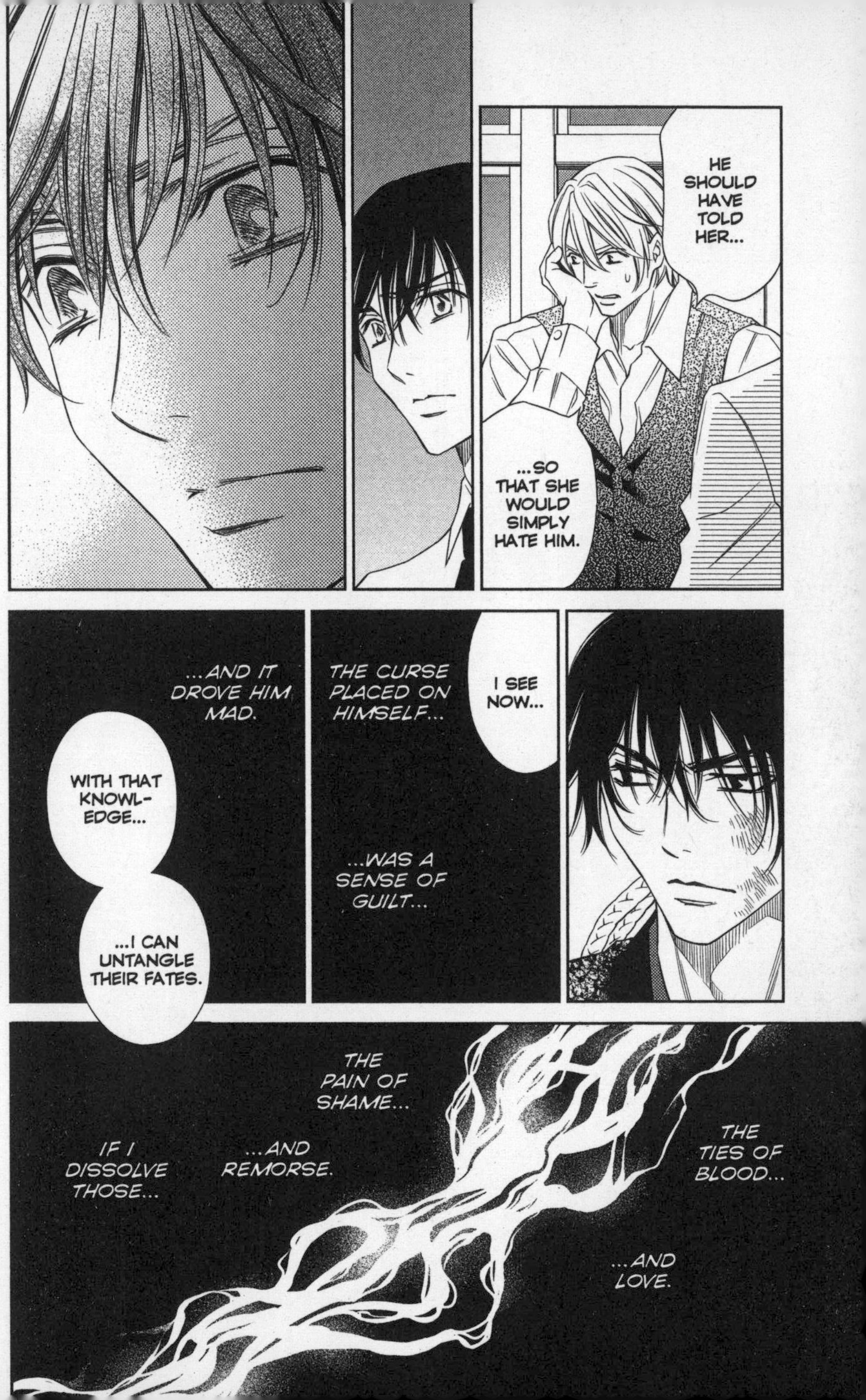
HE SHOULD HAVE TOLD HER...
...SO THAT SHE WOULD SIMPLY HATE HIM.
I SEE NOW...
THE CURSE PLACED ON HIMSELF...
...WAS A SENSE OF GUILT...
...AND IT DROVE HIM MAD.
WITH THAT KNOWL-EDGE...
...I CAN UNTANGLE THEIR FATES.
THE TIES OF BLOOD...
...AND LOVE.
THE PAIN OF SHAME...
...AND REMORSE.
IF I DISSOLVE THOSE...

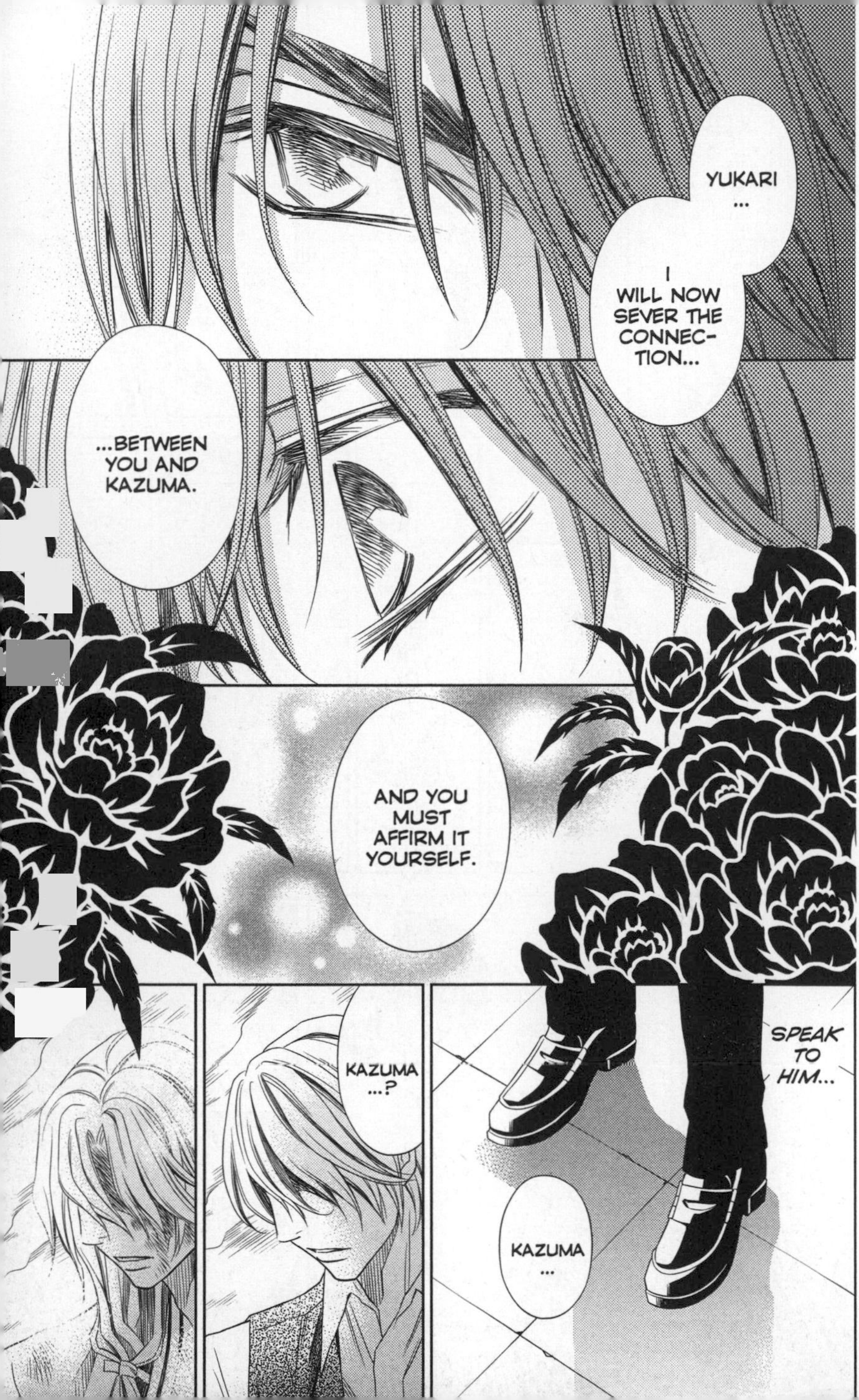
YUKARI ...
I WILL NOW SEVER THE CONNECTION...
...BETWEEN YOU AND KAZUMA.
AND YOU MUST AFFIRM IT YOURSELF.
SPEAK TO HIM...
KAZUMA ...
KAZUMA ...?

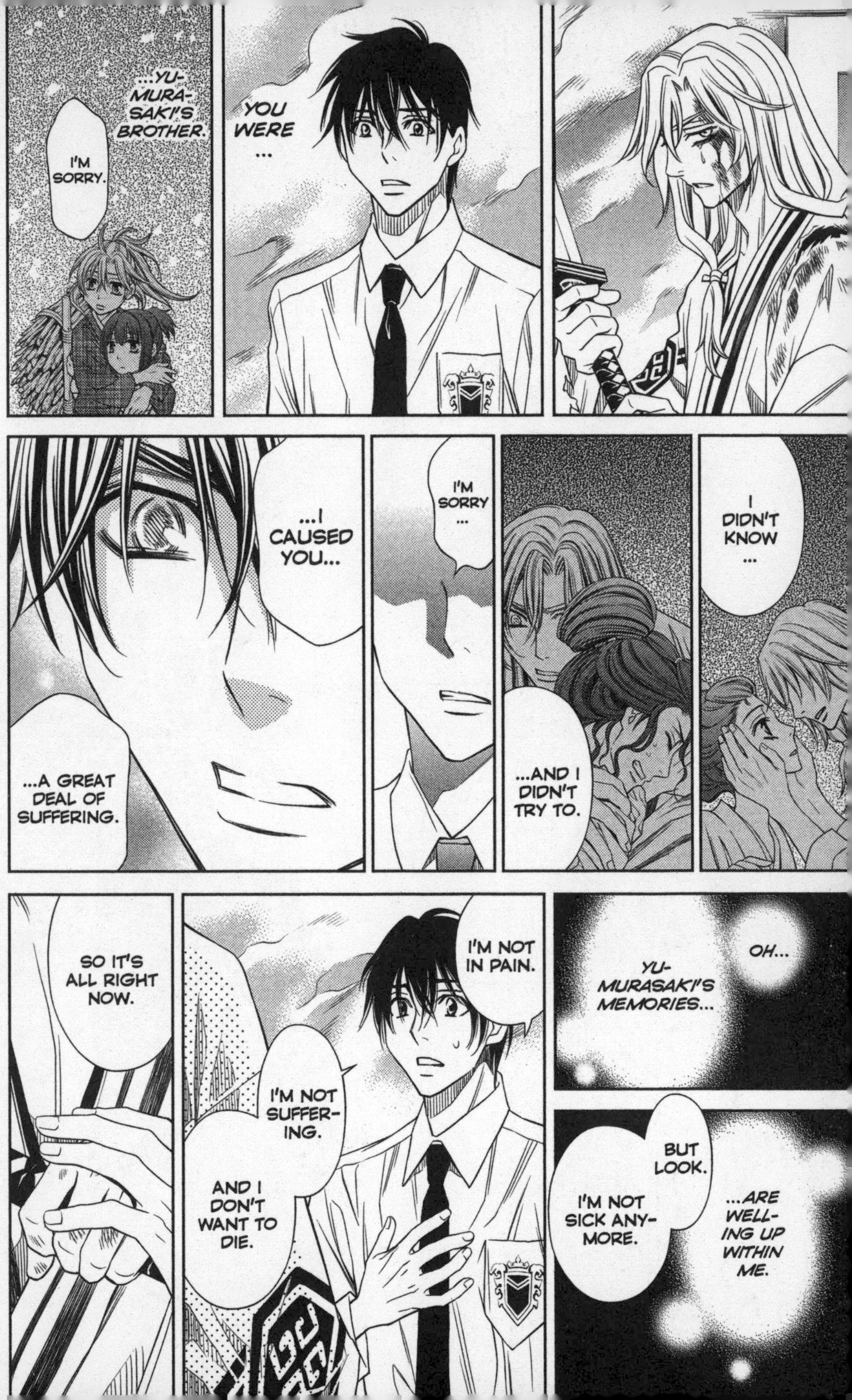
YOU WERE ...
...YU-MURASAKI'S BROTHER.
I'M SORRY.
I DIDN'T KNOW ...
...AND I DIDN'T TRY TO.
I'M SORRY ...
...I CAUSED YOU...
...A GREAT DEAL OF SUFFERING.
OH...
YU-MURASAKI'S MEMORIES...
...ARE WELLING UP WITHIN ME.
BUT LOOK.
I'M NOT SICK ANYMORE.
I'M NOT IN PAIN.
I'M NOT SUFFERING.
AND I DON'T WANT TO DIE.
SO IT'S ALL RIGHT NOW.

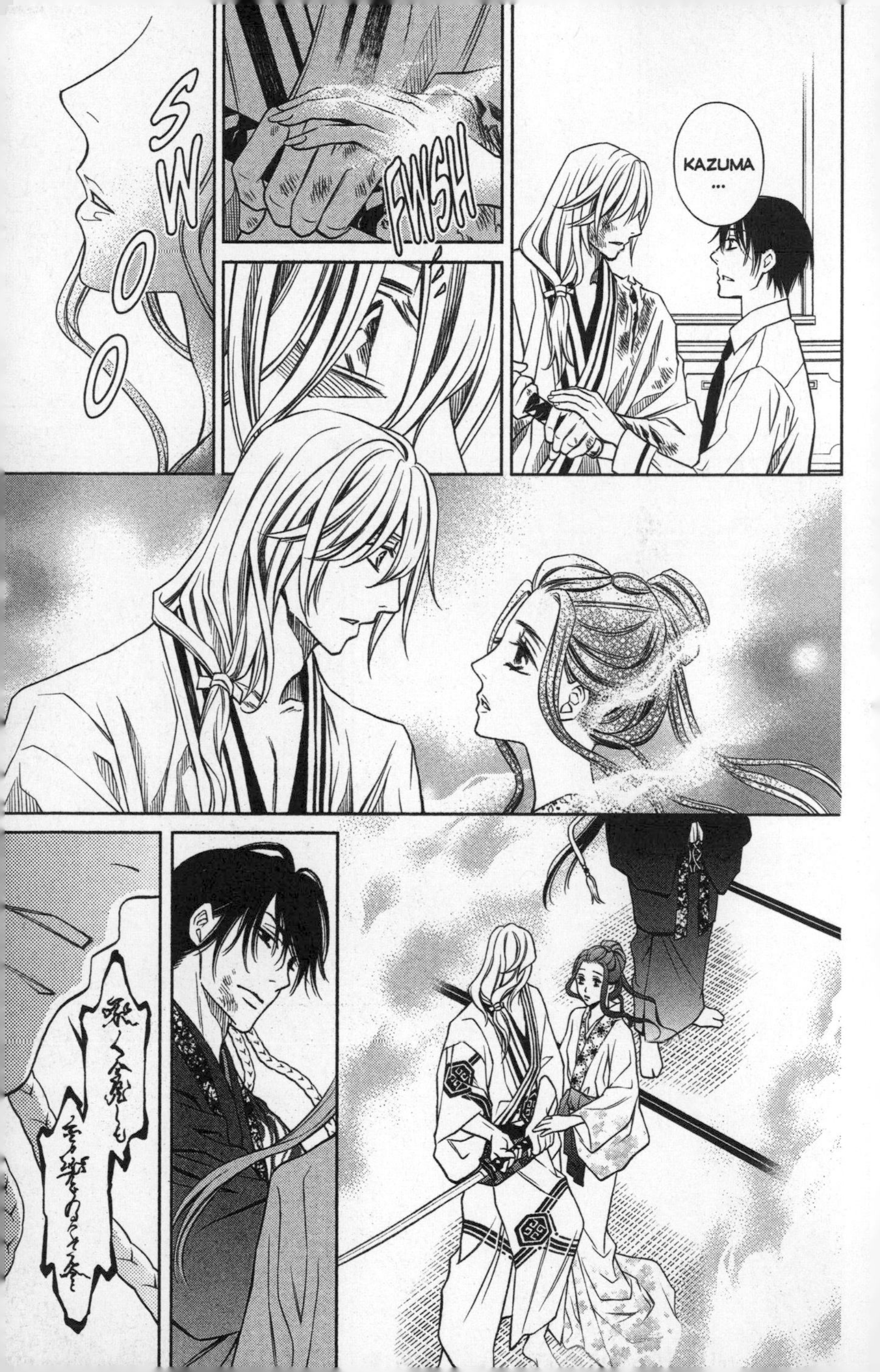
KAZUMA ...
FWSH
SWOOO

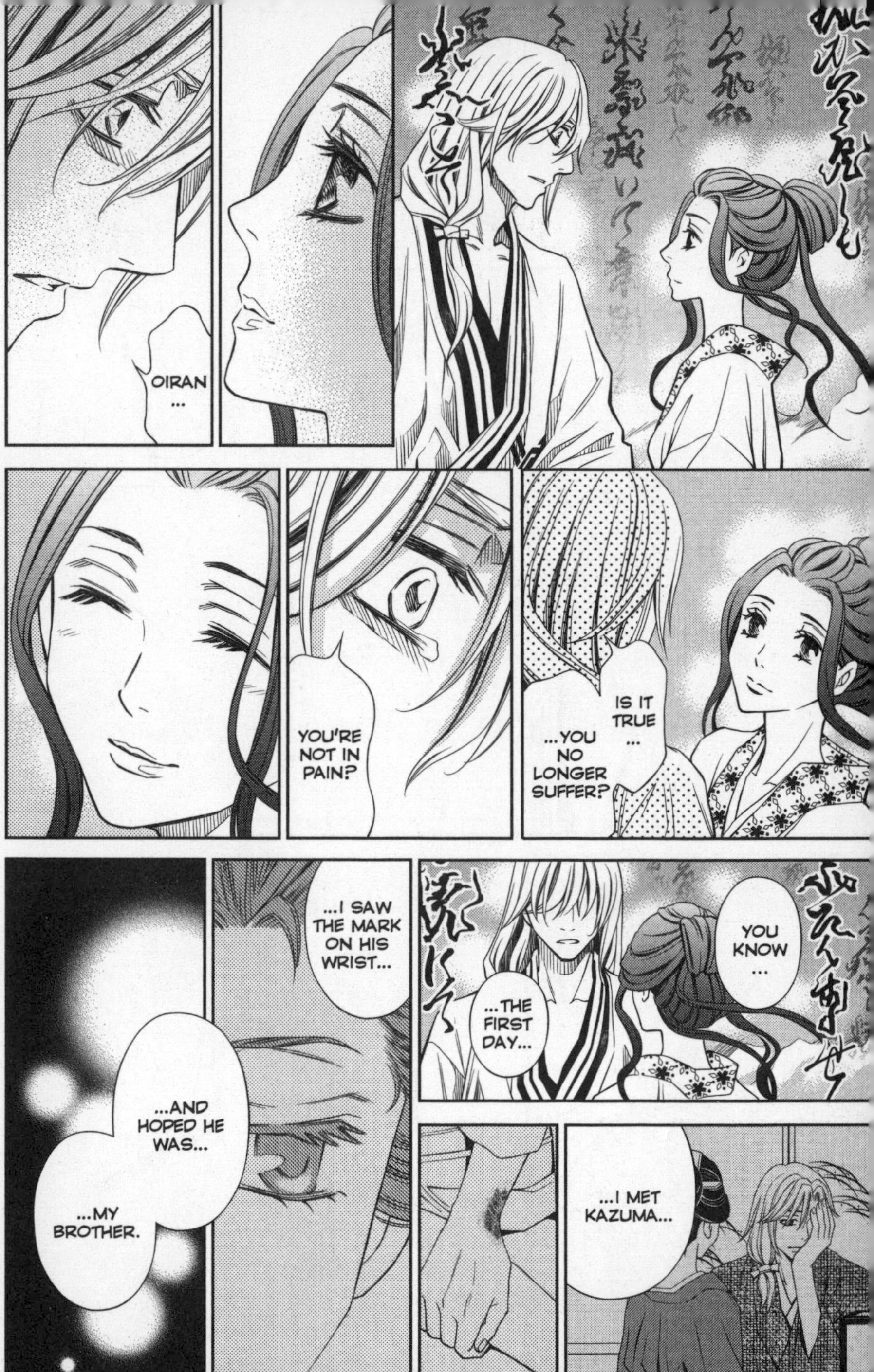
OIRAN...
IS IT TRUE...
...YOU NO LONGER SUFFER?
YOU'RE NOT IN PAIN?
YOU KNOW...
...THE FIRST DAY...
...I MET KAZUMA...
...I SAW THE MARK ON HIS WRIST...
...AND HOPED HE WAS...
...MY BROTHER.

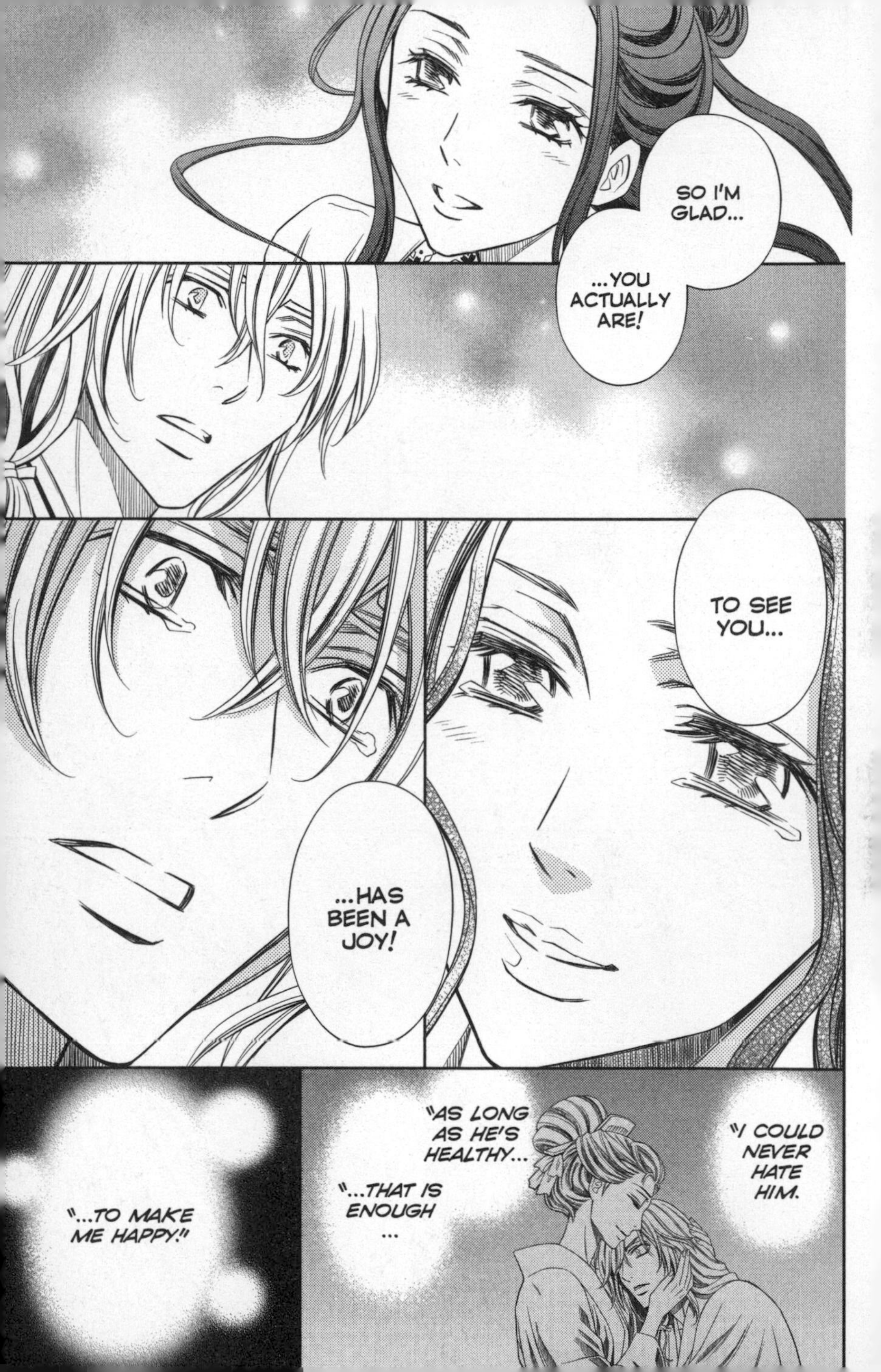
SO I'M GLAD...
...YOU ACTUALLY ARE!
TO SEE YOU...
...HAS BEEN A JOY!
"I COULD NEVER HATE HIM.
"AS LONG AS HE'S HEALTHY...
"...THAT IS ENOUGH ...
"...TO MAKE ME HAPPY!"

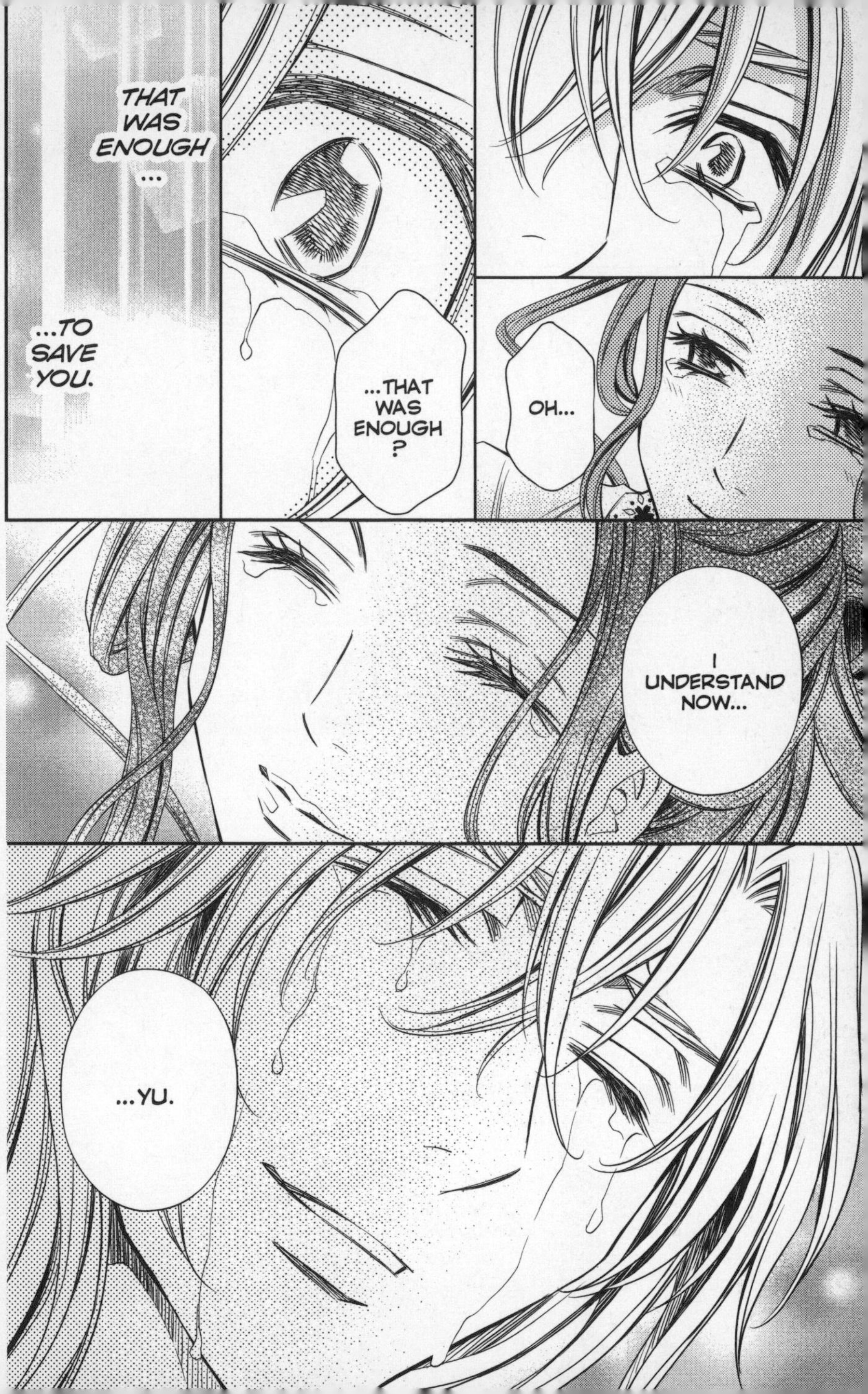
OH...
...THAT WAS ENOUGH?
THAT WAS ENOUGH...
...TO SAVE YOU.
I UNDERSTAND NOW...
...YU.

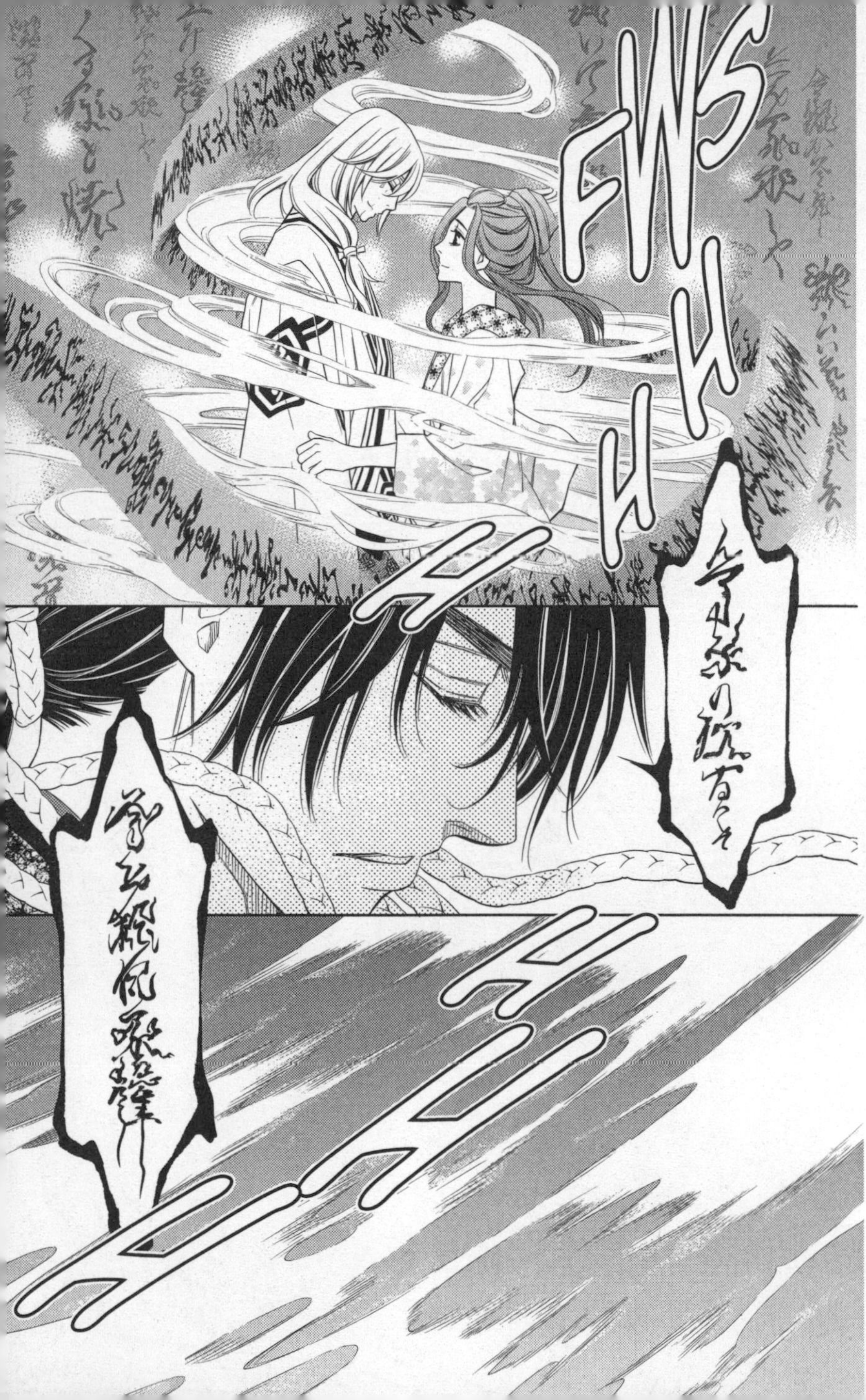
FWSHHH
HHHH

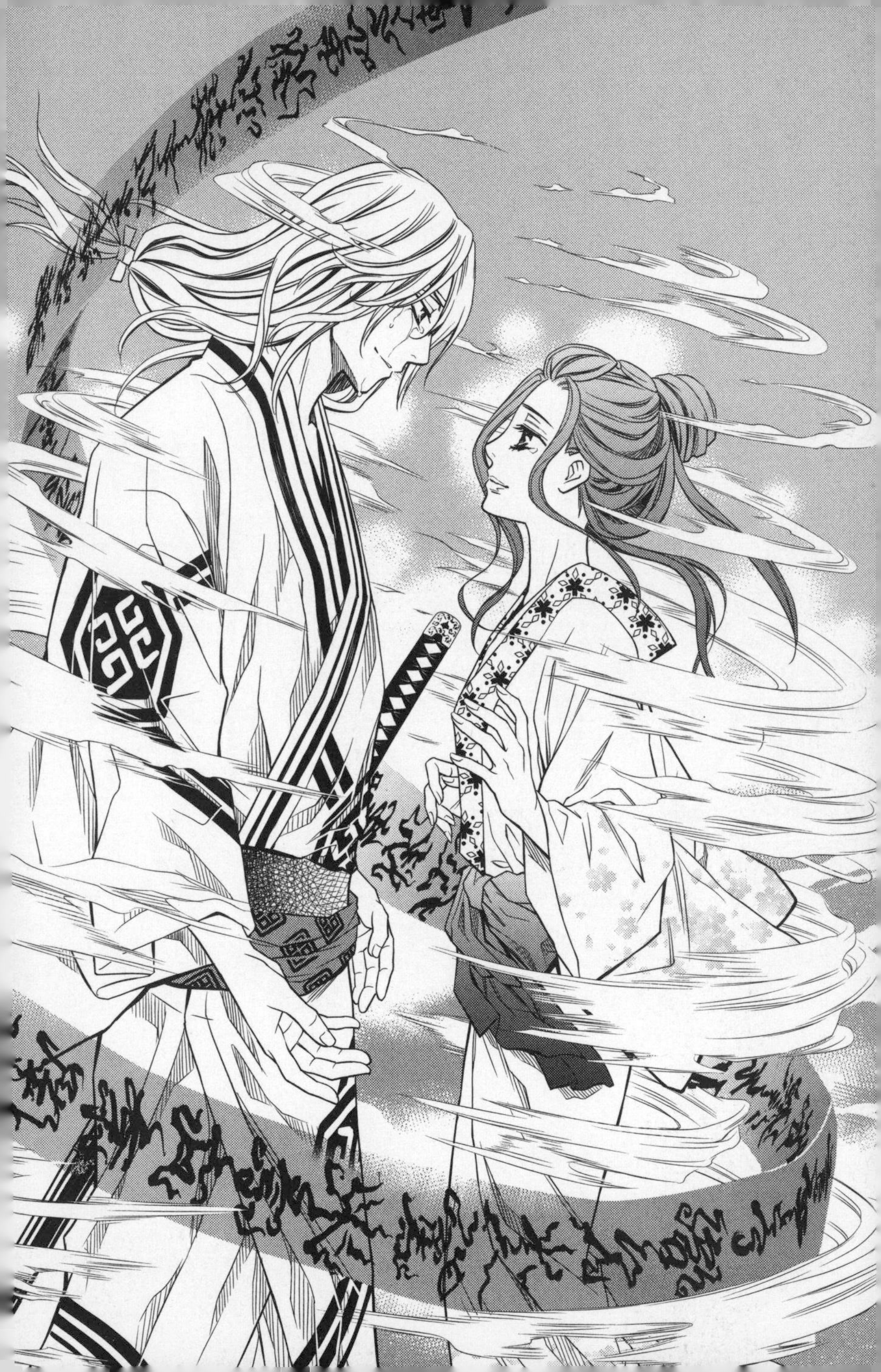

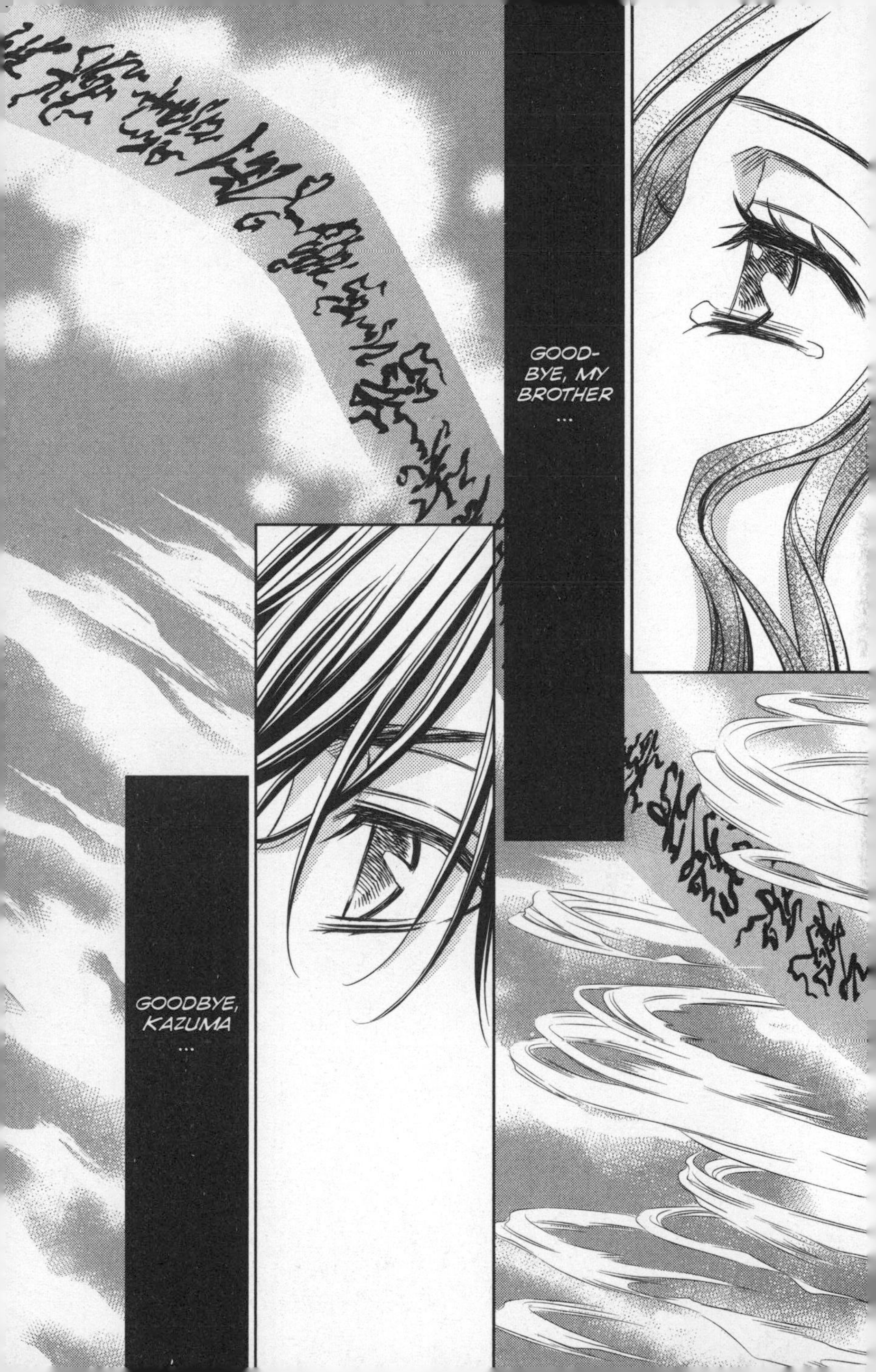
GOOD-BYE, MY BROTHER ...
GOODBYE, KAZUMA ...

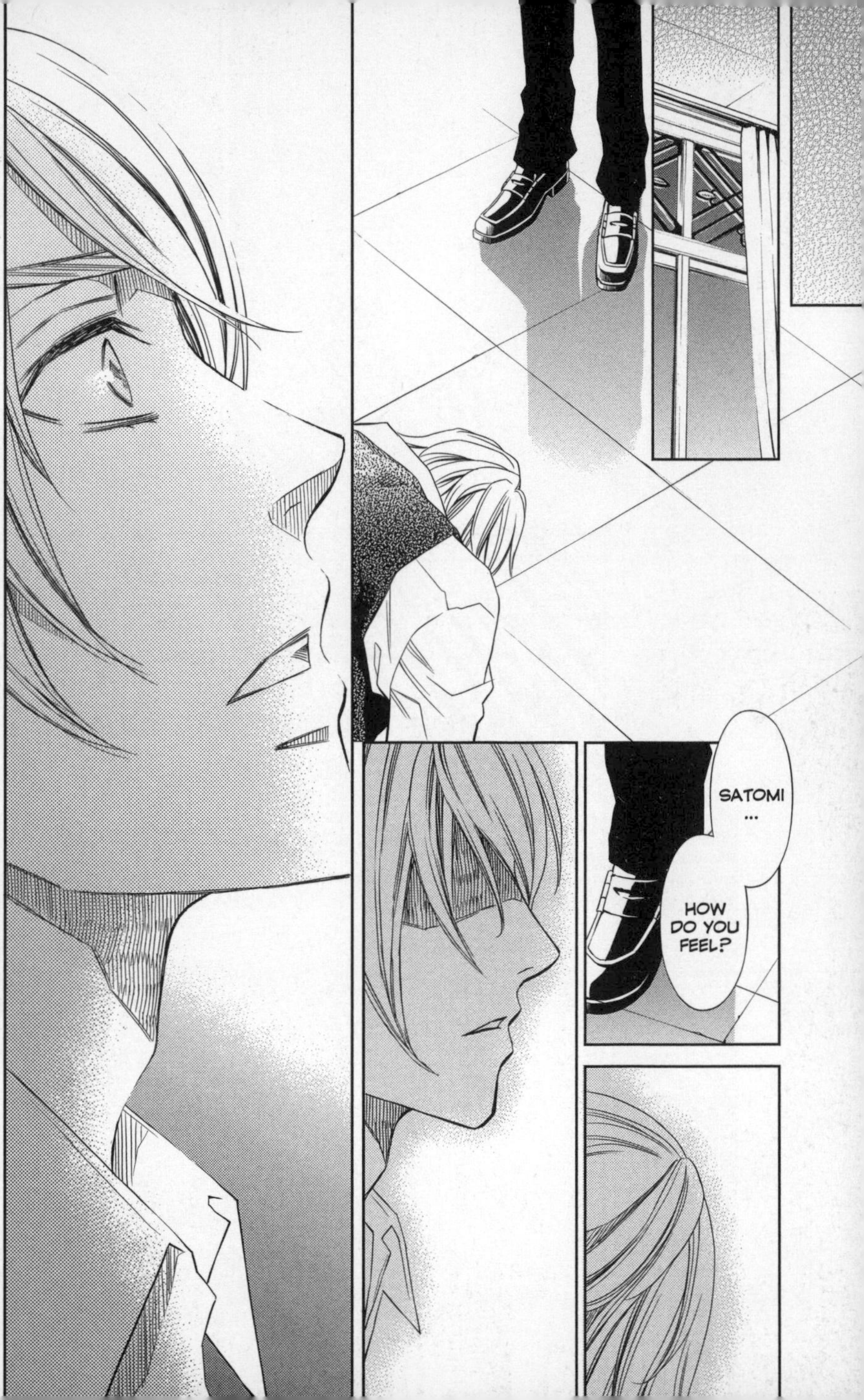
SATOMI ...
HOW DO YOU FEEL?

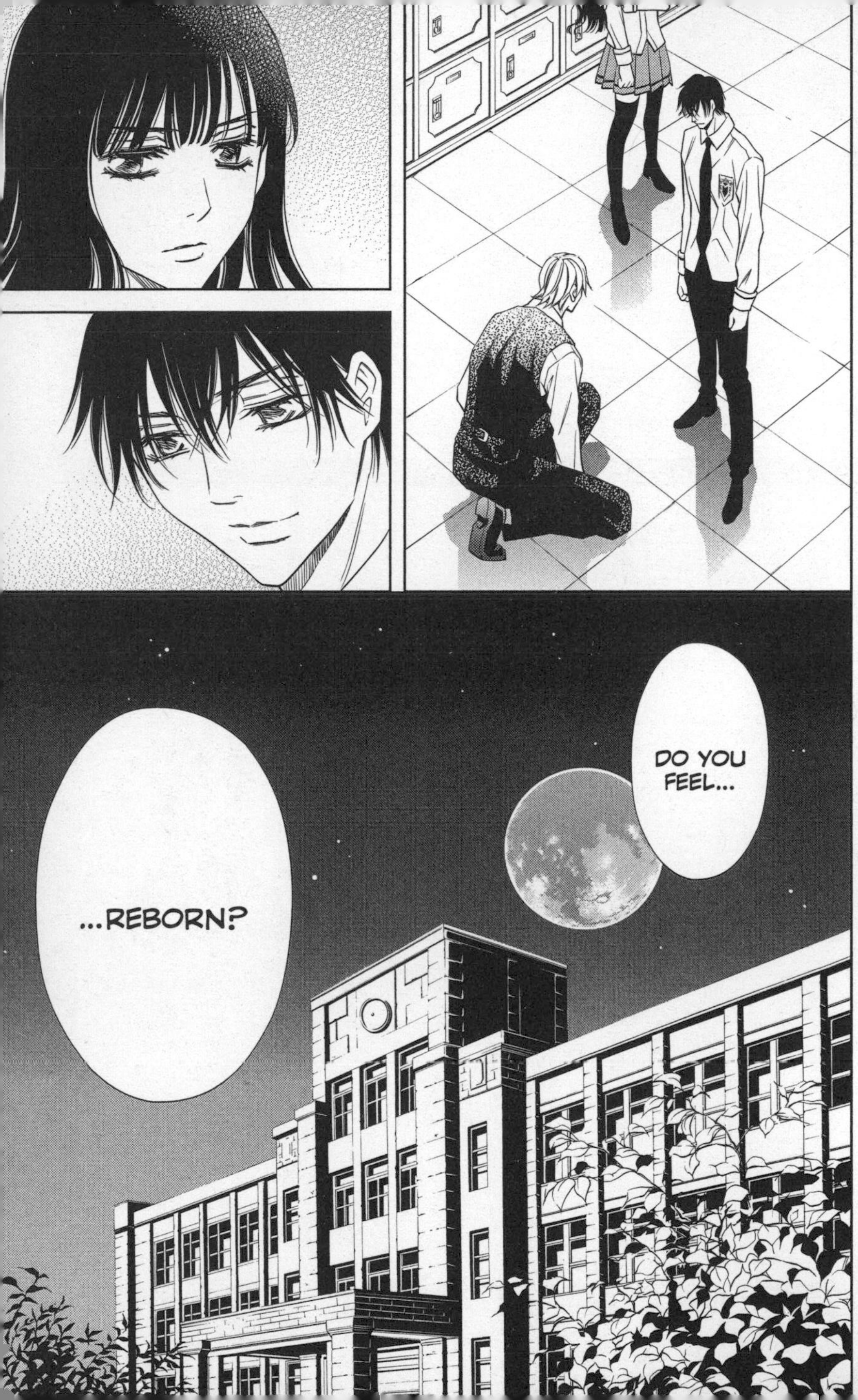
DO YOU FEEL...
...REBORN?

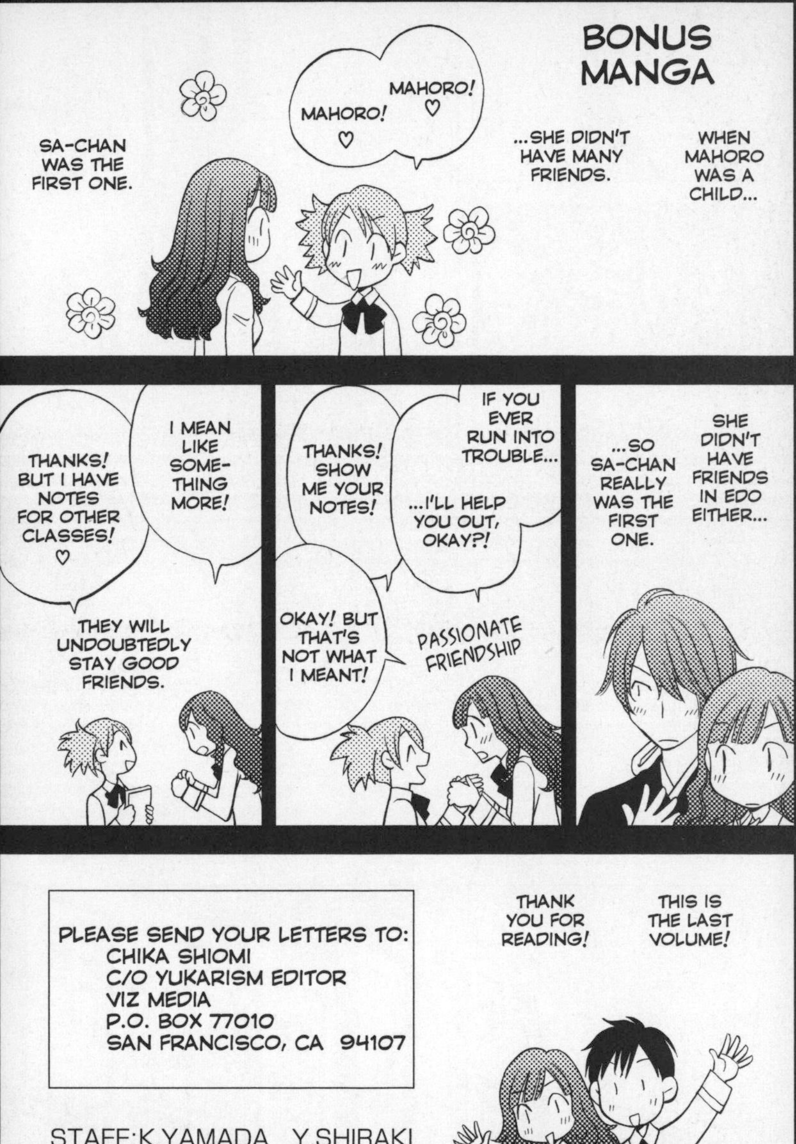
BONUS MANGA
WHEN MAHORO WAS A CHILD...
...SHE DIDN'T HAVE MANY FRIENDS.
MAHORO! ♡
MAHORO! ♡
SA-CHAN WAS THE FIRST ONE.
SHE DIDN'T HAVE FRIENDS IN EDO EITHER...
...SO SA-CHAN REALLY WAS THE FIRST ONE.
IF YOU EVER RUN INTO TROUBLE...
...I'LL HELP YOU OUT, OKAY?!
THANKS! SHOW ME YOUR NOTES!
PASSIONATE FRIENDSHIP
OKAY! BUT THAT'S NOT WHAT I MEANT!
I MEAN LIKE SOME-THING MORE!
THANKS! BUT I HAVE NOTES FOR OTHER CLASSES! ♡
THEY WILL UNDOUBTEDLY STAY GOOD FRIENDS.
THIS IS THE LAST VOLUME!
THANK YOU FOR READING!
PLEASE SEND YOUR LETTERS TO:
CHIKA SHIOMI
C/O YUKARISM EDITOR
VIZ MEDIA
P.O. BOX 77010
SAN FRANCISCO, CA 94107
STAFF:K.YAMADA Y.SHIRAKI
CG WORKS:ERII MISONO

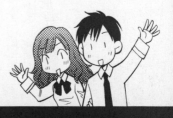

Chapter 17

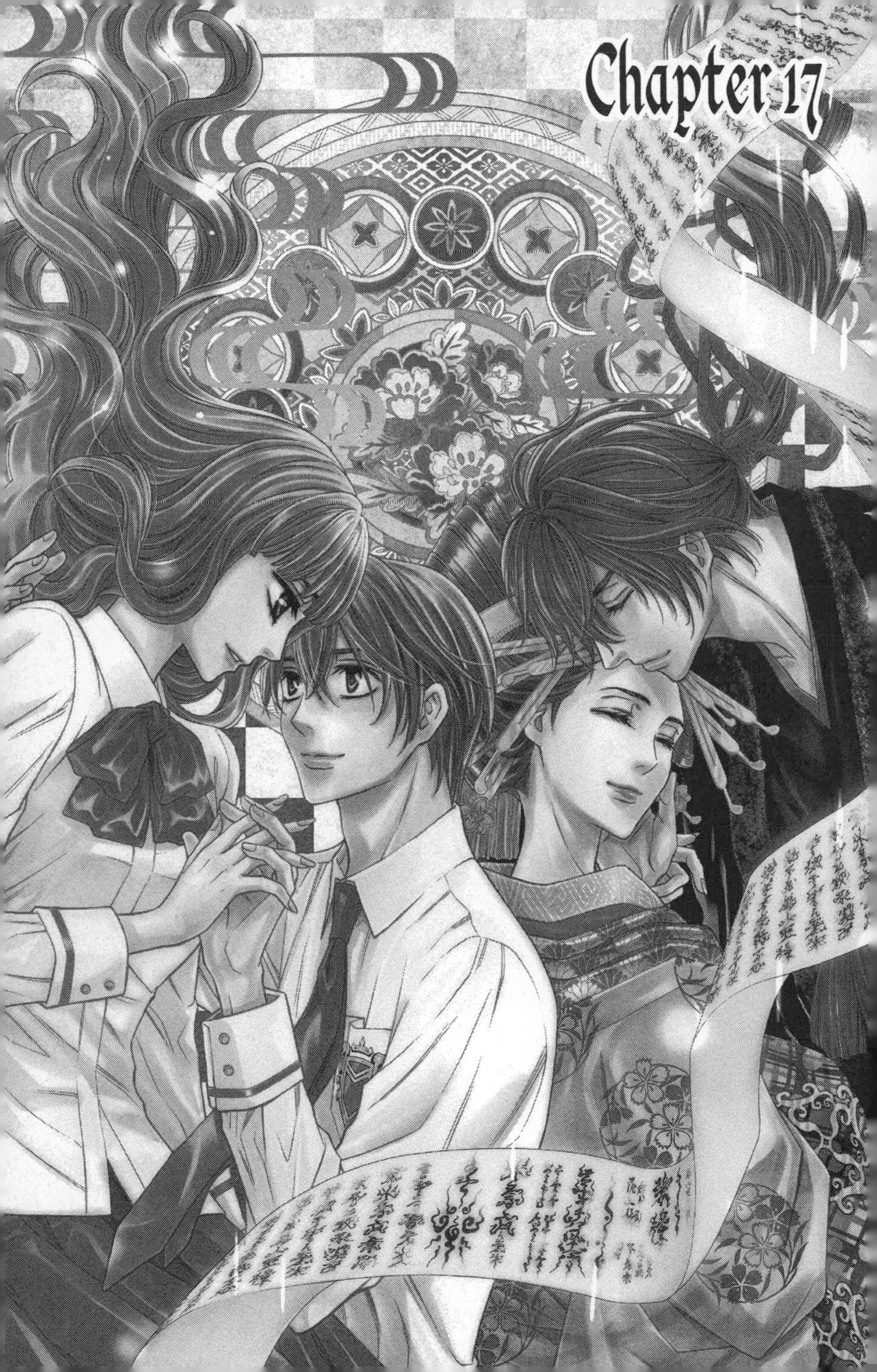

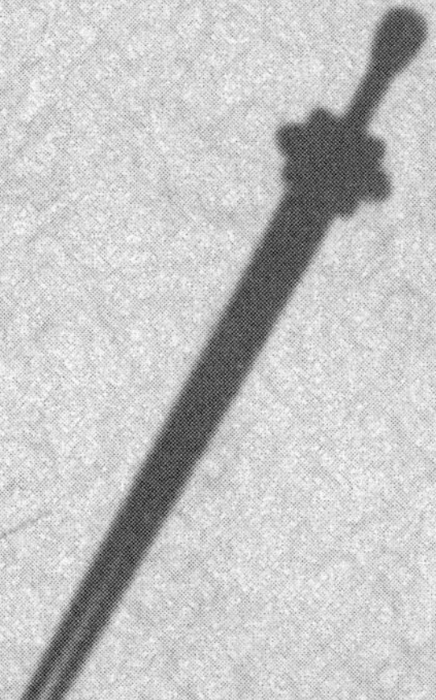

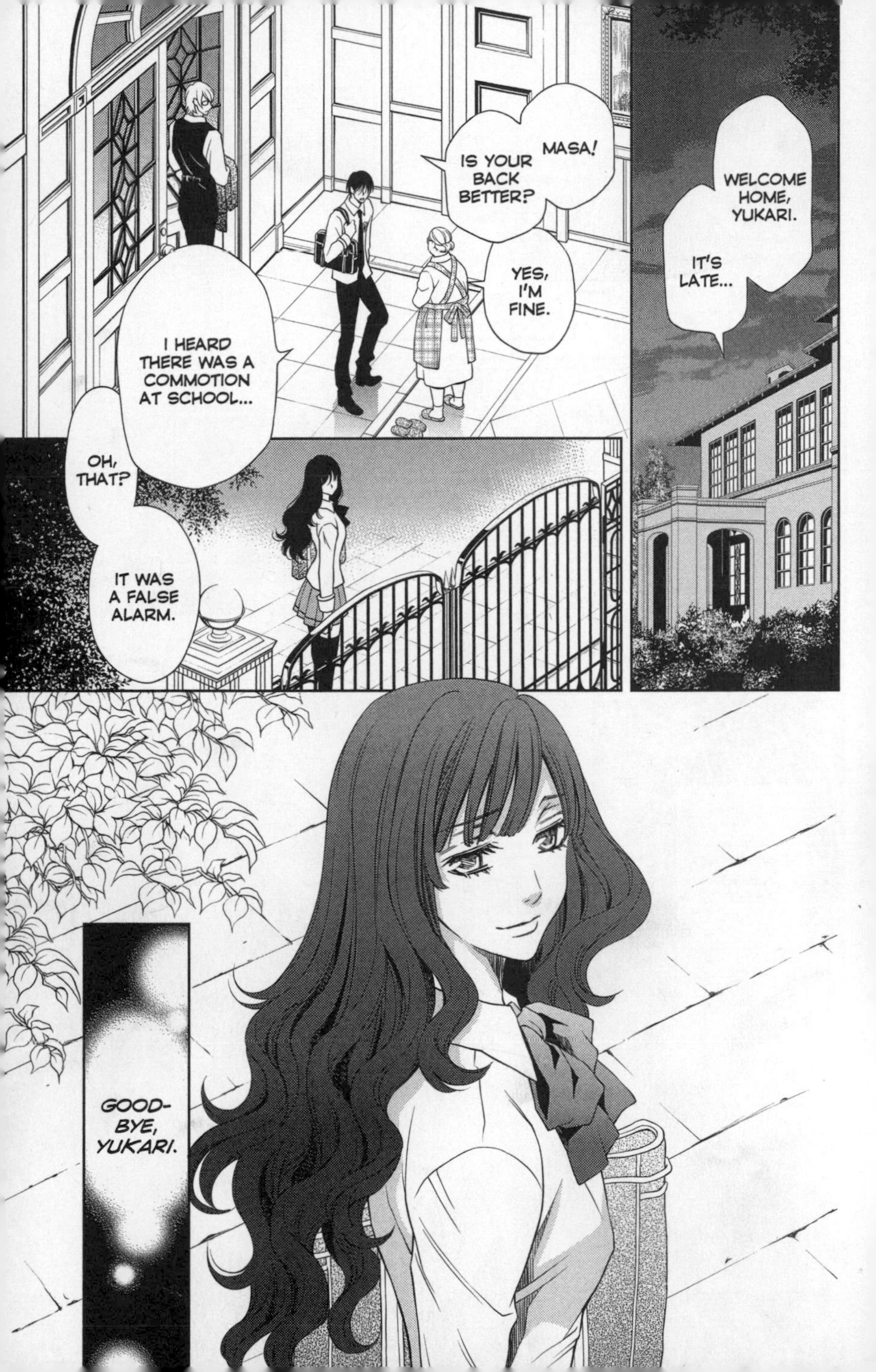
WELCOME HOME, YUKARI.
IT'S LATE...
MASA!
IS YOUR BACK BETTER?
YES, I'M FINE.
I HEARD THERE WAS A COMMOTION AT SCHOOL...
OH, THAT?
IT WAS A FALSE ALARM.
GOOD-BYE, YUKARI.

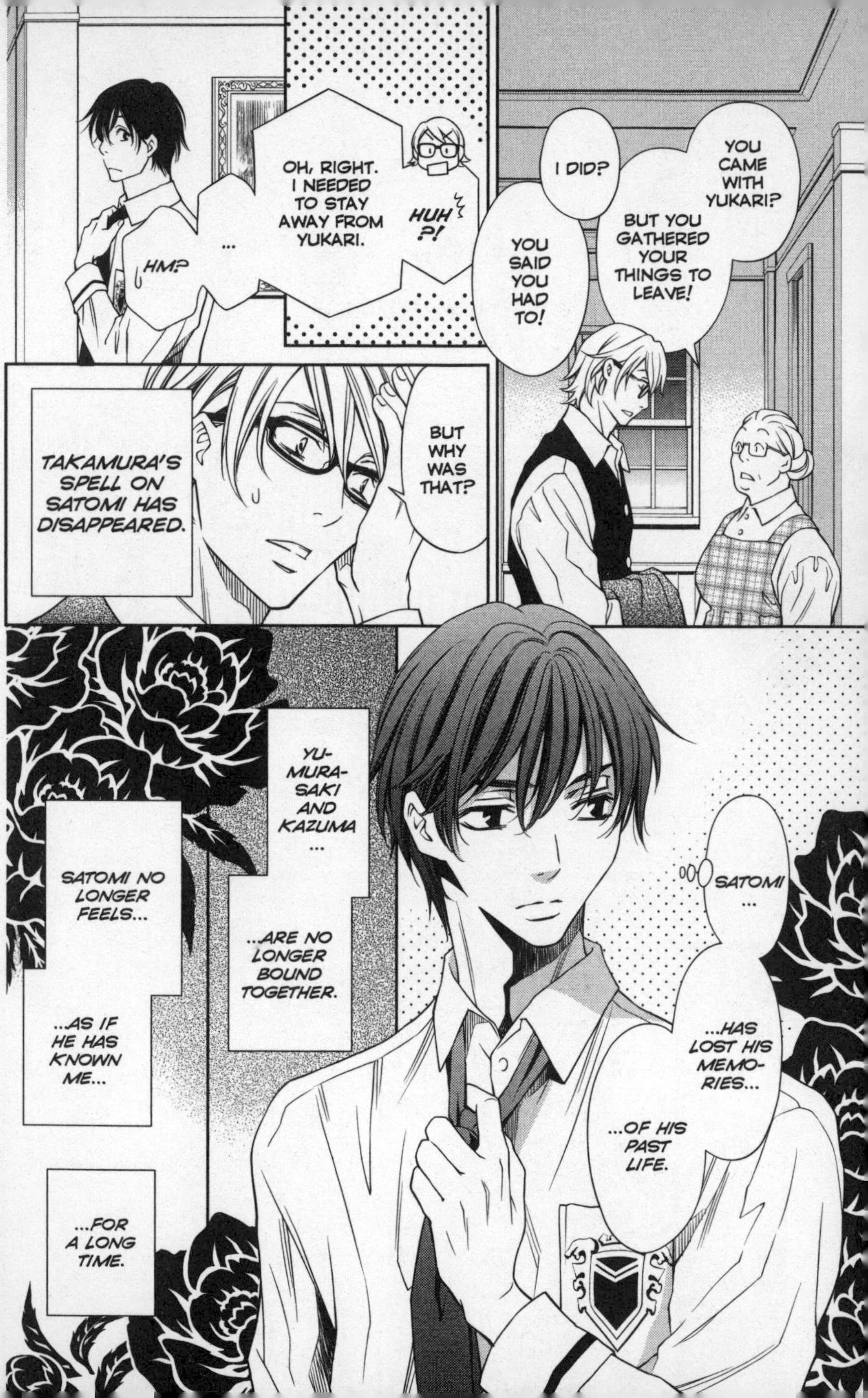
YOU CAME WITH YUKARI?
BUT YOU GATHERED YOUR THINGS TO LEAVE!
I DID?
YOU SAID YOU HAD TO!
OH, RIGHT. I NEEDED TO STAY AWAY FROM YUKARI.
HUH ?!
...
HM?
BUT WHY WAS THAT?
TAKAMURA'S SPELL ON SATOMI HAS DISAPPEARED.
SATOMI...
...HAS LOST HIS MEMORIES...
...OF HIS PAST LIFE.
YUMURASAKI AND KAZUMA...
...ARE NO LONGER BOUND TOGETHER.
SATOMI NO LONGER FEELS...
...AS IF HE HAS KNOWN ME...
...FOR A LONG TIME.

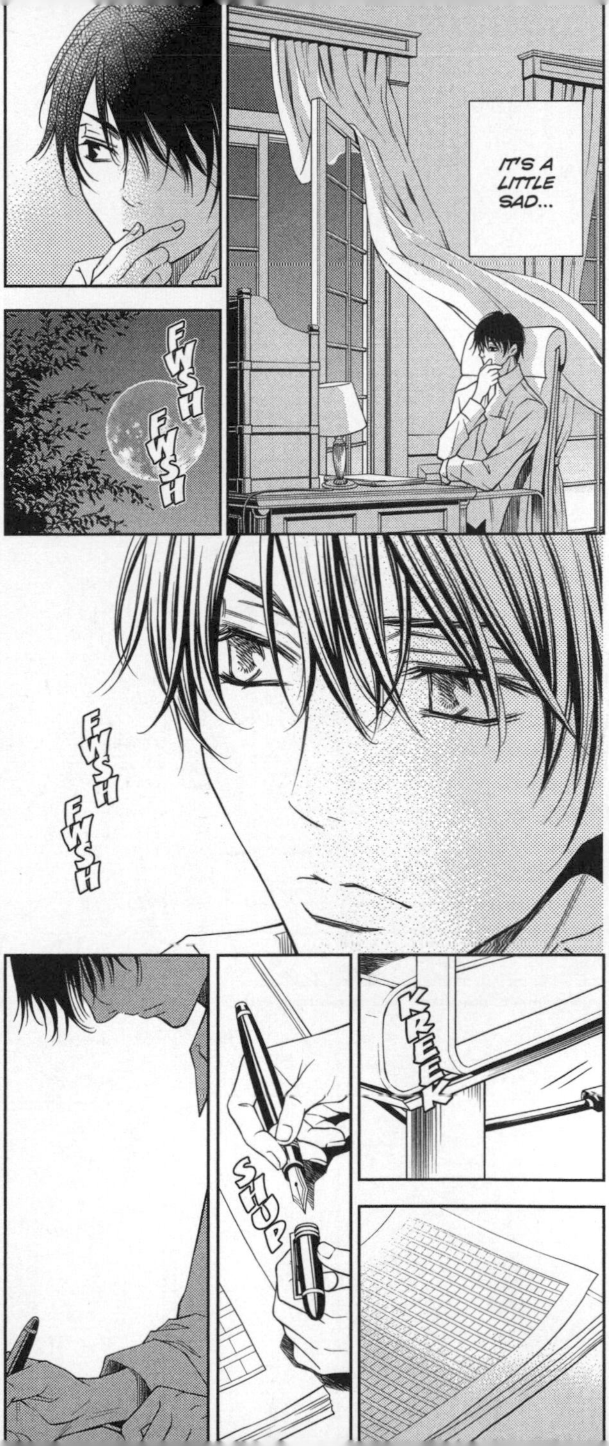
IT'S A LITTLE SAD...
FWSH
FWSH
FWSH
FWSH
KREEK
SHUP

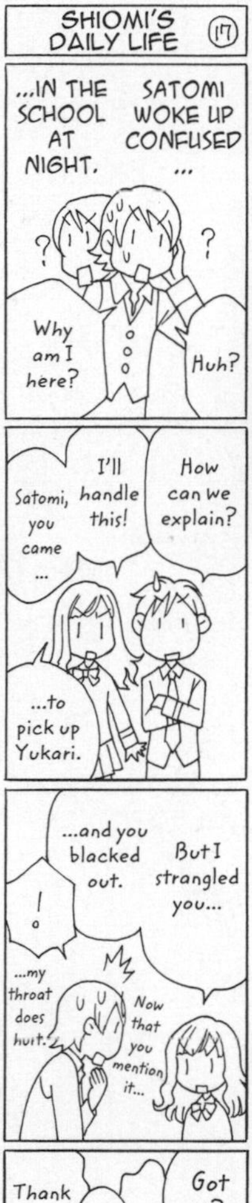
SHIOMI'S DAILY LIFE 17
SATOMI WOKE UP CONFUSED ...
...IN THE SCHOOL AT NIGHT.
?
?
Huh?
Why am I here?
How can we explain?
I'll handle this!
Satomi, you came ...
...to pick up Yukari.
But I strangled you...
...and you blacked out.
!
Now that you mention it...
...my throat does hurt.
Got it?
...
Here are your glasses.
Thank you...
Okay, bye.
That made sense?!

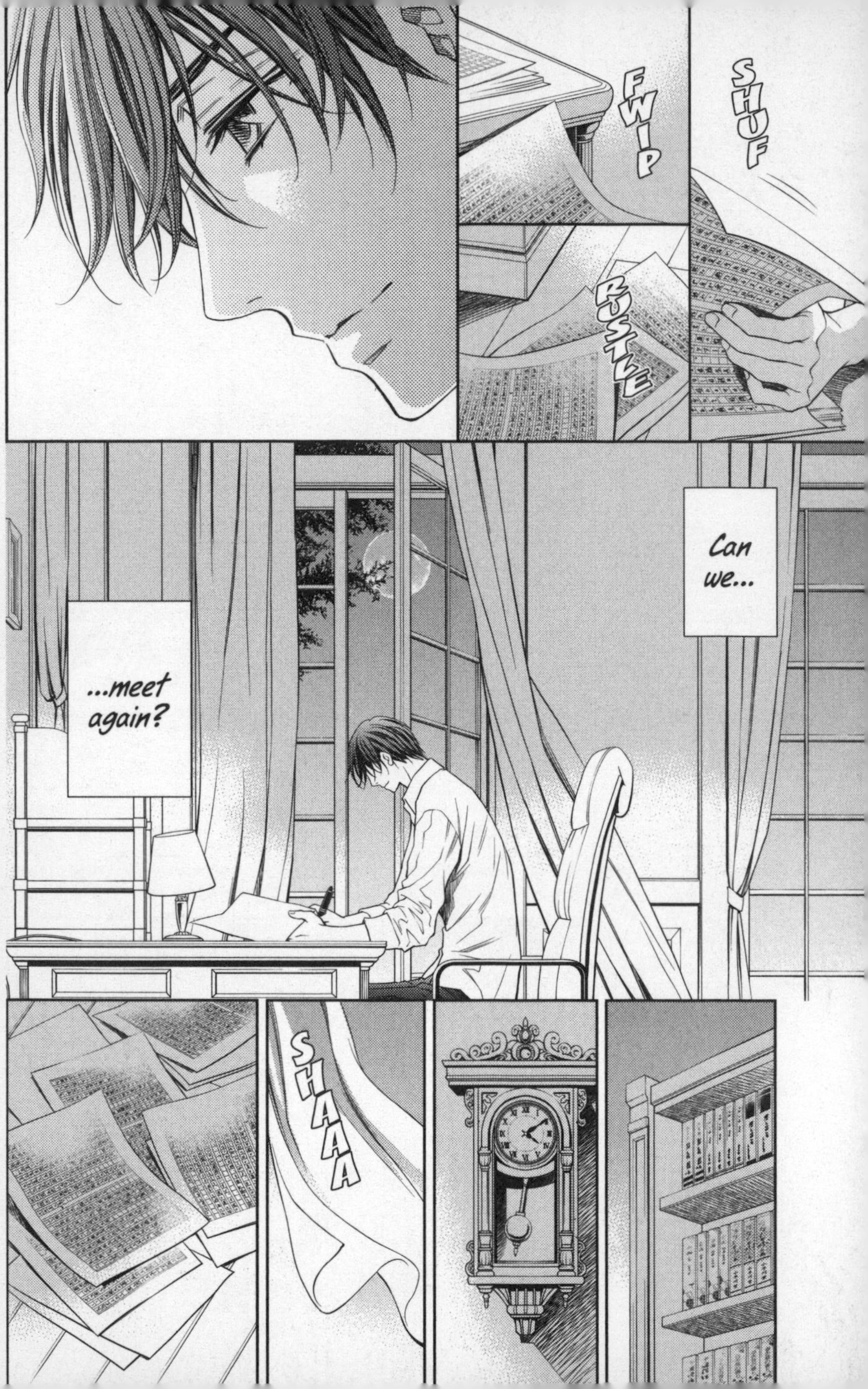
SHUF
FWIP
RUSTLE
Can we...
...meet again?
SHAAA

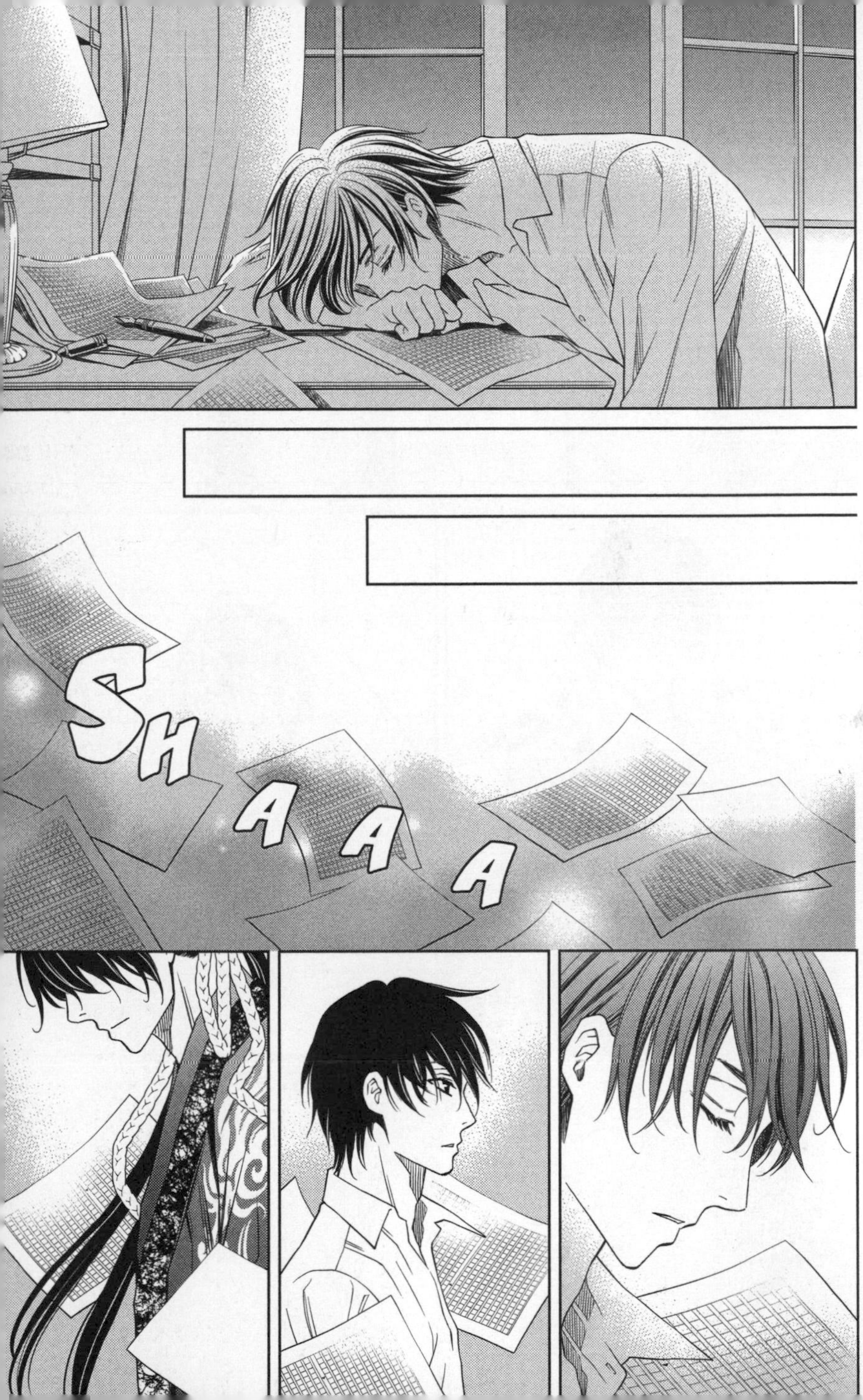
SHAAAA

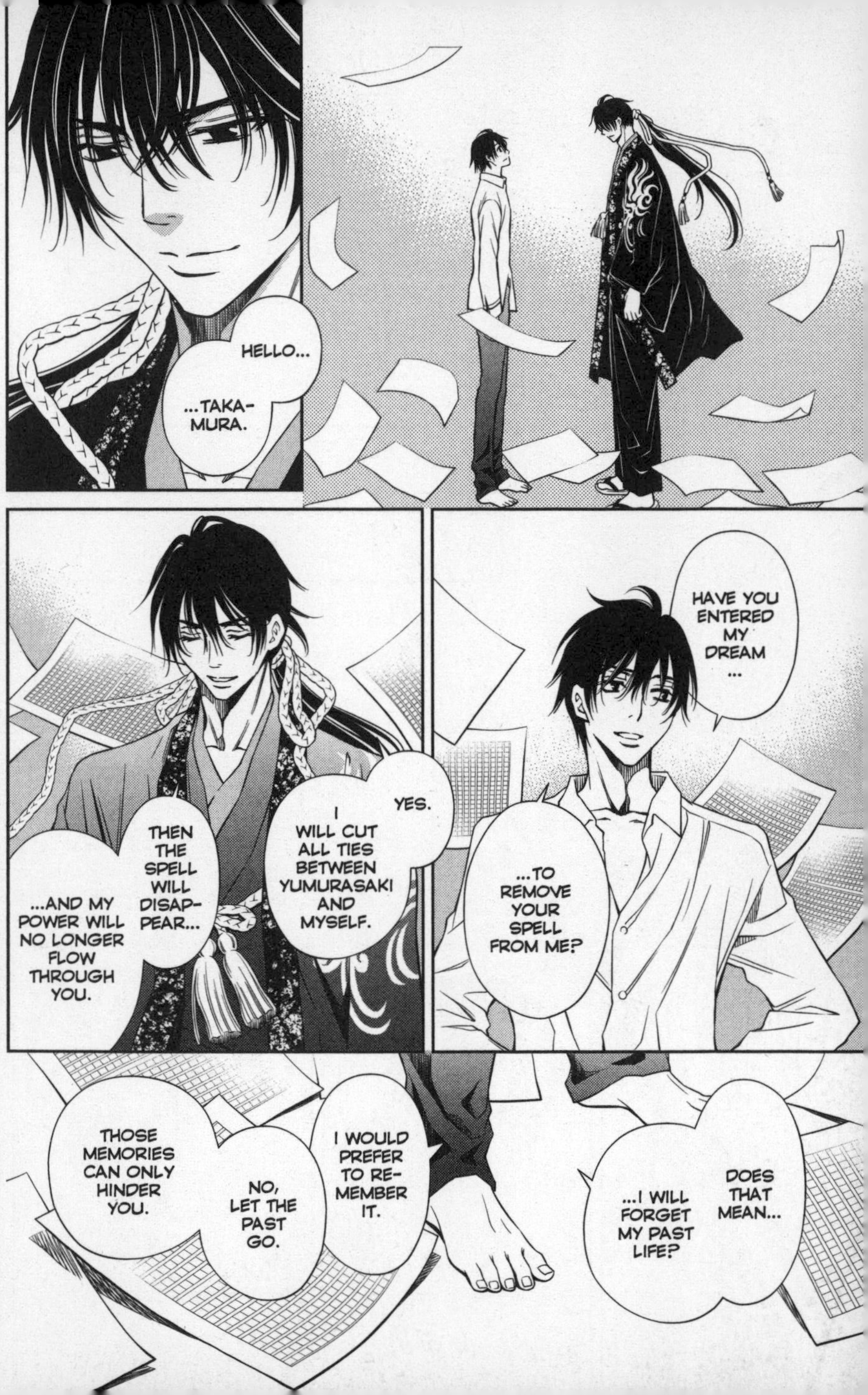
HELLO...
...TAKA-MURA.
HAVE YOU ENTERED MY DREAM ...
...TO REMOVE YOUR SPELL FROM ME?
YES.
I WILL CUT ALL TIES BETWEEN YUMURASAKI AND MYSELF.
THEN THE SPELL WILL DISAP-PEAR...
...AND MY POWER WILL NO LONGER FLOW THROUGH YOU.
DOES THAT MEAN...
...I WILL FORGET MY PAST LIFE?
I WOULD PREFER TO RE-MEMBER IT.
NO, LET THE PAST GO.
THOSE MEMORIES CAN ONLY HINDER YOU.

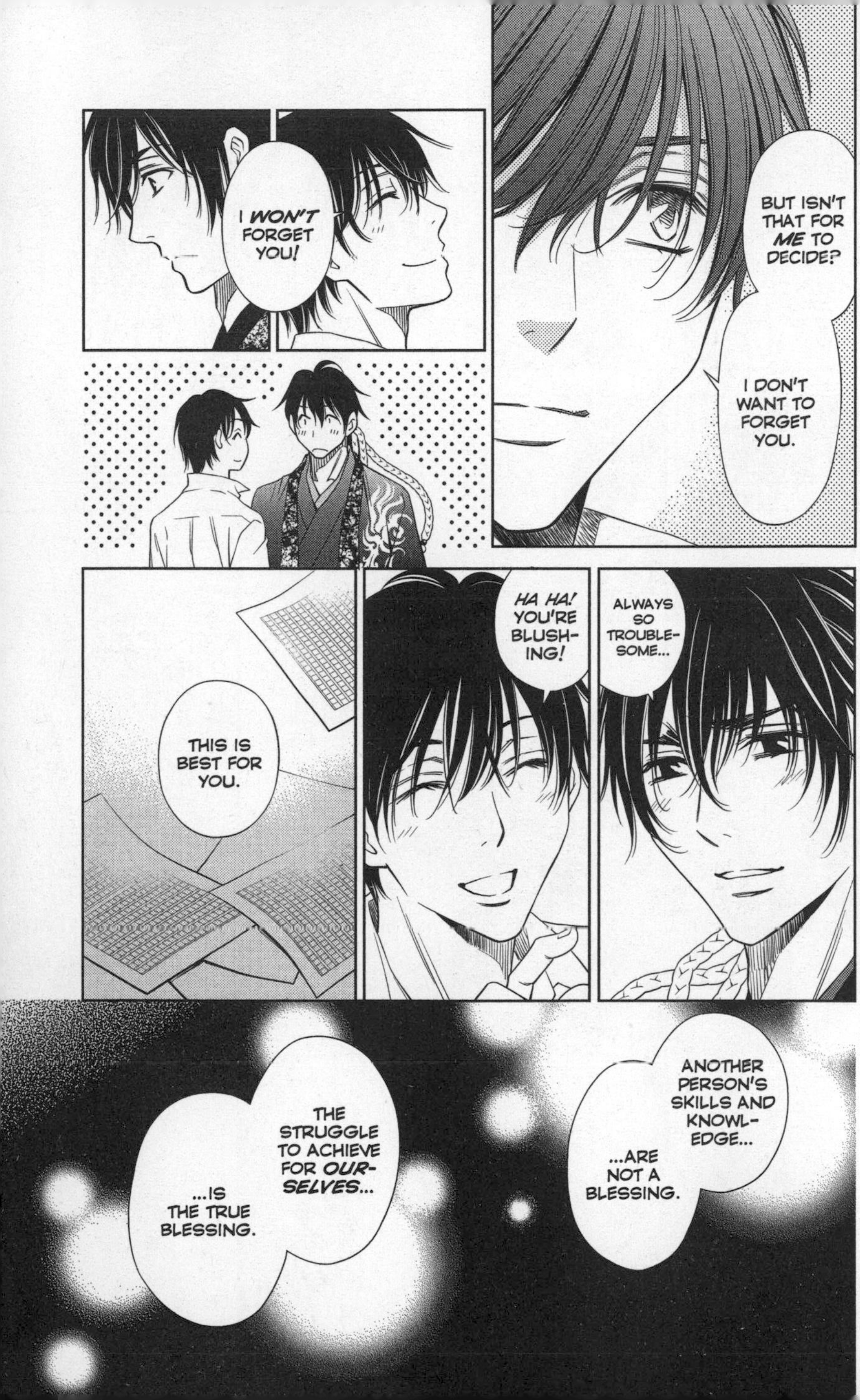
BUT ISN'T THAT FOR *ME* TO DECIDE?
I DON'T WANT TO FORGET YOU.
I *WON'T* FORGET YOU!
ALWAYS SO TROUBLE-SOME...
HA HA! YOU'RE BLUSH-ING*!*
THIS IS BEST FOR YOU.
ANOTHER PERSON'S SKILLS AND KNOWL-EDGE...
...ARE NOT A BLESSING.
THE STRUGGLE TO ACHIEVE FOR *OUR-SELVES*...
...IS THE TRUE BLESSING.

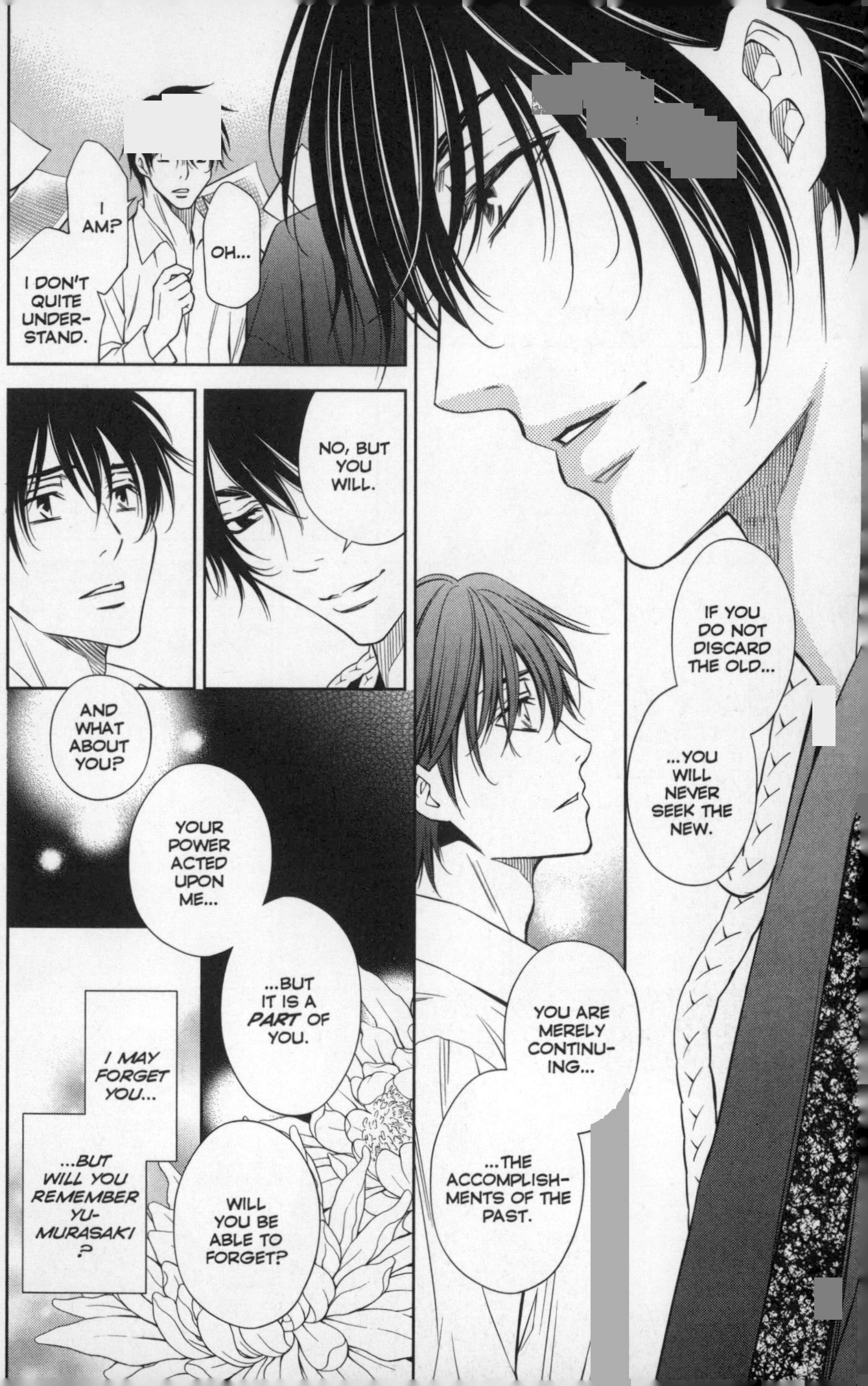
IF YOU DO NOT DISCARD THE OLD...
...YOU WILL NEVER SEEK THE NEW.
YOU ARE MERELY CONTINUING...
...THE ACCOMPLISHMENTS OF THE PAST.
OH...
I AM?
I DON'T QUITE UNDERSTAND.
NO, BUT YOU WILL.
AND WHAT ABOUT YOU?
YOUR POWER ACTED UPON ME...
...BUT IT IS A *PART* OF YOU.
WILL YOU BE ABLE TO FORGET?
I MAY FORGET YOU...
...BUT WILL YOU REMEMBER YU-MURASAKI?

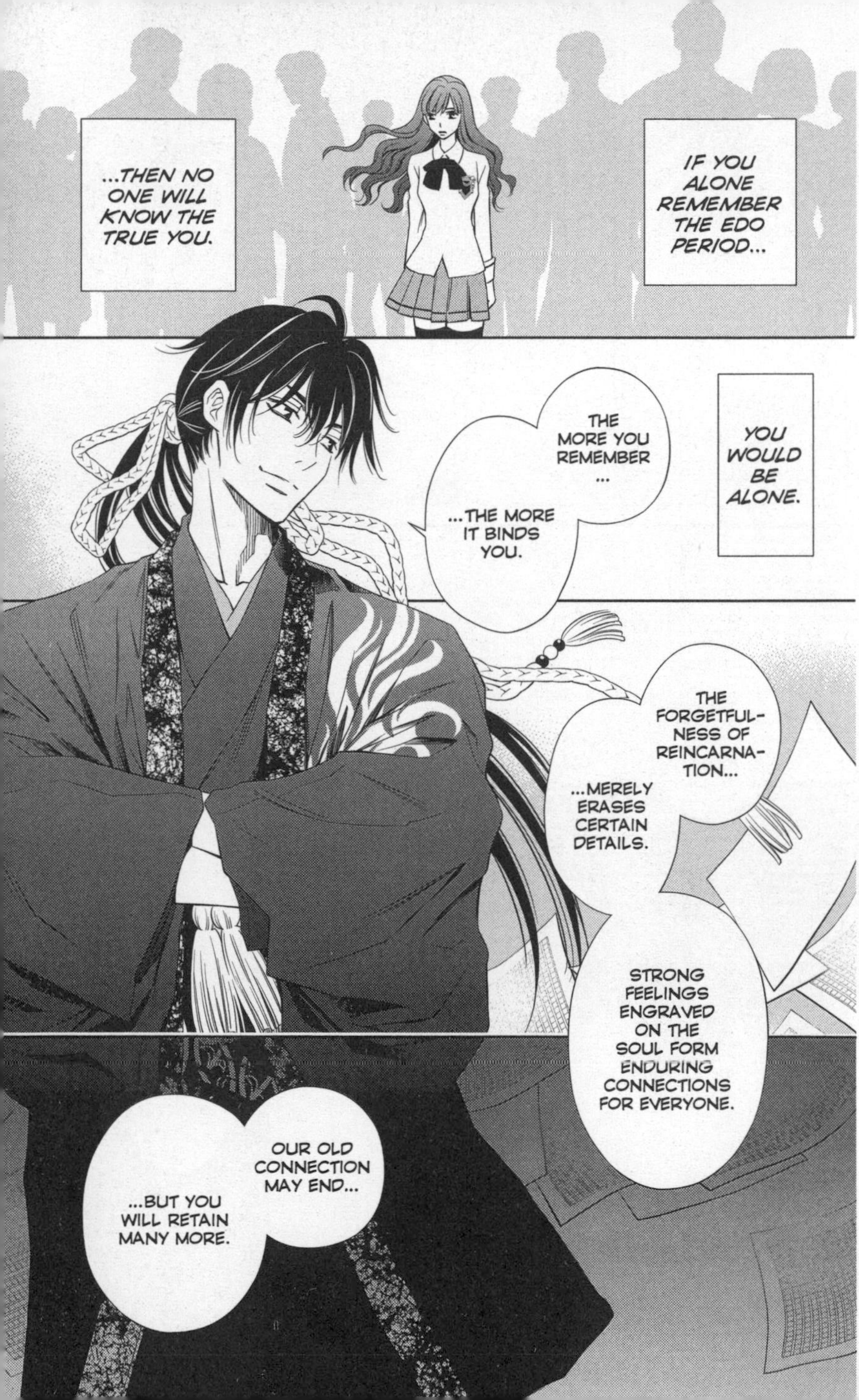
IF YOU ALONE REMEMBER THE EDO PERIOD...
...THEN NO ONE WILL KNOW THE TRUE YOU.
YOU WOULD BE ALONE.
THE MORE YOU REMEMBER ...
...THE MORE IT BINDS YOU.
THE FORGETFUL-NESS OF REINCARNA-TION...
...MERELY ERASES CERTAIN DETAILS.
STRONG FEELINGS ENGRAVED ON THE SOUL FORM ENDURING CONNECTIONS FOR EVERYONE.
OUR OLD CONNECTION MAY END...
...BUT YOU WILL RETAIN MANY MORE.

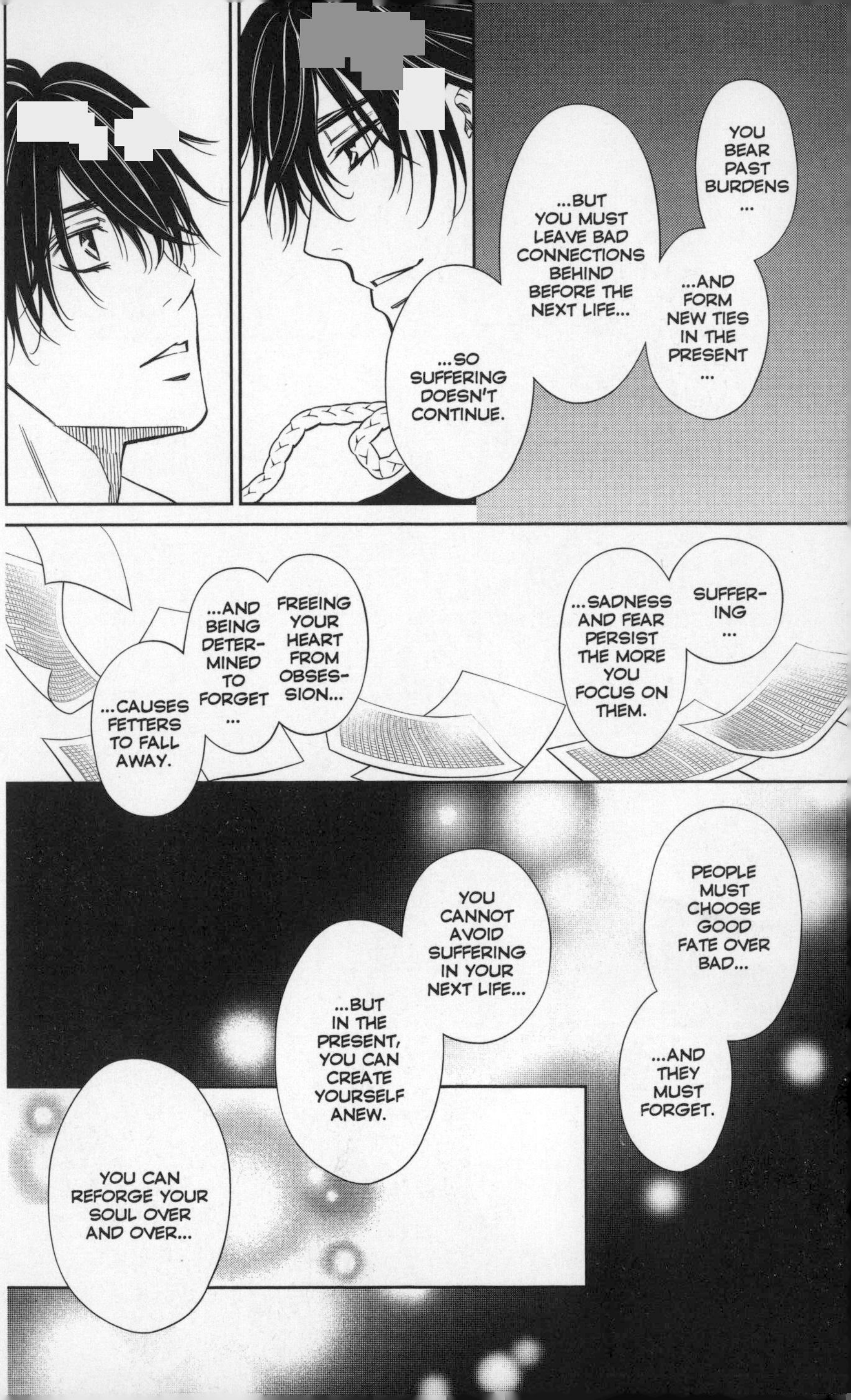
YOU BEAR PAST BURDENS...
...AND FORM NEW TIES IN THE PRESENT...
...BUT YOU MUST LEAVE BAD CONNECTIONS BEHIND BEFORE THE NEXT LIFE...
...SO SUFFERING DOESN'T CONTINUE.
SUFFERING...
...SADNESS AND FEAR PERSIST THE MORE YOU FOCUS ON THEM.
FREEING YOUR HEART FROM OBSESSION...
...AND BEING DETERMINED TO FORGET...
...CAUSES FETTERS TO FALL AWAY.
PEOPLE MUST CHOOSE GOOD FATE OVER BAD...
...AND THEY MUST FORGET.
YOU CANNOT AVOID SUFFERING IN YOUR NEXT LIFE...
...BUT IN THE PRESENT, YOU CAN CREATE YOURSELF ANEW.
YOU CAN REFORGE YOUR SOUL OVER AND OVER...

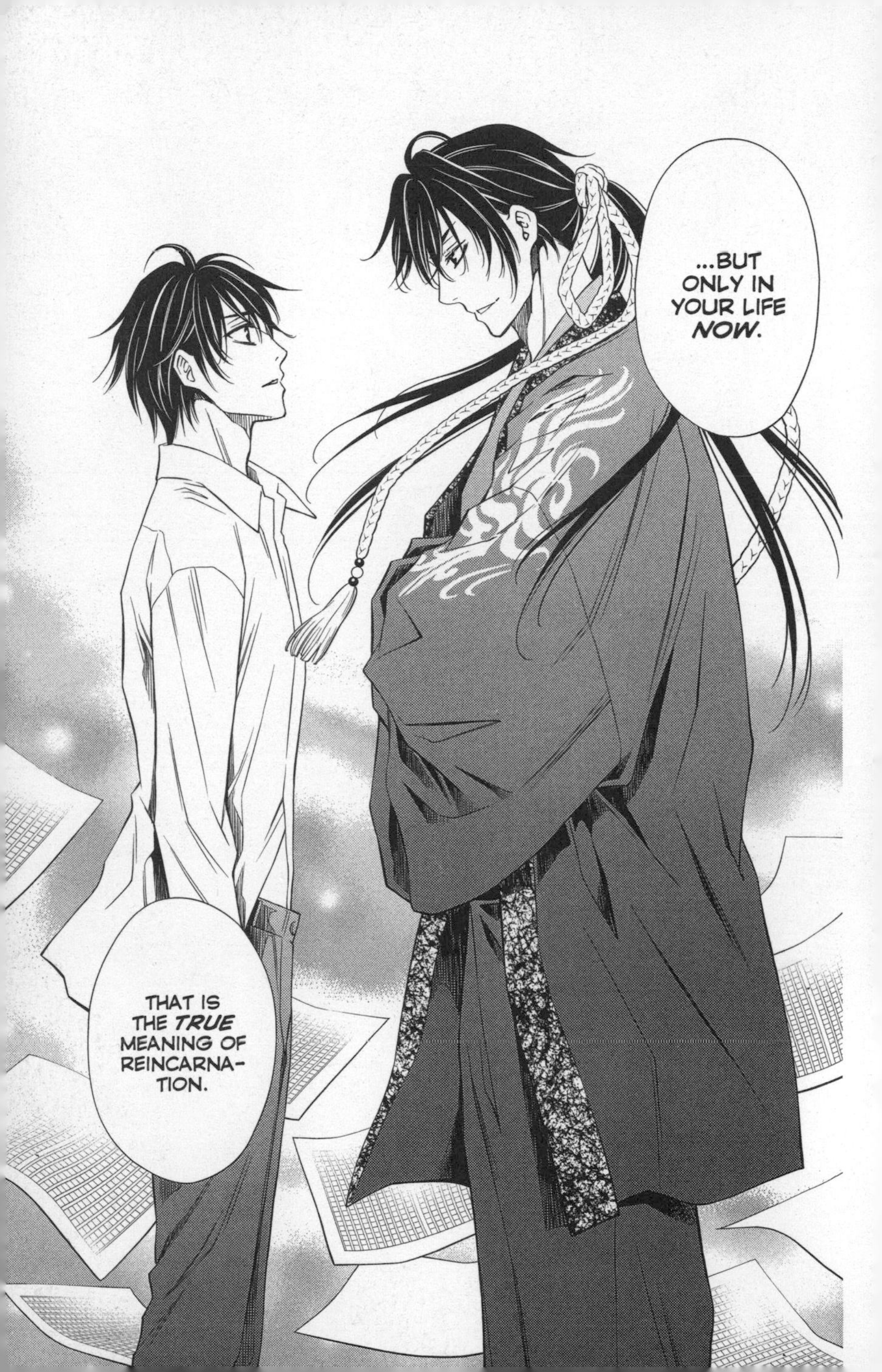
...BUT ONLY IN YOUR LIFE *NOW*.
THAT IS THE *TRUE* MEANING OF REINCARNA- TION.

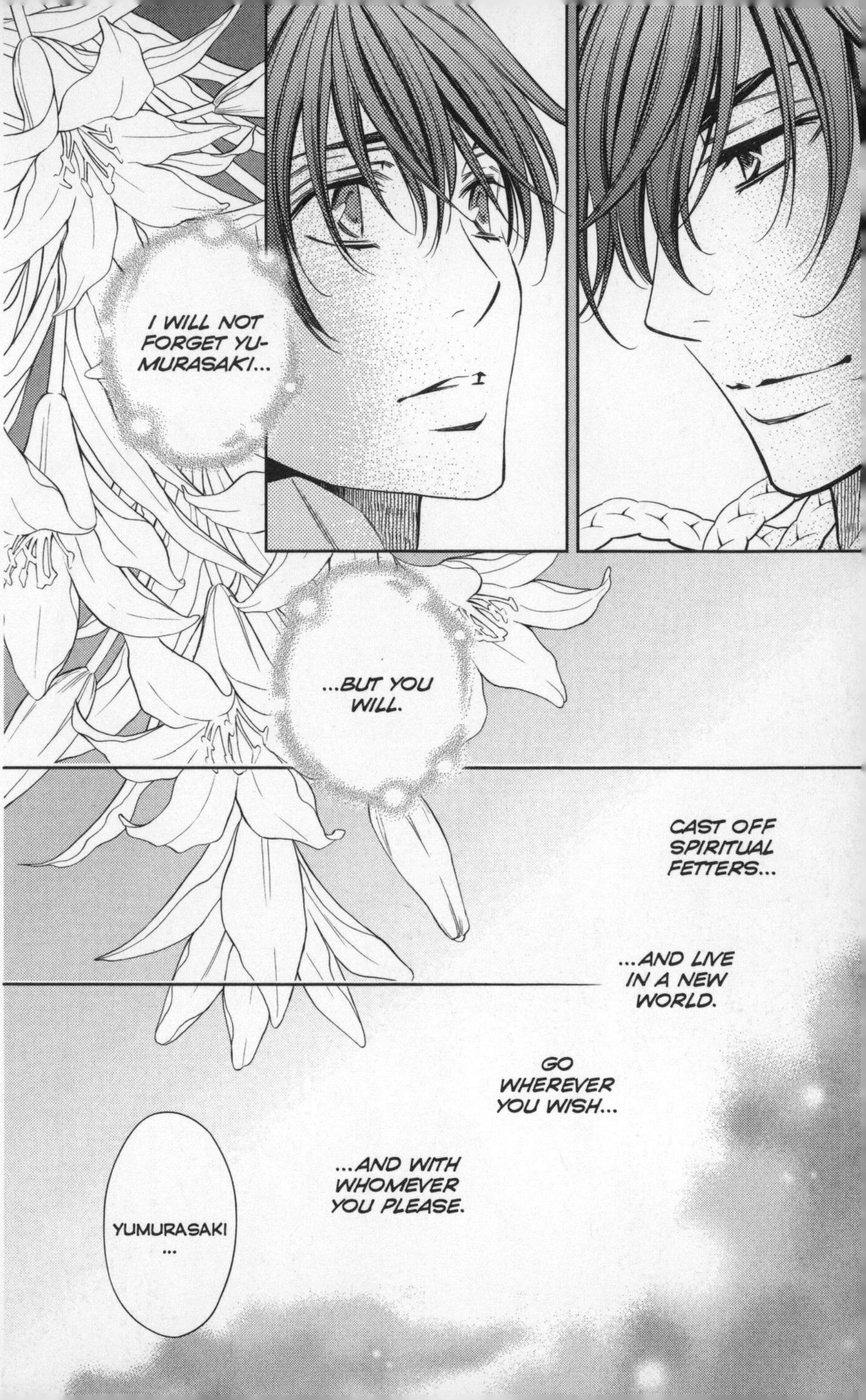
I WILL NOT FORGET YU-MURASAKI...
...BUT YOU WILL.
CAST OFF SPIRITUAL FETTERS...
...AND LIVE IN A NEW WORLD.
GO WHEREVER YOU WISH...
...AND WITH WHOMEVER YOU PLEASE.
YUMURASAKI ...

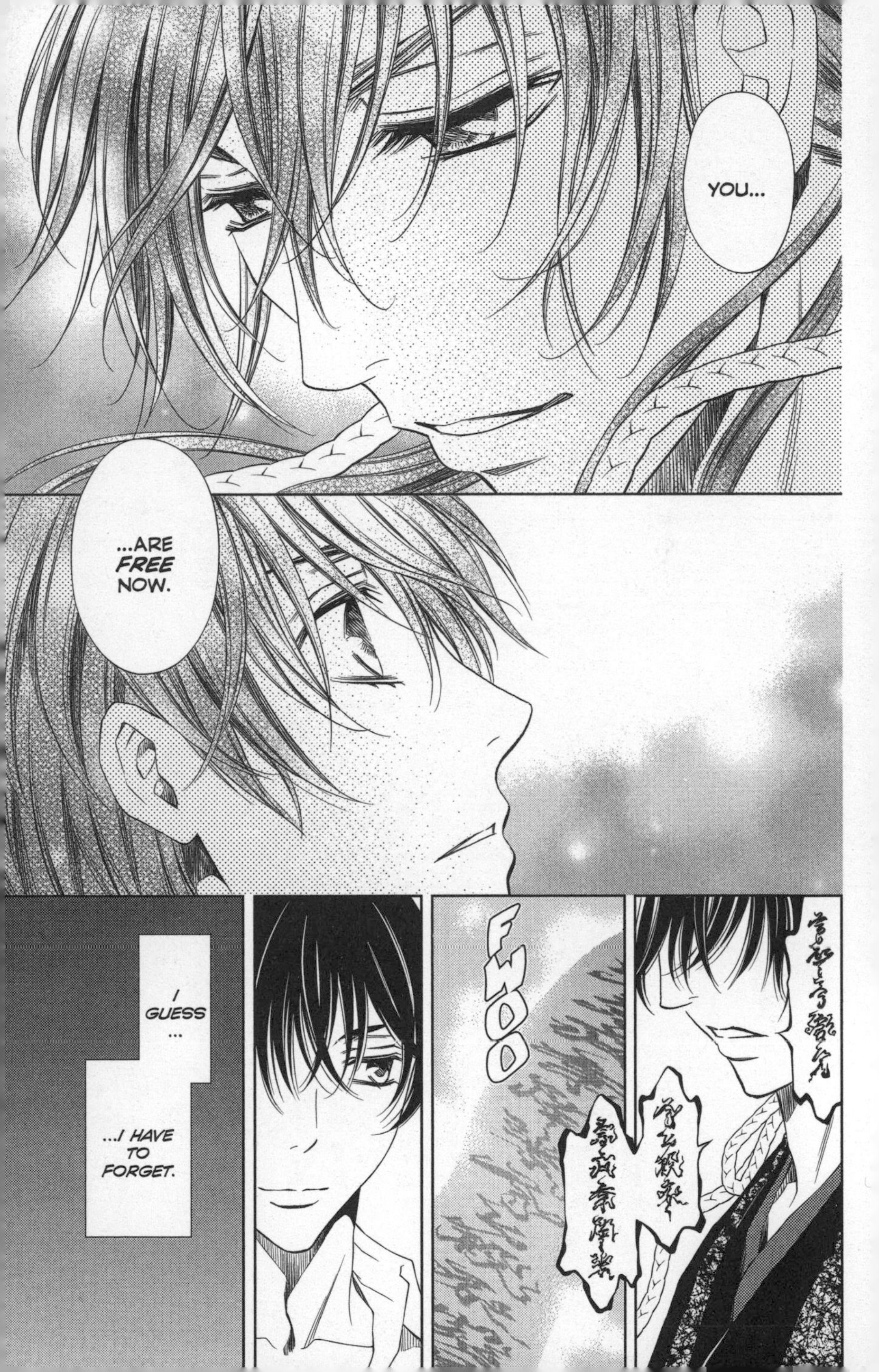
YOU...
...ARE *FREE* NOW.
FWOO
I GUESS ...
...I HAVE TO FORGET.

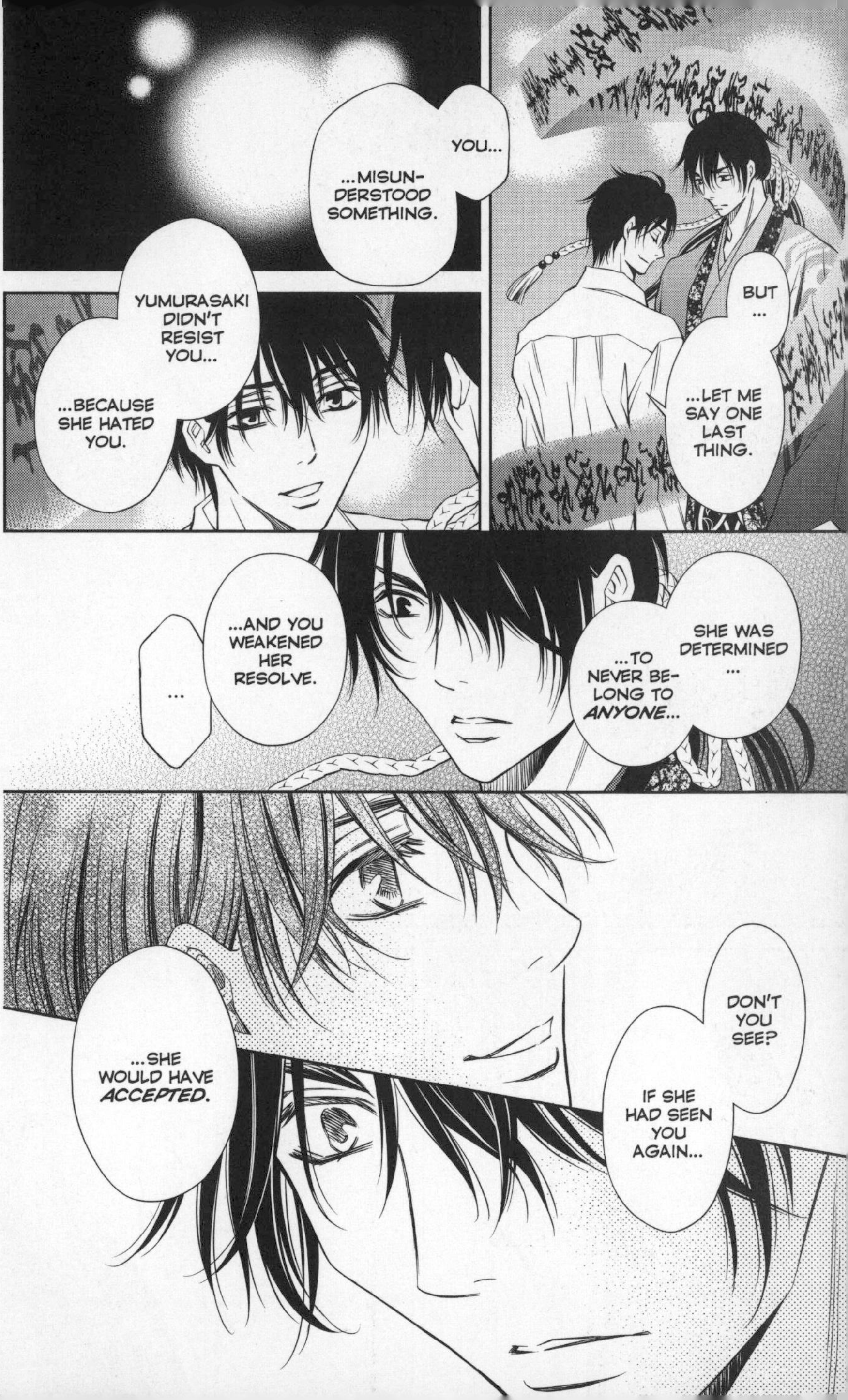
BUT ...
...LET ME SAY ONE LAST THING.
YOU...
...MISUN-DERSTOOD SOMETHING.
YUMURASAKI DIDN'T RESIST YOU...
...BECAUSE SHE HATED YOU.
SHE WAS DETERMINED ...
...TO NEVER BE-LONG TO *ANYONE*...
...AND YOU WEAKENED HER RESOLVE.
...
DON'T YOU SEE?
IF SHE HAD SEEN YOU AGAIN...
...SHE WOULD HAVE *ACCEPTED*.

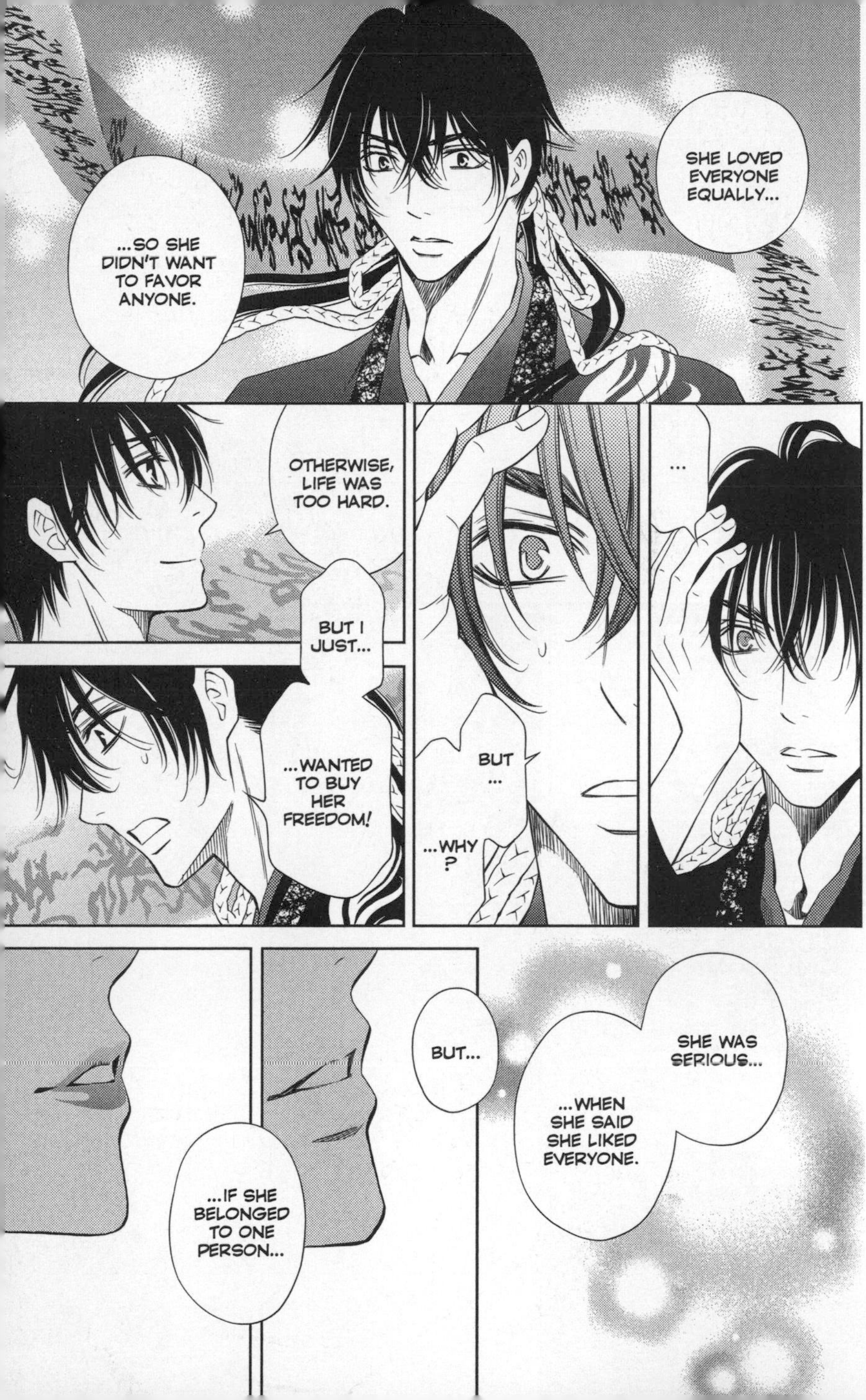
SHE LOVED EVERYONE EQUALLY...
...SO SHE DIDN'T WANT TO FAVOR ANYONE.
...
BUT ...
...WHY ?
OTHERWISE, LIFE WAS TOO HARD.
BUT I JUST...
...WANTED TO BUY HER FREEDOM!
SHE WAS SERIOUS...
...WHEN SHE SAID SHE LIKED EVERYONE.
BUT...
...IF SHE BELONGED TO ONE PERSON...

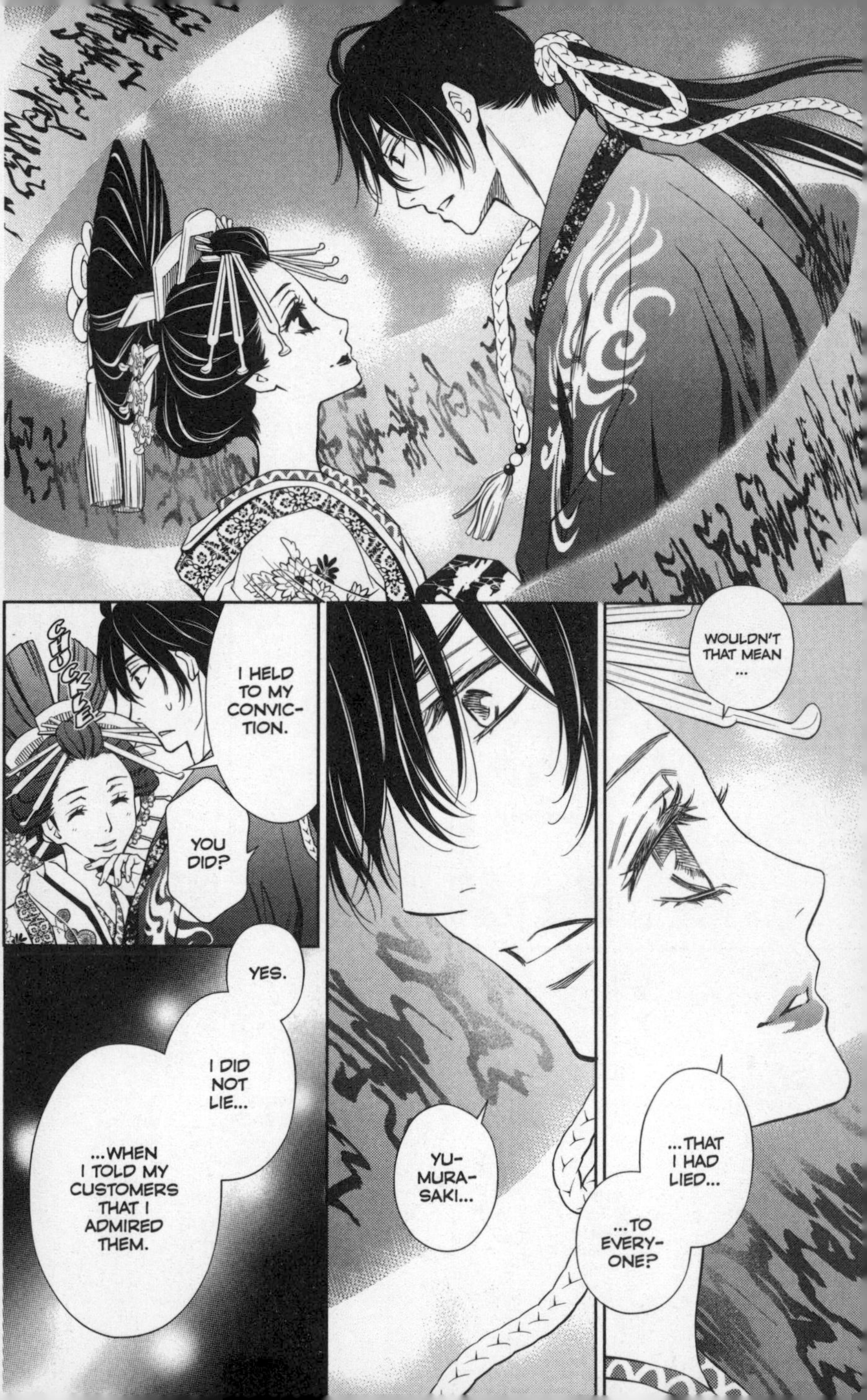
WOULDN'T THAT MEAN ...
...THAT I HAD LIED...
...TO EVERY-ONE?
YU-MURA-SAKI...
I HELD TO MY CONVIC-TION.
CHUCKLE
YOU DID?
YES.
I DID NOT LIE...
...WHEN I TOLD MY CUSTOMERS THAT I ADMIRED THEM.

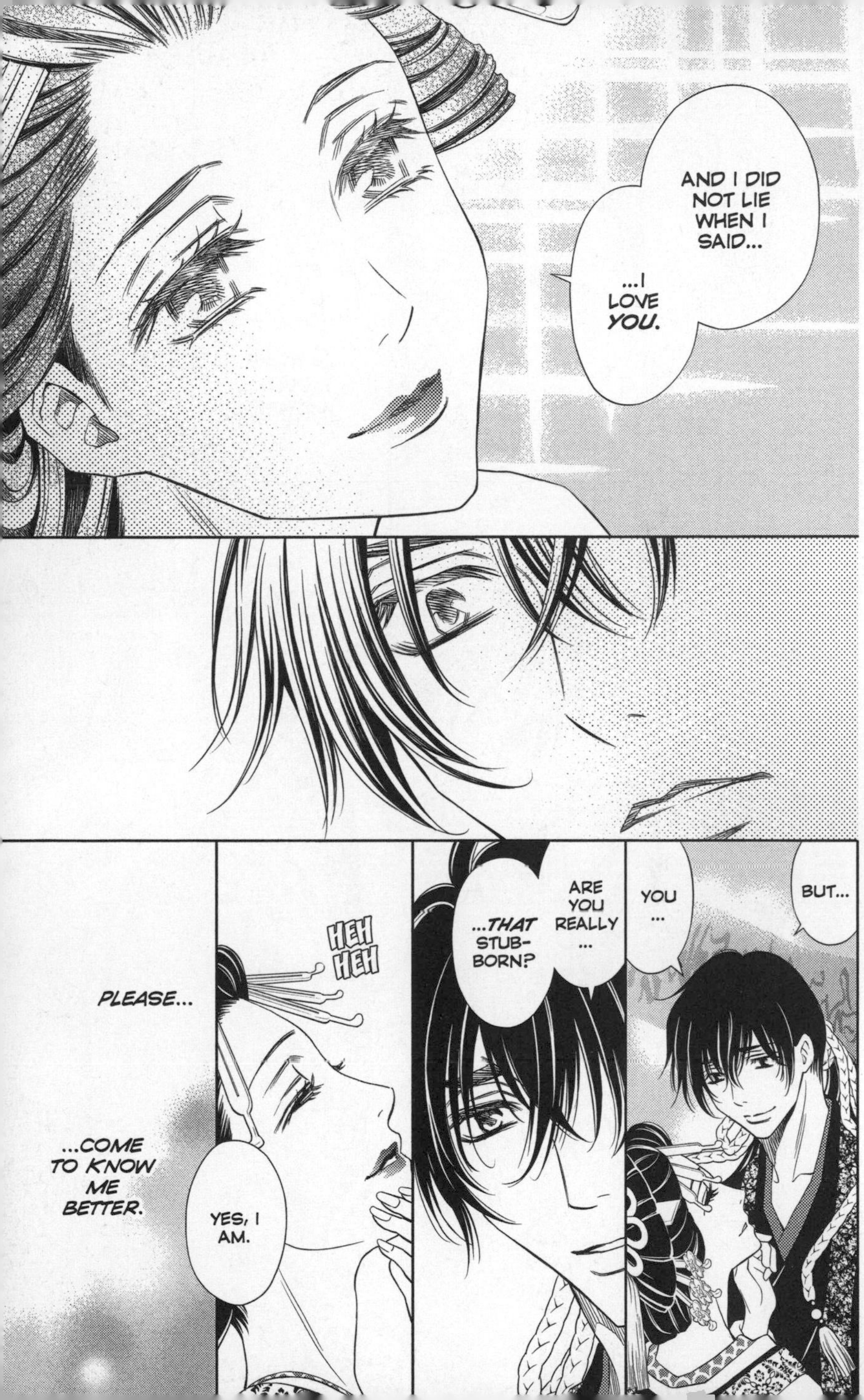
AND I DID NOT LIE WHEN I SAID...
...I LOVE *YOU*.
BUT...
YOU ...
ARE YOU REALLY ...
...*THAT* STUBBORN?
HEH HEH
YES, I AM.
PLEASE...
...COME TO KNOW ME BETTER.

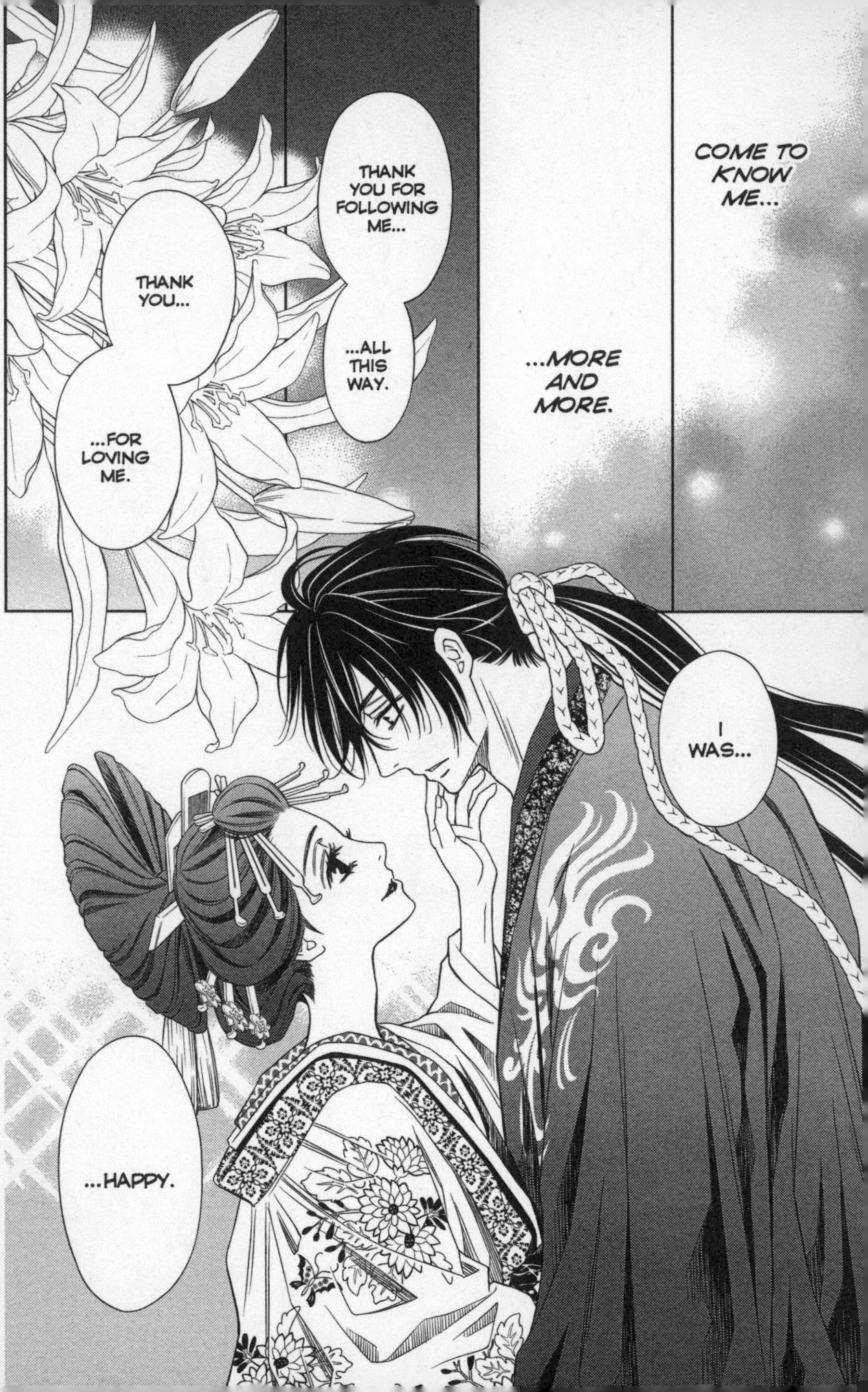
COME TO KNOW ME...
...MORE AND MORE.
THANK YOU FOR FOLLOWING ME...
...ALL THIS WAY.
THANK YOU...
...FOR LOVING ME.
I WAS...
...HAPPY.

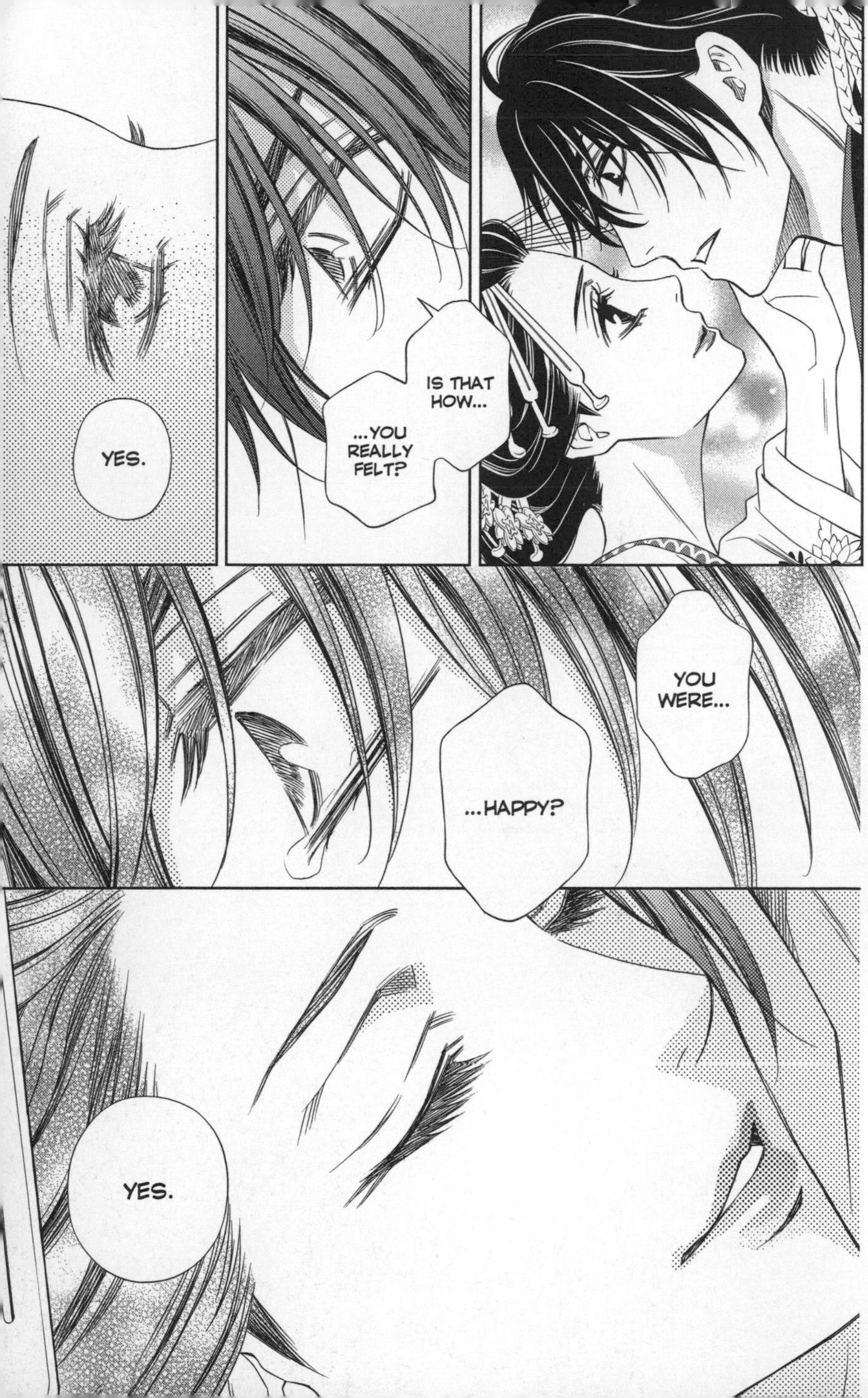
IS THAT HOW... ...YOU REALLY FELT?
YES.
YOU WERE...
...HAPPY?
YES.

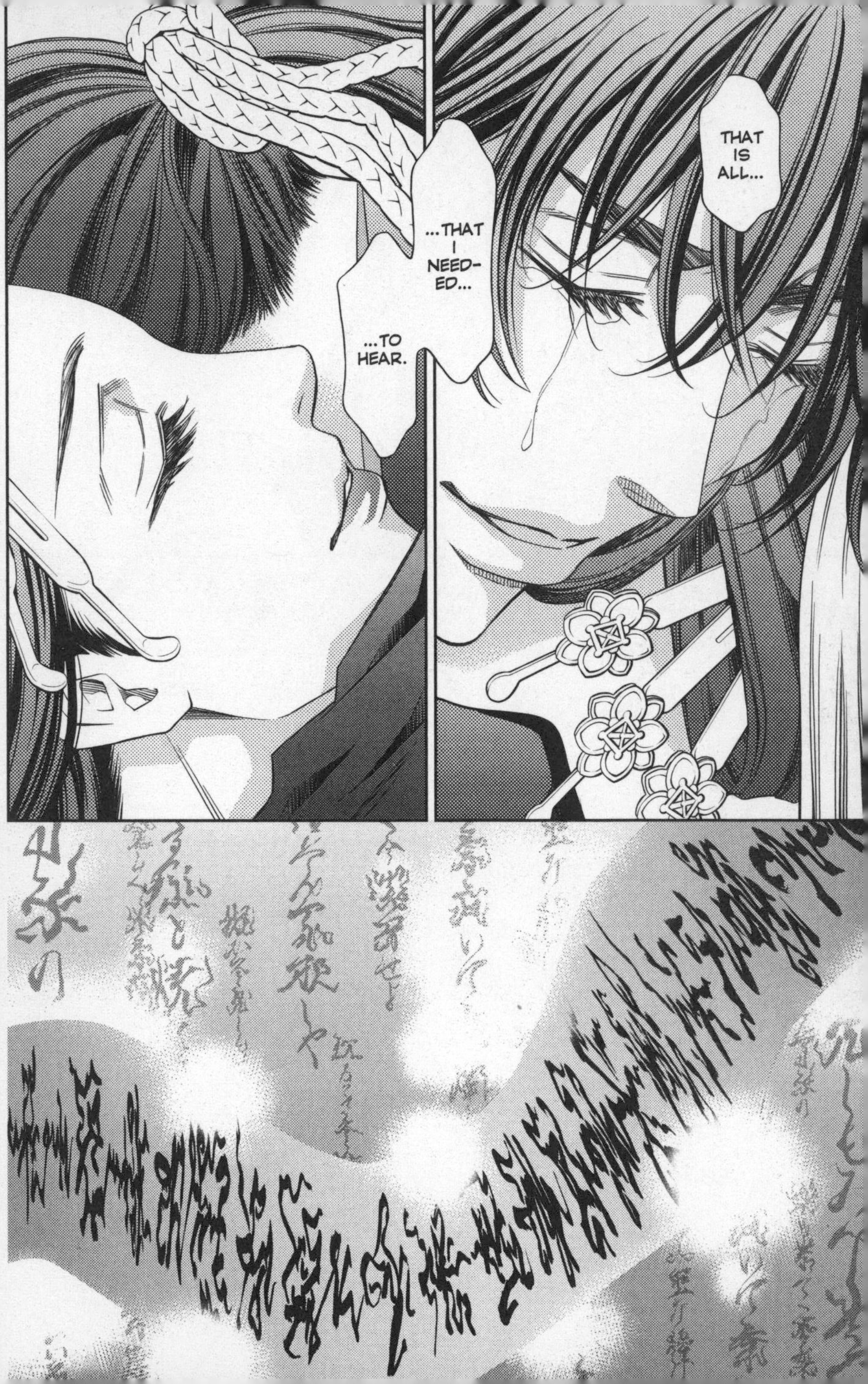
THAT IS ALL...
...THAT I NEEDED...
...TO HEAR.

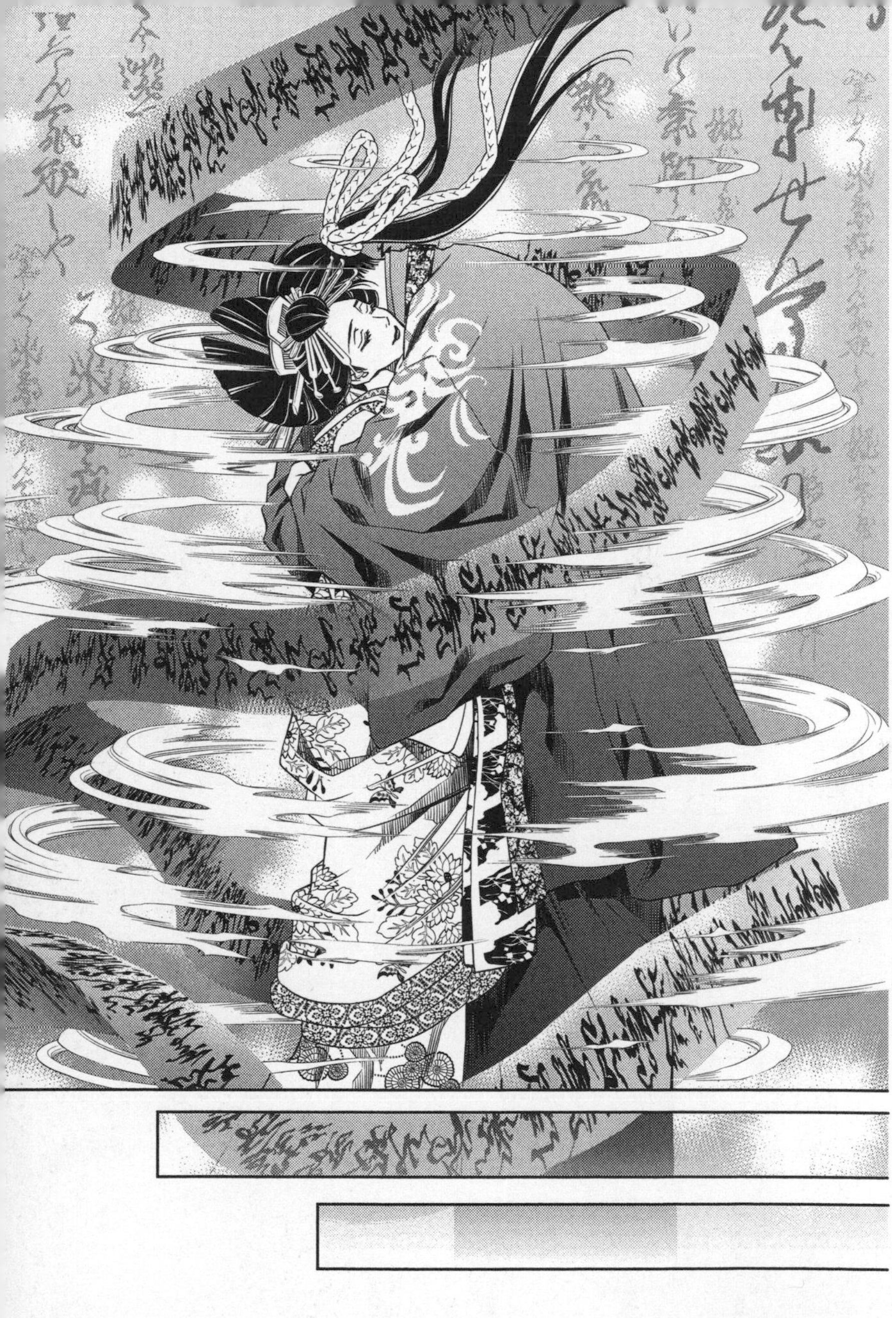

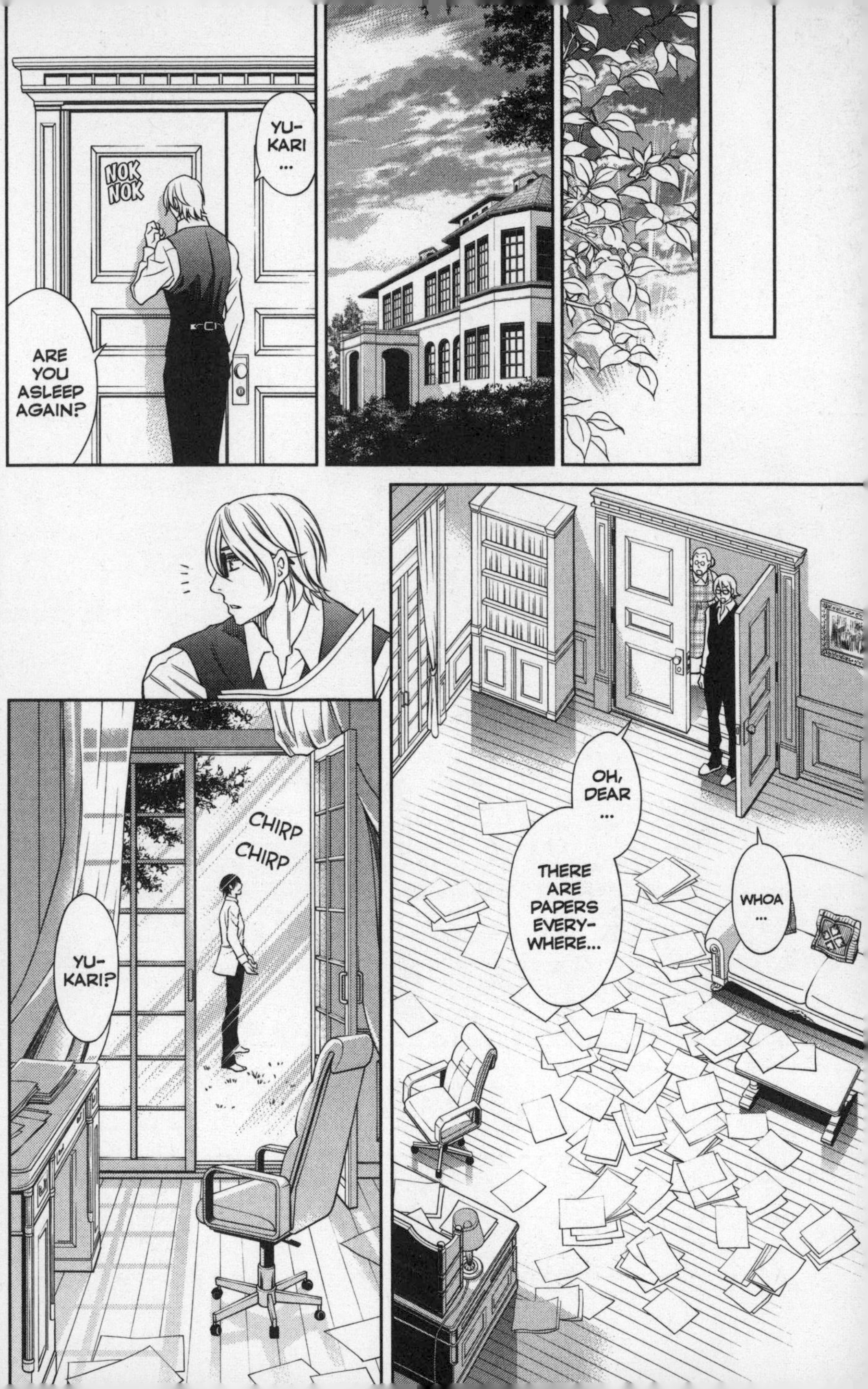
YU-KARI...
NOK NOK
ARE YOU ASLEEP AGAIN?
OH, DEAR...
THERE ARE PAPERS EVERYWHERE...
WHOA...
CHIRP CHIRP
YU-KARI?

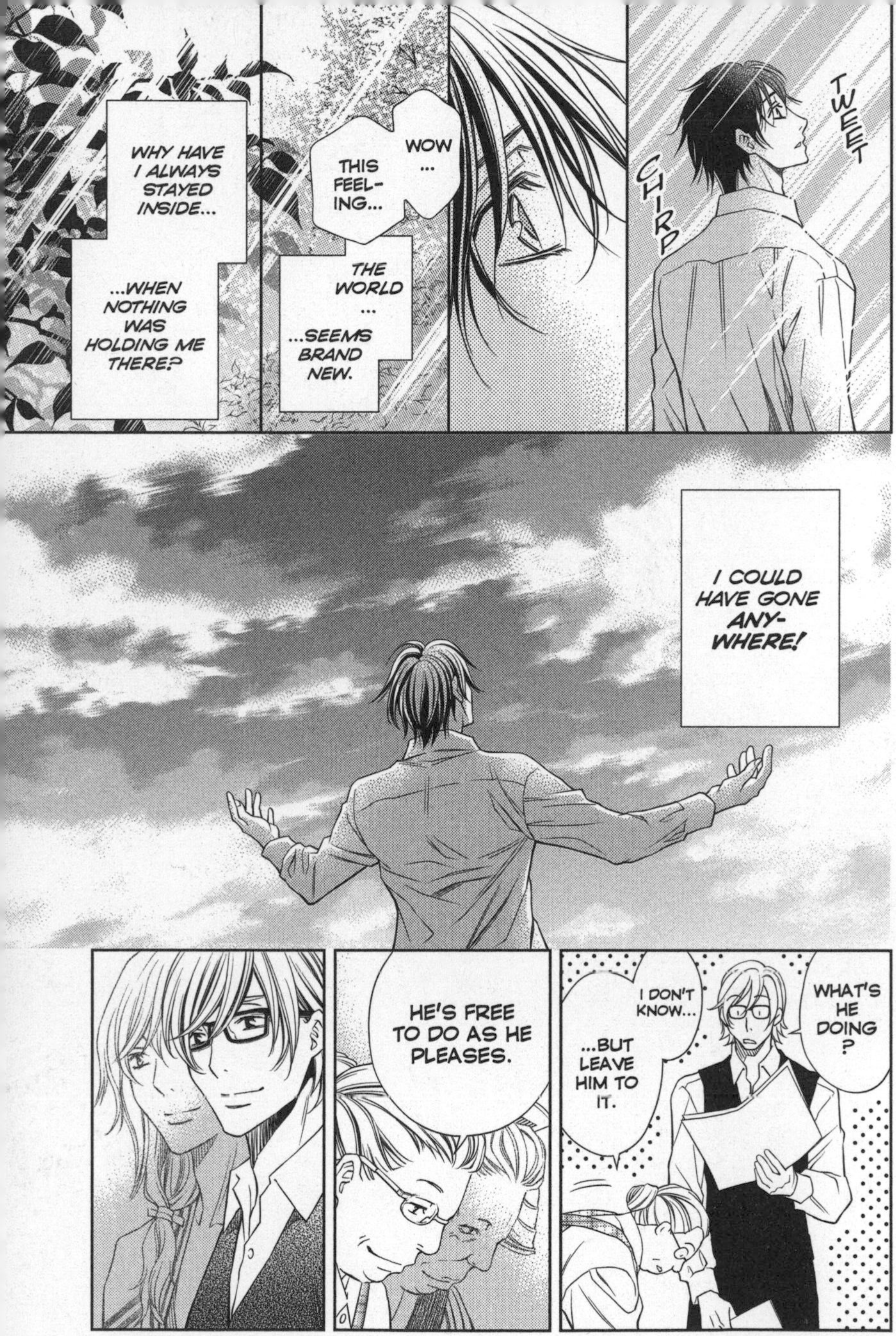
TWEET
CHIRP
WOW...
THIS FEEL-ING...
THE WORLD...
...SEEMS BRAND NEW.
WHY HAVE I ALWAYS STAYED INSIDE...
...WHEN NOTHING WAS HOLDING ME THERE?
I COULD HAVE GONE ANY-WHERE!
WHAT'S HE DOING?
I DON'T KNOW...
...BUT LEAVE HIM TO IT.
HE'S FREE TO DO AS HE PLEASES.

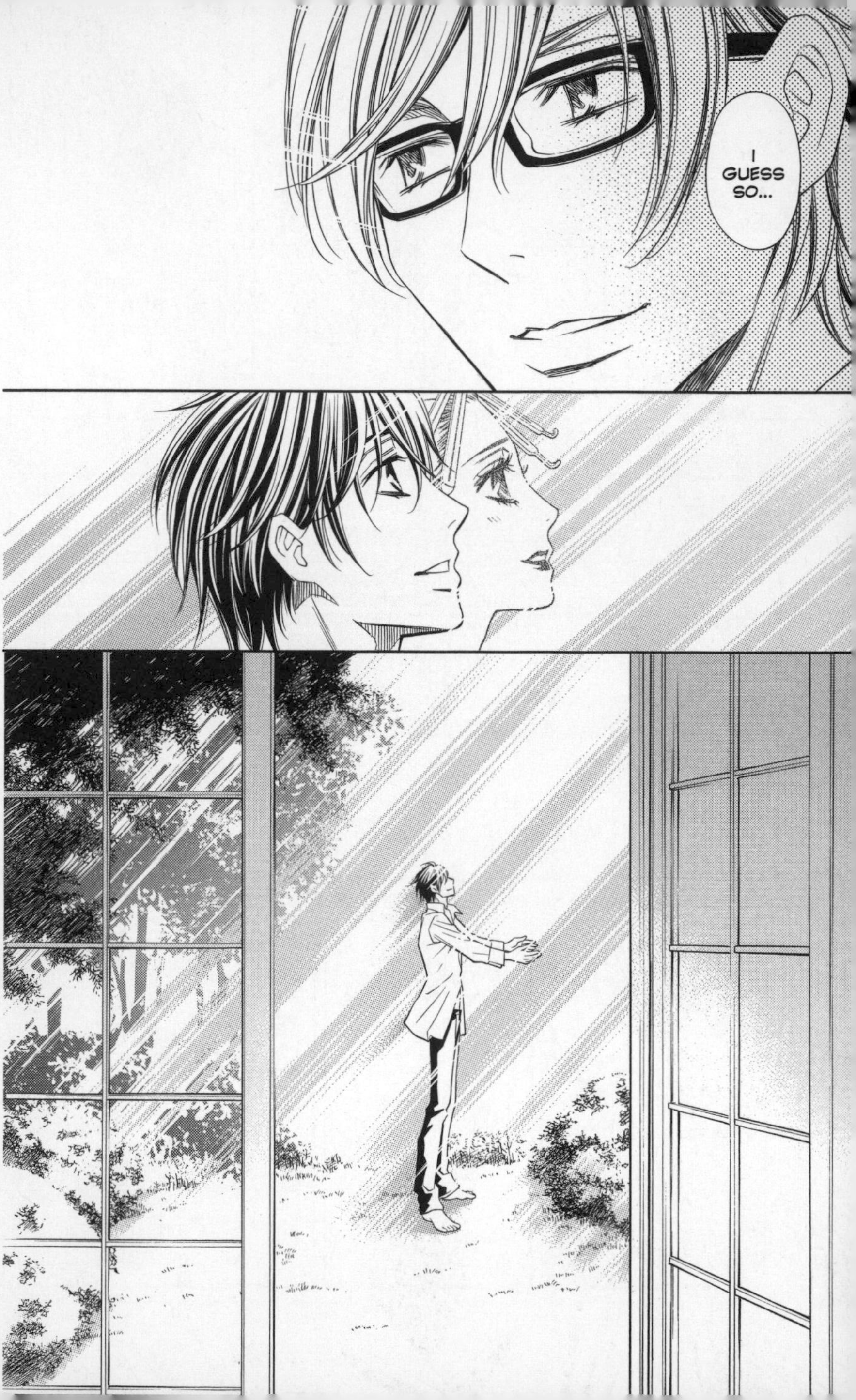
I GUESS SO...

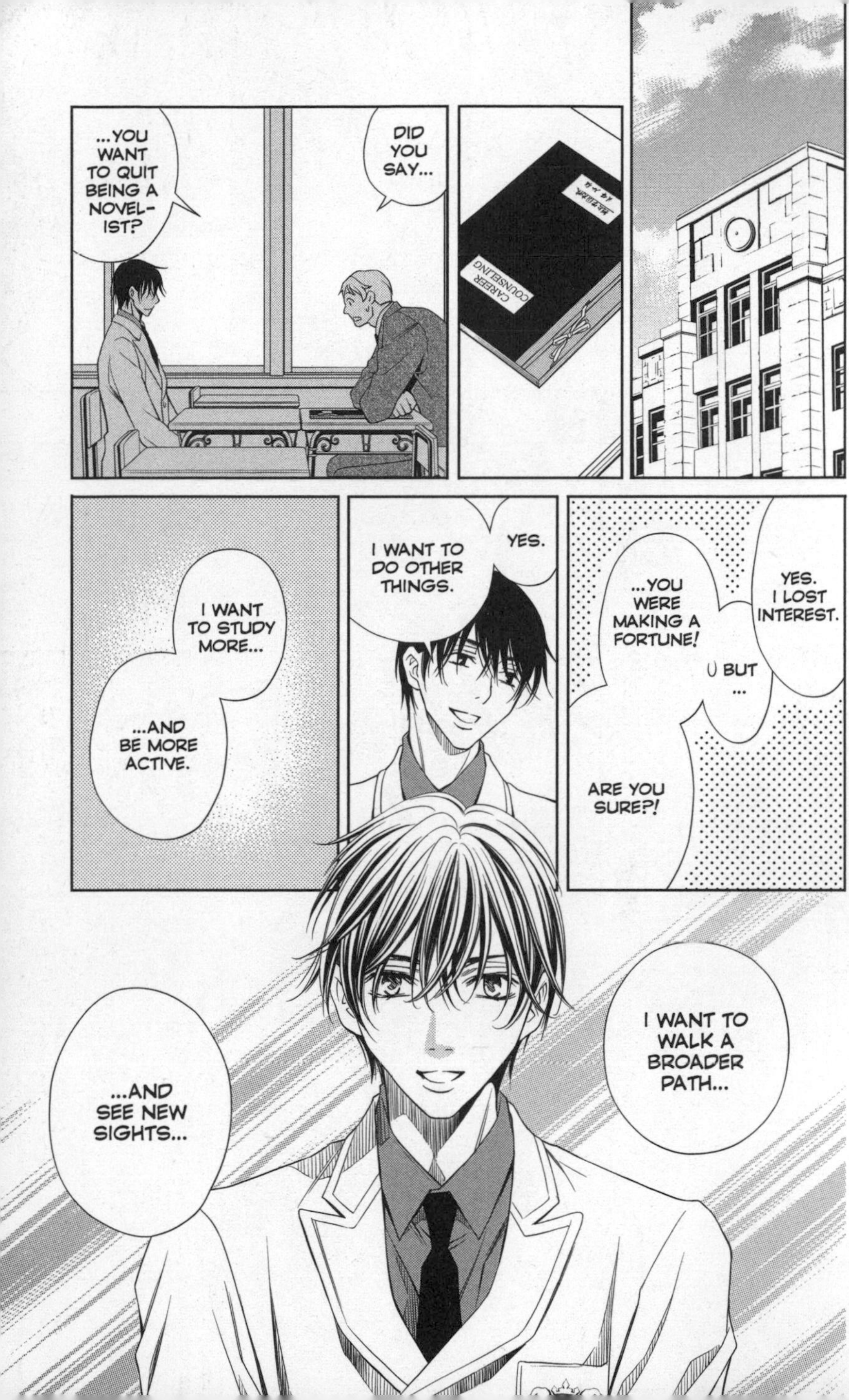
CAREER COUNSELING
DID YOU SAY...
...YOU WANT TO QUIT BEING A NOVELIST?
YES. I LOST INTEREST.
BUT ...
...YOU WERE MAKING A FORTUNE!
ARE YOU SURE?!
YES.
I WANT TO DO OTHER THINGS.
I WANT TO STUDY MORE...
...AND BE MORE ACTIVE.
I WANT TO WALK A BROADER PATH...
...AND SEE NEW SIGHTS...

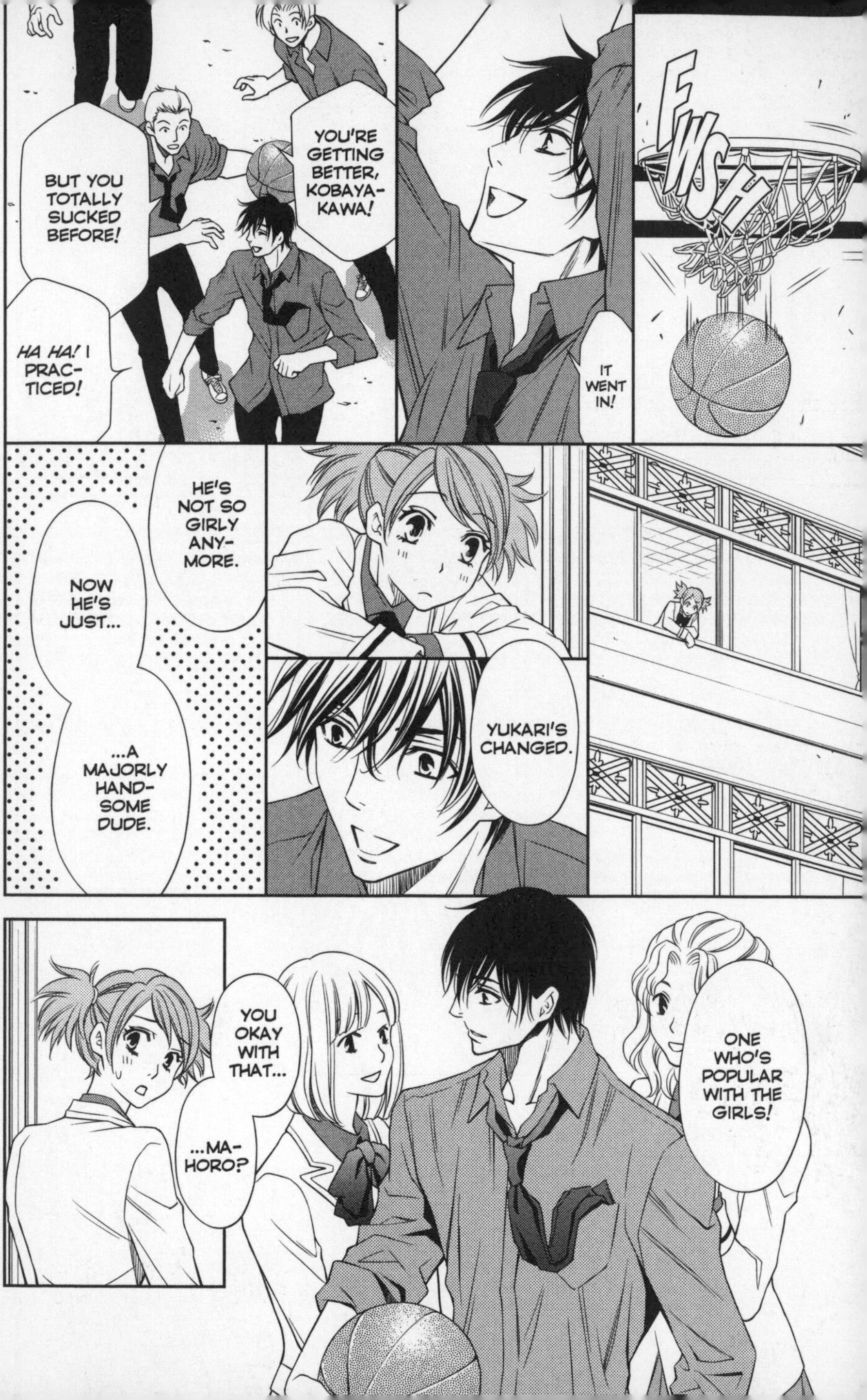
FWSH
IT WENT IN!
YOU'RE GETTING BETTER, KOBAYAKAWA!
BUT YOU TOTALLY SUCKED BEFORE!
HA HA! I PRACTICED!
HE'S NOT SO GIRLY ANYMORE.
YUKARI'S CHANGED.
NOW HE'S JUST...
...A MAJORLY HANDSOME DUDE.
ONE WHO'S POPULAR WITH THE GIRLS!
YOU OKAY WITH THAT...
...MAHORO?

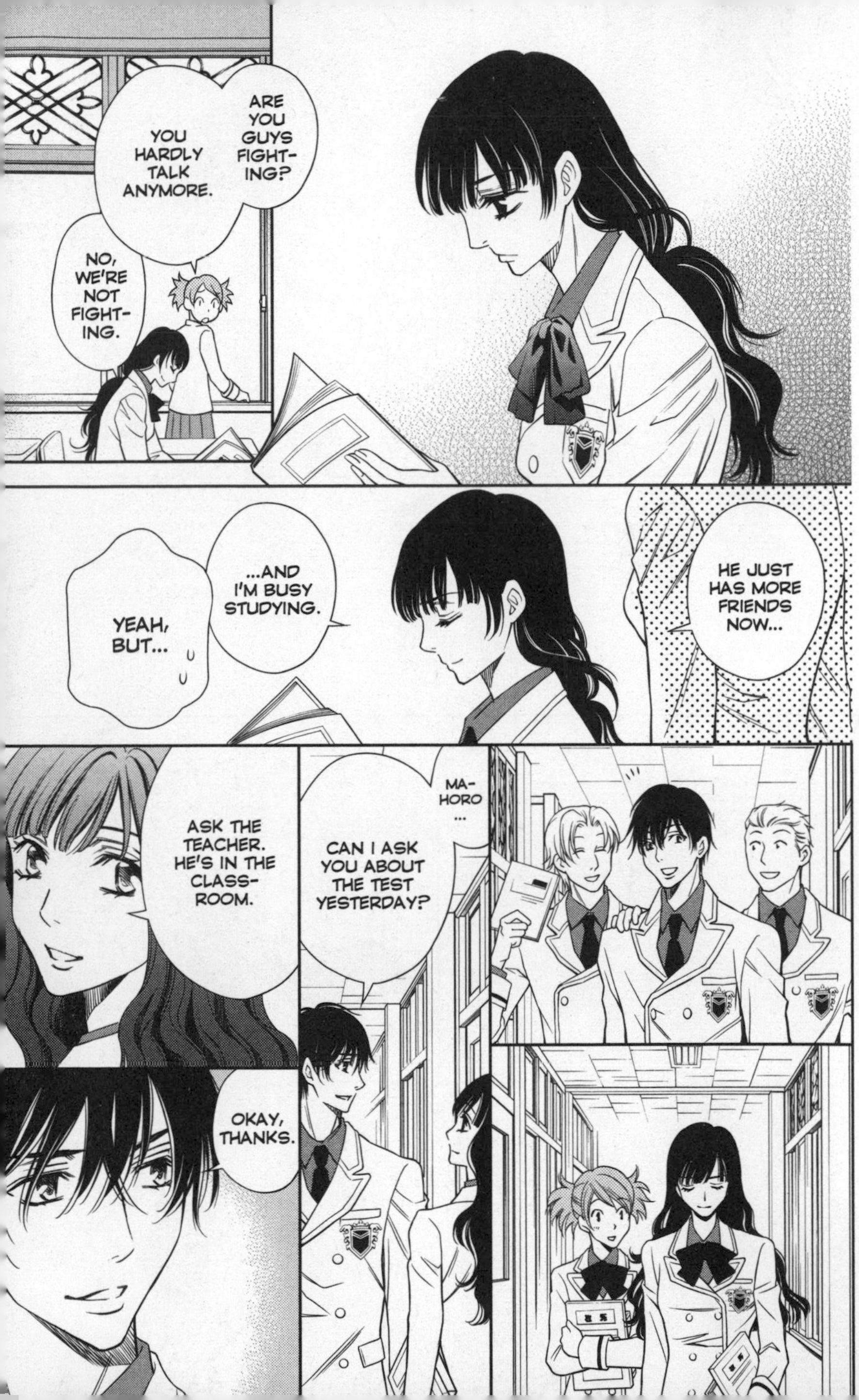
ARE YOU GUYS FIGHTING?
YOU HARDLY TALK ANYMORE.
NO, WE'RE NOT FIGHTING.
HE JUST HAS MORE FRIENDS NOW...
...AND I'M BUSY STUDYING.
YEAH, BUT...
MAHORO...
CAN I ASK YOU ABOUT THE TEST YESTERDAY?
ASK THE TEACHER. HE'S IN THE CLASSROOM.
OKAY, THANKS.

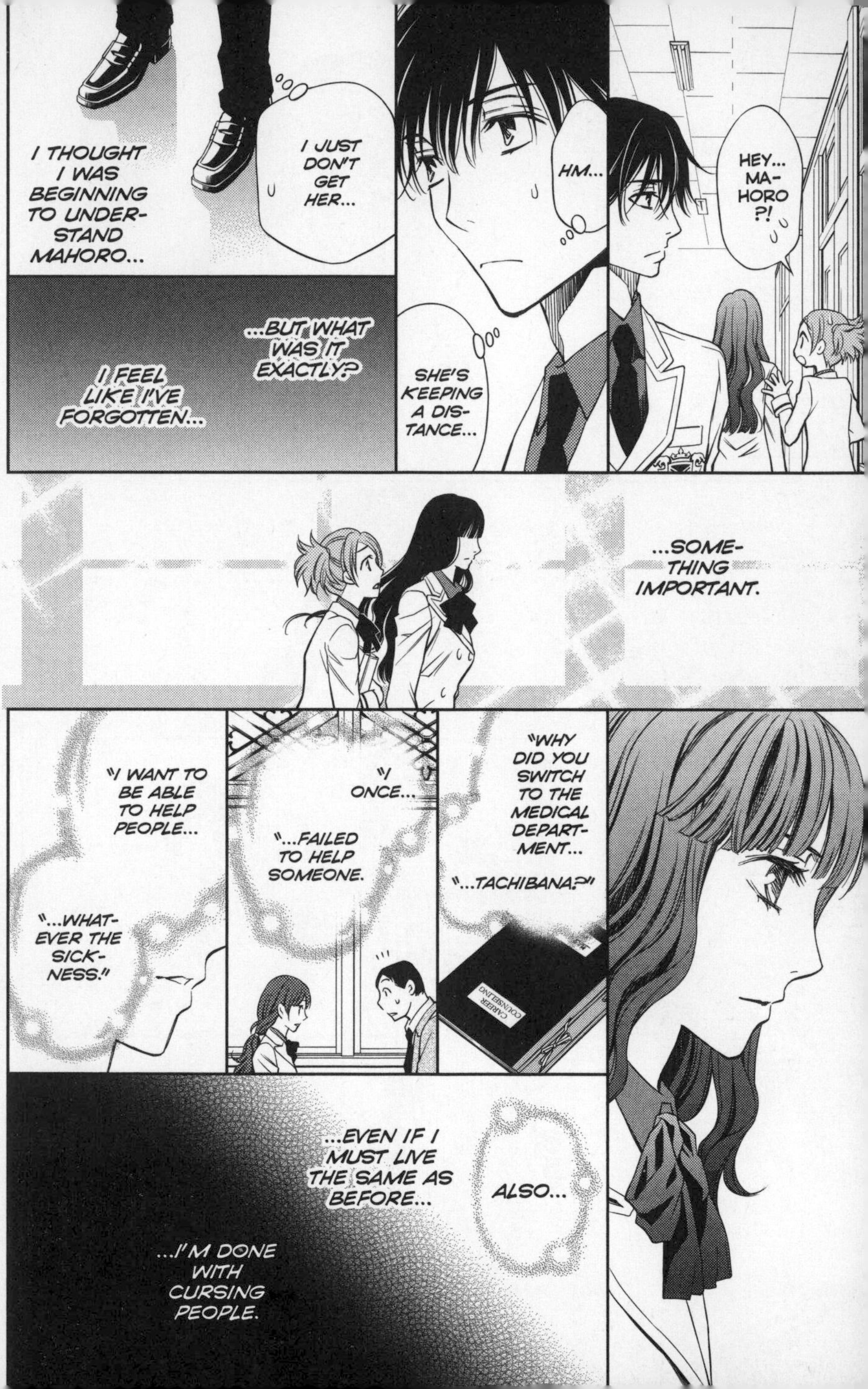
HEY... MAHORO?!
HM...
SHE'S KEEPING A DISTANCE...
I JUST DON'T GET HER...
I THOUGHT I WAS BEGINNING TO UNDERSTAND MAHORO...
...BUT WHAT WAS IT EXACTLY?
I FEEL LIKE I'VE FORGOTTEN...
...SOMETHING IMPORTANT.
"WHY DID YOU SWITCH TO THE MEDICAL DEPARTMENT...
"...TACHIBANA?"
CAREER COUNSELING
"I ONCE...
"...FAILED TO HELP SOMEONE.
"I WANT TO BE ABLE TO HELP PEOPLE...
"...WHATEVER THE SICKNESS."
ALSO...
...EVEN IF I MUST LIVE THE SAME AS BEFORE...
...I'M DONE WITH CURSING PEOPLE.

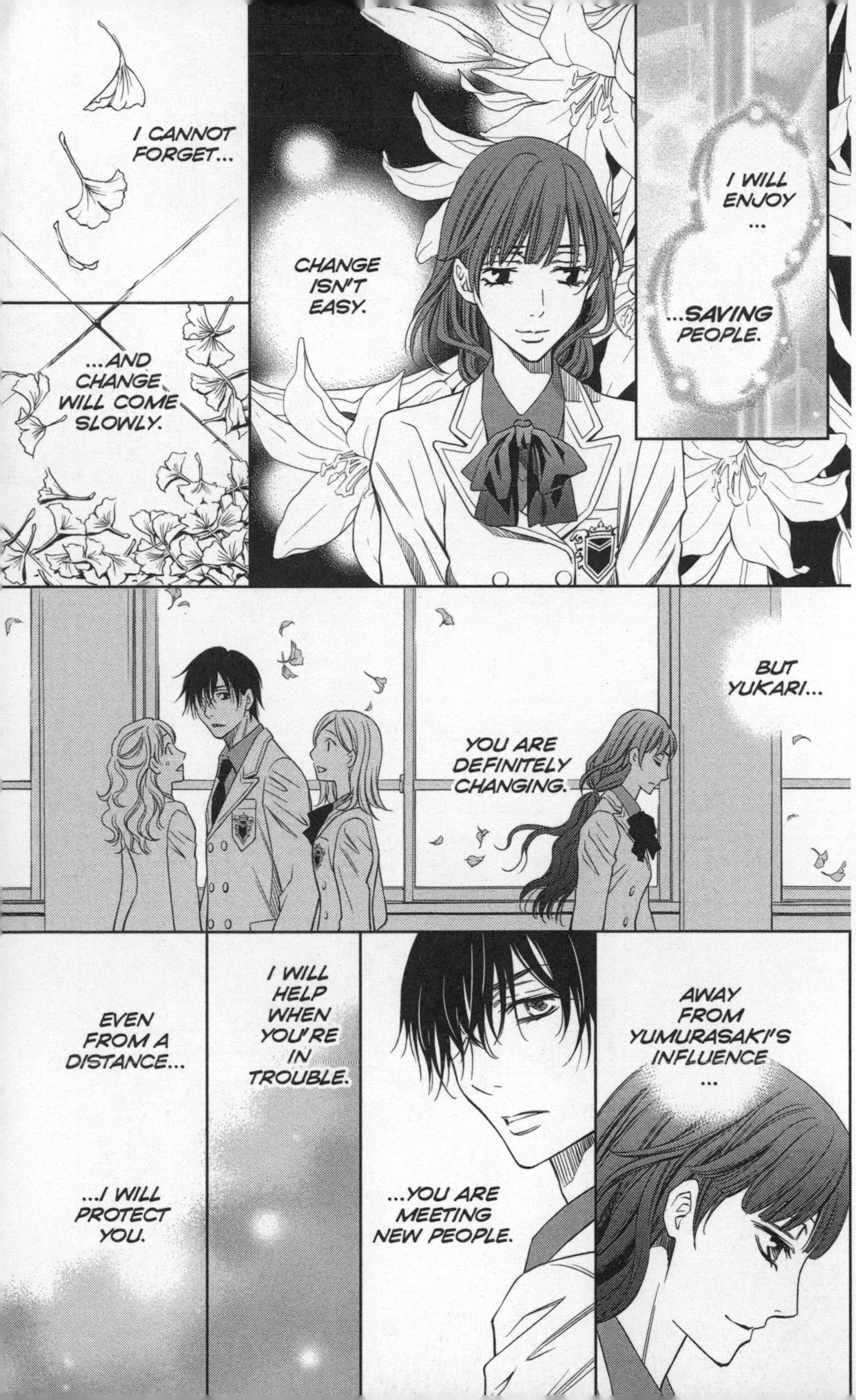
I WILL ENJOY ...
...SAVING PEOPLE.
CHANGE ISN'T EASY.
I CANNOT FORGET...
...AND CHANGE WILL COME SLOWLY.
BUT YUKARI...
YOU ARE DEFINITELY CHANGING.
AWAY FROM YUMURASAKI'S INFLUENCE ...
...YOU ARE MEETING NEW PEOPLE.
I WILL HELP WHEN YOU'RE IN TROUBLE.
EVEN FROM A DISTANCE...
...I WILL PROTECT YOU.

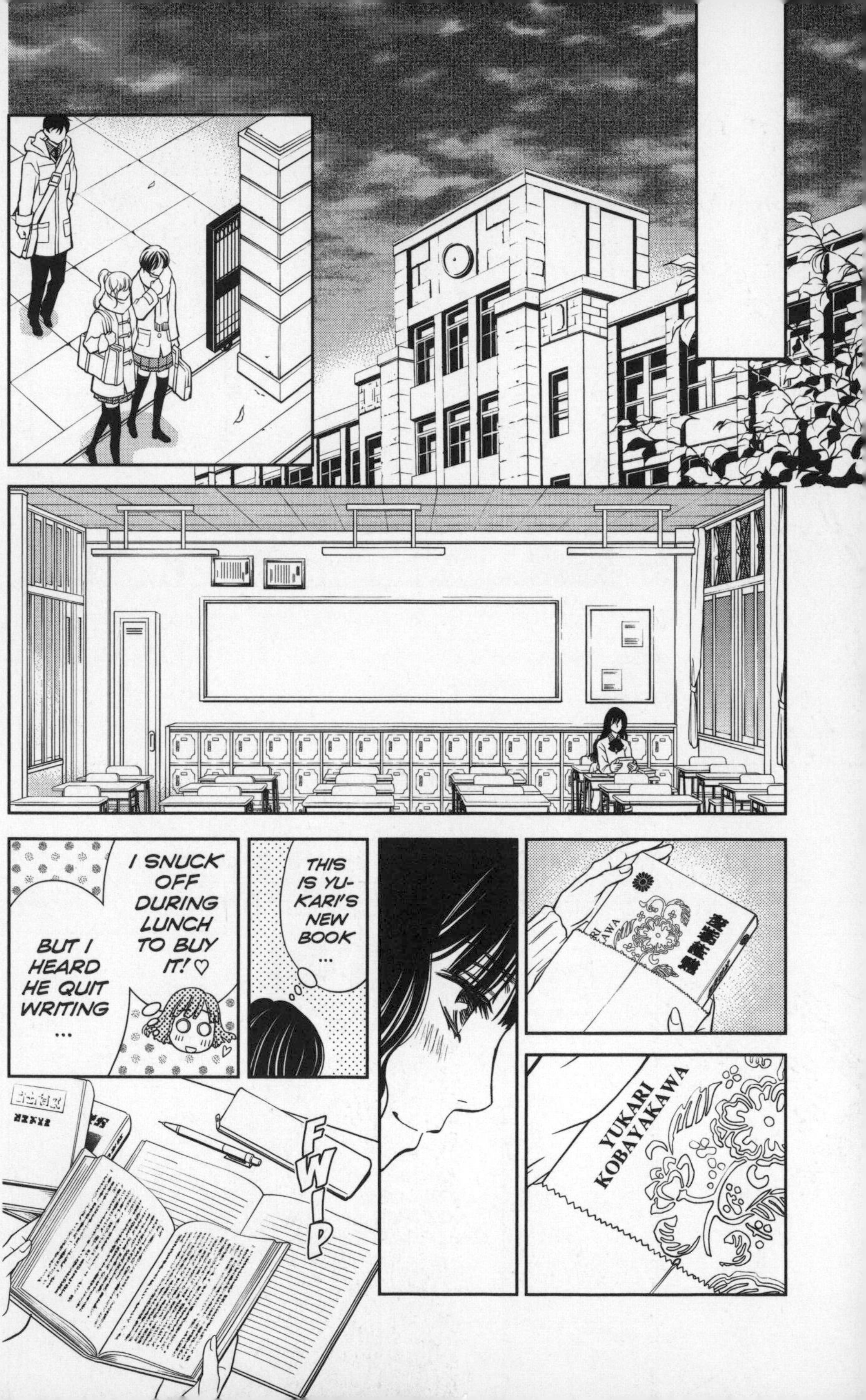
YUKARI KOBAYAKAWA
THIS IS YU-KARI'S NEW BOOK ...
I SNUCK OFF DURING LUNCH TO BUY IT! ♡
BUT I HEARD HE QUIT WRITING ...
FWIP

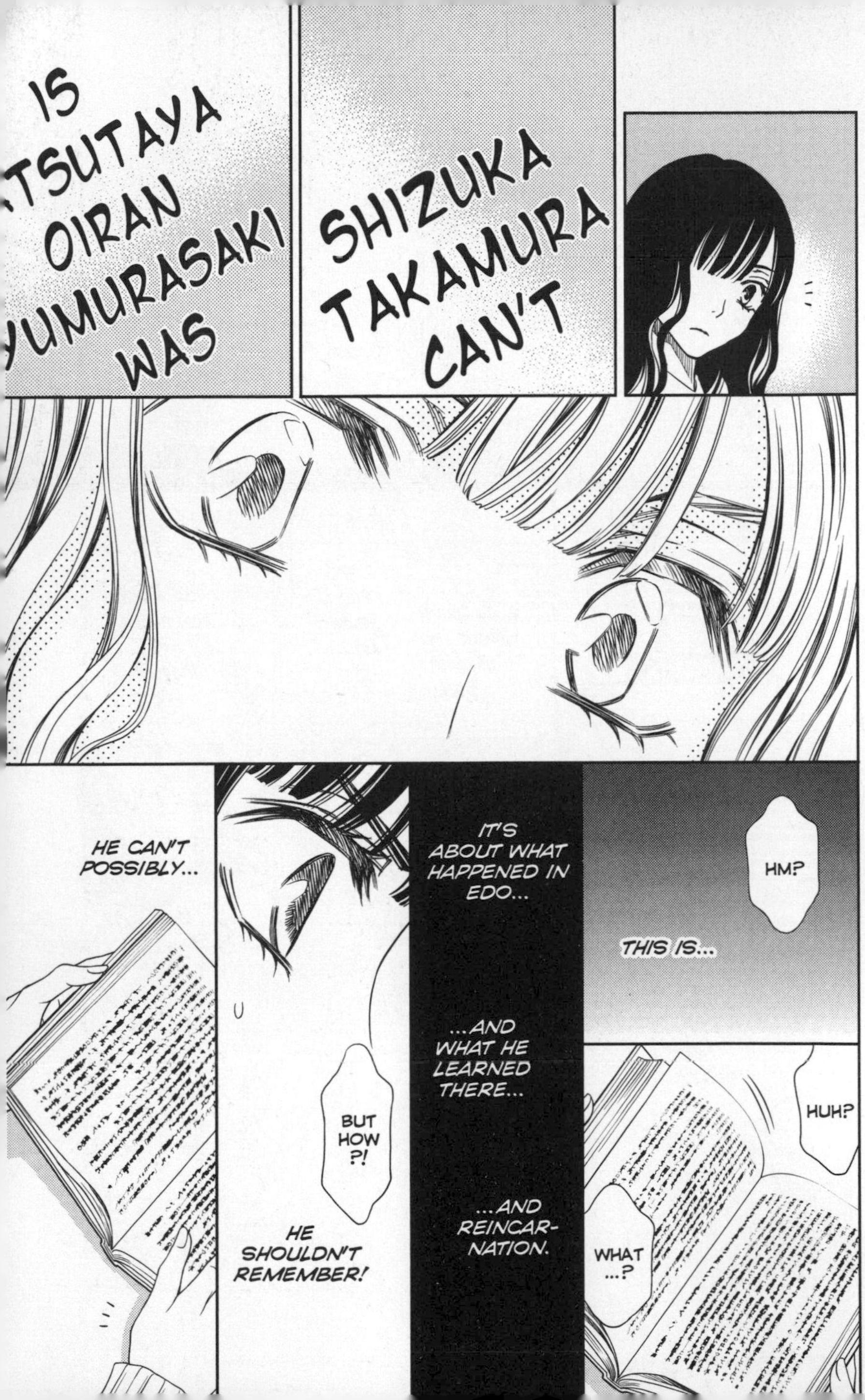
SHIZUKA TAKAMURA CAN'T
IS TSUTAYA OIRAN YUMURASAKI WAS
HM?
THIS IS...
HUH?
WHAT ...?
IT'S ABOUT WHAT HAPPENED IN EDO...
...AND WHAT HE LEARNED THERE...
...AND REINCARNATION.
BUT HOW ?!
HE SHOULDN'T REMEMBER!
HE CAN'T POSSIBLY...

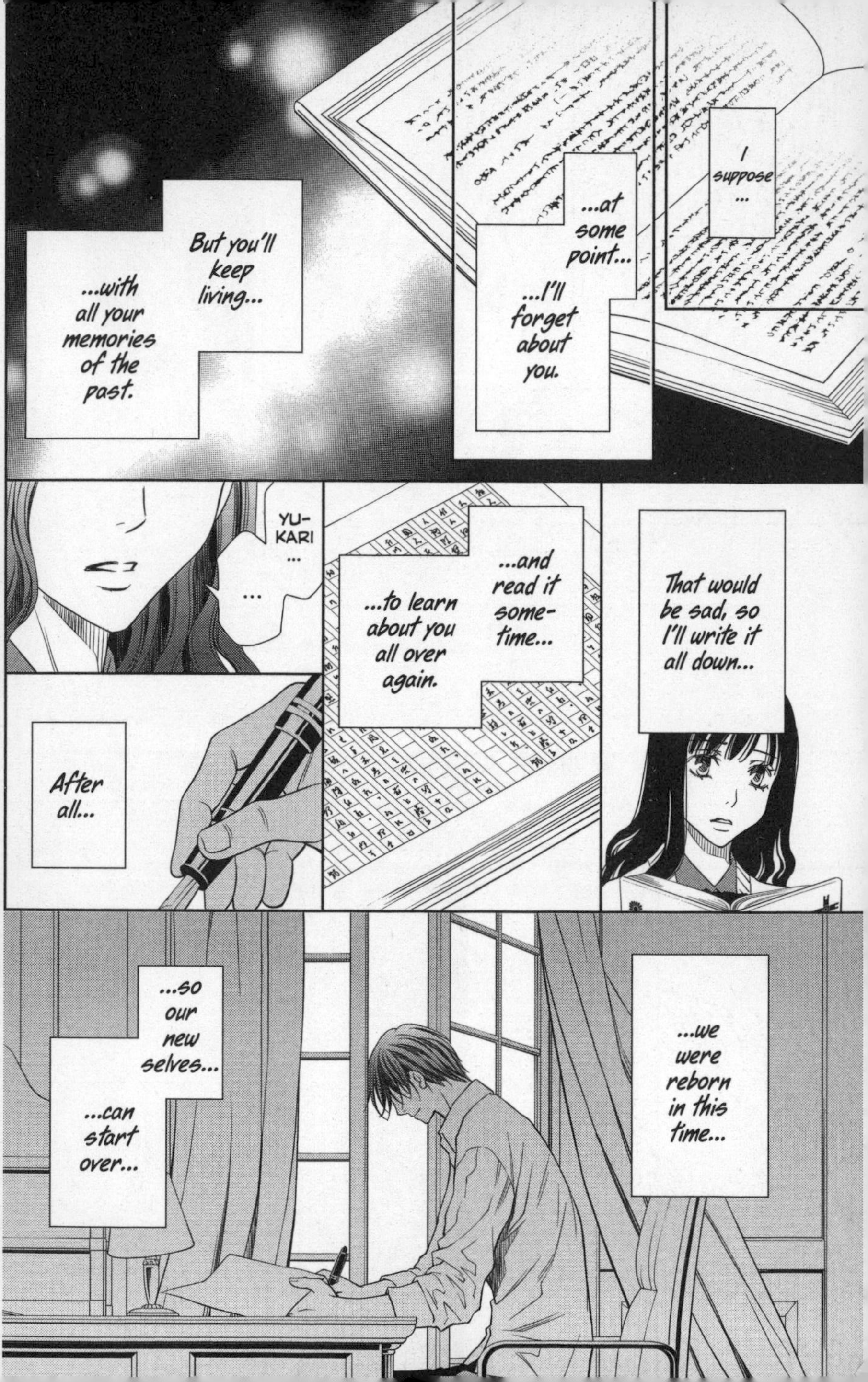
I suppose...
...at some point...
...I'll forget about you.
But you'll keep living...
...with all your memories of the past.
That would be sad, so I'll write it all down...
...and read it sometime...
...to learn about you all over again.
YU-KARI...
...
After all...
...we were reborn in this time...
...so our new selves...
...can start over...

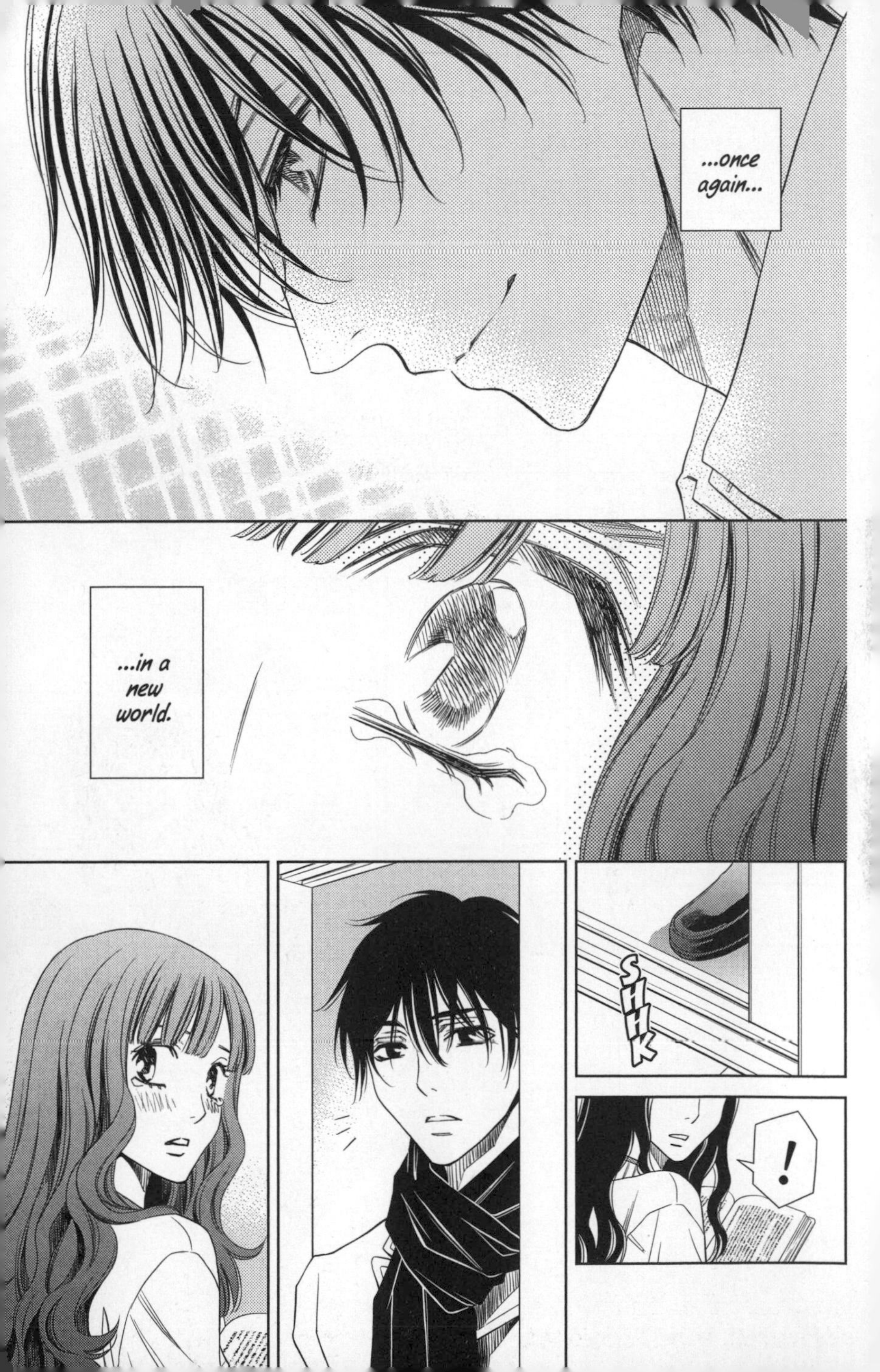
...once again...
...in a new world.
SHHK
!

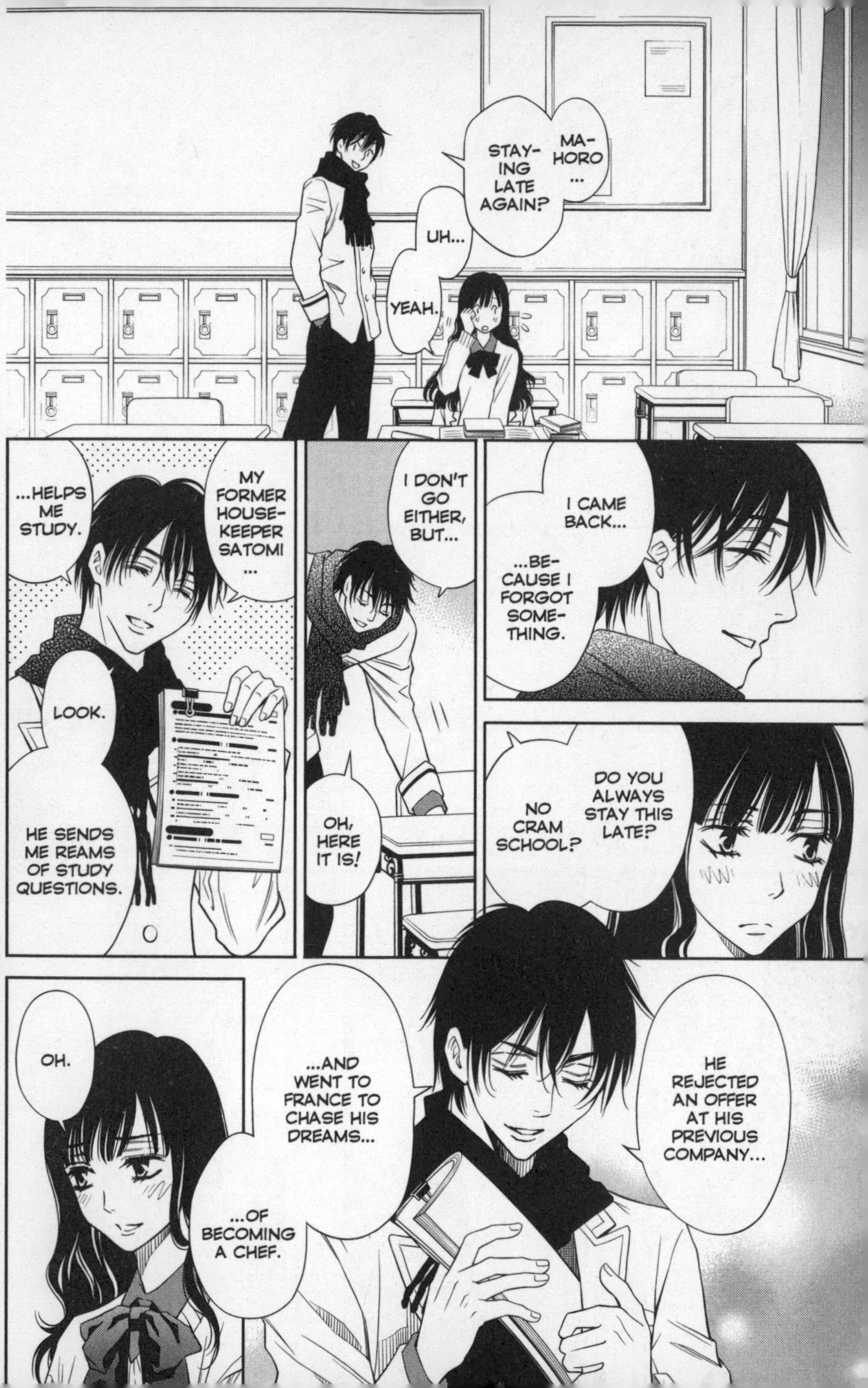
MAHORO...
STAYING LATE AGAIN?
UH...
YEAH.
I CAME BACK...
...BECAUSE I FORGOT SOMETHING.
DO YOU ALWAYS STAY THIS LATE?
NO CRAM SCHOOL?
I DON'T GO EITHER, BUT...
OH, HERE IT IS!
MY FORMER HOUSEKEEPER SATOMI...
...HELPS ME STUDY.
LOOK.
HE SENDS ME REAMS OF STUDY QUESTIONS.
HE REJECTED AN OFFER AT HIS PREVIOUS COMPANY...
...AND WENT TO FRANCE TO CHASE HIS DREAMS...
...OF BECOMING A CHEF.
OH.

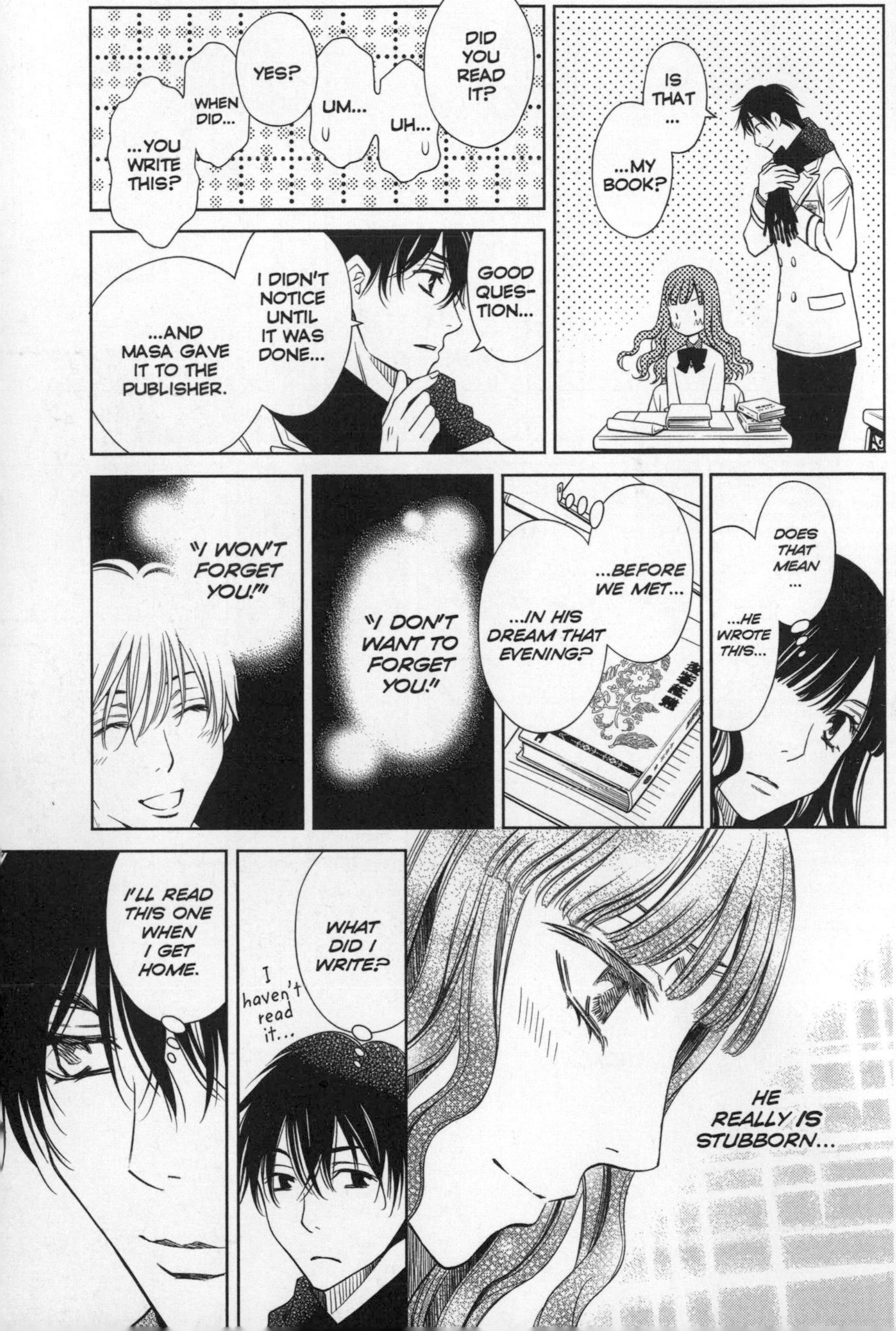
IS THAT ...
...MY BOOK?
DID YOU READ IT?
UH...
UM...
YES?
WHEN DID...
...YOU WRITE THIS?
GOOD QUES-TION...
I DIDN'T NOTICE UNTIL IT WAS DONE...
...AND MASA GAVE IT TO THE PUBLISHER.
DOES THAT MEAN ...
...HE WROTE THIS...
...BEFORE WE MET...
...IN HIS DREAM THAT EVENING?
"I DON'T WANT TO FORGET YOU!"
"I WON'T FORGET YOU!"
HE REALLY IS STUBBORN...
WHAT DID I WRITE?
I haven't read it...
I'LL READ THIS ONE WHEN I GET HOME.

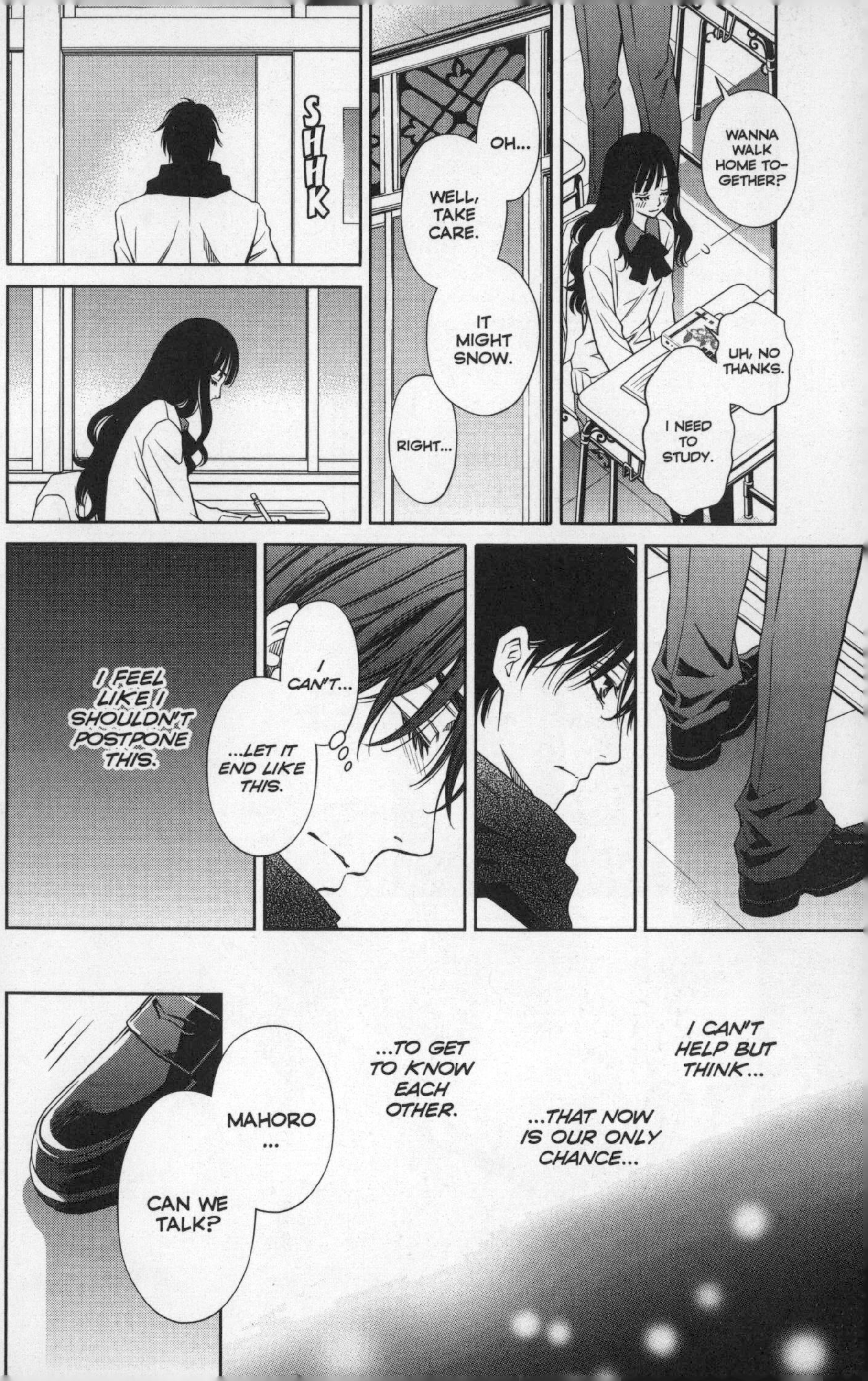
WANNA WALK HOME TO-GETHER?
UH, NO THANKS.
I NEED TO STUDY.
OH...
WELL, TAKE CARE.
IT MIGHT SNOW.
RIGHT...
SHHK
I CAN'T...
...LET IT END LIKE THIS.
I FEEL LIKE I SHOULDN'T POSTPONE THIS.
I CAN'T HELP BUT THINK...
...THAT NOW IS OUR ONLY CHANCE...
...TO GET TO KNOW EACH OTHER.
MAHORO...
CAN WE TALK?

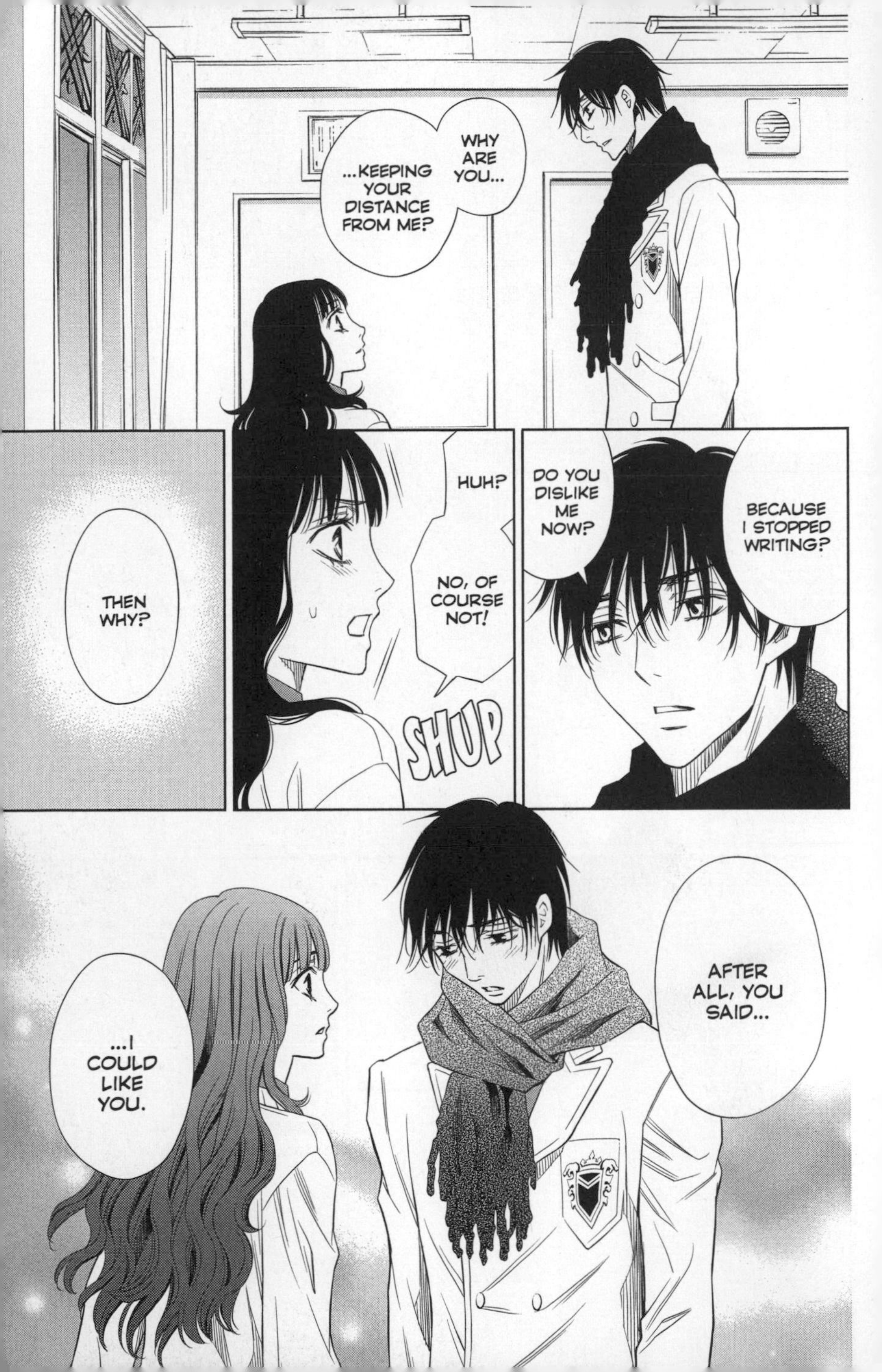
WHY ARE YOU...
...KEEPING YOUR DISTANCE FROM ME?
BECAUSE I STOPPED WRITING?
DO YOU DISLIKE ME NOW?
HUH?
NO, OF COURSE NOT!
SHUP
THEN WHY?
AFTER ALL, YOU SAID...
...I COULD LIKE YOU.

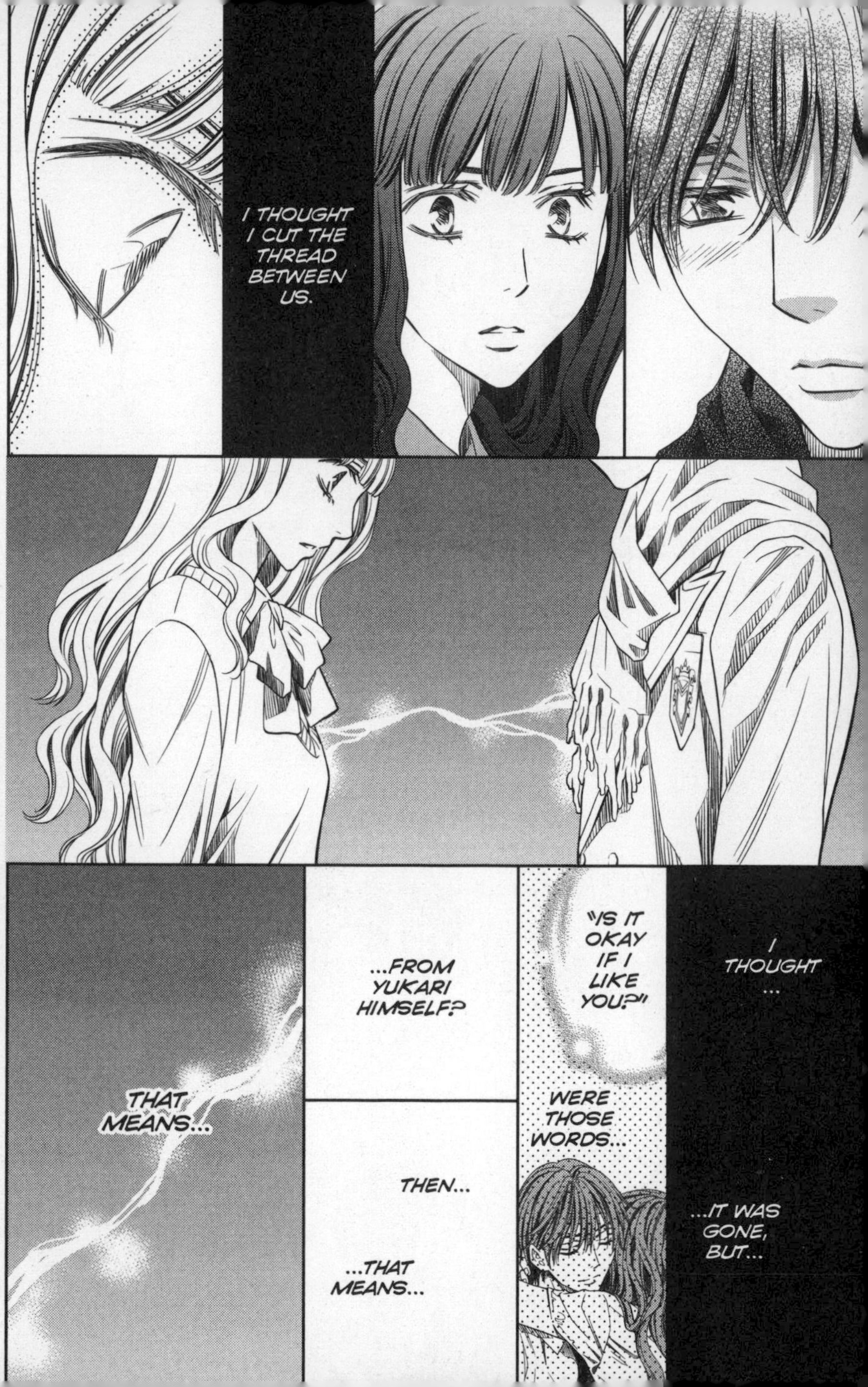
I THOUGHT I CUT THE THREAD BETWEEN US.
I THOUGHT...
...IT WAS GONE, BUT...
"IS IT OKAY IF I LIKE YOU?"
WERE THOSE WORDS...
...FROM YUKARI HIMSELF?
THEN...
...THAT MEANS...
THAT MEANS...

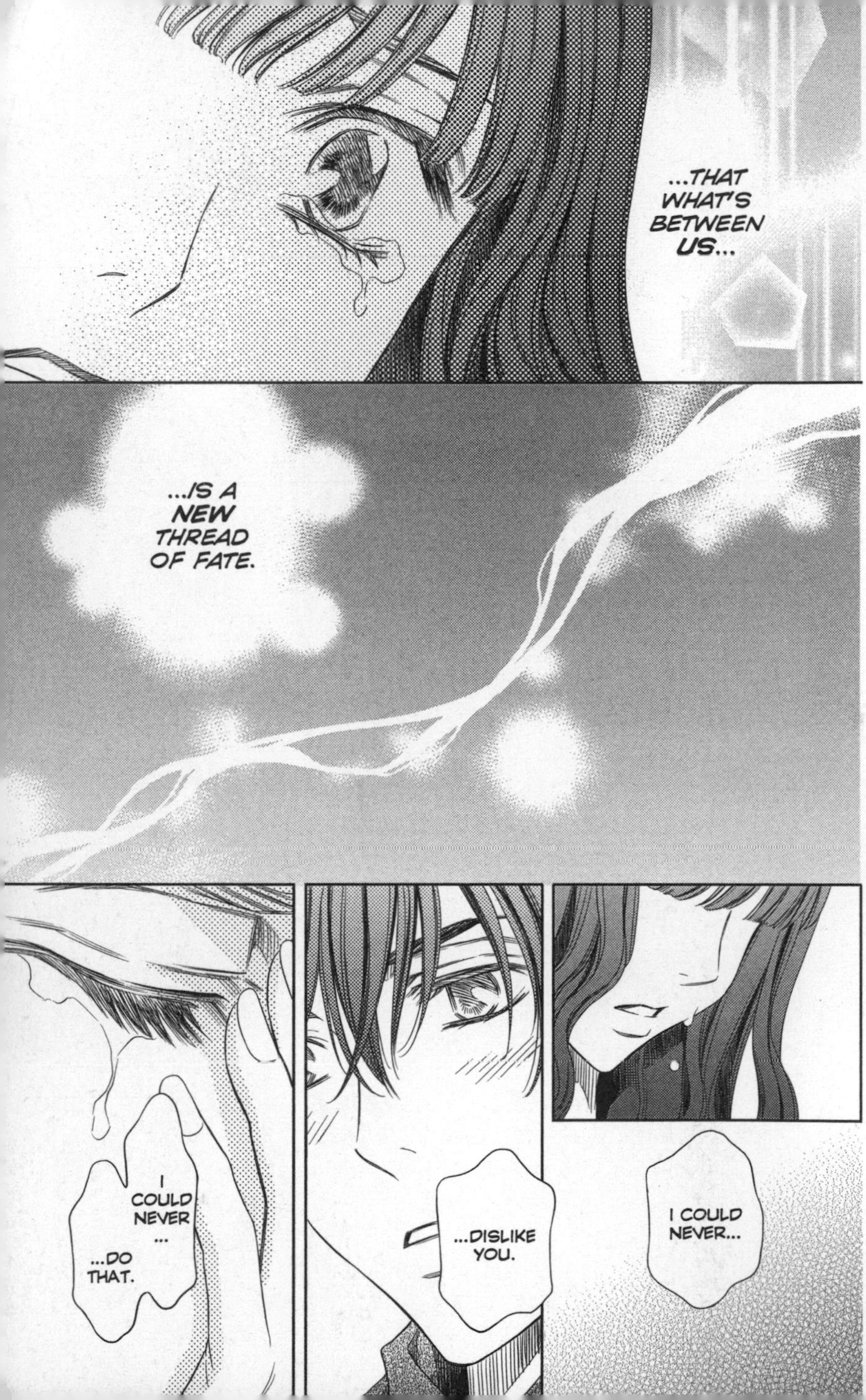
...THAT WHAT'S BETWEEN US...
...IS A NEW THREAD OF FATE.
I COULD NEVER...
...DISLIKE YOU.
I COULD NEVER ...
...DO THAT.

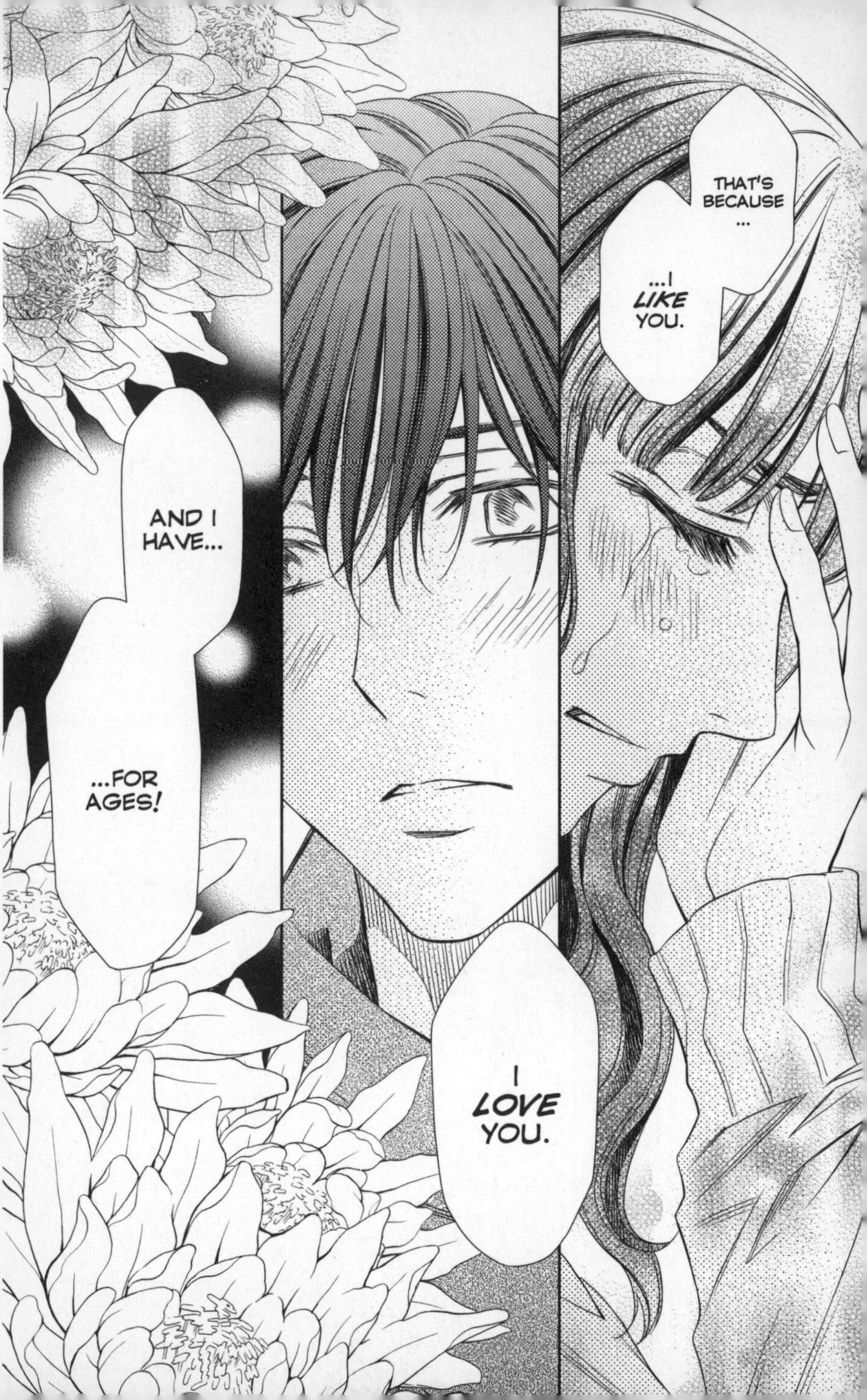
THAT'S BECAUSE ...
...I LIKE YOU.
I LOVE YOU.
AND I HAVE...
...FOR AGES!

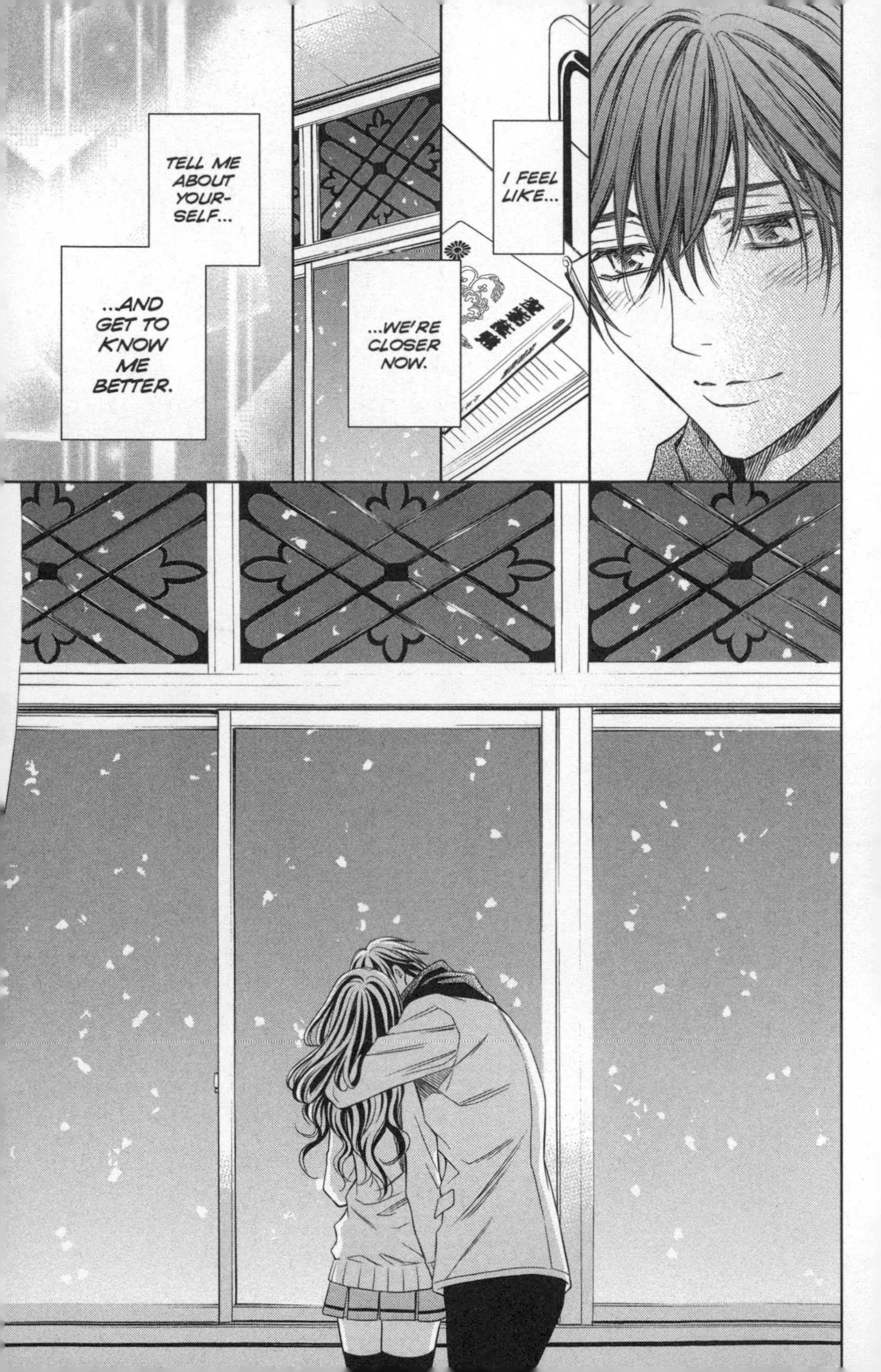
I FEEL LIKE...
...WE'RE CLOSER NOW.
TELL ME ABOUT YOUR-SELF...
...AND GET TO KNOW ME BETTER.

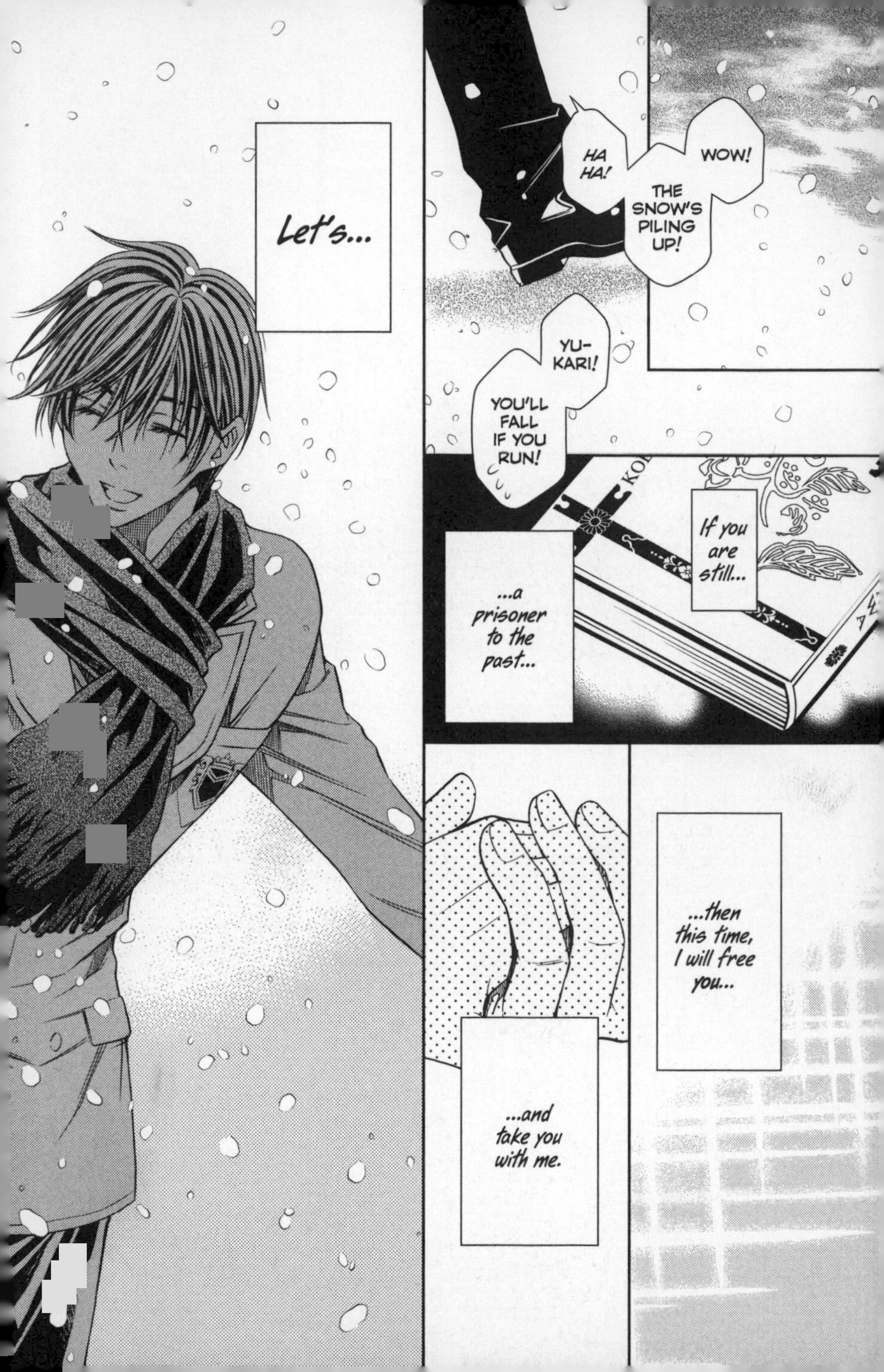
WOW!
THE SNOW'S PILING UP!
HA HA!
YU-KARI!
YOU'LL FALL IF YOU RUN!
If you are still...
...a prisoner to the past...
...then this time, I will free you...
...and take you with me.
Let's...

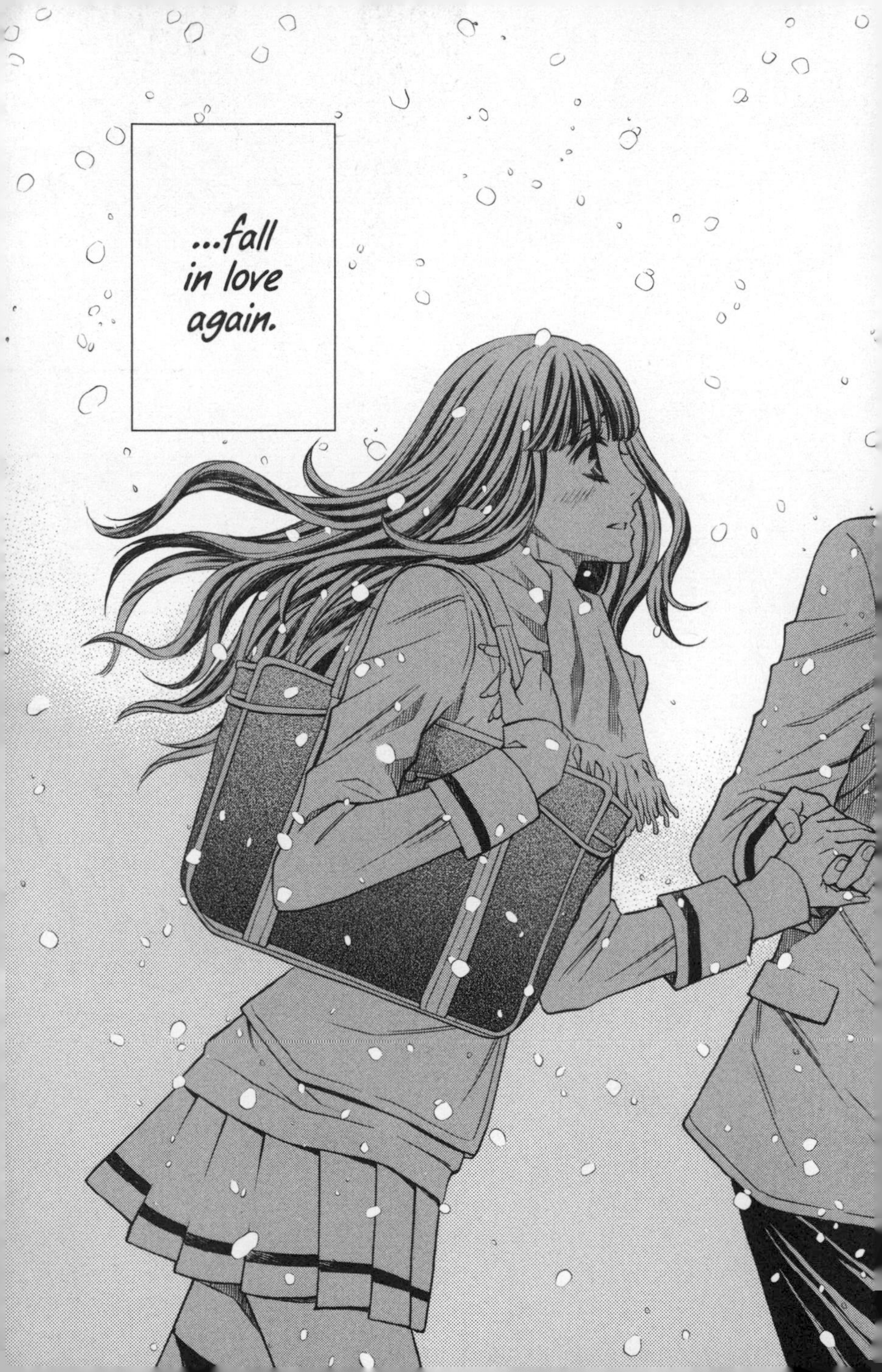
...fall in love again.

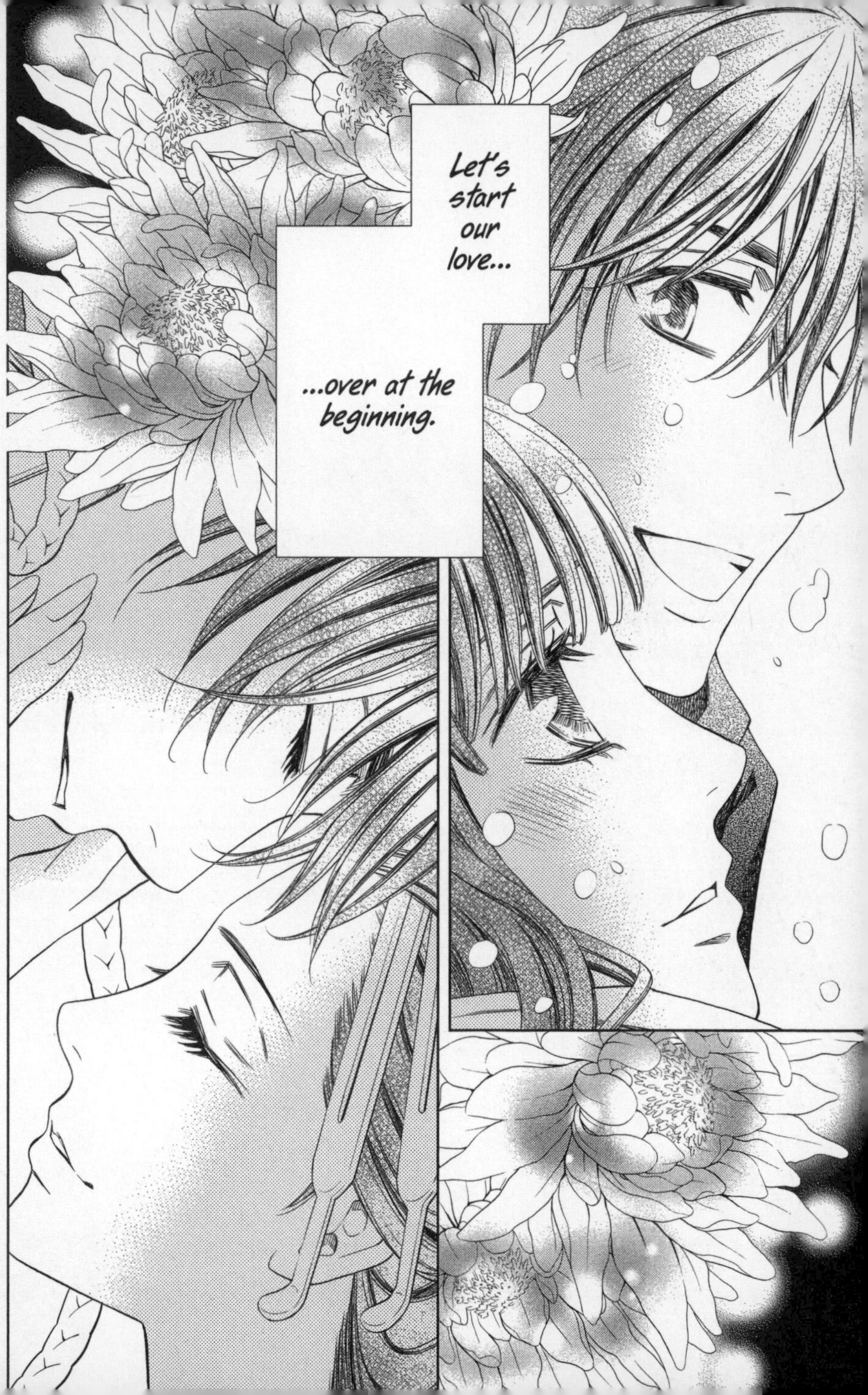
Let's start our love...
...over at the beginning.

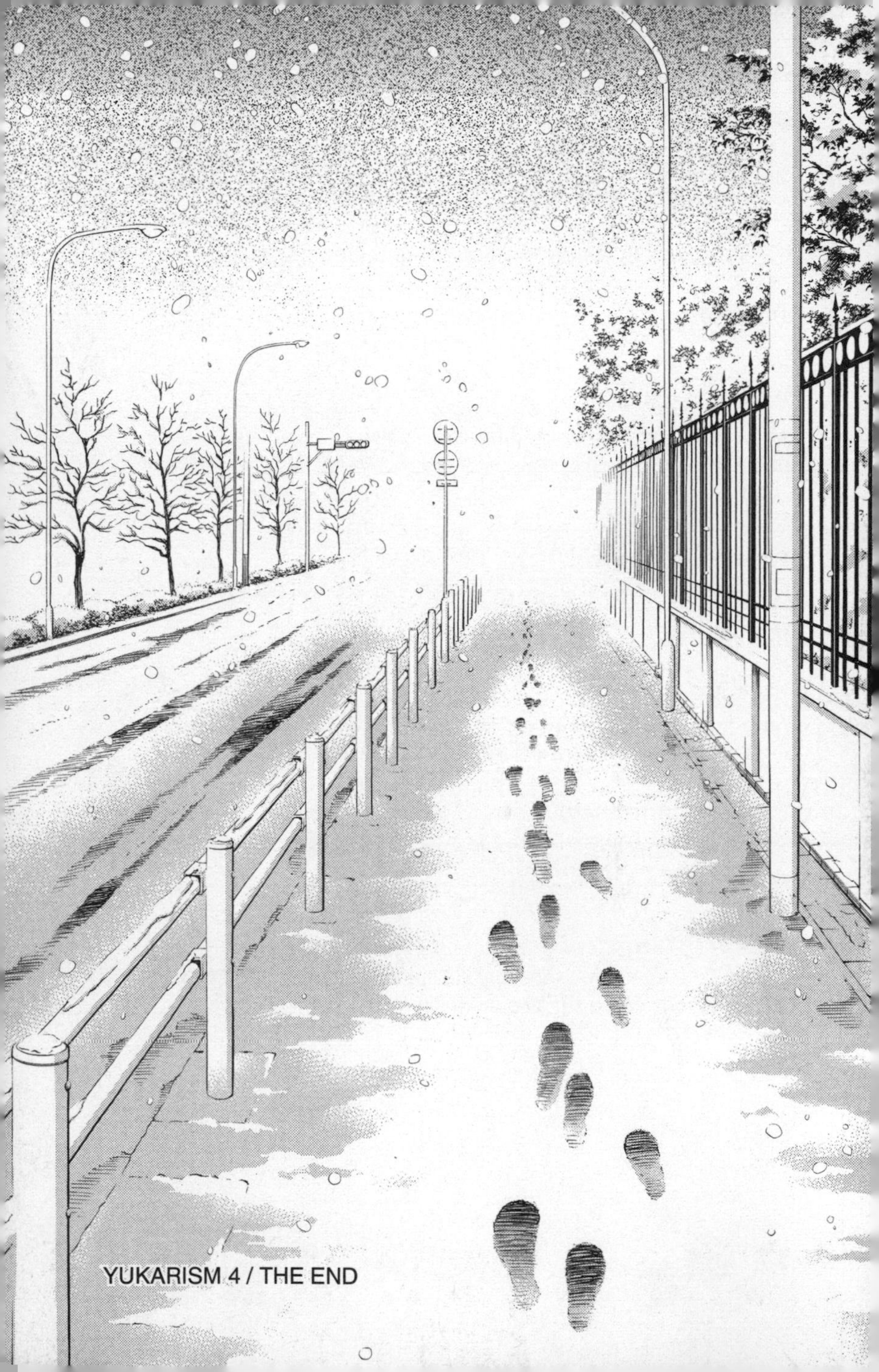
YUKARISM 4 / THE END

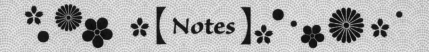

Yukari's past life occurs during the Edo period of Japan.
Check out the notes below to help enrich your understanding of
Yukarism.

Page 2: Yukari
The kanji character 縁 (pronounced "yukari") means "connection"
or "bond." The actual kanji for Yukari's name (紫), however, means
"purple."

Page 2: Edo period
Also known as the Tokugawa period, the Edo period lasted from
1603 to 1868.

Page 2: Katana
A traditional Japanese sword used during feudal Japan that has a
moderately curved, slender, single-edged blade.

Page 3: Yumurasaki
The kanji characters for Yumurasaki's name (夕紫) mean "evening"
and "purple."

Page 3: Oiran
A class of courtesan, especially during the Edo period. The kanji
characters for *oiran* (花魁) mean "flower" and "harbinger,"
respectively.

Page 25, panel 3: Ne-san

An honorific that means "older sister," *ne-san* is used to address an older sister figure (similar to calling someone "Miss").

Page 56, panel 1: Sama

An honorific used to address a person much higher in rank than oneself.

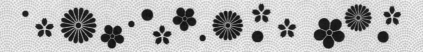

Author Bio

Chika Shiomi debuted with the manga *Todokeru Toki o Sugitemo* (Even if the Time for Deliverance Passes), and her previous works include *Yurara* and *Rasetsu*. She loves reading manga, traveling and listening to music by Aerosmith and Guns N' Roses. Her favorite artists include Michelangelo, Hokusai, Bernini and Gustav Klimt.

YUKARISM

Volume 4
Shojo Beat Edition

STORY AND ART BY
CHIKA SHIOMI

Translation & Adaptation/John Werry
Touch-up Art & Lettering/Rina Mapa
Design/Izumi Evers
Editor/Amy Yu

Yukarism by Chika Shiomi
© Chika Shiomi 2014
All rights reserved.
First published in Japan in 2014 by
HAKUSENSHA, Inc., Tokyo.
English language translation rights arranged with
HAKUSENSHA, Inc., Tokyo.

The stories, characters and incidents mentioned in this
publication are entirely fictional.

Printed in the U.S.A.

Published by VIZ Media, LLC
P.O. Box 77010
San Francisco, CA 94107

10 9 8 7 6 5 4 3 2 1
First printing, November 2015

www.viz.com   www.shojobeat.com

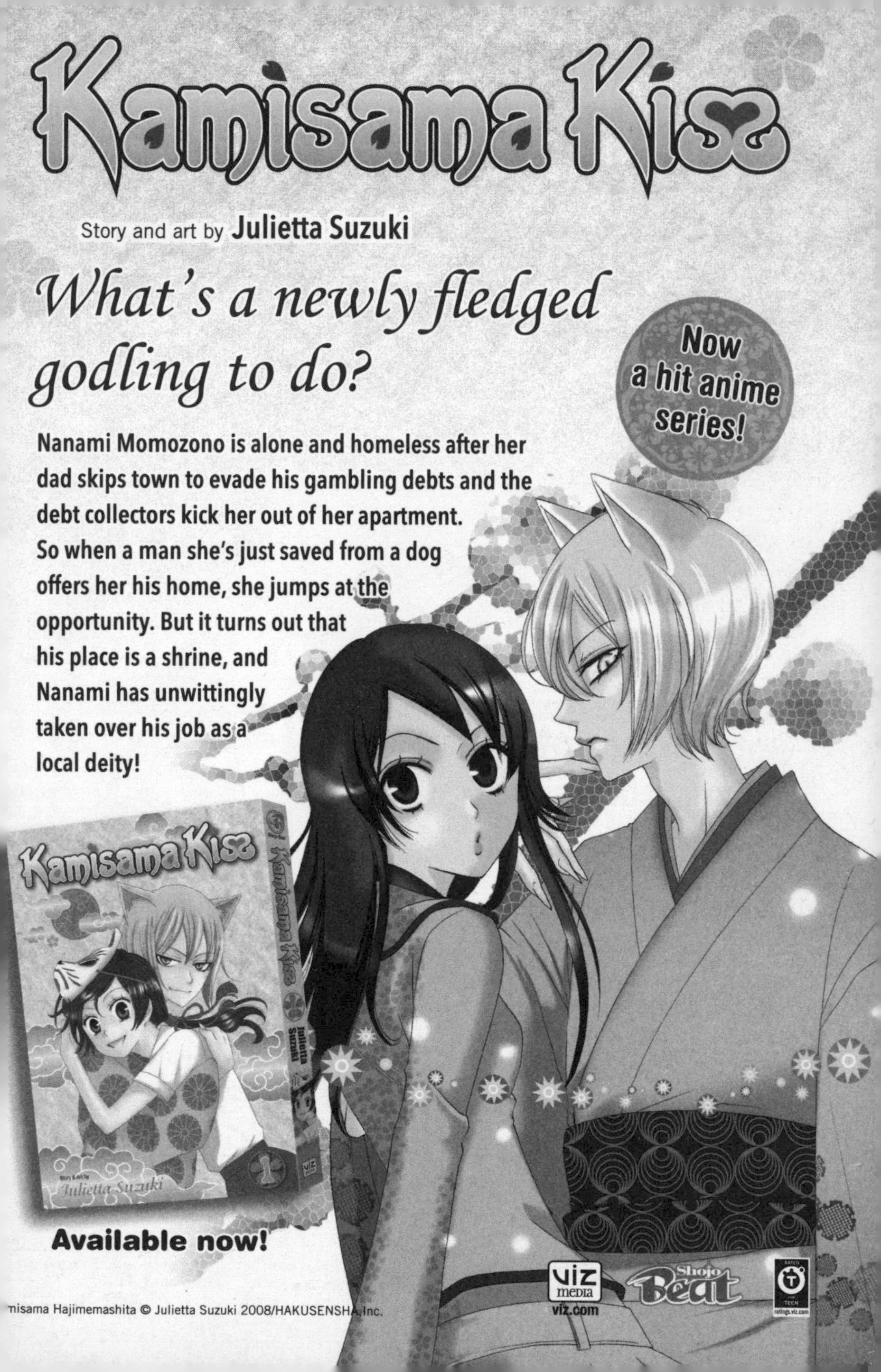
Kamisama Kiss
Story and art by Julietta Suzuki
What's a newly fledged godling to do?
Now a hit anime series!
Nanami Momozono is alone and homeless after her dad skips town to evade his gambling debts and the debt collectors kick her out of her apartment. So when a man she's just saved from a dog offers her his home, she jumps at the opportunity. But it turns out that his place is a shrine, and Nanami has unwittingly taken over his job as a local deity!
Kamisama Kiss
Kamisama Kiss
Julietta Suzuki
1
Julietta Suzuki
Available now!
VIZ media
viz.com
Shojo Beat
RATED T TEEN
ratings.viz.com
misama Hajimemashita © Julietta Suzuki 2008/HAKUSENSHA, Inc.